GOD'S COACH

The Hymns, Hype, and Hypocrisy of Tom Landry's Cowboys

SKIP BAYLESS

A FIRESIDE BOOK
PUBLISHED BY SIMON & SCHUSTER
New York   London   Toronto   Sydney   Tokyo   Singapore

FIRESIDE
Simon & Schuster Building
Rockefeller Center
1230 Avenue of the Americas
New York, New York   10020

First Fireside Edition 1991

FIRESIDE and colophon are registered trademarks
of Simon & Schuster Inc.

Designed by Irving Perkins Associates
Manufactured in the United States of America

10 9 8 7 6 5 4 3 2 1

Library of Congress Cataloging in Publication Data

Bayless, Skip.
God's coach: the hymns, hype, and hypocrisy of Tom Landry's
Cowboys / Skip Bayless.
    p.   cm.
1. Landry, Tom. 2. Football—United States—Coaches—
Biography. 3. Dallas Cowboys (Football team) I. Title
GV939.L28B39   1990
796.332′092—dc20   90-39634
[B]   CIP

ISBN: 0-671-70896-1
ISBN: 0-671-74865-3 Pbk.

To God, who gave me the strength.

ACKNOWLEDGMENTS

In these few sentences, I ask many people to forgive me for abusing my relationship with them through the writing of this book. I thank John Buzzetta, Roy Bode, and especially Gary Hardee of the *Dallas Times Herald* for their patience. I thank Mike Fernandez for his invaluable research and friendship. I thank Kevin Shepherd and Craig Humphreys for their support. I thank Shari Wenk for her guidance. I thank Jeff Neuman for sharing my passion for this project. I thank those who had the courage to speak out.

I thank Peggy Black, for listening and waiting.

And I thank Levita Anderson for making this book possible. It's time to say something I haven't been able to say to her: I love you, Mom.

PREFACE

AS I covered the inevitable collapse of Tom Landry and America's Team, I sometimes thought of *The Wizard of Oz*. Yes, while writing newspaper columns in press boxes across the NFL, I flashed on Toto. Remember? As Dorothy & Co. cowered before the giant screen that flamed and roared with "the great and powerful Oz," Toto smelled a rat.

It was Dorothy's dog Toto who slipped away and opened the curtain with his teeth.

And there, frantically yanking levers that controlled "Oz," was a very average little man. Stunned, Dorothy flamed and roared with indignation. How dare this silly little man impersonate a power in which so many people believed! Near tears, Dorothy said, "Oh, you're a very bad man."

And the wizard answered, "Oh, no, my dear. I'm a very good man. I'm just a very bad wizard."

In the end Tom Landry proved to be a very bad wizard. But how had he become the great and powerful Landry? Did it start when his image was projected up on the giant NFL screen? Had he been swept into the role of wizard for a city desperately in need of one? Had he given in to the ego and greed made famous by Dallas? Had he watched in frantic awe as his belief in God made him a god to millions? Had the Dallas Cowboy media machine helped make an image Landry couldn't live up to? Did others in the organization use "God's Coach" as a front for their corruption?

Was the real Landry basically a good man who found himself in a bad situation? Or was he more of a snake-oil salesman, like the Kansas "wizard" who inspired Dorothy's dream? Perhaps you want to know only the great and powerful Landry who was projected on your TV screen. But if you dare, this book will open the curtain for you.

Bear with me and I'll take you over the gold-brick road to Dallas, through the twelve years I closely observed Landry. Who was this man? He was so simple, so complicated. So famous, so unknown. So dull, so fascinating. So Christian, so criticized. So all-knowing, so oblivious. So perfect and mortal, powerful and average. I looked to him for courage, for heart, for brains, and he sometimes failed me. I looked to God's Coach for the answer, and he didn't always have it. Again and again he and Dallas tested my faith in God. I stumbled often. But in the end Tom Landry taught me a lot, an awful lot.

So come along, if you dare, through the Lions and Bengals and Bears. We're off to see the wizard.

GOD'S
COACH

1

JERRY JONES felt as if he had been tackled in his sleep by "Too Tall" Jones. His head, his stomach—Jones hadn't hurt so bad since August two-a-day practices back at the University of Arkansas. "Lord have mercy," said Jones, getting more religious with each throb.

For Jones, the hotel room in Cabo San Lucas was beginning to rock like a fishing boat on high seas. The hotel—"some famous place," Jones remembers—was built into the cliffs above the Pacific. Below, a charter boat waited in the harbor to take Jones, forty-six, and his oldest son Steven, twenty-three, out after marlin. But Jones had spent half the night at a place called the Giggling Marlin, where *turistas* are strung up by their feet, like a prize catch, and allowed as many free margaritas as they can drink while upside down. Sick?

Jones was. The mere thought of stinking fish and a rocking boat made him even queasier. "You go on," he told Steven, who couldn't help grinning. Oh, wait till the boys back home in Little Rock heard that Jerral Wayne Jones, honky-tonk king, had met his match in old Mexico.

The day before, Jones and son had been at an oil and gas

convention in San Diego. Jerry Jones had done in the oil fields what
he did on the football field: overachieve. As a two hundred pound
guard he had co-captained Arkansas's undefeated national championship team of 1964. He had married a former Miss Arkansas USA,
a title commonly known as Poultry Princess. Then, hustling and
plunging, Jones kept striking it richer than Jed Clampett. Only in
America. Or Arkansas. Jones was worth, what, $300 million? He
didn't know for sure.

But now, in early September 1988, Jones was getting bored
with gushers. Steven had done him proud by playing football at
Arkansas and graduating with honors and an engineering degree.
Daughter Charlotte had graduated from Stanford with a biology
degree and had done some modeling. Jerry Jr. had left home to
attend Georgetown. Now Jones was restless for a second career, a
new challenge, something fun. He had tired of the convention and
decided to fly on down the Baja Peninsula—in his Lear 35 with
full-time pilot and copilot—to do some deep-sea fishing. That fired
him back up. "I love to smile," Jones says.

Jones often smiles so hard his head seems stretched sideways—
Steve McQueen in a funhouse mirror, eye teeth glinting. His nose
flattens like a prizefighter's. His thin, wavy, light-brown hair, still
short enough for '60s football, is pulled even tighter to his skull. His
pale blue eyes bug. The veins bulge in his short, thick neck.

But now, the morning after, Jones was not steroid-smiling. He
was wasting away in Margaritaville. Steven went on fishing. Jones,
through one eye, passed the time scanning a day-old San Diego
sports section he had tucked in his suitcase. His hangover, miraculously, was cured by an item buried on page five. It said, "Dallas
Cowboys owner H. R. 'Bum' Bright has retained Salomon Brothers,
an investment banker, to find a buyer for the team. . . ."

Jones was up, throwing on some clothes. *Damn, the Dallas
Cowboys!* he thought. Soon he was downstairs in the lobby asking
the *"ay-meego"* at the front desk how you call Dallas, Texas, U.S.A.
Jones was led to a room with a single telephone. The international
operator told Jones she'd call him back when she reached Salomon
Brothers.

Jones paced. The phone rang. The connection was terrible.
Jones fairly yelled into the mouthpiece, "You don't know me, but
my name is Jerry Jones and I'm going to buy the Dallas Cowboys."

With those garbled words from Mexico, "America's Team" was

no more. In effect, three of the most powerful images in sports history—Landry! Schramm! Brandt!—crumbled in a Bible Belt Rome called Dallas. The organization known for nearly thirty years as "the most stable in sports" was in reality that fragile. Perhaps coach Tom Landry's spiritual life was "founded upon a rock" (Matthew 7:25), but his "business," as he called the Cowboys, was built on prairie dust. On Texas-sized egos. On greed. Excess. Sex appeal. Adultery. Lies. Oil. Alcohol. Arrogance. Gusher luck. On a towering media-made facade known as Cowboys Mystique. "This thing, this monster," as Cowboys public relations director Greg Aiello calls what the Cowboys became. No longer were they just a pro football team.

To many, the Cowboys were a televangelist crusade led by the Reverend Landry. To many, Dallas Cowboys Football Club, Inc., was the right wing of IBM, led by team president Texas E. Schramm. To millions more, they were the Dallas Cowboys Cheerleaders, safe-sex goddesses who starred in TV movies.

They were a weekly episode of the country's hottest TV show, "Dallas," with the no-good Cowboys (like J. R. Ewing) winning by hook or crook. They were a George Lucas creation, exploding across the TV screen with special effects right out of *Star Wars*. They were billions and billions of words in newspapers and magazines the world over. They were the tallest Texas tale.

They weren't what they appeared.

"I wouldn't have believed it," says Jones, "unless I'd seen it from the inside out."

Holy Cowboy, was Jones's reaction.

For around $150 million, Jones would buy "this monster," and it would nearly devour him. He would suffer an arrythmia, an irregular heart rhythm caused by stress, too little sleep, and too many cocktail parties. A guy who had been interviewed "maybe once or twice" in his life would spend "three or four hours a day" giving his views on everything from the Shotgun formation to gun control. After all, he was the Cowboy owner.

"Jethro" Jones would be ridiculed across America for trying to turn a lavish religion back into a profitable business. He would get reeled in like a marlin in a public relations game with three master media manipulators: Landry, Schramm, and vice president Gil Brandt. For them the team built on illusion had led to monstrous self-delusion. The team that had won by distracting opponents with an ever-shifting "multiple offense," a bizarre defensive scheme known as the Flex, spaceman uniforms of metallic blue and silver, halter-topped cheerleaders, and diabolical computers finally had fooled its creators, too. Long before the team fell to an NFL-worst 3–13 in 1988, Landry-Schramm-Brandt had come to believe their exaggerated media images.

Tom Landry: God's Coach. Tex Schramm: Most Powerful Man in the NFL. Gil Brandt: Draftmaster.

Don Beck, a sports psychologist who for years counseled Landry and Schramm, says, "It was impossible for Jones to know what he'd gotten himself into. He wasn't dealing with real people. These are myths. And they were created because they just happened to come together at the absolute right time in the right city in the right business. It was like a—what was the phenomenon a while back?— yes, like a Harmonic Convergence. There has never been anything quite like it in sports, and there probably won't be again. Good gosh, you had a coach from *Mission*, Texas, who flew bomber *missions* and was on a *mission* for the Lord. You had a Schramm who actually was named Texas.

"But none of them really planned any of this. It just took off. Individually, you wouldn't consider Tom or Tex or Gil a genius by any stretch of the intellectual definition. But we're all made up of little intelligences, and each one provided little intelligences that created overall genius."

Magical, fragile genius. Imagine: Rome was falling because Jerry Jones had a hangover.

Thomas Wade Landry, God's Coach, waited near the putting green of a golf course outside Austin. It might as well have been called Gethsemane Hills. The sun was setting on February 25, 1989. Landry's Saturday golf game had been interrupted by word that this Jerry Jones was on his way from Dallas. On his way to fire Tom Landry? Landry was surrounded by thirty or forty disciples, club members angry enough to string up this "yokel" from Arkansas who dared treat Tom Landry like some Tom, Dick, or Harry.

This man was a god.

Yes, through coaching a brutal game played on the Sabbath, Landry had become one of America's most influential religious leaders. Thanks to twenty-nine years of sideline TV closeups, he was the

Man in the Hat. Mount Landry. The Great Stoneface. The Genius. A silent televangelist assuring millions each Sunday that God still loved the world and the Cowboys. In pictures he looked like a cross between the Pope and Gary Cooper. To many he was the last bald eagle, the last American Hero.

For Dallas, "the city that killed Kennedy," Landry was something of a peace offering. Here, America, was another brilliant war hero who inspired millions. Here was an inhuman burden.

Like Schramm and Brandt, Landry had become a prisoner of his myth. He, too, had been overwhelmed by the team's runaway fame. Beneath Landry's "best dressed" awards was just a small-town guy with a mild speech impediment who sometimes couldn't remember the names of his players. The real Landry was called "nerdy" by some around him. The real one, according to many assistants and players, at times was overwhelmed by major game plan or personnel decisions and sometimes made irrational moves seldom criticized by the media. After all, God's Coach worked in mysterious ways.

The real Landry at times seemed to blank out under pressure on the sideline, forgetting plays or calling ones that didn't exist or made no sense. As the losses mounted in 1988, the real Landry kept "losing it" during close games, according to several assistants. Yes, beneath the stoneface facade, the coat and tie, Landry sometimes came unraveled, at the expense of his quarterback. Yet the real Landry was too insecure to ever accept any blame.

Many players accused the real Landry of lying to them and the media in the name of "business" and hiding behind the Bible. He motivated by fear and devastated players by criticizing their mental lapses in front of the team. His locker rooms echoed with Big Brother paranoia. He seldom offered one-on-one encouragement. He never let a player—even a great one—know what he really thought of him. The real Landry created his personal mystique by saying as little as possible.

In front of the team or media, the highest compliment Landry could pay a player was, "He's a pro." That meant he played when he was hurt. That meant he agreed to take painkilling injections. That meant he risked serious or permanent injury to a knee, a vertebra, a brain. That meant he ignored the doctor's warning and all the screaming signals with which God so wondrously equipped the body. Is that what God wanted? That a player dedicate his knees to

. . . to what? To Landry's glory? Is that how you got to heaven? Sure, this was pro football. Most teams were run as cold businesses. But the Cowboys were run by a man who traveled the country speaking God's word.

The real Landry left many ex-stars suffering from what you might call PLS (Post-Landry Syndrome). One, Pete Gent, who left the team in 1968, still writes Cowboy-based novels as therapy for Cowboy trauma. "What many guys wanted was for Tom to be their father figure," Gent says. "The two guys he had the most trouble with, Duane Thomas and Thomas Henderson, had lost their fathers, and they looked to Tom. But there was this erratic split in Tom's personality, the business and the religion. Here's a man dealing in human flesh and crippling injuries, betraying men, possibly lying to them about their physical conditions, deceiving them about why they've been released, keeping them ignorant and scared. I just don't believe a man can preach moral ethics and do what he did.

"It's like, man, there better be a fucking God. Didn't he realize the human carnage he could inflict?"

But didn't players realize Landry was just as scared as they were? Couldn't any of the many players Landry drafted for their intelligence see through his image? In the end, a few did, but a very few. "My personal theory," says D. D. Lewis, who played fourteen years under Landry, "was that the Cowboys gave you all those psychological tests before they drafted you because they wanted guys with a fear of abandonment. They wanted guys smart enough to play Tom's system but too scared to question it or ask for more money when the team won."

Only one Cowboy questioned it successfully. Ironically, he was the perfect Cowboy, Roger Staubach, God's Quarterback. Landry won two (of five) Super Bowls mostly because Staubach, the Naval officer, was courageous and instinctive enough to stand up to the myth, to ignore the play sent in by The Genius and run his own, damn the torpedoes and consequences. All the great Cowboy plays—from the Hail Mary pass on down—came after Staubach changed or modified Landry's call. "In theory," Gent says, "the system was brilliant, but ultimately the offense rested on the quarterback's ability to improvise."

So much for computers and for an image that nearly destroyed a nice guy, called Tommy by his nice wife Alicia. "Tom," says psychologist Beck, "was coming apart emotionally."

The real Landry seldom spoke with his business partners, Schramm and Brandt. Somehow Landry kept coaching, Schramm inventing and promoting, Brandt drafting—and this Harmonic Convergence continued for twenty-nine years. Somehow they stayed together but totally separate. No real interaction. No socializing. Each was content to grow famous and powerful in his domain. No power plays. They needed each other too much.

Early on, the Schramms had the Landrys over for dinner, but the Landrys didn't return the invitation. For years Schramm smoldered. He said, "You know how many times that son of a bitch asked me over for dinner?" And his thumb and forefinger formed a zero.

But after all, how could Landry justify his relationship with two men who did not practice what Landry preached? How could he live with two made-for-Dallas businessmen who used Landry's godly figurehead to shield what often was an ungodly organization—even to justify their life-styles and ethics? How many people had trusted Schramm or Brandt because, heavens, they were partners with Tom Landry? Yes, it was more of an Unholy Trinity. Even owner Bright came to resent Landry's "unapproachable arrogance" and asked Schramm to fire him as early as 1987.

Holy Cowboy.

Landry was a guy—just a guy—torn between football and religion, which Texans often confuse. America's fascination with Dallas and the Cowboys provided a powerful image for Landry, with which he won souls for the Lord. Yes, away from football, Landry could be a very different guy. He could be so kindly, so caring. Away from business, Landry could be as faultless a Christian as ever passed through the national media's mettle detector. He "walks his talk," as Billy Graham says.

Says Fellowship of Christian Athletes leader Chuck Bowman, "Without the incredible amount of time Tom Landry has dedicated, I'm not sure the FCA would have survived. Through the years Tom has been unblemished and unstained. We had to have him for credibility." Speaking nearly 100 times a year, coast to coast, Landry has affected perhaps as many lives as Graham through the 1980s. Yes, the coach often criticized by players for his inability to motivate became one of the country's most popular motivational speakers. Did that justify selling a little of his soul to Schramm and Brandt? Landry dedicated his off-seasons to God and family while his team went to hell.

But Landry couldn't quit. Tom Landry never quits. He had let the Cowboy talent fade into the sunset, but *he* couldn't. How many more 3–13s could he and his image endure? At what point would he have to be dragged into the sunset?

Then, coming toward Landry through the winter twilight, was the guy from Arkansas who was about to "release" him, as Landry would call it. Yes, the Lord was about to work in a very mysterious way.

Up in Dallas that morning, Jones and Bright had struck a deal. Jones had outfinagled about fifty bidders, including Los Angeles Lakers owner Jerry Buss and a partnership headed by Staubach. Jones's strongest qualification—other than cold cash—may have been the coach he brought to the bargaining table. From his first conversation with Salomon Brothers, Jones made it clear he wouldn't waste anyone's time negotiating if he couldn't bring along University of Miami coach Jimmy Johnson, a roommate and teammate of Jones's at Arkansas. Bright liked the idea. Many bidders had shied away from what was known around Bright's office as the "Landry problem." Who wanted to pay Bright's asking price of $180 million for the inevitable responsibility of having to fire Tom Landry? In effect, Landry had just named himself offensive and defensive co-ordinator. He had indicated the Cowboys would continue running the same offense and defense they basically had used since 1960. He had said he would coach "into the '90s," if not forever.

Bright had asked Schramm to tell Landry to "stay in pocket," just in case a deal was made. But with rumors flying, Landry had flown to Austin, where he has a getaway home on the eighteenth hole of The Hills of Lakeway. Landry had made himself even harder to find by driving seventeen miles to play another course, appropriately named Hidden Hills. After a five-hour telephone search, Bright had reached an employee at Hidden Hills and told him, "Go out on the course and find Tom and grab him by the arm. And if you need to, take somebody with you to grab the other arm. Then take him somewhere and hold him."

Foolishly, Jones volunteered to fly with Schramm to Austin to "look Coach Landry in the eye and tell him about my relationship with Jimmy Johnson." Jones was about to go down, down in Cowboy history as the Man Who Fired Tom Landry. Bright says, "It was my decision to fire Tom, and Tex's responsibility. I had no idea Jerry would take the fall."

Near the putting green, Schramm introduced Jones to Landry and his family. Wife Alicia and daughter Lisa began to sob, along with several bystanders. Son Tom Jr. accompanied his dad, followed by Jones and Schramm, up a hill to an empty sales office that overlooked the course. Jones sat on a couch that faced an open picture window. Landry and Schramm faced each other in chairs to Jones's left and right.

Landry couldn't seem to believe this was really happening. How dare this . . . this chicken-fried Judas. *Hey, I'm Coach Landry. I invented the Flex. I had twenty straight winning seasons.* He told Jones, "You didn't need to come here. This is just a publicity stunt."

"No, Tom," said Schramm, "I don't think that's why Jerry came down."

Jones cleared his throat and said, "Coach Landry, some day I hope you'll realize what great respect I have for you, but . . ."

Jones glanced away for a moment and locked eyes with a lynch mob. Through the picture window, family, friends, and fans were watching Tom Landry be fired. "It wasn't the best of circumstances," Jones says. "I didn't stay in the room more than ten minutes or so, then I left Tex and Tom together. Walking back to the car past all those people outside was the longest walk of my life."

In the next few weeks a private investigator would be hired to deliver "dirt" on Jones to Dallas newspapers. Jones would be told the P.I. was paid by a group of religious zealots enraged by the way God's Coach had been treated. *This thing, this monster.*

That night back at a bar in Dallas, eight or ten Cowboy starters and ex-stars mock-toasted the only ex-coach the Cowboys had ever had. One player who was there says, "Guys kept raising a glass and saying, 'Here's to the baldheaded motherfucker. He got it just the way he gave it to so many of us.' "

Two months or so later, Jerry Jones sat across a makeshift desk from a raging Schramm in the sandstone palace Schramm ruled. "Fucks" and "goddamn its" were flying. At one point Jones feared Schramm was going to "come over the desk" at him. Jones tried to defuse Schramm's anger with a big smile and a "Tex, you know I'm forty-six and you're sixty-four . . ."

"Cowboys Center" was a monument to Texas Ernest Schramm's rule-the-world ego and spending—and a symbol of Dallas's economic collapse. Schramm's was a ranch-style palace: one story, eighty thousand square feet, surrounded by a housing development called Valley Ranch northwest of Dallas. As team president, and 3 percent owner, Schramm spent as if he were the majority owner. After all, as NFL commissioner Pete Rozelle says, "There hasn't been an innovation in this game in the last twenty-five years that Tex didn't have something to do with."

Showgirl cheerleaders. Computerized drafting. Instant replay. Thirty-second clocks. Referees' microphones. In a way, Schramm even invented Rozelle. While Schramm was Rams P.R. director in 1952, he hired Rozelle as an assistant. Some said Rozelle remained Schramm's assistant even as commissioner.

Just think: All this from a guy who had struggled as a $30-a-week sportswriter in Austin. Yes, the Schramm who so brilliantly used sportswriters to help create Cowboy Mystique couldn't hack it as a writer. Schramm became the stories he wanted to write. He created his own newspaper, Cowboys Weekly, with a peak circulation of nearly one hundred thousand, and wrote the lead column. He had his own radio show, "Ask Tex Schramm," and local TV show, "Cowboys Weekly," which at its peak outrated "Miami Vice." ("Miami Vice" was Landry's favorite show. Was Schramm Landry's alter ego?)

Until the end, owner Bright didn't question Schramm, whom he called "the best CEO in the NFL." Bright says he went to Cowboys Center only three times in the five years he owned the team: twice for Christmas parties and once on October 22, 1987, to suggest his CEO fire Landry. But as the records fell toward 3–13, Bright discovered Schramm was taking advantage of his trust. Bright says, "Tex was like Phineas T. Barnum—an all-time great promoter. He was like Phineas T. and Jumbo the elephant. Jumbo wasn't really the world's biggest elephant. Tex just convinced everybody it was.

"But Tex was one of the worst businessmen. Inherently he was not straightforward. . . . I was blinded by the mystique. It was my fault."

Bright had blindly carried on the Cowboy tradition of invisible ownership begun by Clint Murchison. Schramm widely boasted about how Murchison had the "class" to stay in the background and accept that owning an NFL team was not a profitable venture. But Bright found that Schramm had signed Landry to a guaranteed three-year contract in early 1986—with annual salaries of $800,000,

$900,000, and $1 million—instead of three one-year deals, as Bright had instructed. Jones found he owed Landry $1 million. Jones found "little expenses" such as about $20,000 a year just to polish the leaves of plants that beautified the two hundred acres of Cowboys Center. Jones found utility bills alone of $100,000 a year, outrageous expense accounts, and inflated salaries and overtime for employees who did little more than polish Schramm's ego.

"I was just a fan," Jones says. "I had no idea."

One thing Jones could not find was his way out of the Cowboys Center's funhouselike hallways. Early on, Jones got so lost he had to call his secretary via a house phone to come find him. "Get me outta this damn place," he told her. Players often joked they were just a sideshow at Schramm's amusement park, through which guided tours constantly passed. Cowboys Center includes a Cheerleaders dance studio, travel agency, memorabilia shop and, oh yes, a locker room and practice field. For an original $70 million Schramm also envisioned a hotel, a golf course, a restaurant pavilion, an ice-skating rink, a sports medicine clinic, and his special project, Cowboys ShowPlace, a high-Tex hall of fame. But while the team's records were falling, the bottom fell out of the Dallas real estate market. Schramm's monument became a sandstone elephant stalked by tusk-hunting creditors.

"I was shocked," says Jerry Jones, who even dared to question why the team left "the NFL's finest facility" for two months a year to train at Cal Lutheran University in Thousand Oaks outside Los Angeles, to the tune of another $500,000 or so.

One reason, Jones discovered, was that so many front-office people and coaches had girlfriends in California. Thousand Oaks was like summer camp for consenting adults. As ex-assistant Paul Hackett said early in his first camp, "This place is incredible. Just about everybody's got something going out here." Landry's team was an irresistible sexual magnet. The players often compared themselves with rock stars. For groupies there was just something about riding a Cowboy in the name of Tom Landry. It was a religious experience. A sacrifice. A duty. Hadn't original owner Murchison begun the team's "eat, drink, and chase Mary" tradition? Murchison biographer Jane Wolfe says Murchison was "the equivalent of fifteen of the worst adulterers you can imagine."

The team's weekly newspaper featured a centerfold spread of a Cheerleader—Bambi or Teri or Toni or Gigi—posing seductively at poolside or beneath a lonesome oak. Somehow Schramm found time to sort carefully through all the pictures and choose just the right ones. "The highlight of his week," an ex-aide says. Schramm had even elevated his favorite secretary and Gal Sunday, Suzanne Mitchell, to Cheerleaders director.

What had Jones stumbled into? No, he's no angel, but after undergoing a routine investigation for NFL ownership approval, Jones was told his "rap sheet was the shortest ever," he says. By Cowboy standards, anyway, Jones was a pretty decent guy. He certainly wasn't in Schramm's league for consuming alcohol. On a flight to Hawaii for the league meetings, a Cowboys staffer claims to have counted as Schramm downed nineteen martinis and seven of his favorite bullshots (beef boullion and vodka). The source also insists Schramm walked off the plane under his own power.

And Landry kept saying Texas Stadium should be renamed Murchison Stadium? Schramm had been named 1987 Father of the Year in Dallas?

Holy Cowboy.

And now, facing Schramm across the desk, Jones could have used a stiff drink himself. Would Tex Schramm actually take a swing at him? Jones was using a temporary desk in the conference room outside Schramm's office. "I really thought Tex and I could work together," Jones says. But Jones had authorized the firing of a long-time employee, a loyal Schrammite named Ann Lloyd whose title was assistant ticket manager. Jones was beginning to "cut away the fat" by eliminating a number of jobs such as Lloyd's, in the $40,000-a-year range, that could be or were already being done by others. But cutting away Lloyd sent Schramm into one of his famed rages. During games Schramm sat in the press box and often pounded his fist the way Khrushchev pounded his shoe. Schramm called refs "goddamn cocksuckers" and worse.

Now, as he challenged Jones, Schramm's jowly bellow could be heard for miles down the endless hallways. To Schramm, it was inconceivable that this rich hillbilly could be taking over his empire. *Doesn't he realize who I am? I broke the players' strikes! I kept Cowboy salaries the lowest in the league! I made a fool of Tony Dorsett in contract negotiations! I kept Lee Roy Jordan out of the Cowboys' Ring of Honor because he dared to hold out on me.*

The only book Schramm ever chose to read was *The Godfather.*

A front office source says, "Tex thought he *was* the Dallas

Cowboys—the creator, owner, operator—but he had the job that Jerry moved to Dallas to do. He was doomed the moment Jerry got involved."

Doomed from the moment Jones couldn't go fishing. Schramm's passion? Fishing for marlin.

As crates of plaques and pictures and commemorative footballs were being hauled out of Schramm's office, Jones's secretary noticed the framed NFL franchise agreement—the title to the team—also was leaving. Jones says, "There was some debate about what belonged to Tex and what belonged to the Cowboys."

The franchise agreement stayed.

About two months later security guard Bill Westfall noticed Gil Brandt on the video arcade of screens in front of him. Westfall was monitoring the many entrances to Cowboys Center. Brandt was breezing into the main administrative entrance as if he still owned the place. Westfall had his orders: Under no circumstances was Gil Brandt to be allowed on the premises. Westfall left the control booth. This was one duty he would relish.

As new Cowboys coach Jimmy Johnson says, "It was amazing how many people on the staff came to me and told me what a tyrant Gil could be."

Of the Unholy Trinity, Brandt created his media image most completely with neon and blue smoke. Gilbert Harvey Brandt was the grand master of illusion. He sometimes told interviewers he had been a defensive back at the University of Wisconsin, but he lied. He didn't even play football in high school. He had bluffed his way into pro football.

Brandt often was portrayed in print as a computer wizard. Yet ex-secretaries say Brandt had a "phobia" about trying to operate a computer. As a rival general manager says, "It took a while, but people around the league finally realized what a joke Gil was. He wouldn't know a football player if he bit him in the ass."

Oh, no? So why did Landry rely almost solely on Brandt's scouting information until the 3–13 end? "Gil Brandt," says Paul Hackett, "made this team in the '60s and early '70s, then he broke it." Yes, Gil Fuckin' Brandt, as he was called around Cowboys Center, helped make and break God's Coach.

Holy Cowboy.

Jones may have felt as if he were upside down drinking margaritas when Bright told him about The Deal. When Bright bought the team, he agreed to honor his friend Murchison's agreement with Brandt. As Mrs. Gil Brandt became Mrs. Clint Murchison in 1975—ironically, the year of Brandt's last great draft—Murchison promised Brandt lifetime security as the Cowboys' personnel director. The Deal may have had a good deal to do with the Cowboys' plunge through the '80s.

"I agreed to honor that," Bright says, "but I told Jerry he was under no obligation to do so."

Given a blank-check budget by Murchison in the '60s, Brandt simply outhustled an NFL still playing in black hightops. "Most teams," says Brandt, "were still drafting out of *Street & Smith's*." Night after night, long after Landry had gone home to his family, Brandt worked. While most teams still drafted out of magazines, Brandt built a network of informants—assistant coaches, trainers, secretaries—that reached schools so small even Brandt could have played for them. Brandt became the Draftmaster on information alone. He didn't know a football player on sight, but he got to know people who did. Brandt didn't need binoculars, just a telephone, and he began stocking Landry's system with superior two-deep talent.

Brandt did whatever it took to make college coaches feel they owed him a favor. He sent them clothes, set up vacations, and staged an annual golf tournament for them in Dallas. Welcome to Fantasy Island, Coach. Whatever made them happy, Brandt arranged.

Brandt tried to turn every college into IOU. In return Brandt wanted info. Brandt's vast network helped him become *Sport* magazine's annual "draft guru." Brandt chose *Playboy*'s all-American teams. Brandt was readily reachable for any sportswriter in any city or town. Brandt traded inside info for publicity—for mystique. Brandt could tell you which college star was bisexual, which slept with a teddy bear or with his coach's wife or daughter. Ironic, wasn't it, that Brandt recommended so many players to Landry who turned out to be flakes, weirdos, druggies, or police blotter regulars? The team known for character actually had the NFL's largest assortment of characters. "So many quirky players," says Gent, one of the quirkiest. So many: Duane Thomas. Thomas "Hollywood" Henderson. Lance Rentzel. Don Meredith. John Niland. Pat Toomay. Harvey

Martin. Tony Dorsett. Larry Bethea. Rafael Septien. All highly intelligent, by NFL standards. All highly unLandrylike.

So many "incidents." Toomay, a defensive end turned novelist,
calls it The Lid. "They kept trying to push The Lid down on us, and
guys kept coming out the sides."

And Brandt, who knew all the right people at the police department and the telephone company, almost seemed to be posting
bail before the arrest had even been made. Vice president Brandt
was more like the president of vice. Brandt knew Dallas's dark side
as well as its spotlight, knew of the gamblers and the pushers, and,
usually, which Cowboys were associating with them.

Dextor Clinkscale, the Cowboy player representative in 1984
and 1985, named his pet snake Gil. Charlie Waters, voted the team's
most popular player in the late '70s, once threatened to "put snakes
in Gil's hot tub." Brandt went from being every rookie's best friend
to every vet's worst enemy. Brandt loved to gloat about his
draftees—and delighted in humbling them come contract time.
Brandt did the dirty-work negotiating for Schramm. Like Schramm,
Brandt's ego was fed by dominating All-Pros. A team executive says,
"When it was time to negotiate, Gil would use anything he knew
about a player's personal life against him." As Schramm once said of
Brandt, "Every organization needs a son of a bitch." No wonder the
guy who seemed to know everybody never seemed to have any real
friends.

Brandt, who may not have even attended college, became the
godfather of college coaching. Many major-college presidents who
needed to hire a coach called Brandt for advice and matchmaking.
Brandt dropped more names than his '80s draftees dropped footballs. Brandt was "tight" with Bo Schembechler and Bobby Knight.
Brandt put H. R. "Bum" Bright (a powerful regent at Texas A&M)
together with Jackie Sherrill. Brandt recommended "my good
friend" Jimmy Johnson to the right people at Miami. Brandt made
sure college coaches and administrators saw him on TV. He was the
lone NFL personnel director who dressed like an assistant coach and
stood on the sideline, holding a clipboard and shaking his fist after
big plays and bad calls. Invariably a camera would find him and an
announcer would say, "There's Gil Brandt, the man behind the
Cowboy drafts."

Brandt built his reputation on exotic discoveries: basketball
players, track stars, unpublicized athletes from unknown schools

who scored off the boards on his special quickness, agility, and IQ tests. But by the late '70s other teams had caught up with Brandt—and with Landry, who mostly left the scouting to Brandt while he spoke to groups, sat on boards, played in golf tournaments, and spent time with his family. Brandt kept trying to live up to his diamonds-in-the-rough image. Brandt began to find flaws in obvious choices and to reach further and further for "finds." Brandt began drafting more "good stories" than good players. Brandt began to miss sensationally.

Brandt's final ten drafts were mostly the work of a man who wouldn't know a football player if he bit him.

But in the end even "good friend" Johnson saw through Brandt. Johnson discovered that Brandt, the superscout, was paying $48,000 a year to subscribe to a scouting service. Sources in the new and old regimes say Brandt's personal expense account for 1988 was around $360,000. Jones's treasurer, Jack Dixon, wouldn't confirm that figure but said, "Well, Gil's expenses weren't *utterly* excessive when you think about all they included." For years Brandt even operated a hotel hospitality suite at college basketball's Final Four. After all, he and Knight were tight, and he had played some basketball in high school. Brandt had become a traveling P.R. evangelist for America's Team. Or was he promoting himself? In the '80s, did Landry's team benefit from Brandt's $1,000 tabs for rookies or college coaches at the Palm restaurant in downtown Dallas?

One of Brandt's scouts says, "He bragged about how he never spent a penny of his own money. He probably has more money than Jerry Jones." And Jones says, "No one benefited more financially from the Cowboys than Gil Brandt."

Brandt was fired the way he fired so many secretaries and gofers: without ceremony.

But Brandt wouldn't leave Cowboys Center. He wouldn't clean out his office. He kept playing racquetball. He kept being Gil Brandt. A Cowboy scout says, "Gil just couldn't believe it was happening to him. This was his whole life. He had nowhere else to go." He was fifty-seven, or maybe sixty-seven or forty-seven.

Brandt claimed the furniture in his office belonged to him. The team made him an offer for it. "But," says a team official, "his wife [who had sued Brandt for divorce] let us know the furniture was paid for by the team."

Eventually Brandt's belongings were boxed up and stored in a shed. The lock was changed on his office door. A locksmith was called to open his office safe, which contained nothing but some old, useless draft information.

The guards were given their orders.

Bill Westfall approached Brandt and said, "Gil, I'm sorry, but I understand you're not welcome here anymore."

"Who said?"

Do you know who you're talking to, pal? I'll have your job and make sure you never work in this town again.

"Jerry and Jimmy said. So let's not have a scene, Gil. If you'll just go quietly, I won't escort you off the property and embarrass you."

Brandt went just as he had come to Dallas—quietly.

2

IN NOVEMBER 1978 I walked into a novel by Larry McMurtry or Pete Gent or Dan Jenkins or maybe even by Texas E. Schramm. If not a novel, then I found myself in an episode of "Dallas," TV's hottest new show. This couldn't really be happening. I'd gone through the looking glass, wildly. This was *Dallas in Wonderland*.

The Cowboys were "streaking," as Landry called it, toward their fifth Super Bowl of the '70s. Little did I imagine it would be their last. Who knew, as Thomas "Hollywood" Henderson big-played his way toward the cover of *Time*, that he was careening toward cocaine hell? Who knew Roger Staubach would play just one more season and retire prematurely, as Don Meredith had before him? Who knew America's Team was about to come quietly apart at its designer seams?

I had arrived at its zenith. Make that Zenith, as in television and radio. The Cowboys were on their way to shattering the NFL record for national TV appearances with (counting exhibition games) nineteen. Beano Cook, then a CBS spokesman, said, "The two most important people to CBS are J.R. Ewing and Tom Landry. We have a rule we go by when we're planning NFL telecasts: Give people the best game possible. And when in doubt, give them the Cowboys. Our ratings are up this season, and there's only one reason: the Cowboys."

The Cowboys were inescapable. They had the largest radio network in sports—225 stations, including 16 in Mexico. The Cowboys dominated the sales of NFL Properties (sportswear, trinkets, bumper stickers, and so forth) with about 30 percent. Of twenty-seven other NFL teams, Pittsburgh was next with 8 percent. The Cowboys—or their Cheerleaders—even scored unstoppably in non-sports programming. A made-for-TV movie wittily titled *The Dallas Cowboys Cheerleaders* was the second-highest-rated boob-tube flick ever. Ever! (I was told this piece of idiotic cheesecake outrated *Roots, Ike,* and, of course, *Jesus of Nazareth.*) And what soon would be showing right across the parking lot from the Cowboy offices on the eleventh floor of Expressway Towers? The movie version of Gent's *North Dallas Forty,* based on his Cowboy nightmares. Naturally it would be a box office smash across the country.

At least thirty books based on Cowboy experiences had or would be written, including this one, which is writing itself.

My first week in Dallas, Schramm told a *Washington Post* interviewer, "It's self-evident we're by far the most popular team in the country, by any available measuring stick. It's even hard to say who's second."

Yes, I had entered a dimension of sight and sound that would dominate my existence. The *Dallas Morning News* had "hired me away" from the *Los Angeles Times,* where my editor was so distraught he sniffed and asked, "How do you get to Dallas anyway, by wagon train?" No, by covered limo. The *News* had thrown open its vault and offered me $40,000 a year to write a daily sports column. Okay, a lot of Dallasites left $40,000 a year in tips. But I was twenty-six years old. I had come from nowhere—well, the humble side of Oklahoma City. And in L.A. I mostly had written magazine-length feature and investigative stories. The truth was, I hadn't written a column before. Not one. All I really had was an "L.A." image.

Yet for weeks before my arrival, the *Morning News* hyped my debut by running mysterious red or blue boxes throughout the paper that said only, "Skip." I soon would be advertised on billboards and buses in a mock-*Playgirl* pose—lying on my side, head propped on hand, in a gray sweatsuit. Pinch me, please.

I had talked my way into this job, just as Gil Brandt, I would discover, had talked his way into his.

Brandt was the first to pop out of his office as I stepped off the eleventh-floor elevator. He introduced himself and said, "So the *Morning News* broke down and gave you a little more money and you decided to come, huh?"

No, I had accepted the first offer. But I nodded sheepishly as if Brandt knew something I didn't. After all, I was looking into the shifting eyes of *Gil Brandt*. The Draftmaster! The Source! The man who could spot a football player from a light-year away. I had been raised in awe of the Cowboys. My parents had taken me to several early '60s games when the expansion Cowboys played at the Cotton Bowl. My father had pointed down to the sideline and said, "That's Tom Landry. He's a great man."

Landry, Schramm, Brandt—hey, I even had a Cowboy trash can in my dorm room at Vanderbilt University. I'm not sure what Freud would have said about that, but I had been fascinated by the Cowboys since I first beheld the phallic-symbol skyscrapers that form the Dallas skyline. The Cowboys were on TV nearly every Sunday in Oklahoma City, which is two hundred miles north. For a kid in Oklahoma, the Cowboys were like watching Saturday morning superheroes on Sunday afternoons. They just seemed faster, stronger, smarter—somehow destined to defeat the forces of evil.

And there I was talking football with Brandt himself. "Lemme tell you what's really happening with this Dorsett situation," he said, referring to Dorsett's latest run-in with the Dallas police. Brandt actually leaned and spoke out of the side of his mouth, which seemed permanently pulled to the left. Brandt had the look of a guy from working-class Milwaukee trying to go Hollywood. His razor-cut, blow-dried, Grecian Formula hair didn't seem to fit with his face, which was mostly nose, lower lip, and chin. One manicured hand was dominated by a Super Bowl ring so big that that shoulder appeared to hang lower than the other. His lips barely opened as he spoke. Brandt, I'd heard, had suffered through dental hell to fix a mouthful of rotted teeth.

He was maybe five-eleven, 190 pounds, but he stood in a five-eight slouch. He didn't stand long, though. He was fidgety. He walked away in a quick, cocky prance, chin high. His body language said, "I know something you don't, and I'm about to know something else."

Gil Brandt! He even called me at home to tell me how much he liked my first column. How he got the number I still don't know. He said, "That was smart that you were real complimentary of Dallas."

Everybody in Dallas was bullish on Dallas. New residents were pouring in by the wagon-train load, especially from the economically depressed North. "Snowbirds," they were called. Corporations such as American Airlines were relocating in Dallas—in the "Sunbelt," where we tried to ignore the two or three ice storms a winter. In the next three or four years the population of the Dallas–Fort Worth "Metroplex" would rise from about 2.7 million to 3.5 million. Dallas was experiencing a sort of twenty-first century gold rush. Money was being made and spent faster in Dallas than perhaps ever before in America. Businessmen were too busy to say "business" in its entirety. "Bidness," they said. Landry was so busy he said "bi'ness."

Dallas was striking oil, selling real estate, lending millions, doing government-funded white-collar work on computers and aircraft. Dallas rhymed with palace. Dreams came true in Dallas. Welcome to Oz. Heaven can wait.

"Can do!" was the city's motto. It was as if people greeted each other with, "Aren't we great?" Yes, we were! Cowboys trailing? No problem. Staubach can do!

Dallas was Neiman-Marcus, the department store for the shopper who had everything. Neiman's Christmas catalogue featured his and hers oil derricks. Jack Miller, then head of the rival Sanger-Harris stores and now a civic leader and sought-after speaker, says, "You came to Dallas [Miller had been in Philadelphia] and the sky was wider, the moon was bigger. There was such a contrast between Dallas and the older cities in the East. There, the feeling was that the only money made was from old money. In Dallas only your own limitations could keep you from making what you damn well pleased. The banks were on a roll. It didn't matter what you paid for real estate because you could sell it for twice as much two years later. Everybody was looking for the latest watering trough [bar or restaurant]. Everybody seemed to be swapping wives. If your neighbor had two cars, you had to have three—a Mercedes, a Rolls, and a Jag. 'The deal' was everything. The most admired people were the ones who knew how to make the most money. Unfortunately, people thought the men with the most money had infinite wisdom, too.

"I actually sent our buyers to games at Texas Stadium to see what everyone was wearing. It was a real fashion show in the suites [which are connected by a hallway that circles the stadium]. People wouldn't really watch the game. They'd just walk up and down the hallway, sticking their heads into different suites to say hi and have a drink. That was Dallas in the late '70s."

I was soon hanging out with a twenty-four-year-old guy from Shreveport who hung out at a disco/bar called Cafe Dallas. "A lot of Cowboys go there," he told me one day by phone from his BMW. He sold commercial real estate. Three weeks in a row he closed shopping center deals that made him $100,000 commissions. And I had settled for $40,000?

Dallas! I was finding the city, like so many of its successful stories, came from nowhere; it had no reason for being. Dallas, which rises off the plains of north central Texas, isn't on an ocean or lake or major river. It isn't in the mountains or even rolling forests. It doesn't offer a tropical or desert climate. Dallas was founded by a pioneer entrepreneur named John Neely Bryan, whose downtown cabin has been preserved. Jack Miller says, "Bryan came to sell his wares to the Caddo Indians, but he found they all had been massacred. So Bryan divided up the land and started selling real estate, and he traveled all around the area promoting it."

Dallas became a new, clean, friendly place to buy and sell, to make and spend, to get rich (and poor) quick. At night the downtown beneath the photogenic skyline turned into a ghost town of street people and winos. How was I to know that this sonic boomtown hung by the same Neiman-Marcus thread its football team did? Who could have imagined Cowboys owner Clint Murchison, with an estimated worth of $600 million, would soon lose nearly all of it? That my real estate buddy would leave town fleeing creditors?

This was late 1978 and the Cowboys were on another Super Bowl roll. They had crushed Denver's "Orange Crush" Broncos in the previous Super Bowl. Ho hum, wouldn't it always rain diamonds through the hole in the Texas Stadium roof?

Just as Dallas could get very hot and very cold, so could its passion for its Cowboys. I hadn't experienced anything like it in sports. There wasn't so much blind devotion to this team as there was blinding interest in it. Everybody wanted to talk and know about the Cowboys, especially if they lost. Dallas had to know WHY and WHAT'S BEING DONE ABOUT IT. Dallasites hated being embarrassed by their Cowboys. In defeat it was as if Dallasites sniffed and disassociated themselves from the team. Like the Cowboys, Dallas was built on image, on a skyline facade of chrome and glass. Dallas cared passionately about how it *looked* to the rest of the country.

Yet what amazed and amused me was that the city's national image was being created by a TV show set on a ranch called South-fork and by a team called the Cowboys, and Dallas didn't really have many genuine cowboys. Journalists came from the coasts looking for downtown rodeos, freeway cattle drives, cattle horns on bumpers of Cadillacs, and I'd tell them to try Fort Worth or Houston. Fort Worth, about thirty miles away on I-30, still had its stockyards and its Billy Bob's Texas, a square mile of honky-tonk packed with urban cowboys and cowgirls doing the two-step. And Houston was far more blue-collar, boots-wearin', snuff-dippin', mechanical-bull-ridin' cowboy than Dallas. Houston was Oilers coach Bum Phillips, who actually lived on a ranch and rode horses and raised cattle.

In Dallas people mostly rode elevators. Dallas was a stainless-steel melting pot. Sure, there were Wild West diehards in the suburbs east and west. "Shit-kickers" or "goat-ropers," they were called. And there were some Rich Old Texans, out of the Jock Ewing mold. But I didn't see many rootin'-tootin' cowboys in the Dallas that fascinated America—North Dallas.

This mink-lined corridor stretched north between North Dallas Tollway and Central Expressway, from the old-money palaces of Highland Park (designed by the same fellow who did Beverly Hills) through the castles of the *nouveau riche* in the Bent Tree and Preston Trail additions. I met many people my age who had been raised in North Dallas and spoke with almost no Texas drawl, not even a "y'all." Too many parents had come from "up North." Most North Dallasites and Texas Stadium patrons wouldn't be caught dead in a cowboy hat. Boots were worn mostly by wealthy wives. While "Texas chic" had spread all the way to Manhattan's garment district, the only ranch I knew of was Southfork, where the TV show was shot. Southfork was a tourist trap maybe an hour's drive north of downtown.

God, Dallas's *image* was even an image.

Dallas, I found, was a nice place to live, but you wouldn't want to visit there. It was as pretty a place as man could erect, but other than Southfork, the only site to take visitors to see was the Texas School Book Depository. Imagine: The city's biggest tourist attraction was the Kennedy memorial.

After business hours there wasn't enough to do in Dallas except go to the latest, hottest Mexican cantina or nightclub and, well, no wonder Dallas was known as the divorce capital. Too many painted ladies from too many places were arriving daily in search of a rich husband, preferably an oil man or a Cowboy. Turn up the disco throb of Donna Summer's "She Works Hard for the Money." Yes, money was the root. Dallas had become the devil's workshop. An area of Greenville Avenue, just behind the Cowboys' office tower, had grown into a three-mile Satan's strip of pulsating meet markets. It looked like one long strip shopping center: Cafe Dallas. Elan. Humperdink's. Biff's. Their names, winking in neon, changed as fast as their clientele. Here today; gone tomorrow night.

Herpes was still something people gave each other in Philadelphia or Detroit.

Divorced mothers were the target audience of the top-rated radio station in the Metroplex, KVIL. The Voice of Dallas, Ron Chapman, knew how to assure "Kay-ville's" many Alimony Annies that a rough life was going to get better, gosh darn it. Chapman's motto for building the number 1 station in Dallas–Fort Worth: "Perception is reality."

Mostly because of Landry, I guess, I'd always thought of Dallas as the Bible Belt capital, but its Christian soldiers seemed to be losing the battle. Racism smoldered. White supremacy flourished. Dallas was pretension and tension. Blacks were just fine as long as they stayed put south of the Trinity River, which trickled past downtown. "Dallas," says psychologist Don Beck, "just hadn't experienced the racial crises that had forced change in so many other cities. Dallas was busy mourning Kennedy."

Blacks also were just fine if they were a Cowboy. Thomas Henderson says, "In 1978 I went to pick up a white girl at her parents' house in Highland Park, and her right-wing Ronald Reagan dad answered the door with a look of horror. I said the magic words: 'Hi, I'm Thomas Henderson of the Dallas Cowboys,' and his eyes lit up."

Cowboys made everything okay.

I met several "religious" people who told me they attended Highland Park Methodist—"you know, where Tom Landry goes." Lots of white Anglo-Saxon Protestants attended church only for show, it seemed. Lots of preachers were becoming stars. Former Cowboy safety Dextor Clinkscale, who regularly attended church and team Bible study and left Dallas to pursue law school, says, "Dallas is a base for political and religious power. If you have a persona and a gift of gab, you can get away with murder from the pulpit. Dallas had more Jim Bakkers than any city around—men who were more religious and less Christian. The wealthy are into the religious atmosphere. They religiously go to church and contribute to charities, and they religiously are deceitful in their business and personal lives."

Dallas religiously followed its Cowboys, too, thank goodness. "We've decided," I was told by a *Morning News* editor, "that the Cowboys will sell this newspaper the way nothing else will." A circulation war was just beginning to rage between the *Morning News* and *Times Herald* (which would hire me away in 1982). The winner, it seemed, would be the paper that could dazzle the reader with the most Cinemascope and Dolby coverage of the Wowboys, as I began to call them in print. Dallas wanted to touch the metallic-blue magic. Through the sports page, readers wanted to be able to say they personally knew Roger (Staubach) and Drew (Pearson) and T.D. (Tony Dorsett). I was honored by the many requests I received to speak to high school and college journalism classes, but nearly every question was something like, "Do you really get to talk to Charlie Waters?" I was becoming a "star" by association. I could have written, "See Charlie run. Run, Charlie, run." And many readers, it seemed, would have thought, "This guy from L.A. has *talent.*"

In Dallas, if you weren't conversant in Cowboy, you couldn't do business or socialize. I began getting letters from women saying something like, "Thanks for writing about things I can understand about the Cowboys. I don't get all that technical stuff, but thanks to you, I now have something to talk about at cocktail parties." A Dallasite's opinion about or inside knowledge of the Cowboys was as critical as what car he or she drove. If you actually knew a Cowboy or even someone who did, who knows what deal you might close? Having a personally decorated $300,000 Texas Stadium luxury box or at least seats on the 50-yard line was as important as what neighborhood you lived in. Says Clinkscale, "It was like everything was one big facade—the city, the organization, even the fans at Texas Stadium. There just wasn't much permanent about it."

I couldn't believe America's Team sometimes had trouble selling out the end zone seats in its own stadium. Yet president Tex Schramm explained, "If we had sixty-five thousand seats between the 40s, we could sell out every game." At any price Dallas just wasn't an end zone kind of town, especially if that Sunday's set decoration was the Giants or Eagles and it was sure to be a boring blowout. Schramm had insisted on leaving the Texas Stadium field open to the heavens because "football was meant to be played in the elements." But the customers had a roof over their heads. This wasn't New York or Philly, where battling the elements was part of the game for fans, too.

This was Dallas, where double-breasted "bidnessmen" stood around at cocktail parties comparing Cowboy opinions as if they were comparing manhoods. Yes, Dallas measured its virility by how tall its buildings were and how much it knew about its Cowboys. In reality it knew only what Landry-Schramm-Brandt wanted it to know. But the point was, the Cowboys had become Dallas's ski slopes, its beach, its recreational reason for being. Dallas *was* the Cowboys.

I soon realized this city was made for—or maybe by—Tex Schramm.

There it was, looming on the endless horizon: Texas Stadium. Or maybe Tex's Stadium. Schramm's domelike sky-blue creation, girded like Dallas with white concrete and steel, was ten minutes from the Dallas–Fort Worth Airport, which was three hours by jet from anywhere in America. In fact, Texas Stadium itself looked as if it could be cleared for takeoff at any moment. It was Battlestar Galactica or the Starship Enterprise or maybe Darth Vader's home away from home.

Who could have imagined America's Team would become the first NFL team ever to lose fourteen consecutive home games?

There it was, where highways 183 and 114 met in the sprawling suburb of Irving. Irving? The Cowboys played in a place that sounded as if it had been named after a wimpy loser? It was my first game at Texas Stadium. I walked past the four white limos parked at Gate 8 and up two flights of stairs to . . . sportswriter's heaven. I was entering a press box in which we mustard-stained wretches were treated like oil and cattle barons. As Cowboy receiver Butch Johnson would tell me, "They treat you guys a helluva lot better than they treat us. You are their lifeblood."

Yes, we had our own giant luxury box. We had a kitchen, an open bar and bartender, and a lounge area (with two big TVs) that could seat around sixty or seventy at a dozen big tables. "Whatever you need" was the motto of Schramm's P.R. machine. Southwestern cuisine? Whenever you wanted, before or during the game, the blue-haired woman in winged-framed glasses behind the cafeteria-style line would slice you up a mess of ribs, ham, or barbecued beef and call you "hon." You could dish up the potato salad and baked beans yourself, hon. Have some pee–can pie. Have a beer. Have some J&B, like ol' Tex. Have a nice day.

This was work? This wasn't how it worked at any other NFL stadium. The lounge area opened into a three-tiered press box fit for a, well, Schramm. He sat on the top row, overlooking "my people," as he called sportswriters. At Washington's RFK Stadium, for instance, we sat on folding chairs wedged into an open-air press box and pulled neck muscles trying to see replays on a mounted TV. But at Tex's Stadium we sat in deeply cushioned swivel chairs protected from the elements and noise by a window. Every two writers had their own miniature TV. Female attendants known as Texettes kept passing by to see if "y'all" needed anything. Another beer? A column idea?

After games the Texettes were even available to give shoulder rubs to ease deadline tension. Ah, America's Team. Some Texettes had failed in the Miss America-like Cheerleader tryouts and wanted to stay close to the team while staying in shape for next year's competition. In the age of the Farrah Fawcett poster, most Texettes were Farrah-wanna-bes. Texettes wore short blue skirts and enough makeup to make a writer see exclamation points. Texettes were highly skilled flirters. A writer's objectivity—*his* lifeblood—could be lost in a cloud of Texette perfume. Surely it was Chanel No. XIII, like the coming Super Bowl. By the way, midway through the season Schramm and staff had flown to Miami to "scout" the Super site.

Where *was* I?

After games Texettes began bringing Xeroxed sheets of quotes from Landry, the opposing coach, and key players from each team. Sheet after sheet piled up to your right and left, covering your notebook, your lineup card, your perspective. You didn't even have to leave your seat to do your job! You didn't have to fight down through the departing crowd to get to the locker room for post-game interviews. You could watch Landry on closed-circuit. Your favorite Texette—Sandi or Suzi or Jacki—would bring you whatever other quotes you needed. Last call wasn't until about three hours after a game.

Incidentally, there was another press box straight across the stadium just for TV and radio people and a third, the auxiliary press box for overflow media requests, in the end zone. The stadium seemed to be an afterthought. This was one big press box.

Schramm had created an atmosphere conducive to Texas-style hyperbole. Schramm, the failed sportswriter, knew exactly what inspired most of us bullfight-covering Hemingways: quotable stars with interesting stories and the time to tell them, a cushy place to work, sexy women, and good food and plenty of drink. Schramm's P.R. staff was known as the NFL's most open, cooperative, and tab-covering friendly. P.R. assistant George Heddleston told me, "A lot of general managers forbid their P.R. guys from getting friendly with any of the writers. Most teams have an adversary relationship with the writers who cover them. The writers are the enemy. But Tex encourages us to socialize with media people. He wants to make everybody feel part of the Cowboy family."

No wonder Schramm had refused for years to spend one blue cent on advertising. Yes, the Cowboys had begun to win big. And yes, NFL gates were split 60–40 with the visiting team, so maybe Schramm didn't really care that America's Team sold out more consistently on the road than at home. But in effect, Dallas–Fort Worth newspapers were taking out three or four full-page ads a day for the Cowboys. Even Schramm couldn't budget that kind of advertising, and he was getting it for the price of the NFL's highest P.R. budget, which allowed Schramm to have his cake and, well, drink it too. Tex was throwing weekend P.R. parties, of which he was the life. Ingenious. His big business was his pleasure. He promoted his legend as well as his team's.

No wonder his Cowboys were leading the league in seating requests from out-of-town writers. Yes, the team's record commanded coverage, but it was just so much more fun writing about the Cowboys than the Steelers or Rams. That week, a writer from Philadelphia wrote: "The Dallas Cowboys aren't just another football team, they are another civilization. They play in a stadium that is as cozy as the palace of Versailles. Their fans sit in super boxes surrounded by crystal and crushed velvet, sipping white wine and discussing the stock market. They are a white gloves and opera glass crowd. They applaud politely, like first-nighters at the Bolshoi.

"The Cowboy front office looks like a branch of Texas Instruments, Inc. Everywhere you look there's some guy who just stepped out of the Neiman-Marcus catalog, studying a computer printout. The coaches sit around like board members, discussing the run-pass ratio and third-down efficiency. The Cowboys approach games with all the emotion of a conglomerate swallowing up a lemonade stand."

I must admit I had written similar mythological prose when I visited Dallas for the *Los Angeles Times*. Editors liked it. Readers liked it. Schramm loved it. Schramm's staff compiled files of everything written nationally on the Cowboys, pro or con. Schramm believed in the axiom "Any publicity is good publicity." He said, "As long as they're writing *something*." Every word in every city added girders to Cowboy Mystique. Every reference to the "computer-brained Landry" and his "bionic superstars" watched by "J. R. Ewings who own ranches in downtown Dallas" made opponents that much more fearful and the Cowboys feel that much more invincible. Why the hole in the Texas Stadium roof? So God could watch His team.

Jim Finks, then general manager of the Bears, said, "You walk into Texas Stadium and immediately feel class. You feel it from the structure itself, from the private skyboxes, the painted field. . . . The Cowboys squad has always been very presentable. You don't see any overweight players or coaches. It's a catching thing, really. I honestly believe when a player becomes a Dallas Cowboy that he often immediately begins playing better than he's really capable of."

Was I writing over my head? One of my favorite writers, Leigh Montville of the *Boston Globe,* wrote, "The Cowboys are the team I would put into the time capsule. . . . No team better illustrates the good, the bad, and the frivolous of the Magic World of Pete Rozelle. . . . The Cowboys reflect our time . . . they seemingly have been in our living rooms forever. They have a bigger-than-life team . . . of people named 'Lance' and 'Billy Joe' and 'Dandy.' . . . Everything seemingly has been extended as far it can go in Big D."

What was happening to me? My second week, Schramm laid a little scoop on me. A little incentive to become part of the Family? Old-days "payola"—money or gifts in exchange for favorable coverage—was now taboo at both Dallas papers, yet Schramm was beating even that new system by paying some reporters an extra $100 or so a week

to do a story for his *Cowboys Weekly*. His aides often left the reporters a bottle of their favorite firewater, to help get them through
the extra drudgery. Good God: Schramm's house organ was edited
by guys who used to cover the team for Dallas papers and had sold
out to float down whiskey river with their Cowboys.

My only hope, I figured, was my sportswriting quirk. Confession: I didn't care for the taste or effects of alcohol. I had thought
about seeking help but I figured I was just, well, different.

But was Schramm, the deep-sea fisherman, baiting another
hook? The scoop was a pretty minor thing: A Schramm staffer told
me he was considering an alternative to post-game interviews in the
locker room. It was simply too crowded for both players and three
press-box-fuls of reporters, who formed rugby scrums for close-
quarter interviews. When I asked Schramm about it, he said yes,
that every Sunday he was opening an interview room across the hall
from the locker room. This also would solve the problems of female
reporters having to interview naked players—a Landry grievance.
This way players would shower and dress first or wear robes across
the hall for interviews.

Ah, another Cowboy innovation. In my laudatory column I
mentioned this NFL first would also appeal to Schramm's "vanity."
At that Sunday's game I watched him make his usual pre-game walk
from the field up through the adoring masses to the press box,
where he jumped me.

Schramm, in his forgettably conservative downtown-Dallas
power suits, could be as alarming as he could be charming. He could
intimidate with his quick fuse and foghorn roar. In a suit he seemed
even bigger than six feet and 190 paunchy pounds. With his thin-
ning, gray, '50s barber-shop hair, Schramm had the look of corporate
dominance. He had an inventive eye for style, but none personally.
Waving his Super Bowl ring, he could have been a CEO atop any
Dallas tower. Tex could have run Texaco. He had a winning laugh.
But he simply had to win, to control. If challenged, his W. C. Fields
nose actually appeared to turn blue with rage—Cowboy blue. The
nose was a Pinocchio-like symbol of Schramm's passion: J&B Scotch
and loyal Schrammites to share it with. Schramm loved to hear
himself expound on anything that concerned his life's work, the
League. The National Football League. When it came to the
League, Schramm had all the objectivity of the Third Reich.

Schramm confronted me in the press box lounge and said, "You should look up the word 'vain' in the dictionary. It doesn't mean what you think it means. I'm not vain."

Schramm was that offended by a single reference in a positive column? Was I somehow being bullied into second-guessing every word I t-y-p-e-d from now on? When I looked up "vain," Schramm definitely wasn't the first definition: "having no real value." Or the second: "marked by futility or ineffectualness." But beside the third might have been Schramm's smiling press-guide picture: "having or showing undue or excessive pride in one's achievements."

Later I was told that Schramm's wife Marty, over post-game cocktails in the press box lounge, laughed and told Schramm, "Oh, you're the most vain man I know."

I was living a novel in a mythological city that loved to look at itself in its mirrored buildings. I was flying to road games on the team charter. I was sitting in first class while the players were "in the back." I was getting to know flight attendants who were juggling affairs with players and assistant coaches. I was having an in-flight feast that included pre-takeoff snack pack (submarine sandwich, almonds, gourmet cheese, crackers, and chocolates), appetizer tray (crab salad, cocktail shrimp, grapes, and rolls), main course (steak the size of Wichita Falls, potato halves mixed with cheese, cauliflower in cheese sauce, and more rolls), topped off by as many pieces of strawberry-swirl cheesecake as I desired.

I was watching in wonder as the coaches and staff around Landry ordered cocktail upon cocktail while Tom got lost in his game plan or one of his favorite Louis L'Amour novels. Naturally, Tom and wife Alicia were "good friends" with L'Amour, she told me.

I was pushing my way through the lobby as Milwaukee-area fans wearing Cowboy jerseys numbered 12 (Staubach) and 33 (Dorsett) and 54 (Randy White) mobbed the Cowboys. Most Dallasites considered themselves too sophisticated to chase Cowboys as if they were Beatles, but on the road it was as if forty or so of Hollywood's hottest young actors were making broken-field runs for lobby elevators. Look, it's America's Team! This was the age of the *Star Wars* movies and Thomas Thompson's best-selling *Blood and Money* about Texas wealth and vengeance. Here were forty Luke Skywalkers who played in Dallas for Darth Vader.

Bob Ryan of NFL Films would suggest two titles for the 1978 highlight film to Cowboy P.R. director Doug Todd: *Cowboys Die Hard* and *America's Team.* Todd said, "I didn't like the idea of us dying. And besides, they had all this footage from around the league of people in other stadiums waving Cowboy pennants or wearing Dallas T-shirts."

I was sitting in the cramped, cold press box in Milwaukee's County Stadium hearing a sellout crowd cheer as loudly when Dallas scored as when the Green Bay Packers did. Schramm was telling me, "I think we caught the public's imagination in the early '60s. We were the good guys, the little kids on the block trying to grow up. We had the Merediths and [Bob] Hayeses—colorful characters. We were willing to try anything: basketball players like Cornell Green and track men like Mike Gaechter. We were always in the news with people like Duane Thomas. And despite Joe Namath's popularity I think the American public still likes their heroes to be all-American boys. We're lucky we've had that in Roger Staubach. I think people even like our uniforms—the colors, the star on the helmet.

"And I think they relate to Tom in a different way. He's not a [John] Madden, stomping around on the sidelines. When all hell is breaking lose, he's the rock."

I was covering games that exploded with column ideas. Something was always happening. Charlie Waters, the team thinker, told me, "You're going to love covering this team. There's just a *dynamic* in the locker room. So many different, strong personalities. Headlines are made."

Day after day I struggled to decide what *not* to write. Walking into the Cowboy locker room was like walking into a multiplex of eight or ten theaters. Now showing in one was Hollywood Henderson. Fighting laryngitis, Henderson did an entire interview for me in sign language, complete with indicating the breast size of his girlfriend. Showing in another was pretty boy Waters, who had done a shirtless beefcake poster but said teenage groupies "don't really want to have sex with you. They just want to imagine it." In another theater was speak-first, think-later Dorsett, who dared date white women in Dallas and had been arrested after a fight with a bartender who called him nigger.

All-Pro Harvey Martin owned a barbecue restaurant, a nightclub, did a radio gig called "The Beautiful Harvey Martin Show," and even made time for football. The receivers constantly vied for

publicity and game plan attention. Drew Pearson was ripping Butch
Johnson for being a "publicity hound." Johnson was criticizing Tony
Hill for being gutless. Hill was whining about how Pearson was
"Tom's favorite." America's Team was on its way to placing nine
players on the NFC Pro Bowl team.

If the players bored you, Brandt was always around the locker
room with an ultimatum for some ungrateful Cowboy. Brandt told a
New York Times reporter he studied biorhythms. He said, "I won't
talk contract with a player on critical days." Hello, column idea.

Schramm had even hired a fortyish fitness guru from California,
Dr. Bob Ward, who was into "focusing" players in sensory depri-
vation tanks and teaching defensive linemen martial arts. Ward,
who experimented with something called steroids, was stronger than
a lot of his players. Sportswriter's heaven.

I mentioned in a column that I'd seen Staubach, crowned by
Sports Illustrated the week before as the "NFL's Sir Gallahad,"
drinking a beer on a charter flight home. Coming home, the charter
turned into a flying drunk tank. Staubach seemed mad/glad about
the reference and told me he was torn between having to live up to
his image as God's Quarterback and having to answer sackfuls of
say-it-ain't-so mail from Bible Belters. How many other NFL quarterbacks had to hire a secretary just to answer mail? I received thirty
or forty letters myself, mostly from mothers saying I'd ruined their
children by printing trash about Roger Staubach's drinking. I'd all
but said there was no Santa Claus.

"You're really going to love Dallas," Staubach kept telling me.

For sure, I loved each Tuesday's "Landry luncheon"—another
NFL first for the Cowboys. Every media outlet in North Texas sent
representatives, which ensured that fans would be bombarded with
Wowboy hype every Tuesday night and Wednesday morning. Some
Tuesdays no legitimate news came out of the luncheon, but I always
wrote about the Cowboys for Wednesday. We were served great
food, then Landry, then Schramm. Then any rival-city writers were
asked to leave, and Ermal Allen, the assistant coach in charge of
quality control, gave us a chalk talk. Yes, we in the Family were
shown the next opponent's strengths and weaknesses and how the
Cowboys would attack the latter. Allen's wink-and-tell sessions
weren't for publication, just "background." They were to help us
better understand the game, which they did. But they also gave us
a deeper appreciation for covering the Cowboys.

I was privileged. I was inside America's Team. I was feeling

NFL macho. Just three years earlier I had been making around
$9,000 a year. Now I was traveling first class with my childhood
dream team. I was stepping off the third of three Cowboy buses, the
one reserved for media and staff, and having people gawk at me as
if I were important. I was hanging out in the road-hotel hospitality
suite, with open bar and five-star hors d'oeuvres. I was watching
special-teams coach Mike Ditka smoke cigars and play poker until
long after curfew. I was talking TV and football with announcers
such as CBS's Pat Summerall and NBC's Dick Enberg. I was lusting
after the team's carefully chosen suite scenery: knockout charter
flight attendants who looked as if they'd been around the world a few
times. No other NFL team I knew of had a hospitality suite. The
one-night, one-morning food and drink alone could approach $1,000.

But this was America's Team, and we were important. The first
time that I was asked to a spare-no-expense road dinner with the
Family—P.R. men and media people—we ran into Landry and Alicia at Bookbinder's in Philadelphia. They had a bottle of wine. Somehow that surprised me more than Staubach's beer.

I no longer was thinking clearly. I was fighting my better judg-
ment. After one particularly potent victory at Texas Stadium, I was
following a Texette back to her apartment. I was sitting in her living
room, wondering if Big Brother were watching. Was I being pho-
tographed for future leverage? What was I *doing?*

During the off week before the Super Bowl, I was granted my first
audience with Landry. I was told he could spare ten minutes during
lunch hour at the practice field.

I won't forget the first time I saw this facility, which was a
twenty-minute drive from the team's classy tower offices, north on
Greenville Avenue, and east on Forest Lane to Abrams. The practice field was squeezed between a faded apartment complex and a
Pizza Hut. Across busy Forest Lane was a shopping center that
featured a Tom Thumb grocery store, where many players grabbed
lunch of fried chicken at the deli. Could it be? America's Team
resided in a one-story prefab of rippled aluminum siding painted
light blue. Butch Johnson called it "a roach-infested tent." It was
like walking into a discarded dollhouse full of giant humans. Everything was incredibly cramped and poorly lit. Naked egos and light
bulbs. Lots of Dallas high school teams had a more spacious train-

ing, meeting, and equipment room. At six-feet-nine, Ed "Too Tall" Jones appeared to walk with a stoop.

Even the parking lot was jammed. I parked across at the Tom Thumb and thought, "I've got the wrong place."

But this was it. This was Tom Landry, one on one. Without chitchat, we sat in two of the desk-top chairs in the meeting room— the torture chamber for many players. Some drank or took drugs to get through Landry's film-session criticism. Maybe I was feeling a little of what they felt. I had interviewed lots of famous people: Ali, O.J., Nicklaus, Chrissie, Reggie, the Bear. But I'd never been nervous. I'd never been much for hero worship. Famous people, I'd found, are often more insecure than those who interview them.

But now I could feel my underarms getting wet. And why not? Like Landry, I was raised Methodist. I was conditioned to believe Landry all but sat at the right hand of God the Father. For me, Landry was the most powerful religious figure on earth. No exaggeration: more powerful than the Pope or Billy Graham. The father of my best friend back in Oklahoma City was on the staff of the Billy Graham Crusade. He often spoke of Landry—who often spoke for the Crusade—as a "force for the Lord." I believed.

How many Sundays had I come straight from church to listen to Landry's silent sermon? Has there ever been a more imposing TV closeup than Landry, in snap-brim hat and Brooks Brothers suit, game plan in hand, jaw set, top lip pursed over bottom, teeth working almost imperceptively on his gum, eyes seeing what only Landry can? Now I was momentarily paralyzed by those eyes. They were the bluest I had ever seen, Technicolor blue, almost metallic blue— the Cowboy color. Blue with electric flecks of white. The eyes sat deep in his head, beneath a high, prominent forehead, giving the bald Landry the look of a superior being with an enlarged brain attached directly to lasers.

You could almost feel the eyes boring hot little holes in your soul, so Landry could glance in at all the cobwebs and rust.

The jaw made the eyes even more arresting. The Landry jaw— for years the cartoonist's delight—was as big as its caricature. No one could have a jaw this big. It looked as if an Old West blacksmith had fashioned it out of horseshoes. The jaw protruded from under his ears and swung down into a double-barrel shotgun of a chin. Everything about Landry was even bigger in person. The neck was thicker. The shoulders were broader. The hands—Lord, the hands

seemed even too meaty for Landry's six-foot-two, 210-pound phy-
sique. I'd seen him lifting weights after practice, but up close the
ex-Giant cornerback looked as if he could still suit up in an emergency. He was wearing coaching shorts, and his calves looked as if
they could win a state fair livestock contest. With his shoulders
locked back and his chest stretching his Cowboy T-shirt, his posture
said, "I'm fifty-four, but you wouldn't want to mess with me."

Further complicating my first impression were Landry's smile
and glow. The initial brief smile was a mysterious little Mona Lisa
flicker, slightly crooked, with the corners of his mouth barely turning up. The glow was that of a clergyman. Landry's face and hands
looked as if he'd just scrubbed down. Landry's pinkish glow gave a
soft tint to a powerful package.

My senses were confused completely by Landry's voice, which
belonged in a guy named Skeeter who worked on cars in Mesquite
and Waxahachie. This was not the voice of Mount Landry. This man
should have the echoing bass of John Facenda, who narrated Super
Bowl highlights for NFL Films. Instead, Landry's cracky twang
sounded like a guitar with a string or two missing. Landry's tongue
kept getting in the way of his teeth, like the feet of a rookie defensive
back in the Flex defense. Landry butchered a lot of words. It was as
if Landry were speaking some dialect of English he learned down in
his hometown of Mission, on the Mexican border. Landry, bless
him, sounded like an incurable Texas hick.

A little shook up, I summoned my courage. No time for warm-
up questions about how the team was looking. I immediately told
Landry I was a born-again Christian. I had rededicated my life to
Christ four years earlier. I did not, however, tell Landry I was going
through a divorce from my high school sweetheart that had shaken
my faith.

I said, "Could you talk about how your faith helps you cope
with the ultimate pressure from the 'ultimate' game?"

In the next ten minutes I took thirty minutes' worth of notes. It
was like the loaf of bread that fed the masses. It was the best interview I would ever have with Landry. I felt such warmth and humility from this coach who could seem so coldly emotionless.

Landry said, "The answer is that I'm a Christian. That's where
I live. It's hard for a secular society to handle. It's a difficult thing to
explain. I don't want to come across as a pious-type person. I suffer
after losses, but fortunately I recover quickly. I have a source of

power I wouldn't without my relationship with Christ. I've reached the point where I feel no pressure in the Super Bowl."

Time out: *No pressure in the Super Bowl?*

None, he said. Landry paraphrased one of his favorite verses, 2 Timothy 1:7. He said, "God does not give us fear, but power and love and self-control. The thing that eats you up is fear and anxiety. Once you commit your life to Christ, it's in God's hands. He has a direction He wants to take you which isn't based on winning and losing. The more you dwell on your own power, the more anxious you become."

The most powerful man in my world, at the top of the NFL's most powerful organization, refused to feel any power? No, he said. "So much of coaching is out of your control. You can be an excellent coach and still be a loser. Look at Tommy Prothro. He could have come out with one of the strongest teams in San Diego, but he didn't. Things are out of your hands."

I fought to remain objective. I thought, *Wait, isn't this the one NFL coach who refuses to delegate authority to his assistants?* The one who basically coordinated his offense *and* defense? Who insisted on calling plays even though his thirty-seven-year-old quarterback, Staubach, was constantly frustrated to the point of early retirement? And things were out of Landry's hands? Completely in God's? Did Landry's relationship with God give him an edge on secular rivals? Did God bless America's Team?

"No," Landry said, "God doesn't interfere. We have great Christian friends all around the league. He just gives you the courage to excel, the confidence to perform to the best of your ability. So many people don't use what they've got. It's how you *think* that makes you successful. If you have a positive attitude, good things will happen. Why has positive thinking become a multimillion-dollar industry? They're just teaching what God gives us in the Bible."

I said, "Okay, I know this is inconceivable, but what if the Steelers beat you badly [in the Super Bowl] and the wheels fall off and you have a bad season or two?"

Landry said, "I could have a bad season and be fired. I would suffer. I'm human. That's why there's a great need for God. I wouldn't stay down too long. I'd know He had something else in mind for me other than football. That's the way I live with it." Pause. "Okay?"

"Okay?" meant the interview was over. Landry had an inflexible schedule to meet. I went back to the office and wrote a column on Landry's faith for the next morning's paper, Saturday's. On Sunday, with Landry in the congregation, the minister at Landry's church used the column as the framework for his Sunday sermon. Laminated copies of the column were distributed among church members, who wrote me many letters of thanks.

I didn't open that batch of mail until I returned from Super Bowl week in Miami. I almost trashed one letter in a Cowboy envelope. All I needed was another Cowboy press release. But inside this Cowboy envelope was a note from Tom Landry. It began, "I've never written to a sportswriter before. . . ." Landry thanked me for "explaining my faith so accurately." So many other journalists, he said, had tried and "failed to understand."

But in a way I felt more confused than ever. So many mixed signals and emotions. So many mixed drinks around Landry. What was happening? There almost seemed to be two Landrys—the Christian and the business partner. He almost seemed to have an *altar* ego. How had Tom Landry come to be partners with Schramm and Brandt? God's will? Demonic design? Harmonic Convergence?

3

BY 1978, if Tom Landry's media-guide biography had said "He was found lying in a manger outside Mission, Texas, on September 11, 1924," few Cowboy fans would have doubted. But the real story was nothing for Matthew or Mark to chronicle. Landry was born beneath the many palm trees in Mission, the "Home of the Grapefruit," deep in the Rio Grande valley. His parents were bigger deals around town than Tommy would be for a good while. Ray Landry Fireman's Park was named after his father, a volunteer fireman and Sunday school superintendent who ran an auto repair shop. "A great man," Tom calls him. Tommy's mother, Ruth, was equally revered for the time she dedicated to First United Methodist Church.

But their second of three children, Tommy, would help put a town of about five thousand on the tourist map. "The Tourist Mecca of South Texas," Mission now calls itself, and some Missionites now remember that, by golly, Tommy may *have* been born in a manger. I did find one, however, whose perspective remains as vivid as his memory. Jimmy Mehis was a boyhood friend of Landry's, the center on a small-class 12–0 high school team quarterbacked by Landry.

Mehis, who retired from Dow Chemical and still lives in Mission, says, "I thought he'd be an average man. I didn't think he'd go on to what he became. There was no way you could see any future greatness in him. Hell, he was just like the rest of us, just an ordinary kid."

Just a big-boned youngster with a slight lisp. Grade school words like sugar came out "tuga." But other kids didn't kid Landry about the way he talked. He was too big, too athletic, too solid a citizen and specimen. Mehis says, "Oh, everyone respected Tommy." As a single-wing quarterback, more runner than passer, Landry didn't turn into what Texans call a blue-chip recruit. He wasn't too fast. But as a junior and senior, at six-feet-one and 180 pounds, Landry ran as if he had no regard for his body—or any tackler's. He played possessed, as if all that mattered was the approval of his coach. (Landry still has trouble with his surgically repaired knees, which prevent him from jogging or playing too much tennis.) Lots of kids in Texas were like that. Small-town life revolved around football. It wasn't until the '70s that kids began to ask why.

Landry was recruited by Texas, SMU, Rice, and Mississippi State, if for nothing else, for his forty-yard punting average. Mehis says, "Tommy was a good football player, but there were a few others on the team better than he was. You know, a lot of people get lucky. The ball bounces up and some people catch it and run, and others drop it. Tommy caught the ball and made the most of it."

The week before Mission's regional title game, Japan bombed Pearl Harbor. Landry went on to the University of Texas the next fall and played freshman football, but he also joined the Air Force Reserve. That spring he was called into active duty. By the next fall he found himself based in London under the command of Maj. Gen. James H. Doolittle, flying missions through black clouds of flak over occupied territory. Landry was a copilot and occasional tailgunner on a B-17, the famed Flying Fortress. An Air Force plane flown by his older brother Robert had exploded inexplicably over Iceland, on its way to London. Landry could have been killed just as easily during any one of his thirty missions spanning four hundred hours.

Once, returning to England over friendly France, the plane ran out of fuel and Landry's crew survived a crash landing among trees in pitch-black countryside. Landry told the *Dallas Times Herald*, "We sheared off both wings. A tree was all the way up to the instrument panel by the time we stopped. But all nine of us walked away. That was really amazing. A four-engine B-17 is really a big plane. How we kept from crashing into those trees, I don't know. I guess, to some extent, it was luck. We just skidded right through and barely stopped in time."

Another time, returning from bombing Czechoslovakia, the B-17 sounded as if it were running out of fuel over occupied Belgium. Landry said, "We were weaving our way down, and the pilot decided it was time to jump." Time to become a prisoner of war? An MIA?

Landry says, "When I got out of my seat, I noticed the fuel mixture was bad, so I just shoved the lever forward and all four engines cut on again. The ack-ack guns were right on our tail all the way back, but they never got us and we got back somehow. Again, I think it was a lot of luck. But as I began to think back on it, I knew God had a purpose for me."

Many Cowboys would wonder. Often I heard from Landry's players, "Remember, the guy was a bomber pilot." At Landry's April 1989 retirement ceremonies, before some fifty thousand in front of Dallas's City Hall, Thomas Henderson watched along with many ex-Cowboys as a retired Air Force general all but decorated Landry for his World War II heroics. Henderson says, "That was the most embarrassed I've ever seen a man. I thought Tom was going to crawl under the carpet. This man was lauding Tom for his bombing! I believe Tom has lived in a pit of remorse, shame, and guilt. He killed a lot of innocent people. You can say it was war, but killing is killing. How can you be a Christian and bomb?"

The Landry who coached Henderson didn't bomb. Landry the copilot was just twenty-three; it was twelve years before he says he gave his life to Christ. At twenty-three Landry was just a shy, sheltered kid from Mission seeing the world for the first time. He had signed up to defend American soil against Germans and Japanese. Landry wasn't thinking about innocent people. He probably wasn't thinking about much of anything, except making his mama and daddy proud. Mount Landry was no Aristotle or Gandhi. He was a small-town guy who played football. Many of his players never could quite understand that.

Perhaps they would have felt more comfortable with Landry if they had known he—like most of them—was a love-'em-and-leave-'em ladykiller. In high school Landry had been too shy to even ask a girl to dance, but back at the University of Texas he was a war vet who had been discharged as a first lieutenant. He had been to hell and back; he had come of age.

He was also a varsity football player at a school that idolized them. In high school he had been voted the cutest boy in his senior class. He was a Longhorn fullback. He was a frat man—Delta Kappa Epsilon. He even had his own convertible.

I've heard this story from several people who knew Landry, though each version is slightly different. I suspect it happened, though perhaps not exactly this way: One weekend when Landry's mom visited him, she was riding in the front seat of his car while two teammates rode in the back. She happened to pull down the sun visor, and a pair of panties fell in her lap.

"What's this?" she asked her son.

"Oh," Landry said, "those are from my score last night."

One source says, "Tom talked openly to his mom about his conquests. He was wilder than a lot of people think he was." The source is another from the Cowboy organization who wants the world to know, "Tom wasn't always Mr. Perfect." No, he was just like a lot of college guys.

But his panty-raiding days couldn't have lasted long. He soon met Miss Perfect, a monied lovely from exclusive Highland Park in Dallas. Alicia Wiggs was the daughter of Herbert, chairman of the board of an insurance company. Alicia was the Classic Texas Blonde. She could make the young Stoneface laugh. She could speak for him when he wasn't sure what to say. Alicia would become his biggest fan and best friend, his salvation away from big "bi'ness." In 1948 Alicia left school in the middle of her sophomore year to marry Landry, who had finished his football eligibility and would graduate with a B.A. in business. He wanted to enroll at the University of Houston and pursue a degree in industrial engineering. But his final game had probably been his best. He had finished as the Orange Bowl's top rusher with 117 yards on seventeen carries as Texas beat Georgia 41–28. He also had played some hellacious cornerback and punted spectacularly. The New York Yankees of the All-American Football Conference offered him a $2,000 bonus and $7,500 a season. "Good money in those days," Landry says. Tom and Alicia decided to go to New York, almost as an adventure.

As a pro cornerback for the Yankees and Giants, Landry earned a reputation for hitting hard and occasionally late. Glenn Davis, Army's Mr. Outside, was a Rams receiver who says Landry "loved to pour it on you when you were hanging high and dry waiting for the football." Davis says that during one fourth quarter of a tight game, he faked a hook route on Landry, who came charging as Davis flew past him. "I caught it in the clear at the 20 and had an easy touchdown. Thing was, when I got to the goal line and started to ease up, I could still hear Landry pounding after me, so I ran right through the end zone. He was still coming . . . I was ten yards beyond when he finally tackled me. Oh, he was pissed off. I was pretty hot myself by this time. I said, 'Here, if you want it so bad, take it,' and I slammed the ball in his face. Then I scrambled up and ran for the bench because I knew I'd be safe there, and I'll be damned if he didn't chase me halfway to the bench."

Yes, this was the Landry with a taste for strong drink. In Tex Schramm's authorized biography, *Tex!*, by Bob St. John, Schramm mentions early that Landry the Giant was "known to partake of a martini." It's almost as if Schramm, the legendary boozer, is saying, "See, Tom drank, too."

But this Landry also was married, with a new son and an old goal to finish his engineering degree during off-seasons. This Landry took everything in his life more seriously than most, if not all, of his teammates. To most Giants, football was still something you played. You certainly didn't study it. But Landry went home to watch movies of football. Current Cowboy P.R. director Greg Aiello says Frank Gifford, a Giant teammate of Landry's, "would come in to do Monday night games and laugh about how people would say Tom was so 'intimidating.' Gifford would say, 'Why? Tom's a nerd. He's so shy, so square. Why does anyone think he's intimidating?' "

Maybe because young Stoneface started taking football as seriously as he did engineering. "I had to," Landry says. "I wasn't fast enough to play cornerback. I had to outthink 'em." Landry became a player-coach. Landry the film nerd came up with this mad-scientist notion of "keying" off different offensive players instead of just chasing the ball or guessing run or pass. This wasn't exactly Einstein stuff. But by early '50s NFL standards, it was the theory of relativity.

Landry and another young coach named Vince Lombardi, an emotional volcano, became the top assistants for coach Jim Lee Howell. Fortunately for Landry, Howell was no Landry. As a head coach, Landry would treat assistants as if they were to be seen and not heard. But Howell gave Landry and Lombardi almost all the daily coaching responsibility—and credit. After the Giants beat the

Bears 47–7 for the 1956 NFL championship, Howell said it was a "great tribute" to Landry and Lombardi. Landry says he was "very lucky"—that word again—to coach under such a secure leader. The more Howell talked about Landry, the greater Landry got. Howell even said once that Landry was "the greatest coach in the NFL." You suppose Howell meant Landry had the best young technical mind in the game, but the quote, carved like a commandment in stone, would follow Landry to Dallas, where it became the bedrock for his early image.

Giants owner Wellington Mara once said, "Lombardi was on the surface a much warmer person than Landry. He went from warm to red hot. You could hear Vince laughing or shouting from five blocks. You couldn't hear Landry from the next chair. Lombardi was more of a teacher. It was as though Landry lectured the top 40 percent of the class and Lombardi taught the lower 10 percent."

Despite his "great coach" image, Tom Landry wasn't much of an instinctive, inspirational teacher. Young assistants named Dan Reeves and Mike Ditka would have to take care of the Lombardi part for Landry. Landry wasn't the kind of player-turned-coach who could see untapped talent in a rookie and coax it out of him. Landry wasn't a screamer or a sweet-talker. Reeves, the former Cowboy halfback, could say to a struggling Cowboy, "Look, hoss, you can play this damn game if you'll just quit thinking so much." Ditka, the Hall of Fame tight end, could yank a Cowboy aside and say, "Do you want to go through the rest of your life being remembered as a pussy?" Landry wasn't "cool." He didn't speak fluent "locker room." Landry didn't have the desire, rapport, or verbal skills to small-talk with his players.

Classic Landry story: From 1984 to 1987 one of Landry's favorites would be receiver Mike Renfro who, like Landry, survived on guile and guts. Teammates shortened Renfro to Fro. During one Landry luncheon he was asked about Renfro's high pain threshold. Landry said, "That's why they call him Pro."

No, Coach—Fro. That's how in touch Landry the film nerd was with his cogs.

Landry taught a system, not an individual player. Landry the engineer was beginning to design something called a "coordinated defense." Landry would be able to lecture the top 40 percent of the class on every subtle movement of what would become known as the Flex. Landry would attempt to draft only the top 40 percent for his Cowboy teams.

But in 1958 Landry wasn't even sure he belonged in pro football. He considered a second career, something closer to Alicia and the kids and their home in Dallas. Should he try making some real money selling insurance for Alicia's father? Or what about college football, which remained far more popular than the NFL? Landry called a Dallas businessman named H. R. "Bum" Bright, who was helping conduct a search for a new Texas A&M coach. After the 1957 season Paul "Bear" Bryant left A&M for Alabama. Bright says he agreed to interview "this fellow Landry." Bright says he was "singularly unimpressed." Can you blame him? Can you imagine Landry, pre-image, trying to sell eighteen-year-olds on A&M? Imagine a film nerd who played for Texas trying to recruit for its rival.

Then again, if Bright had hired Landry in 1958, perhaps he wouldn't have had to worry about firing him as owner of the Cowboys in 1988.

Again, fate bounced as oddly as a football. Rejected, Landry drifted spiritually for another season. Then, he says, "my life changed forever." Consider these words, written twelve years later for "Lenten Guideposts," a syndicated newspaper series of Christian inspiration. If Landry penned them himself, he writes far more powerfully than he speaks off the cuff. These words give you a 50-yard-line seat for what became Landry's thirty-year-old struggle between his ego and soul.

When my playing days were over and I became a full-time coach on the New York Giants in 1956, I used my college training in industrial engineering to devise a complex and, it turned out, highly successful defense that had never been tried in professional football. Another accomplishment, but a sense of dissatisfaction remained. After the 1958 season I returned to Dallas. I was thirty-three years old. I had achieved almost every goal I had aimed for and had every reason to be happy and content. Yet inexplicably there was an emptiness in my life.

One day a good friend casually invited me to attend a men's breakfast at the Melrose Hotel. "I think you'll like it, Tom," he said. "We probe the Scriptures and have some good fellowship together." What happened in the weeks that followed is not easy to explain, but I do know these informal sessions of probing, questioning, and searching the Gospels began a whole new era of my life.

In looking back I find it hard to pick out any one specific turning point, but my early attention was certainly grabbed by this passage: "Therefore I tell you do not be anxious about your life, what you shall

eat or what you shall drink, nor about your body, what you shall put
on. Is not life more than food and the body more than clothing?"

"Is not life, then, more than football?" I asked myself, uncom-
fortably. Challenged by this statement, I turned my thoughts to the
Challenger. Who was He, this Jesus? Did I accept Him really? For, I
reasoned, if I accepted Him, then I accepted what He said. And if I
accepted what He said, then there was something unsatisfying in the
way I was living my life.

I began reading about Jesus. As a football coach I measure things
in terms of results. During each game we keep a chart of the players'
efficiency in carrying out their assignments. If most players perform
well, we will probably win the game. Therefore, I couldn't help thinking about Jesus in terms of what He did, of the results of His life. The
impact of His life on the lives of countless millions down through the
years is impressive, compelling.

Finally, at some period during the spring of 1959, all my intellectual questions no longer seemed important, and I had a curiously
joyous feeling inside. Internally, the decision had been made. Now
while the process had been slow and gradual, once made, the decision
has been the most important of my life. It was a commitment of my life
to Jesus Christ, and a willingness to do what He wanted me to do, as
best I could by seeking His will through prayer and reading His word.

The result was that I learned what He meant when He said, "I
came that we may have life and have it abundantly." He didn't ask me
to give up football or my ambition to be the best coach in the business,
but to bring Him into my life, including football. I begin each day now
with a person-to-person effort to contact Him. "Lord, I need Your
help today when we make squad cuts," or "Please give me the right
words to say to the coaches at our meeting," or "Help me to forget
football today when I'm with Alicia and the children." At the end of
the day I take inventory. Was my criticism of the quarterback handled
right? Did I get across to the squad my moral convictions without
preaching? Was I too stern with my daughter Kitty over her report
card? The main evaluation concerns whether I had brought the Lord
into these situations or whether I was barging ahead on my own.

When I get out of touch with Him, I flounder. Power seems to
ebb away, and that restless feeling returns. When God is in control of
my life that gnawing sense of dissatisfaction is gone.

The impact of Landry's life on countless thousands would be
impressive, compelling. Words like these would uplift many drifting
souls. Yet they also would torment the many Doubting Toms who
played for or worked with Landry. Was God helping Landry be-

come the best in *this* business? Was a morning prayer Landry's way of confessing his sins before committing them? Would his "faith" be a way of justifying a white lie to a player or the press—or his relationships with Tex Schramm and Gil Brandt?

Even as Landry was being born again, Schramm and Brandt were in Dallas signing players to counterfeit contracts to play for an unborn team.

Schramm needed a coach who could sell some tickets. He planned to share the Cotton Bowl—and Dallas customers—with the AFL's Dallas Texans and their loquacious coach, Hank Stram. For some reason Schramm kept winding up in the same place as Tom Landry. They had attended the University of Texas at roughly the same time. Both had left to serve in the Air Force, then returned to Austin. They didn't know each other, but Schramm knew all about Landry. While Schramm had worked for CBS in New York, he kept reading about the "young genius" who coached under Jim Lee Howell. Hmmm. Why not? Landry would appeal to Texas Exes, as UT grads were called. He was a religious family man who took football very seriously. That would attract some Bible Belt fans. And the press could have a field day with the "greatest coach in football" stuff.

Landry even lived in Dallas. Landry just might be the ticket.

Landry has said often that God moved him to coach the Cowboys. He was pursued by Bud Adams, who owned the AFL Houston Oilers, but he wanted to stay with the more established NFL. He wanted to stay in Dallas. God had spoken.

But sometimes in the early '60s it was as if a frightened young coach had bailed out of a B-17 over a magical city on the plains of North Texas. It was as if he had parachuted down into a field of wide-eyed natives. Many would say, "Look, a god has descended." They would build him a pedestal, bow to him, see only his greatness. Overwhelmed, he would blink and smile and nod.

Each time he was sure that the natives had figured out he was mortal, Tex Schramm would convince them otherwise.

Maybe Tex Schramm created himself. How else can you explain him? Yes, he sat down one day in his native Hollywood and made himself up. Maybe CBS or Paramount would buy the script and Schramm could watch himself go down in history. "I want to be remembered," he once said. "The only difference between me and most people is that I'll say it."

How about this for a plot? *Hyperactive kid named Texas flunks first, second, third, and sixth grades in Los Angeles while being kidded unmercifully about his name but shocks teachers and school friends by creating the most famous team in sports history—in Texas!*

For years I thought Texas E. was born in San Antonio, Texas. It often said so in newspaper and magazine articles. Only recently did I discover Schramm was born in San Gabriel, California. Technically Schramm was born in a hospital in Los Angeles. But why spoil a good story? Who wanted a Dallas Cowboys president named Los Angeles Schramm?

Texas Schramm, Senior, our Tex's father, was born in San Antonio. Tex Sr. moved his family west and became a successful stockbroker. Tex Jr. was raised in the far-right wing of Nixonian Los Angeles; at least Schramm says he was raised in San Gabriel. Schramm, like Hollywood, sometimes doesn't let the facts get in the way of a good story.

Schramm says his dad wanted him to attend the University of Texas, as Tex Sr. did. But as a journalism major Schramm discovered he needed a high school credit in typing. Typing can come in handy for a sportswriter, but Schramm hadn't finished high school typing. Schramm says he called a friend who worked at his high school and had his transcript changed to show he had a credit in typing. He later took an English literature course even though he was too antsy to sit and read a book, so his wife Marty read all the novels and summarized them for Schramm, who says he passed the course.

Schramm tells many of these beat-the-system stories in *Tex!* He seems proud that he occasionally fudged and fibbed his way to greatness. What mattered was that he, Texas E., was clever and courageous enough to triumph against all odds.

Schramm went out for freshman football at UT; I checked—he did. But it remains unclear how a guy who went a year to junior college was allowed to play freshman football. The rules must have been different then. Anyway, Schramm didn't last long. Ex-Cowboy star Duane Thomas indicates Schramm played football only to please others. Thomas says Schramm once told him about "all the problems he had with his parents when he was growing up. He said he went into football because it was accepted. He was forced into it, and it was demoralizing for him."

When Schramm returned to Austin after the war, no one would rent an apartment to him and his wife because (he says) they had a two-year-old daughter. Schramm ran a newspaper ad that said something like, "Is there someone in Austin who feels a child is not an outcast of society? If so, and you have a two-bedroom house or apartment, let us show you our daughter. If you think she will not demolish your property, you will not only have reliable tenants but honest friends. Veteran. 6876."

In 1982, when a *Dallas Morning News* reporter called to ask Schramm if anyone took the bait after he ran the ad, Schramm said, "You know, I can't remember for sure. Which way would be better for your story?"

For sure, Schramm left his sports desk job at the *Austin American-Statesman* to become P.R. man for the L. A. Rams. For a dedicated newspaperman this would be considered selling out, but for Schramm it was just moving up to what he did best—selling, period. After all, Schramm admits he "couldn't write." He knew his limitations in sportswriting but saw none in life. Schramm wanted to make money and history, and he wasn't going to do it in a poor-paying profession for which he had no talent.

The Rams became the model for Schramm's ultimate selling job. In his book Schramm says, "We wanted to make the Rams Southern California's team, and that included Hollywood. We took advantage of what we had. We had star players [Norm Van Brocklin, Bob Waterfield, Elroy "Crazylegs" Hirsch, Tom Fears, Bob Boyd] and merchandised them. It was the same approach we used with the Cowboys later—to try to make everybody you can feel a part of the team. You want the players to want to play for you. You want all the free agents to want to sign with you. You win and establish an image and then, when the players come in, they're prepared to adapt to your ways because of that success. I think you can compare the Rams when I was there to the Cowboys—glamour, speed, the type of players."

Ah, those were the days when Schramm could write mythological stories about the Rams, drop them off at the L. A. papers, and often read them verbatim in the next day's edition. Those also were the days, as Schramm says, that Americans were becoming "watchers instead of doers." Television, he says, was exploding. Schramm was fascinated with the way images in a living-room box were beginning to control people's lives. He left the Rams after ten years to work for CBS. Schramm sold the network on televising the 1960

Winter Olympics in Squaw Valley. A Winter Olympics hadn't been televised before, and some CBS higher-ups scoffed that the ratings would tumble down a ski slope.

Now Schramm, along with vast American audiences, proudly watches the Winter Olympics. What the Flex defense was to young Landry, the Winter Olympics were to young Schramm. Schramm just had a sense for what people would watch and buy. Says psychologist Don Beck, who worked with Schramm, "Tex had lots of what Howard Gardner [in his book, *Frames of Mind*] calls multiple intelligences. Tex wasn't what you'd call intellectually intelligent. He was intuitive. Instinctive. It wasn't here [Beck points to his head] but here [he points to his stomach]. His gut feelings were almost always right."

Even before the Olympics, Schramm had accepted the general manager job with a proposed NFL expansion team in Dallas. Yes, he was made for Dallas. Schramm, from his Austin days, understood the Texas Myth and how to sell it to Texans. Schramm's gut feeling: Dallas or bust.

Straight from Squaw Valley, Schramm did a snow job on prospective team owner Clint Murchison. Schramm told him he would lose $2.5 million before the team would ever be good enough to draw fans and make money. Murchison argued but bought it. Schramm had found an owner who, in effect, would let Schramm operate and spend as owner. Unheard of. A source who was close to Murchison says, "Tex was a fabulous manipulator and maneuverer. He was a genius at knowing when to bully, when to charm."

So why didn't Schramm attempt to manipulate his young head coach? And wouldn't Landry have been even vaguely uncomfortable entering into a working relationship with a general manager from L. A. who had an eye for pretty women and a taste for liquor and cigarettes? About the only time Schramm said "God" was in conjunction with "damn." For Schramm, fall Sundays were Roman holidays. Game days. Schramm pumped himself up as if he were playing and walked among his players, checking his field, as his crowd gathered. He always said he took losses harder than anyone in the organization. He once said, "When everyone else has gone home and gone to bed, I'm still sitting there with saucer eyes, drinking J&B, alone."

When Schramm hired staffers, he told them, "The job has to come first, even ahead of your family."

Was this the organization Landry wanted to head?

Probably not. But he and Schramm soon found they did share a driving desire to dominate, to be famous, to be recognized as highly successful businessmen, to erect a monument that would stand forever, to reach millions of people—and dollars.

Landry and Schramm needed each other to achieve their goal. Landry had little to say to Schramm, who mostly kept his distance from Landry. Even when one disagreed with what the other was doing, he kept it to himself. Landry wasn't confrontational, and he was the one man Schramm was afraid to confront. Schramm didn't make strategy or personnel suggestions to Landry, who didn't tell Schramm how to run the business side.

What are the odds Landry would hook up with one of the few general managers who didn't want to be involved in making personnel decisions? Schramm always said, "I'm not a football man." Schramm wasn't interested in scouting or game planning. For Schramm, football was a means to fame.

Did God bring these two together? Tougher question: Did God match Landry and Gil Brandt?

Saturday night, November 11, 1978. Mob scene, motel lobby, Milwaukee. The Cowboys had arrived. I bumped, literally, into Cowboy P.R. aide George Heddleston, who had spent the week in Milwaukee "advancing" the game with the Packers. He told me an intriguing tale about his Friday night with Gil Brandt.

Brandt was from Milwaukee. Right there in the Cowboy media guide it said: "A native of Milwaukee and graduate of the University of Wisconsin . . ."

Heddleston said he and Brandt had an expense-account-style dinner at a downtown hotel where Brandt seemed to know everyone from the maître d' to the busboys. "Gil didn't have anything but his Diet Cokes, though," Heddleston said. "You know how he is: He gets silly on two glasses of wine." Brandt, who logged around 150,000 air miles a year, collected miniature bottles of liquor from each flight. But he seldom drank alcohol.

Then Brandt surprised Heddleston by taking him back to the "old neighborhood." The temperature had fallen into the twenties, but Brandt wore only his suit coat. Heddleston chuckled fondly and said, "Gil was really being macho—really strutting. It was like his triumphant return." Or so Heddleston thought. "We walked all through the neighborhood, and I was freezing. But each time we came to a house where he said his mother or sister or somebody lived, we just stood out on the sidewalk looking at it. I thought maybe we'd go up to the door, but he just looked and stayed mysterious. I didn't know what to say or think."

Had those really been the homes or even ex-homes of Brandt's family? Did this man *have* a past? Or had Schramm simply suggested in 1960 that someone invent him a workaholic left-hand man?

From a 1960 story in the *Dallas Morning News*: "Brandt himself never played professional football. Indeed, he didn't even play varsity football in college, for an automobile injury after his freshman season at the University of Wisconsin benched him permanently. Football was in his blood, though, and he made a hobby his last year in college of making up his own pro talent lists. He wrote to colleges to borrow game films and did for fun much of what he does today for a living.

"A neighbor of his back in his hometown of Milwaukee was astonished at the reports Brandt made up for his own amusement. So the neighbor, Elroy (Crazylegs) Hirsch, then a great star with the Los Angeles Rams, introduced Brandt to that club's general manager, Tex Schramm. He was quickly put on the Rams' payroll. . . ."

Looking back, you wonder if Schramm wrote that story and dropped it off at the newspaper. I'm ashamed to admit I covered Brandt for ten years without once thinking to check his background. After all, he was part of the Cowboys' Holy Trinity. In a 1979 interview Brandt told me he was a defensive back and physical education major at Wisconsin. Not until I began researching this book did I discover otherwise. Even Schramm's authorized biography says Brandt was a high school quarterback.

Brandt grew up in what was described by an official at Brandt's high school as a downtown German-Jewish neighborhood. His father was a foreman at National Tea Company. Brandt's home was across the street from North Division High, where he was an average student with good grades in mechanical drawing, chemistry, and physics. But a search of yearbooks turned up no Gil Brandt on the football teams or in any other school activity. A classmate says, "Gil was always a hustler. He always had some money-making scheme going down on the tough side of town."

Perhaps Brandt graduated from another high school or via some alternate program, but no record could be found that he graduated from North Division. None could be found that he enrolled or played football at the University of Wisconsin in Madison or the branch in Milwaukee. Crazylegs Hirsch says he doesn't know anything about being Brandt's neighbor: "I didn't know Gil Brandt from Milwaukee. The first time I ran into Gil was at the 1952 College All-Star Game [in Chicago]. We [the Rams] were playing the All-Stars and Gil was doing some scouting for us. He wound up giving us a good scouting report on the All-Stars, and when the Rams asked [later] I told them that. Gil and I never really talked much. I just knew he hung around football and was really interested in that phase [scouting]."

Yet Schramm says his recollection is that Hirsch first recommended Brandt to the Rams. So why, as Hirsch says, was Brandt preparing a scouting report for the Rams at the 1952 All-Star Game? It appears Brandt was nothing more than the original Draftnik. Today, thousands of Gil Brandts write away for college media guides, tape obscure cable channel college games, subscribe to insider reports, and rank prospects for the NFL draft. Now hundreds of wacko, weirdo Draftniks make the annual Draft Day pilgrimage to New York for a cult gathering.

The Draftmaster was the original Draftnik. Here was a Walter Mitty whose daydream came true. Today the odds against a Draftnik talking his way to the top of an NFL organization's scouting department would be laughably high. But in the '50s, Schramm's Rams were the only team to budget for part-time scouts across the country who actually evaluated prospects all season. Most teams went (and spent) no further than reading college preseason magazines and newspaper reports, and making telephone inquiries. As yet no team had thought to make the draft a year-round, spare-no-expense priority.

Brandt just happened to come from nowhere at the right time. He didn't know much about the technical aspects of football. He had no eye for undiscovered potential. But he had a computer of a memory, a relentless work ethic, and a thirst to know everything about a college star. Brandt was a superfan who loved to hang around college and pro teams. He was one of those guys who could convince a gate guard he was, say, Elroy Hirsch's neighbor and needed to give him a very important message. It sounds as if Brandt convinced

Hirsch he had prepared a scouting report on the All-Stars for Schramm and that Schramm thought Hirsch knew Brandt.

Brandt was persistent and prepared. He always knew far more about you than you knew about him, and he went right for your ego. *Elroy, do you realize your Wisconsin high school rushing record is a national record?* It was hard not to like Brandt, who could be so charming.

Former Cowboys and Jets executive Al Ward once listened to a friendly debate among several writers over which Cowboy could win a heavyweight title fight. Ward said, "I'd go with Gil Brandt. If he hadn't bribed the referee, he'd talk the other guy out of it."

How was Brandt making ends meet before Schramm brought him to Dallas at age twenty-seven? Brandt ran a baby picture operation, once making $10,000 a year, according to a newspaper story. Some accounts say Brandt gave cameras to nurses at three hospitals. Each hospital would add $3 to the maternity bill and keep twenty-five cents; Brandt got the rest. A coach who knew Brandt says he took pictures of kids of all ages: "Gil was great working with the kids, putting them on horseback, getting them to smile." Brandt was even said to take high school graduation pictures.

This became the story angle behind which Brandt hid his past. Early on in Dallas, Brandt let it be known he took baby pictures. So for thirty years nearly every feature story written on Brandt played up the ex-baby photographer handle promoted in the media guide. That made Brandt another only-in-Dallas story—a "cute story," as Schramm called them—and gave Brandt the same kind of canned image he liked his draftees to have, the kind that made easy, reliable stories for writers. Yet, in retrospect, isn't Brandt's real story more writable and admirable? What he achieved against such odds should have made him at least as proud as Landry and Schramm were. "A hell of a success story," Elroy Hirsch calls Brandt.

But Brandt was tormented by the past he didn't have. Instead of playing to his one remarkable strength—hustling information—he constantly tried to convince the world of his football genius. John Wooten, Brandt's chief scout for fourteen years, says, "Where I think Gil did the biggest disservice to himself was that he never learned the details of the game. I don't know why he didn't want to. It just had to do with desire and patience. He could have sat right here like anyone else and learned the game by running [the game tape in the VCR] back and forth."

Bulletin: *Gil Brandt did not study film.* Brandt spent his time asking others for their opinions and telling others how much film he watched. An early *Dallas Morning News* story said: "Brandt, with the aid of coaches, has studied players in nearly five hundred films." The truth was, Brandt was living a Hollywood film. Living a lie. Of course, without his acting prowess, maybe no one would have noticed Brandt in the first place.

He would live and die by a rubber sword.

The truth was, Schramm didn't hire Brandt to scout college players but to do a little part-time dirty work. Schramm says he didn't really know Brandt but "I knew of him, I knew . . . when you wanted to get something done, he'd get it done." And in late 1959, Schramm desperately needed something done. The NFL draft had already been held in November. League owners wouldn't meet until January. Only then could the NFL approve an expansion team for Dallas. And if it did, the new team would have no players. Schramm's plea for a standard NFL contract was denied, so Schramm, uh, borrowed one and had copies made. Schramm armed Brandt with counterfeit NFL contracts and told him to sign as many free agents as he could before the league meeting.

A rival general manager says, "Remember, Schramm was fighting the AFL and Lamar Hunt's Texans, too. The competition for players was cutthroat, so he brought in Gil because he was persistent enough to find players and hide them out if he had to—you know, babysit them until they signed."

Remarkably, Brandt signed twenty-eight free agents. Schramm's book says, "This became one of the deciding factors in Dallas's being awarded a franchise."

So did Schramm say, "Thanks, Gil, you can go home now"? Maybe he thought about it. But Brandt, as usual, just kept hanging around. Schramm says Brandt just "worked into the job" of personnel director. Just kept hustling. Producing. Doing whatever it took to ingratiate himself.

Brandt was living his superfan fantasy. What luck! The coach Schramm had hired wasn't like any coach Brandt knew. This Tom Landry wasn't interested in studying film of a college senior and saying, "That kid's a player." Landry only wanted to study film of opponents. Landry wasn't much of a college or even pro football fan. Landry didn't even know the names of a lot of college stars. Landry's attitude seemed to be, "Just give me players who can play my system." Landry wanted to dedicate his time to designing and perfecting an offense and defense. Young Landry seemed to believe the systems were more important than any one player playing them. Landry definitely wanted to make the first few choices on Draft Day. But he seemed perfectly willing to let Brandt provide him with information.

A Cowboy scout says, "Tom's ego dictated that he make the choices, but he relied heavily on Gil's reports."

Didn't Landry take time to research Brandt's background? No, Landry never got to know Brandt. Maybe, after a while, he didn't want to know much about Brandt. Landry once said, "Nobody knows Gil very well. He doesn't sit down long enough for anyone to know him." Landry had an almost inhuman capacity for blocking out everything around him except his religion, his family, and his game plan. He often came off as small-town: "Heck, I'm too busy to know about any of *that*." But perhaps he was naive by design. For sure he wanted to do as little on-the-road scouting as possible.

So Gil Brandt hit the road the way Landry used to hit receivers. Brandt introduced himself to famous college coaches. He charmed their secretaries with Cowboy T-shirts and pens. He shared inside info with assistant coaches and trainers. He found other Draftniks in remote places and put them on the Cowboy payroll. He learned the birthdays of coaches and their wives and children and called every last one on their special day. "That Gil," coaches would say, "is somethin'."

That Gil was even rumored to be able to arrange companionship for lonely college coaches at the College All-Star Game. For years, as Brandt's legend grew, I heard these stories from scouts and players. Says John Wooten, "I always heard coaches laughing about what Gil could do for them, but I never actually saw it myself. I think Gil almost liked having that reputation. He didn't do anything to discourage it."

And coaches and their wives, secretaries, assistants, and trainers began to share information with Brandt. The coach at IOU would confide, "I think I got something special here, Gil." Brandt was told about George Andrie at Marquette, Jethro Pugh at Elizabeth City State, Rayfield Wright at Fort Valley State, and Larry Cole at Hawaii. For Schramm, Brandt was building a CBS-like network. Brandt, who hadn't played football, was outrunning rivals who had. While lots of teams were more interested in regional college stars for their gate value and accessibility, Brandt turned all of America into Draftnik heaven.

Says Bob Ackles, who shared personnel duties with Brandt from 1968 on, "His memory was amazing for names and statistics. He'd glance at a list of one hundred guys who had taken physical examinations and be able to tell you every last injury and what the doctor thought of it."

Need a trivia answer? Brandt became the Source. An Eagles P.R. man once called Brandt and said, "Gil, what was the name of that one-armed . . ." Brandt interrupted the question with: "Ellis Jones. Tulsa, 1942–43–44. Played in three bowl games. Played in the College All-Star Game against the Bears in 1945. Played one season with the Boston Yanks."

Need a coach? College presidents and athletic directors began to call Brandt because he knew every college coach's strengths and unpublished weaknesses. He knew their contract length and how much money they'd want. He even knew whether their wives would be happy in College Station or Eugene. Brandt could arrange clandestine meetings. Brandt could even serve as arbiter in negotiations. Brandt was on his way to becoming the godfather of college football—another job nobody had thought of doing. Soon college coaches would lay inside info on Brandt because he could lay a better job on them.

Need a scoop? Sportswriters from everywhere were calling Brandt, one NFL executive who quickly returned their calls. Brandt knew everything and often shared it, off the record. If a "source" said Michigan coach Bo Schembechler had turned down Texas A&M's offer but Jackie Sherrill wouldn't, it probably was Brandt. The Nowhere Man was becoming one of the most powerful men in sports.

Ditto in Dallas, which was becoming Power City. Brandt was quoted in the papers almost daily. Brandt was growing as famous as Landry and Schramm. Brandt was getting to know all the right maître d's, telephone company insiders, airline executives, military and law enforcement officials—even well-known gamblers. Brandt said, "You can never have enough good information."

Schramm always seemed a little uncomfortable with the monster he had created. He seemed to roll his eyes at having to share billing with this one-time part-timer. But Schramm and Landry needed Brandt. He did what had to be done. Imagine: Mission, Texas, had met Hollywood and the wrong side of Milwaukee in Dallas. What were the odds?

4

FALL, 1960. Bedford Wynne tried to keep smiling his "ain't we lucky" smile as he watched the convertible move dramatically out of the Cotton Bowl tunnel and past the stands. It was halftime. The first-year Cowboys were losing again. Wynne, a Cowboy owner, sat in the hollow middle of maybe eight thousand fans who dotted the lower stands of a stadium that held nearly eighty thousand.

Perched on the convertible's trunk, with their feet in the backseat, were none other than Roy Rogers and Dale Evans. Wynne had arranged for this special appearance and was taking Roy and Dale to a private wingding that night. What better sideshow attraction for a Dallas Cowboy game than Mr. and Mrs. Cowboy? Where was everybody? And why the hell was the convertible beginning to speed up?

"I was appalled," Wynne said recently. "People were throwing ice at Roy Rogers and Dale Evans."

That was the Cotton Bowl on Sunday afternoons in the early '60s. Pro football was just something you watched as a mildly amusing hangover remedy after a big Saturday of college action. Dallas was a college football capital with loyalties split like an atom. No city in America had (and has) so many rabid rivals from so many schools: Southern Methodist University was fifteen minutes up Central Expressway from downtown elevators jammed with blood-and-money supporters of Texas, Texas Christian (in Fort Worth), Texas A&M, Texas Tech, Baylor, Rice, Arkansas, and Oklahoma. At best the city's two pro teams attracted rowdy cult followings as they shared the Cotton Bowl. Lots of North Dallas college fans considered the stadium, just east of downtown on the fairgrounds, an unsafe place on a "pro" day: too many blacks in the end zone seats and surrounding neighborhood.

Lamar Hunt, who owned the AFL Texans, says, "We had an impossible situation for two teams. We both did lots of promotions, like five free kids with one paid adult. And the crowd figures were severely inflated by both teams. But neither team was drawing flies. Actual records later were subpoenaed for a lawsuit, and in the third year [1962] we won the AFL championship and had 10,100 paid per game and the Cowboys had 10,050 paid.

"But the one thing we noticed was that there was tremendous interest in pro football in Dallas. The team that was on the road would have its game televised back in Dallas, and the ratings would be very good."

But at the Cotton Bowl, handfuls of customers threw handfuls of ice at Roy and Dale.

For the Cowboy "in-crowd" the games were just a necessary evil before post-game parties. On the fairgrounds near the Cotton Bowl was a roller skating rink that had been converted into the Cowboy Club. Smiling wistfully, Bedford Wynne said, "Oh, was that ever the place to be. That was the age of the miniskirt and . . ."

Wynne and Clint Murchison (pronounced Mur-ki-son) had been best friends since boyhood. Murchison's father and Wynne's uncle were partners in American Liberty Oil. Clint and Bedford shared a thirst for alcohol and women in miniskirts. The Cowboy Club overflowed with both. There were very few morals to this story.

Clinton Williams Murchison, Jr., was a namesake who never could quite live up to his father. Clint Sr. made the cover of *Time* in 1954. "Clint Murchison," said the caption, "a big wheeler-dealer." Big Clint was known for his gut feelings, guts, and rather large gut. His beloved wife Anne died of jaundice when Clint Jr. was two years old, leaving him a frail, sickly child dominated by a wildcatter father. Clint Sr. once called Clint Jr. "the worst spoiled brat any parent ever had to deal with."

But while little Clint couldn't match big Clint in oil-man macho, he could impress his father with brain power. Clint Jr. was a Phi Beta Kappa graduate of Duke with a degree in electrical engineering. At MIT he earned his master's in mathematics while carrying an A-plus average. At MIT, perhaps to please his father, Clint Jr. played football on a student-coached team. At 130 pounds he played halfback, or tried to. "I wasn't a star by NFL standards," he once told me with a slight dry grin. "When you're little, you have to be shifty."

And Murchison appeared even smaller than he was, at five-feet-seven. He had the physical presence of an empty suit. Even his voice was a very small, very Texas drawl. He always wore his dark-brown hair in a flattop, and his wallflower face was framed by appropriately plain black glasses. The man who would own the most stylish team in sports had no style. The man who would inherit around $300 million took an almost defiant delight in wearing white short-sleeve shirts and black ties. In her book, *The Murchisons*, Jane Wolfe writes, "In and around Boston, Clint Jr. frequented a milieu of intellectuals from Harvard, MIT, and Wellesley. Even in this environment Clint Jr. was viewed as a scientific genius and an eccentric. He loved to spend an evening at the home of a professor or a fellow graduate student where the conversation about mathematical or scientific theory lasted well into the morning hours. On such evenings Clint would not say a social word, but on the subject of math and science he talked at great lengths. He was a voracious reader of dozens of technical journals, and, given the chance, he could explain the latest theories he had read, explanations so complex in their detail that the hosts and other guests were astounded and often baffled."

Of all the men who helped create the Cowboys, Murchison had real genius. But would he become an engineer and design a better tomorrow? No, regrettably, his father's iron-fisted hold was too powerful. Clint Sr. wanted sons Clint and John to run Murchison Brothers, which held stock in companies all over the country. In 1949, Clint Sr. ordered Clint Jr. home to Dallas, and a brilliant mind was unplugged. Little Clint did not inherit big Clint's business instincts. Wolfe writes: "Clint Sr. believed that while Clint Jr. was a genius, he was also unbalanced. He frequently failed to see the practical side of ideas, the bottom line."

Yet little Clint rather desperately wanted to prove his manhood to big Clint. What better way than a Texan's ultimate test—football? After Clint Jr. tried unsuccessfully to buy the San Francisco 49ers and Washington Redskins, Wynne suggested they pursue an expansion team.

Wynne, who graduated from the University of Texas and SMU's School of Law, was a rather bored attorney in his family's firm. Wynne was drawn to limelight and nightlife. Wynne loved to rub elbows and egos with football stars. Wynne wanted to go 50–50 on an NFL team, but when told it would cost $200,000 cash and $600,000 over five years, he backed off and took only 5 percent of the team. Why plunge when Clint would? Murchison put his money where Wynne's mouth was. Wynne became known as the "front man" for the Cowboys. Wynne made all the initial contacts with the league. Wynne got hold of Schramm at CBS and soon became one of Tex's drinking buddies. Wynne: "Clint wasn't a mixer at all. I was the buffer between Tex and Clint. He'd say, 'Call Tex and find this out.' Clint did not like to get out in public."

Bedford Wynne: Could you make up a better name for the owner of a pro football team in Texas? Wynne was a drink-buying, joke-telling fixture wherever in-crowd glasses clinked. Wynne was a Wallbanger to Murchison's wallflower. Wynne's face was ablaze with spirits, his hair was a white gray, and his chest hair was highlighted by gold chains. He had a way with the ladies and was what people called "a helluva guy." Wynne personified quick-money Dallas in the '60s: Life was a bottomless well. Oil-rush Dallas was still a big small town. Its most famous resident, Mickey Mantle, had put in a bowling alley.

A good friend of Wynne's who worked in the Neiman-Marcus hierarchy says, "The Cowboy Club was the wildest place in the history of the world. Nothing but tables and booze. The men all wore these blue blazers with big Cowboy helmets on the pocket and took their wives. But everyone seemed to have a girlfriend there, too, and it was like a big game keeping the wives from finding out. It's almost inconceivable now how much we drank and how unfaithful everyone was. It seems so foolish now. But no one ever questioned it. That's just the way it was in Dallas in those days.

"But Clint was so quiet that it was hard to see him operate. Bedford became something of a procurer."

Wynne introduced Murchison to women he was too shy to approach. While Clint Sr. was known as a fiercely faithful husband, little Clint, married with an eventual four children, began to rebel obsessively. Once, Cleveland owner Art Modell was at Clint Jr.'s home watching the College All-Star Game. Modell was impressed that Murchison and Wynne seemed to be taking notes on college players. On closer inspection, Modell discovered they were going over lists of Braniff stewardesses. Murchison flew Braniff instead of company jets and even sat in the back row at graduation ceremonies for Braniff's stewardess school, quietly noting Phi Beta Kappas.

He had come a long way from MIT. Was he ever proving his manhood.

Naturally, Braniff became the official carrier of the Dallas Cowboys. Murchison and Wynne dedicated many business hours to choosing which stewardesses would get to work the charter flights. As one veteran charter "stew" proudly told me, "Bedford got me on originally. It wasn't easy."

In June 1961, Clint Jr. and brother John appeared on the cover of *Time*. What power Clint Jr. had to be feeling. How many Braniff stewardesses would make a fantasy come true for a math professor? How many sportswriters would chronicle the every wink of some engineer in Boston? Who cared if the Cowboys were drawing only flies and losing money? The kid called a recluse by an embarrassed father was now the invisible life of the wildest party in town. He was shocking Dallas with his quirky behavior and unpredictable moves. He was playing a rich kid's game of who'll-blink-first with Lamar Hunt. Loser leaves town.

A reporter told Lamar's father, H. L. Hunt, that if Lamar kept the Texans in Dallas, he would continue losing $1 million a year. "In that case," H. L. said, "it will take him 150 years to go broke."

Murchison loved that quote, that challenge. And Murchison loved his team's nickname. While Wynne pushed for Jets or Rangers, Schramm suggested Cowboys. "At first blush," Wynne said, "you thought, 'That's ridiculous. It's corny.'" Yes, it was perfectly corny for Murchison. Oddly enough, the nickname was so stereotypically Texan that people everywhere were fascinated by it. Wynne said, "We found that everywhere we went, it was a source of mystique. There was just an intrigue nationally with Dallas—the oil, the wealth."

And Murchison was going to move his team out of town? Losing $1 million a year, he wouldn't go broke for three hundred years.

*   *   *

Once, the story goes, twenty-five-year-old Lamar Hunt stood outside the Cotton Bowl after a Texans practice and watched one of his
stars hop in a convertible driven by a beautiful blonde. Hunt sighed
and said, "Some guys have all the luck." Yes, God had shortchanged
Hunt by only making him the son of one of the world's richest men.
Lamar owned a team that soon would win the AFL championship.
He would help forge the AFL-NFL merger and come up with the
name Super Bowl for America's biggest single game. He would
become one of the NFL's most respected owners and operate a
successful franchise in Kansas City, the Chiefs. But other guys—like
Clint Murchison—would have all the luck.

By 1963, Hunt's business head overruled his heart, or maybe
his greed defeated his ego. Whatever, Kansas City was on its knees
for a pro football team. Hunt was offered free use of a stadium for
two years and guaranteed sales of twenty-five thousand season tickets. "It just would have been a standoff situation in Dallas," Hunt
says. "I don't know if either one of us would have made it."

Murchison even agreed to pay "financial considerations" for
Hunt to move. Whatever they were, they weren't enough. Hunt
continued to live in Dallas and fly to Kansas City for games. Morning
after morning he was greeted by headlines about the Cowboys, who
soon turned into Hunt's dream team. Some guys. . . .

In November 1962, Bedford Wynne went to Washington. "I was
somewhat active in Democratic politics," he said, "and I put on the
first big dinner for Jack Kennedy, a thousand dollars a plate."
Wynne's fondest memory was of arriving in the presidential motorcade and following Kennedy and his wife Jackie inside . . . followed
by Lyndon Johnson and his wife Lady Bird. "Everybody laughed
about how I had upstaged the vice president."

Wynne was everywhere. It's a wonder he didn't drive Jack and
Jackie through downtown Dallas on Friday, November 22, 1963.
Instead, Wynne's services were needed at the Apparel Mart, where
Kennedy was to speak after waving to thousands gathered along the
motorcade route. "I was supposed to help the Secret Service guys
identify the congressmen," Wynne said.

The atmosphere was uneasy. A group of powerful young Republicans had taken out a full-page, black-bordered, anti-Kennedy ad in that morning's *Dallas Morning News*. Clint Murchison was said to be the biggest financial backer of Richard Nixon's unsuccessful campaign against Kennedy in 1960. Murchison had boasted to Wynne about how he once had kept Nixon waiting on the phone while Murchison finished a sexual liaison.

Just after noon Wynne was standing next to a Secret Service man with a walkie-talkie who turned to another and said, "The boss has been hit." At first, Wynne thought Kennedy had been hit by, what, a cup of ice?

Minutes later, as the Cowboys prepared to practice, middle linebacker Jerry Tubbs noticed an agitated team official telling Tom Landry something. Tubbs says, "I thought it was a little strange, so I asked Tom if anything was wrong. He said, 'Oh, some nut just shot Kennedy.' We went on about our business."

Landry was a Republican. Tubbs, who would play and coach under Landry for twenty-nine seasons, didn't vote for Kennedy, either. Tubbs says, "I wasn't emotionally involved, but I thought it was a great tragedy." Commissioner Rozelle decided the NFL show would go on that Sunday, so the Cowboys went on to Cleveland. Tubbs says, "It was a little somber, and we got the expected catcalls and boos. But I don't see how anyone logically could think that Dallas did it [shot Kennedy]. Here was a guy [Lee Harvey Oswald] who had been to Russia. This had absolutely nothing to do with the people of Dallas. When I'd hear [a rival fan] say, 'You killed our president,' I thought it was the epitome of stupidity. It disgusted me. It could have happened anywhere."

Yet the shame and guilt began to echo through the steel canyons in downtown Dallas. Very quietly Boomtown U.S.A. began to ask itself if it was really the City of Hate. Dallas's image had several bullet holes in it.

The final shot was fired by a Dallasite well known to those who toasted the downtown dawns. A nightclub operator named Jack Ruby pulled the trigger. Oswald's death grimace was frozen forever on front pages around the world. Frontier justice? An eye for a sharpshooter's eye? Conspiracy? Communists? Or were Oswald and/ or Ruby somehow products of a Sodom on the Trinity?

Dallas began to grope in the darkness for a new image, to sift through the prairie dust for something other than the Grassy Knoll. "The Cowboys," Tubbs says, "became a vehicle that projected Dallas as a winner instead of the killer of Kennedy."

Landry now tells interviewers that "the Cowboys gave the city something to rally around after the assassination. Looking back, that probably was the most important thing we did."

But Landry's Cowboys didn't do it immediately. Beginning that Sunday in Cleveland—Jack Ruby Day—the Cowboys lost three of their last four to finish 4–10. This was a team picked by some Dallas sportswriters to go at least 10–4. Landry blamed the positive pre-season publicity. He said, "I was hopeful for a 7–7 year, and there is no doubt we would have achieved this if the publicity had been different in the beginning."

Some poison-penned fans weren't buying Landry's logic. One letter to the editor asked for Landry to show some class and resign. It said, "It just could not be any worse, even with any of the Dallas high school coaches taking over. . . . Why should people throw $5.50 away just to watch another frustrated, poorly coached team?" Another letter to the editor said, "If Tom Landry, as the majority of sportswriters clamor, is a genius, what in the hell is Vince Lombardi?"

Already Landry was struggling to live up to what Gary Cartwright, who covered the Cowboys for the *Morning News*, called The Image. Before the 1963 season Cartwright had written about how a coach-of-the-year award for the Texans' Hank Stram had been sent to the Cowboys' offices. Cartwright: "Stram is in his customary role as Dallas's 'second coach' . . . the long shadow of The Image burns his cheeks daily. His is the misfortune of anyone who rides in after the public has inhaled an opinion. There will never be another Gene Tunney, another Sarah Bernhardt, another Orville Wright, another Felix the Cat. There will never, for that matter, be another Tom Landry, just as there never was."

No, there never was a "greatest coach in football," as christened by Jim Lee Howell. Cartwright: "On this foundation [the Howell quote] The Image was erected, permanently, with a dogma as unshakable as motherhood and the Easter bunny."

But Landry was beginning to sweat under the weight of The Image. His four-year record in Dallas was 13–38–3. Cowboy fans were beginning to wonder why Landry couldn't coach as successfully as he dressed. Why did a small-town guy eschew the ball caps and sweaters worn by many coaches? Was it because Landry, struggling with the conflict of football on Sunday, wanted to at

least honor God with the appropriate apparel? Perhaps. Or was it
that in New York, Landry had learned you live up to an image by
creating one? Surely Alicia, who chose his clothes, had impressed
upon him what a powerful impression he made in suits. He was
losing some hair on top, so the hat didn't hurt, either. Was Landry
thinking, "If I can't quite be the greatest coach, I'd better look like
one"?

Later, in 1982, Landry would say, "I've just always dressed this
way. I've always enjoyed wearing hats and felt comfortable in them.
A hat finishes off a coach's dress on the sidelines." From the start
Landry insisted the Cowboys wear coats and ties on the road. "It's
important for a team to dress well because how you dress and look
has something to do with your attitude and success on the field.
Players take pride in their performances and should do likewise in
their clothes."

But in 1963 the Cowboys often dressed much more sharply
than they performed. Perhaps it should be no surprise that Landry
occasionally dropped by road-hotel hospitality suites for one drink
(Scotch, according to veteran Dallas columnist Blackie Sherrod). Of
the Howell quote, Landry said, "It was very nice for Jim Lee to say
that, but it put me on the spot. It's not easy to live up to that sort of
thing."

He wasn't coming close. Rumored replacements for Landry
included Oklahoma's Bud Wilkinson. All Landry had going for him
was that Murchison had taken a distant fancy to him. Murchison
could empathize with Landry, a thinking man's coach with a nowhere man's personality. Imagine the awkward silences if these two
attempted small talk. The point is, they didn't.

Murchison eased into Landry's peripheral vision just once, to
suggest a play. Murchison said, "You know, Tom, if, uh, Frank
Clarke is averaging seventeen yards a reverse, well, shoot, you have
to wonder how far a guy as fast as Bob Hayes would go if he ran one."
Years later Murchison told me, "Tom gave me all this mumbo jumbo
about strong and weak side, and I nodded sagely and walked away."
Three or four games later Murchison watched Hayes lose four yards
on a reverse and said, "That's Tom's way of telling me to stay out of
football."

But now, in late 1963, the pressure built for Murchison to make
a coaching change. Predictably, he did just the opposite. Yes, the
man who seldom ventured into public loved to attract attention to

himself by venturing out on a limb. If public opinion told Murchison to fire Landry, Murchison would rehire him.

For ten more years.

Yes, Murchison announced Landry had been given a ten-year extension. Landry still had one year to go on his original deal, so now a 13–38–3 coach had been given a vote of confidence through 1974. "I was shocked," Wynne said, "and I was as close to him as anyone. That was totally Clint's decision." Some Dallasites had to rank Murchison right up there with John Beresford Tipton for eccentricity. To some fans, no doubt, the ten-year contract was the equivalent of picking a name out of the telephone book and sending Schramm to give the guy $1 million.

If the public had also known the inside story about the Cowbelles, the original Cowboy cheerleaders, Murchison would have been pursued by vigilantes. Murchison focused his binoculars on Cowbelle tryouts just as he watched Braniff graduations. Cowbelles were high school girls. Murchison made it known to his favorites that they'd be a cinch for the squad if they got to know him a little. As Murchison said, "There are two things in life in which logic plays no part, and one of them is sports."

A third may have been business. FBI wiretaps and federal investigations would indicate Murchison was doing some business with organized crime figures. Did Murchison need Landry as a God-and-country facade for his off-camera activities? Did that influence Murchison's decision to give Landry such inexplicable security?

Landry credits Murchison as the key to his success. He has said, "I felt the contract was God's way of saying football was the place for me. I decided then and there I'd make a career of it."

Had God worked through Clint Murchison? Or do some guys have all the luck?

On Draft Day, Landry always made the first five or six picks and went home to the family. On Draft Day, 1964, Brandt had just selected Jake Kupp, an end from the University of Washington, in the ninth round. Schramm had a suggestion for the tenth. He was thinking of Heisman Trophy, Cotton Bowl, box office. Thinking Roger Staubach.

Apparently no other NFL team was. Because Staubach had spent a year at New Mexico Military Institute, improving his grades for the Naval Academy, he technically was eligible for the NFL draft a year early. But even after winning the Heisman Trophy in 1963 and completing a Cotton Bowl record twenty-one passes in a 28–6 loss to Texas, Staubach's NFL stock was not exactly at high tide. As Staubach says now, "I really didn't think I'd ever get the chance to play again when I finished at the Naval Academy. I didn't think anyone recognized that I was more than just a running quarterback. People were telling me, 'Oh, too bad you can't play pro ball.' "

It wasn't that Schramm foresaw a great passing quarterback. Schramm saw a great American hero who had been featured on *Time*'s cover. Could Schramm ever sell this Heisman winner to newspaper and TV audiences. A devout Catholic midshipman? Anchors aweigh.

Brandt, naturally, had talked his way into the Cincinnati home of Staubach's parents and had "nearly been thrown out," Staubach says. Hey, Brandt was just checking to see if Roger had considered passing up his final year of eligibility or maybe even trying to get out of his four-year U.S. Navy commitment. Brandt just wanted to make sure the Staubachs understood the financial advantages of playing pro football, especially in Dallas. But the Staubachs wouldn't hear of pro football until their son had completed his obligation to his country.

Still, Schramm had a gut feeling and pushed for spending the tenth-round pick on a guy who might be five years away from playing for the Cowboys, if then. The Cowboys took Staubach—but nearly lost him to the AFL. To, naturally, Lamar Hunt. Some guys have all the rotten luck.

Gil Brandt struck again. Brandt had struck up a relationship with an assistant basketball coach at Michigan State named Danny Petersen, who had recommended the Cowboys sign a six-foot-five, 225-pound Spartan basketball player named Pete Gent. Brandt did so, in a motel room in Lansing. "He wouldn't turn on the lights until I signed the contract," Gent says, grinning. Gent, who hadn't played football since high school, would become Landry's pass-catching tight end. Petersen soon would take an assistant's job at the Naval Academy, where he would get to know Staubach, who often shot hoops in the gym. One day Petersen asked Staubach if he planned to sign with a pro football team. Staubach said yes, sir, he was leaning toward the AFL's Kansas City Chiefs. "Lamar Hunt," Staubach told Petersen, "is such a nice guy."

Besides, Staubach had played twice in Dallas, and lost twice, bitterly. SMU had upset Navy 32–28 during Staubach's Heisman season. Then, after the Kennedy assassination, Navy had been man-handled by Texas in the Cotton Bowl. Later, at a dinner, Staubach wound up sitting next to Ethel Kennedy, who criticized Staubach for not "representing the country" in losing to Texas "down there." Kennedy was a hero of Staubach's. Kennedy had visited the Navy team during the preseason. Staubach admits he didn't like Dallas, yet he was destined to become Dallas's most dynamic ambassador.

Assistant Petersen told Staubach he should think strongly about signing with the Cowboys. "They're really a team on the move," Petersen said, "and the NFL has a much stronger image." Petersen was a coach, an authority figure, a superior, and his advice had an impact on midshipman Staubach. "That really got me thinking about the Cowboys," Staubach says.

Petersen called Brandt and told him of Lamar Hunt's offer. Staubach agreed to let the Cowboys make one, too. The Cowboys had the advantage of knowing the basics of Hunt's proposal. Staubach signed with Dallas for a $10,000 bonus plus $500 a month while he was in the service, plus another $100,000 (spread over ten years) if he made the team in 1970. Translation: Staubach became the steal of the century. Whatever "bonus" Petersen got from Brandt—slacks, Cowboy shirts, ballpoints—wasn't nearly enough.

"Lamar," says Staubach, "was disappointed we didn't give him a chance [to top the Cowboy offer]."

Brandt's influence was growing, but he still couldn't pull long enough strings to keep Staubach out of Vietnam. (Gent: "I was two days away from going to 'Nam, and I ended up failing my physical four or five times. Gil knew the right people.") Yet Brandt sent Staubach footballs and game films, even in 'Nam. Staubach spent a year as a supply officer, based just south of Da Nang, and wore out his first football throwing to nervous receivers on a field pocked by mortar shells. Brandt sent another. Staubach says, "I was possessed to come back and play for the Cowboys, especially after so many people said there was no way a guy could lay out four years and play."

There should have been no way. And without Staubach, there probably would have been no America's Team. Without him it's doubtful Landry would have won a single Super Bowl. Staubach was the key. And without Schramm's hunch and Brandt's hustle, Staubach almost certainly would have been a Chief.

Without Murchison, Landry very possibly would have been fired after the next season, his fifth, when the Cowboys lost four of their last five to finish 5–8–1. That made "the greatest" 18–46–4 overall. How many NFL owners would have ignored the pleading of friends, fans, and media, and stuck with Landry? Most owners are more egocentric than eccentric.

What if Lamar Hunt had chosen to stick it out in Dallas? Would Dallas have rallied around two pro teams? America's Teams? Would there have been a God's Coach without Brandt? Schramm? Murchison?

5

ON NOVEMBER 21, 1965, Bedford Wynne was not alone in the Cotton Bowl stands. No, Roy and Dale weren't there to keep him company, but an announced crowd of 76,251 was. What? Weren't Landry's 4–5 Cowboys underdogs against the Browns? Yes, but the *Dallas Morning News* quoted a Cowbelle cheerleader as saying, "The lack of cheering really threw me for a loss my first year (1964). But now cheering seems to be catching on in Dallas."

The Cowboys lost to the Browns 24–17. The Cowboys were building a national reputation for folding in the clutch. On record alone, Landry had no national reputation. In his sixth season he was an overall 22–52–4. Yet the *Dallas Times Herald* said, "Suddenly, tickets are hard to get. Even the youngsters usually show up three hours before kickoff to get a cherished end zone seat for a dollar. . . . [Fans] have got to be on hand when the Cowboys unloose a scoring bomb. Dallas's private airports are crowded whenever the Cowboys are at home. Fans fly in from all over the state."

Was this a P.R. story planted by Schramm? No, something was happening. The city was getting closer to a team that kept coming

close. Civic pride, what was left of it, was being refocused on the
Cotton Bowl, on Sundays. The once prominent SMU Mustangs of
Doak Walker and Kyle Rote had gone 1–9 in 1964. The Cowboys
weren't winning a lot of games, just fans. Even when they lost, no
one lost interest. At least Dallas had the most interesting team in the
NFL. Its coach didn't appear to have much life, but *it* sure did. It
had SMU's own Don Meredith going bombs away to Bob Hayes, the
"world's fastest human" who was revolutionizing NFL offense. It
had ex-basketball players at cornerback (Cornell Green) and tight
end (Pete Gent), and an ex-track man (Mike Gaechter) at safety.
Defensive lineman Bob Lilly out of TCU was beginning to leave
lilies on blockers' chests. Middle linebacker Lee Roy Jordan from
Alabama, a ruggedly handsome leader who just looked and sounded
like a Dallas Cowboy, was fitting into Landry's Flex as if it were the
Marlboro Man's leather jacket. The team had stars on its helmets
and shoulders, and the fans had a few in their eyes.

Sportswriters everywhere had stories up to their cigarette
butts. Merrill Swanson of the *Minneapolis Star* once told Cowboy
advance man Curt Mosher, "Boy, am I glad to see you guys come to
town. Other teams come in here . . . well, take the Bears. I do
stories on Butkus and Sayers, and what have I got left? With your
bunch I could go on for two weeks—Meredith singing 'Honky-Tonk
Angels' in the huddle, Hayes, Lilly, Mel Renfro, What-is-a-Jethro
Pugh, Reeves the free agent. . . ."

There was just one hitch: Before Meredith took the snap, his
linemen stood up in unison, then returned to their stances. "The
Hitch," Landry called it. Landry's offense looked like a Chinese fire
drill. Landry wasn't afraid to try trick plays he called "exotics."
Cowboy games were like some wild new bar or restaurant, the place
to be. This was a team on the rise and verge. It was easy for Dallasites to invest emotionally in this team because it just seemed to
have so much talent.

If nothing else, the Cowboys took everyone's mind off the Texas
School Book Depository.

Lord, it was always something. Fans kept waiting for their
Cowboys to be the first team to draft Cassius Clay or Billie Jean King
or the Amazing Kreskin or Ringo Starr. This Gil Brandt was something, with his "best athlete available" philosophy. Brandt was beating the bushes and rival scouts. Brandt didn't care if his "finds"
played football or not. He saw Pro Bowl tight ends in college bas-

ketball stars Pat Riley of Kentucky (round fourteen) and Minnesota's Lou Hudson (round twenty), but both passed up chances of a lifetime for the NBA.

Landry's Cowboys were beginning to put the fear of God in their opponents. The joke circulated that you could take a page of Landry's playbook to a Chinese laundry and exchange it for a bundle of shirts. Pete Gent's classic warning to a rookie opening a playbook was: "Don't bother reading it. Everybody gets killed in the end." Very little about the Cowboys was normal, most of all their defense. Was the Flex beginning to work, or were its cogs making it work? Did Brandt's drafts make the Flex? Or did it make Brandt's drafts?

Jerry Tubbs, who played and coached the Flex for twenty-nine years, speaks for most players and assistants when saying, "By 1965 we just got more players than other teams had. Of course, Gil was spending three times as much as any other team to find them, and the players we had were getting to know the System. But players— that's the name of the game. [Bob] Lilly had turned into a terror, an unbelievable combination of quickness, agility, and strength. [Linebacker] Chuck Howley was coming into his own. Lee Roy [Jordan] was starting to play in place of me. . . ."

Sometimes I wanted to interview the Flex defense. I wanted to go to the Dallas–Fort Worth Airport hangar where I figured Landry probably kept it and bang on the steel door and see if the thing would open up and explain itself. In the D-FW Metroplex, as it's called, Landry's scheme became the MetroFlex. It dominated the city's thoughts like a downtown volcano. It was our Diamondhead, ever looming. Some Sunday, would it suddenly unleash its awesome fury on everyone in the stadium? Would it level the entire city as well as the visiting team? Would it assume the form of a godless Godzilla, tear Cowboy Tower out of the ground, break it in half, start munching it like a carrot, grin at swerving motorists and say, "What's up, Doc?" Would it take the shape of a Frankenstein in a snap-brim hat and too-little Brooks Brothers suit, and turn on its creator, Landry? Would it force Landry to squat like a constipated frog atop a downtown skyscraper for all Dallas to laugh at?

What in the name of Lucifer was the Flex?

The best explanation I ever heard came from Dextor Clinkscale, Landry's defensive quarterback and strong safety from 1982 to 1985. "Dextor," said Landry, "was as smart as anyone we ever had." Clinkscale says,

What opponents didn't understand with the Flex was that it was stupidly simple. Growing up as a huge Cowboy fan, I always read how complicated the Flex was, but all it really had was a lot of fancy names and terms. If you just looked at the playbook, it was intimidating. It was like taking advanced placement English and having the teacher assign you this 450-page book by some guy named Dickerson or Dickens. You say, "Damn, this big book?" I wasn't well-read (as an honors student at South Carolina State), and neither were most players who played the Flex. Most only read their press clippings. But you always heard Summerall and Madden talk about how intricate the Flex was and how Landry was such a scholar and theologian. You (as a rookie) are thinking, "I can't be looking at a coach. He's not draped in blue and white [team colors]. He looks astute. He's a thinker." Then you try to read his playbook, and these things are just tearing up your mind. You try to figure out little things like the technique on [a safety's] end-run force, and it becomes a logic game like on an SAT test. It's not like that.

The Flex is probably the simplest defense in the world because unless you're the middle linebacker, you have only one thing to do. You just have one gap to control. Of the front seven, the middle linebacker is the only one with two gaps. The object is to control every gap. There are only so many gaps an offensive line can create for a ball carrier, so by their initial movements, the center and two guards tell the middle linebacker where to go. They are his keys. The defensive linemen keep the offensive linemen off the middle linebacker so he can make the tackle. The middle linebacker has one gap and one "tango," usually to the weak side of the Flex. He can "tango" weak, meaning an immediate "scrape" by the middle linebacker to get to an outside gap.

This sounds simple for everyone but the middle linebacker, who might as well be reading a Dickerson novel.

More Clinkscale:

You see, it was necessary to set two of our four defensive linemen a yard off the line of scrimmage in a frog stance because this allowed them to sit back and see what was going on. They could read the actions of the offensive line, which would tell them which specific area they would control. You didn't control a man, you controlled an area. In the regular 4–3 [four linemen, three linebackers], you tried to control a man, but the Flex took away your natural instincts of pursuit. In effect, you held your ground and waited for the ball to come to you.

In the '60s and '70s this was an absolutely brilliant concept. Lee Roy Jordan was a student of the game and very quick and agile at around 200 pounds. Then came Bob Breunig in 1976, who was very smart and had some jets on him so he could get outside. He wasn't big (maybe 220) or strong, but he at least could pull down a ball carrier. When he retired [in 1984] all Landry had was Eugene Lockhart, a poor middle linebacker for the Flex. Eugene doesn't have the speed or agility to get outside, and he isn't a thinker like Breunig and Lee Roy. The Flex might have been more dominant in the '80s if the Cowboys hadn't passed over [Baylor's] Mike Singletary (in the 1981 draft). Gil, as I recall, decided Singletary was too short.

Landry depended on Brandt to stock his Flex with bright, quick athletes who could absorb it the way it began absorbing foes. Clinkscale, for instance, was one of some one hundred undrafted free agents the Cowboys signed in 1980. Right away strong safety Charlie Waters, who had a Ph.D. in Flexology, told me, "Watch this Clinkscale. He's picked up the Flex faster than anyone I've ever seen." Clinkscale had the Gift.

Clinkscale continues:

Coach Landry was a genius of preparation and technique. On film he could see tiny little mistakes I knew I'd made. His strength is simply knowledge of the game. He knew his opponents better than they probably knew themselves. On offense he knew how to dress something up. He knew what gave his defense trouble, so he came up with all that "multiple" offense crap in the '60s. Take the Raiders, for instance. They'd run a fullback dive over left guard, but the Cowboys would come out in a weird formation, shift into another weird formation, throw a wideout in motion one way, then a back would take off in motion the other way, then they'd run a fullback dive over left guard.

It was the same thing with the Hitch. It was just a gimmick to distract the defense before the snap. It was militaristic. It showed discipline. It was intimidating. In the '60s and '70s it was always in perfect unison, but by the '80s it looked like a bad halftime show, where the girls aren't all together. But the point of everything was deception. It was a mask for what you really were going to do, which was simple. The easiest way to beat the Flex was just to blow off the ball and block it, the way the Steelers and Raiders finally did. But in the '60s and '70s other teams kept trying to figure it out, and they'd fall prey to the Flex itself. You look across the line at Lilly or Randy White or Ed Jones in his Darth Vader helmet lined up in these weird places and stances, and it just looks like doom.

So now that we've passed Intro Flexology, let's try the advanced course taught by the creator. Only after Landry's Cowboy days were over did he say,

> When I created the Flex in about 1964, it was a completely different concept because it actually was based on engineering principles, which is why it was called the Flex. It took a real commitment from the players to play it because it took away a lot of natural instincts. Lombardi wrote *Run to Daylight,* and we wanted to take away the daylight. When you just go after the ball, bouncing off blocks, there's just going to be some daylight. Lombardi took to Green Bay the idea of pulling a lineman to get the flow going one way, then the back would take a counter step back into the hole. But we wanted guys to hold their position, control their area, see the point of attack, then have three or four guys close in. It took a lot of character to play the Flex. A guy like Bob Lilly could have just pushed people off him and gone for the ball, but he didn't. And we had a great defense through the '70s. It's a defense that would still work today if the players would play it.

Yet there were times Lilly's Cowboys were most dominant after an embarrassing loss when they worried more about playing football than playing Flex techniques. Says former defensive end Pat Toomay, "It wasn't that the players got together and scrapped the Flex. What was scrapped was the fear—the psychological baggage. The defense worked; the fear made you fail. Finally, you just gave up and quit worrying about making a mistake and paying for it during film sessions. You were taught to take this precise six-inch step, then read A, then B, then C. But you finally had to achieve what Charlie Waters called the thought of no thought: You just played. You became more like a Raider than a worried Cowboy. You were jaunty, more 'fuck you.' "

Toward opponents and, in effect, toward Landry. Says former linebacker D. D. Lewis, "Tom would choke you if you let him, by giving you too much to think about. At some point you just had to play football."

You wonder how much better Landry's teams would have been, especially in the late '70s and '80s, had he encouraged his more talented players to just play football. What, ultimately, was the goal of the Flex? Merely to win football games? Or to win a "genius" title for Landry? Was Landry still competing against fellow assistant Lombardi for head-of-the-class honors? Landry wasn't just asking his players to sacrifice their bodies for him. He wanted their very competitive instincts. "You simply had to annihilate your instincts," says Toomay. "You had to focus elsewhere, on a precise key, while the Art Shell across from you was going to kill you."

But how many of Landry's good players might have been great if they had been allowed a little more freedom? Wasn't the mark of a great coach that he adapted his system to the talent available and kept on winning? How many of Brandt's draftees of the '80s would have lived up to their publicity if Landry hadn't so inflexibly stuck with the Flex? Again and again we were told that a high draft pick had failed to "grasp the Flex." Was that subconsciously what Landry wanted? To prevail with inferior talent? To win with Clinkscales? To inspire sportswriters everywhere to shake their heads and say, "Man, that Landry can win with whatever the cat or Gil Brandt drags in"? Was Landry quietly building a monument to himself? Was the Flex his graven image?

While Landry's life well may have been "in God's hands," his Cowboys were absolutely in his.

That year, 1965, the Cowboys disappeared in a Halloween game in Pittsburgh, 22–13. Afterward Landry told his Cowboys he was "ashamed" of them because they had lost to a team "that had no business being on the same field with you." Young Landry was just about out of answers and self-control. He said, "I guess it's my fault. . . . I don't know what else to say."

You could have heard a tear drop—Landry's. Tears appeared on his cheeks.

Later, Landry was asked what he was going to do at quarterback. He said, "It looks like there's only one thing we can do—go with the rookies." With Craig Morton, the first-round choice, or Jerry Rhome.

Ah, yes, another vote of confidence for Don Meredith, his sixth-year quarterback.

One gap Landry couldn't control was the one that widened between him and Meredith. Dandy Don and Landry were as different as Saturday night and Sunday. Meredith was as country cool as Landry was country-church rigid. Meredith partied almost as hard as he played. Meredith didn't take the game so seriously that he sacrificed his bourbon and smokes and many female admirers. Meredith's attitude was, "We'll give 'em hell, then raise a little." His angels all floated through honky-tonks. If he worshiped a god, it probably was Merle Haggard or Johnny Cash, or maybe Conway Twitty. Meredith probably took losing as hard as Landry did, but it wasn't his *life*. Meredith definitely wasn't trying to build a monument that would loom forever above the Dallas skyline. Meredith played more for his teammates than for credit. He played with cracked ribs and a collapsed lung mostly because his buddies needed him. Winning, as a team, satisfied him even more than anything he could touch or taste.

Don Meredith played football because he was pretty good at it and because, hell, it was fun. At least it was until he met his Grinch Who Stole Football. For Landry, fun was what you had playing golf in June or eating Mexican food with your wife one night a week.

Here was live-it-up versus must-live-up.

The Cowboy computers couldn't have selected a personality profile more incompatible with Landry's. In fact, Landry hadn't selected Meredith; Murchison had signed him right off SMU's campus before the Cowboy franchise had been granted. Murchison had shelled out some serious cash—$150,000 for five years. Murchison was banking on Meredith's gate appeal—his looks, his wit, his Mount Vernon, Texas, heritage.

But by 1965 the offense was no longer introduced before Cowboy home games because Meredith was being booed so unmercifully. Behind an expansion-team line, Meredith's body had been battered as badly as his psyche. Roger Staubach says, "Don took an incredible amount of punishment, and he always played hurt. You cannot underestimate how much respect those teams had for Don. He was their leader."

Theirs—not Landry's. This had to shake Landry to his very foundation. Landry, the one-time quarterback, wanted his quarterback to be an on-field extension of his mind and mind-set. He wanted Meredith to operate as if by remote control. Often, in post-game interviews, Landry used "we," as in, "We had the right play called, we just didn't make the right read" or "We had the guy open, we just didn't make a good throw." But Landry and Meredith were not a "we." Meredith male-bonded with just about everyone in the locker room except Landry. He tried to loosen up "Tom" by cracking an occasional joke. He got nothing but Stoneface. You think Landry wanted his televised, publicized extension to be a guy who smoked and drank in public? You think he wanted his team's "spiritual" leader to be a guy who led a growing contingent of Southern good-ol'-boys on wild-bunch raids through a city all but spreading its legs for the Cowboys? Here was classic Epicurean versus Stoic. Meredith: Eat, drink, and have Mary, for tomorrow you may be paralyzed by a Ray Nitschke. Landry: Never let anyone know what you're thinking or if you're feeling.

Landry wanted his quarterback to take orders and, if necessary, blame. Anything to preserve the general's aura of invincibility. Yet in the heat of battle, Meredith began to see a stoic who was susceptible to panic. Holy smoke, Meredith would think, Mount Landry is *human*. Some days Meredith hated Landry for his hypocritical, holier-than-thou image and the way he surgically removed the pride of Meredith's teammates during two-drink-minimum film sessions. Other days Meredith felt sorry for a Landry who put inhuman pressure on himself to run the defense, call the plays, and live up to The Image.

Pete Gent, who was one of Meredith's closest friends, says, "Tom was great until game time. Then he was a mess. I always got a kick out of the public perception of Tom as cool as a cucumber. Believe me, I know he wasn't because I was a play messenger for him. He'd send me in with goal line plays at midfield and long-yardage plays on the goal line. He'd call plays we didn't have for players we didn't have. Sometimes Meredith would just wave the play messenger back to the sidelines.

"I mean, it was a genius system that really appealed to me. On my routes I was supposed to check the linebacker, then the strong safety, and know I was in man-to-man if he stays deep. I'd look for a roll zone and hook up into the hole. But the point is, Tom couldn't run the offense from the sideline. He needed a Meredith or Staubach who ultimately would challenge the System. After Staubach was gone, Tom had too many guys who had grown up in awe of the Cowboys, and they thought the System was this magical, mystical thing.

"But Don finally just got tired of challenging Tom. Don was a real lightning rod, the bravest man I ever saw on a football field. But after, what, nine years of it . . ."

For nine seasons this unhappy marriage survived because Landry and Meredith needed each other. Meredith was too loved by teammates (and writers who loved his one-liners) for Landry to risk a permanent demotion or trade. Meredith was too experienced, too clever, too talented. If Meredith criticized Landry through the newspapers, it was cloaked in humor. Later, Meredith always could say, "Aw, you know you should never take anything I say seriously." Meredith was too shrewd to openly challenge Landry and give him an excuse.

So the week after the '65 Halloween loss, Landry announced he was sticking with Meredith. And the team responded by winning its last three and a trip to Miami for its first post-season game, the Playoff Bowl, which matched the two second-place teams for no particular reason. It lost to Baltimore 35–3, but the countdown had begun. In 1966, with talent coming up around him like a tequila sunrise, Meredith two-stepped into his prime at twenty-nine. Hello, world: The 10–3–1 Dallas Cowboys won five of their last six and found themselves in the NFL championship game. Nine Cowboys made the Pro Bowl all-star squad: Bob Lilly, Cornell Green, Mel Renfro, Chuck Howley, George Andrie, Dave Manders, Don Perkins, Bob Hayes, and Don Meredith.

At the Cotton Bowl, though, Vince Lombardi's Packers beat Landry's Cowboys 34–27. The loss had to be devastating for Landry's personal pride, but it certainly didn't do anything to hurt The Image, which now cast a national shadow. Landry was named NFL coach of the year by the Associated Press.

And who had become nearly as big a Dallas hero as Landry? Murchison. The *Times Herald* called him "the most popular figure in town." Isn't it amazing what owning a football team can do for you? A month after the loss to Green Bay, Murchison announced plans to move the team to Irving. Murchison said he would build "the finest football stadium to date in the world." He said he owed that "to the thousands of Cowboy fans who don't have parking passes, who don't have comfortable box seats, and who are the real reason it is possible for the Cowboys to remain in Dallas."

*   *   *

Every good Cowboy fan can tell you where he or she was the moment Bart Starr followed Jerry Kramer's frozen-frame block over the goal line to win the Ice Bowl 21–17 for Green Bay. That NFL title game was played on New Year's Eve, 1967. I was at the VA Hospital in Oklahoma City visiting my dad, who was in the detox unit for alcoholics. We didn't take the loss too hard. It was obvious the Cowboys would have won if the temperature had been zero or above. The Cowboys had added Lee Roy Jordan and Ralph Neeley to their all-star list. They simply had more talent than Lombardi did. No way the Packers could have stopped Meredith-to-Hayes on a thawed field.

Cowboy arrogance was born that day. A good Cowboy fan never accepted that the Cowboys had been beaten. Always, there was a valid excuse. In my mind, anyway, the '67 Cowboys were champions. They wouldn't become known as "Next Year's Champions" until the next year.

The Cowboys went 12–2 in 1968. Meredith had his finest season and again was named to the Pro Bowl. The Cowboys were to play the Browns in Cleveland for the Eastern Conference title. The Cowboys had beaten Cleveland three straight times, including 52–14 in the '67 playoffs, but Landry prepared as if the Cowboys were in trouble. They sometimes were, when Landry overcoached.

As game plans were passed out, hands went up. Gent says: "A lot of us immediately saw there were no goal line running plays. But of course Tom hadn't made a mistake. He showed us the percentages of how Cleveland's defense bends but doesn't break, and how we just couldn't run on 'em at the goal line. It was weird. The whole week was weird. Tom changed the game plan about three times.

"Naturally, we quickly found ourselves first-and-goal at the one. So Don is throwing passes and looking like a complete fucking idiot. Afterward, all Tom would say was, 'Poor execution.' He was good at leaving you holding the bag."

This would inspire the line from offensive guard (and Stanford grad) Blaine Nye that epitomized Landry's Cowboys: "It's not whether you win or lose, but who gets the blame."

At Cleveland, Meredith got it by the ton, some of it deserved. He had a poor first half and Cleveland hung in, 10–10. His first pass of the second half was intercepted. Cleveland scored. Another Meredith pass glanced off a Cowboy's hands and was intercepted. Cleveland scored again to lead 24–10. And with just two minutes gone in the third quarter, Landry pulled his Pro Bowl quarterback. Did Landry have that little faith in—and respect for—his ninth-year leader? Did he seize the opportunity to humiliate a quarterback who had humiliated him a few times?

Final: Cleveland 31–20.

Afterward, Landry told the press, "Don was having a bad day, and I just thought Craig [Morton] might give us a spark."

Gent says, "The team couldn't believe it because we still had plenty of time. It was almost like Tom just gave up. What if he had yanked Staubach like that in years to come? Don was really hurt by it. We got on the team plane to go home, and he looked at me and said, 'Let's get the fuck outta here.' And we walked off and flew to New York and hung out with Frank Gifford for a few days."

The next June, as training camp approached, Meredith requested a rare office audience with Landry. Their exchange was brief. Basically, Meredith told Landry he was tired of taking the mental and physical beating and that, hell, he'd just go ahead and retire. Landry listened and said, "Well, if that's the way you feel, that's probably the right decision."

That was about it. That and the old ice-blue stare. No "Gee, Don, you had a great year last year, and it would be a shame if you quit at your peak." Not even a "Sleep on it a night or two." Just awkward silence. Prides colliding. Meredith cleared his throat. Silence. Meredith said, "I guess that's about it" and left.

Meredith drove to Gent's place.

"At first he was feeling that intense euphoria," Gent says. "You know: 'I don't have to do this shit anymore!' But I believe in Don's mind he just wanted Tom to talk him out of it, and Tom wouldn't. Eventually the reality sets in that you're going to have to become a stockbroker or something."

At thirty-one, with perhaps four or five good seasons left, Don Meredith retired. Landry had called his bluff, and Meredith called a press conference. Landry even managed to take the credit one last time with a backdoor tribute: "I know many still disagree, but I firmly believe that my decision in '65 to stick with Don was the most important made in this club's history and led directly to our conference championships in '66 and '67."

Meredith's touché: "I won't be remembered as a great passer or signal caller, but I hope I'll be remembered as a nice guy."

Even as Meredith made his announcement, a twenty-seven-year-old rookie was wondering if he had a snowball's chance in one-hundred-degree Dallas of making the team. That very day, July 5, Staubach had been discharged from the Navy. What timing. Staubach says, "I couldn't believe Don retired. If he hadn't, I really believe I'd have wound up with another team. I was too old to sit behind Meredith and Morton for three or four years. I needed to find someplace I could play quickly."

If Meredith hadn't retired, there probably wouldn't have been a Captain America, at least not in Dallas. Had God spoken again? Had Meredith sacrificed his body, psyche, and finally his prime for Landry's rise?

After meeting Staubach at a previous minicamp, Meredith had half-kidded by saying, "Staubach is going to have to learn what an NFL quarterback is like. He's going to have to grow his hair long and start smoking and drinking to keep up the image."

Oh, no, Dandy. Tex Schramm was about to behold the perfect Cowboy.

Same time, next year, 1969: Eastern Championship game versus Cleveland. This one was even in Dallas. This time, Cleveland left nothing but doubt in Dallas. It got so bad that a backup QB named Staubach mopped up. Only Staubach's late touchdown pass to Lance Rentzel cut Cleveland's final margin to 38–14.

Meredith had stewed all season about "his" decision to retire. That night he called Landry at home and told him he wanted to drop by. "The first and last time I was at his house," Meredith says.

Again, perhaps, part of Meredith wanted Landry to hug him and say, "We need you back," but this time Meredith told *Landry* to retire.

Meredith later told the *New York Times:* "I listened to some of the game on the radio, and it had to be the worst game I ever heard. Tom asked me, 'What can I do?' And I told him to hang it up, forget it, get out. Obviously he didn't follow my advice. He is such a fine man . . . it was kind of sad for such a dedicated, disciplined man to wind up in such a situation. His philosophy was challenged and all but destroyed."

Meredith told the *Los Angeles Times:* "I told Tom to get out of the rotten business because he wasn't giving himself a chance to live. That's the most regimented organization in football. He has goals and itineraries for everything. He makes it impossible for anyone to mature in that atmosphere. He's so organized that he doesn't even need to communicate. Discipline is essential, but it has to come from within the players. Tom can't keep trying to run their lives with so many rules. The purest form of success is being satisfied with yourself, and I don't see how Tom can be."

That night, after Meredith had gone, Landry sat in a bedroom chair and prayed. In a "Lenten Guideposts" column Landry said he asked, " 'Lord, what went wrong today?' As always happens in these sessions with Him, I soon found perspective. A crushing setback today, yes, but I've learned that something constructive comes from every defeat. I thought over my relationships of the day with the players, coaches, officials, friends, family. Nothing wrong there. No bad injuries, either. 'Thank you, Lord, for being with me out there.' And with that prayer the bitter sting of defeat drained away. Disappointment remained, but I've found that it doesn't sap energy or creativity. One football game, after all, is quite a small fragment of one's total life."

Skip ahead for a moment to the fall of 1988. Jack Veatch, conducting the sale of the Cowboys for Salomon Brothers, told me, "A dark horse has entered the picture, and I think you'll love this guy. When you talk to him on the phone, just close your eyes and you'll hear Don Meredith."

Veatch referred to eventual owner Jerry Jones, who had contacted Salomon Brothers from Cabo San Lucas. Weird? Please continue.

Soon after Meredith's visit to Landry's home, he and Gent took off for Cabo San Lucas. Meredith was to do a swimwear promotion there. Gent:

> When Don gets down, he can really be self-destructive. We both were about broke. His marriage was in trouble. He had a retarded daughter who I believe had been institutionalized. He was still think-

ing about playing again. And he nearly killed himself about three times. We go in some desert cantina, cinder blocks with a tin roof, and these workers are in there wearing machetes. Don starts insulting them in pidgin Spanish, and I really thought we were dead. I guess they thought Don was so crazy that he just didn't matter.

Then we're out on a boat in the bay and there are big signs that say DON'T SWIM IN BAY—SHARKS. So Don jumps out of the boat and says, "Let's swim in." I say, "Don, what about the sharks?" He says, "Fuck the sharks," and swims all the way in.

Then we're on these two motorcycles, and Don takes off over this rise and wipes out and somehow finds the only soft spot within miles or he would have been dead. He destroyed the motorcycle. He dislocated his shoulder and had a spiral fracture of the right arm. . . . Thank goodness ABC called pretty soon after that with this new idea.

And Meredith will be remembered by millions of fans as a nice guy with a great voice and wit who kept even Howard Cosell from taking football and himself too seriously. "Monday Night Football" hasn't been quite the same since the days Dandy Don put the country needle to Humble Howard's hot-air balloon of an ego. *Turn out the lights . . .*

The voice on the phone was unmistakable. It was not Jerry Jones. This voice is an octave deeper, more C&W resonant. I still hear this voice all over my radio dial, doing commercials.

It was November 1989. Don Meredith apologized for not getting back to me sooner. He had needed a little time to decide if he wanted to answer my questions about his days in Dallas. He said, "Well, it sounds like you've got an interesting project going, but I don't believe I want to get involved. That was a long, long time ago—like another life. I've got something even worse than Alzheimer's disease. I've got CRS—you know, Can't Remember Shit. I'm just really happy with Don Meredith right now—who I am and where I am."

He lives in Santa Fe, New Mexico, far from the maddening crowds. He made his money in broadcasting, acting, commercial-making—in show biz, as he called playing quarterback for the Cowboys. He went from an acting job in Dallas to several in Hollywood. In the end he used the Cowboys just the way they used him. He took Landry to the edge of greatness. Landry and the Cowboy image took Meredith to the edge of Hollywood. Meredith and Landry helped make each other famous. They were partners just the way Landry-Schramm-Brandt-Murchison were.

It all worked out, didn't it? What if Meredith had quarter-backed the Cowboys through three or four more "next years"? What if he had been tattooed a loser? Most ex-players say there was only one man—Staubach—who could have taken Landry over the top. I told Meredith about an interview I'd just had with Staubach, about how he and Drew Pearson changed or modified Landry's calls on so many big plays. Meredith seemed to know all about that. He chuck-led and said, "Every time I see Roger I kid him and say, 'I thought only Protestants had guilt.' "

6

IT WAS fitting that Don Meredith provided the color commentary on the Cowboys' first "Monday Night Football" appearance, November 16, 1970. That infamous night at the Cotton Bowl the Cowboys were otherwise without color. In fact, they looked dead. As I recall, Meredith sang "Turn Out the Lights" sometime in the third quarter. St. Louis won 38–0, but it wasn't that close.

Fans chanted, "We want Meredith!"

On the air, Meredith responded, "You're not getting *me* back out there."

That could have been the title of a country-western ode to Meredith's career.

There was something very wrong with this very talented team. A month earlier it had lost at Minnesota 54–13. This team seemed to have the heart of a computer. It was 5–4. The party seemed to be over. Only three more years to go on Landry's contract.

"Tom," says psychologist Don Beck, "always needed an external event to motivate his team. He couldn't really inspire players by anything he said or did. He needed something dramatic to happen to bring the team together."

A man who would inspire so many from the pulpit couldn't seem to find the words to lift a football team. He needed some shocking development beyond his control. That week he was blessed—blessed?—with two. The first was that 38–0 devastation, prime time Monday night.

The next morning players braced for another Texas Chainsaw Massacre film session. But in walked Landry with a bewildered look. The older players had seen it before, in Pittsburgh after the Halloween humiliation in '65. Landry was near tears. His facial muscles twitched between fury and despair. Clearly, Landry had no answer. He had done everything *he* could.

Landry stood before his team and said, "Y'all can just play *flag* football if you want." And he tossed his clipboard and walked out. For Landry, that was out of control. That also proved to be precisely what his team needed. Sometimes Landry was at his best when he was at his least.

After a moment of silence Bob Lilly took the floor. The night before, after the media had cleared out of the locker room, Lilly had lifted the spirits of a few teammates by saying, "Aw, we got 'em right where we want 'em now. We'll trick-fuck 'em." That line became a winking battle cry for the early '70s Cowboys.

Now Lilly told the entire team to forget about Landry. "He doesn't win games," Lilly said. "We do."

"Hell with him!" said one Cowboy. And another. Lee Roy Jordan spoke. Then Herb Adderley. Then Walt Garrison. Just about everybody spoke in a meeting always dominated by one man. Landry's "robots" had turned themselves on, seized the remote controls, and pressed the "emotion" button. This team finally had come to life.

Says former defensive end Pat Toomay, a rookie that year, "It was amazing because the staff just sort of gave up and blamed it on the 'jerk players.' We were 5–4. It was over. We were able to 'give up,' too, and just play without worrying. It was like, 'We'll show the coaches.' But after we made it to the Super Bowl, I knew we were in trouble. I saw some press guide or program with Landry, Schramm, Brandt, and Murchison on the cover, so I knew who was taking credit for what happened. I knew Tom would never give up again."

But that was still a ways away. On this day, after Landry tossed his clipboard, his robots went outside and played flag football. At first the attitude was, "If Landry wants flag football, we'll give him flag football." But after the first TD pass from an offensive lineman to a kicker, the Cowboys actually started having a good time playing football. The pressure was off—the strangling pressure generated by a man in search of the Perfect Game.

"We had a helluva good time," D. D. Lewis says. If only Dandy Don could have been there, playing middle linebacker with a cigar in his teeth.

The week's other event was not so lighthearted.

Lance Rentzel was one of my Cowboy favorites, and not just because he was from my hometown of Oklahoma City and had starred at the University of Oklahoma. Rentzel, playing wide receiver in Number 19, was the first "pretty" football player I'd seen. He ran pretty, caught pretty, looked pretty. He had come from a private high school known for academics and from a neighborhood, Nichols Hills, in which homeowners had to have a whole lot of nickels. It was as if he operated on a new plane far above football's mud and blood. Playing receiver for my intramural team at Vanderbilt, I pictured myself as Lance Rentzel.

It was no wonder the Cowboys traded with Minnesota for him in 1967. Rentzel was no Viking. Rentzel had just the image Tex Schramm loved to sell. He was personable and quotable, bright as a klieg light, white as North Dallas. Rentzel, who had taken music lessons as a child, even had recorded a country-western song, "Looking Like Something She Ain't."

Rentzel didn't have just any ol' gorgeous girlfriend. His wife was every man's fantasy, Joey Heatherton, of mattress-commercial fame. Joey showed up at the Cowboys' California training camp in a limo. Who knows? Maybe Joey, in hot pants and halter top, first gave Schramm the idea of creating *real* cheerleaders.

You don't think Lance Rentzel was the toast of Cowboy ticket buyers? His parents had moved to Dallas's Highland Park. His father had come from oil money. During the season, while Joey performed in Las Vegas, Lance lived with his folks. Here was a Cowboy who could have been a typical Cowboy fan.

On the Thursday after the Monday Night Massacre, Rentzel drove his car through Highland Park at about 4:15 P.M. He had just come from practice. Was he depressed over his performance or that of his fading team's? Did he need an escape? Who knows?

He called a ten-year-old girl over to his car, exposed himself, then drove away. Her father happened to be a lawyer. He insisted on pressing charges—Cowboy or no Cowboy.

No one in Cowboy Tower would be able to get Rentzel out of this one. Landry said he tried to keep it out of the papers, but the *Oklahoma City Journal* decided to go with it. This was no local story. This wasn't another dumb jock arrested on a DWI, marijuana, or wife-beating charge. This was Lance Rentzel, Joey Heatherton, Tom Landry, Dallas, Cowboys. This was a powerful image, darkly blemished. This was a national shocker. Walter Cronkite told America about it on his CBS newscast.

Why, I wondered from a distance, would a guy who had it all need to do something like that? Had Rentzel been looking like something he ain't? Why did so many inexplicably sick things seem to happen in Dallas?

The fact was, Rentzel had been involved in a similar incident four years earlier in St. Paul, Minnesota. But the girl's father hadn't been a Highland Park lawyer, and the Vikings had been able to keep it out of the headlines. In Dallas, as a highly publicized Cowboy, Rentzel didn't have a prayer. He would plead guilty and be sentenced to five years' probation requiring continued psychiatric treatment.

Before a hotel film session, Rentzel apologized to the team. When he finished, fighting sobs, Landry said nothing and turned on the projector, but in the darkness several Cowboys gripped Rentzel's shoulder and whispered, "That took courage" and "We're with you."

Rentzel had provided an external event that helped unite and motivate Landry's team. It refocused media attention on "the incident" instead of "the massacre." It allowed the Cowboys to think, "Man, what else can go wrong? Let's just go out Sunday and have fun."

They had fun beating the Redskins in Washington 45–21. Then they beat Green Bay. Then Washington again. Then Cleveland. Then Houston, to finish the regular season 10–4. Then Dallas 5, Detroit 0 in a playoff game. Then Dallas 17, San Francisco 10 in the NFC championship game.

From 38–0 and "Lance Without Pants" to Super Bowl V. Only in Dallas. "Weird stuff just kept happening," Toomay says. "Three or four things had to happen with other teams for us to make the playoffs, and they did. Then we won, and won again, and we were in the Super Bowl. In those days the Super Bowl wasn't yet an orgy. Schramm wasn't saying, 'Everyone who's anyone is at the Super Bowl.' I'm not sure if anyone realized what had happened until we were there."

Stranger still was a story Rentzel told in his book, *When All the Laughter Died in Sorrow.* A "touch of Hitchcock," Rentzel called it. His parents had a schnauzer named Scarlett O'Hara. Shortly after Rentzel's arrest, the dog disappeared. Rentzel's mother found it several blocks away in the front yard of the lawyer and his daughter, "romping" with their dog. "This was to happen several more times," Rentzel said.

What dark forces drew the Rentzels' dog to that house? For that matter, what drew so many intelligent, talented "robots" with one loose screw to Landry's Cowboys? Were the Cowboys, with their Hitch, something right out of Hitchcock? Or were less publicized teams better able to cover up their share of "incidents"? These were, after all, child-men trained to wreak havoc. Were Cowboy arrests sometimes blown out of proportion because they were so highly publicized and scrutinized? Did fans overreact when Craig Morton, the playboy QB, was arrested for urinating in public? Or when linebacker Steve Kiner, a rookie wild man, was arrested for hitting an off-duty policeman with a folding chair? Did other teams hide their Lance Rentzels in ways America's Team couldn't?

Tough to answer. But it certainly seemed the Cowboys had more than their share of strange behavior. Mama, don't let your babies grow up to be Cowboys?

After his story broke, Rentzel played no more for the Cowboys. Rentzel says Joey Heatherton soon dumped him. The next spring he was traded to the Rams. Landry said, "It's what's best for Lance."

As late as 1969, black Cowboys complained to the media about living in "Oz." Star running back Don Perkins told an Associated Press reporter in Albuquerque, "It's not easy for a Negro athlete to live in Dallas. My wife and I would be embarrassed for you to see our home. . . . When I was in college [at New Mexico] and we played a road game, I always roomed with a white player. At Dallas it's Negro with Negro. I don't believe any of the Negro players on the Cowboys feel like an integral part of the club or the city of Dallas."

Schramm pointed out that the Cowboys had helped integrate some Dallas hotels in which the team stayed the night before games. Landry said, "When I talk to a player, I never see color."

Yet whether or not Landry saw it—or let himself see it—the Cowboys had a racial problem as deep as Dallas's. It would flare again and again. Black players didn't consistently condemn any one Cowboy coach or official but felt an overall repression. Black Cowboy scout John Wooten, once known among black players as Brandt's bobo, says, "There was a plantation mentality." Black Cowboys were beginning to make little ripples about being paid "slave" wages. Calvin Hill, a black running back from Yale, spoke out about how black stars weren't offered a single endorsement or commercial opportunity. Dennis Thurman, a black team leader of the '80s, says, "In the '60s Coach Landry got used to the type of blacks who would just do what they were supposed to do. The old-guard blacks just said, 'I have a job to do, I'm happy to be here, I won't rock the boat.'"

But by 1970 the USS *Landry* was beginning to rock. And fortunately for Landry two team leaders materialized to stabilize it. Says D. D. Lewis, "Tom had a bit of a racial problem, and a key addition in 1970 was getting Herb Adderley (a black cornerback from Green Bay). He came preaching brotherly love. He said what football was all about was winning a championship. He was the enzyme we needed."

He and the unMeredith, Roger Staubach. One of Staubach's prized possessions is a picture that came from Dallas's Scottish Rite Hospital for Crippled Children. A little white boy is kissing a little black boy. "They don't know they're not supposed to do that," Staubach says.

Staubach would help keep the Lid from flying off Landry's pressure cooker. Staubach may have been more loved by black teammates than white. Says Thomas Henderson, "He is the genuine article." What would Landry have done without him?

Perhaps one indication came on January 17, 1971, in Miami's Orange Bowl. Landry had given Staubach a brief chance midway through the season but had gone back to Craig Morton. Landry could change quarterbacks the way most coaches changed expressions. Staubach was a little too hot-blooded for Landry—too quick to call an audible, bolt from the pocket, look for a secondary receiver. Staubach didn't grasp technical concepts quickly enough. He didn't always have the right answer in QB class. Staubach wasn't Landry's idea of the ideal quarterback-as-extension. Staubach was too confounded emotional and instinctive. He had the nerve to openly challenge Landry in quarterback meetings about why he wasn't getting a fair chance to win the job. Landry kept saying it takes every quarterback at least three years to learn the pro game. But Staubach didn't really have three years. He was already twenty-nine. After Super Bowl V he planned to ask Landry for a trade.

Morton played well enough for the Cowboys to win their first Super Bowl. But then, had Meredith been at quarterback that Sunday, his epitaph probably would have read the same: Baltimore 16–13. In the future a "next Staubach" named Danny White would play well in several monumental losses. Some QBs win; some don't. Morton, at six-feet-four with a NASA arm and brain, was as perfect as a computer could make him. But as even Gil Brandt would later admit, "The only thing the computer can't measure is heart."

Late in the game, score tied at 13, Morton was driving the Cowboys for what might have been the winning field goal. He threw a perfect pass to Dan Reeves, who usually caught passes as easily as Bedford Wynne made them. The ball glanced off Reeves's fingers and was intercepted by Mike Curtis. The rest is Roman-numeral history: Jim O'Brien, game-winning field goal, five seconds left.

Craig Morton: near-great.

But as any good Cowboy fan can tell you, the refs stole the game from Dallas. With Dallas leading 13–6, Baltimore fumbled the second-half kickoff. On second-and-goal from the Baltimore 1, a Cowboy fumble was awarded to Colt Billy Ray Smith—perhaps prematurely. Smith later indicated he didn't have the ball. Cowboy center Dave Manders emerged from the pileup confusion with the ball and screamed to the refs that he had recovered it. If only Tex Schramm had invented instant-replay officiating sixteen years earlier.

The Cowboys came that close to leading 20–6.

But teams fumble and drop passes for some QBs; teams win for others. Maybe the difference is just luck; maybe it's leadership that adds that slight edge to a player's concentration. On the plane home Landry told Staubach he would get his first real chance the next July.

By the way, the Cowboy who fumbled near the goal line was a rookie named Duane Thomas.

In October 1978, as I prepared to leave Los Angeles for Dallas, a colleague mentioned that Duane Thomas was "an actor" at Twentieth Century–Fox. I took a chance and called the switchboard. Before I started writing about the Cowboys, I wanted to talk to the ex-player who called Tom Landry "a plastic man," to Duane Thomas, the silent-movie star of Super Bowl VI. I was in luck. The operator put me through.

"Microfilm," somebody answered. Microfilm? I asked for Duane Thomas. "Hang on." The phone was passed to him. I told Thomas I was moving to Dallas to work for the *Morning News* and wanted to chat. He was hesitant at first but finally said, well, okay, meet him at a park where he coached a kids' football team.

That evening I discovered that Thomas was the fourth assistant on a four-man coaching staff. The kids, who were around twelve years old, didn't pay much attention to him. They would have been around five years old the day Thomas turned CBS announcer Tom Brookshier into a tongue-tied fool following Super Bowl VI.

Thomas, I found, wasn't an actor. He was working for an hourly wage in the microfilm department. "I'm working my way up to acting," he said. He had hitched a ride to football practice and wondered if I could take him back to a relative's home where he was living. On the way he asked if we could stop at a burrito stand in West L.A. so he could grab some dinner. I assumed he knew I'd buy. At least he didn't casually mention he had made reservations for us at La Scala.

We leaned against the car and consumed enough grease for a lube job. Thomas tore into his deluxe burrito with extra onions as if he hadn't eaten in a week. Between mouthfuls he talked about his days under Landry. "What," I asked, "did you exactly mean by the 'plastic man' quote?" I thought Thomas meant Landry was devoid of emotion.

"What I was saying," Thomas said, "was that his image wasn't the reality." He eyed me for a flicker of comprehension or compassion.

But it would be several years before I realized just how perceptive Duane Julius Thomas was. This man was as complicated as the Cowboy offense he ran in. What a sad contradiction of intelligence and foolishness, strength and weakness. He could see through just about everyone but himself. Landry always said, "Duane knew his assignments and everyone else's and never missed a one." But Thomas had no idea how to play The Game—the image scrimmage constantly won by Landry-Schramm-Brandt. For Thomas, reality was perception, and that wouldn't work in Dallas. In order to play football—Thomas's first and last love—he had to play The Game, had to become an off-the-field actor. And here Thomas was in L.A., seven years later, still working in the microfilm department, living from meal to meal, baking and selling pies to subsidize his income, saying, "Green Bay may let me come up there and try out."

What a waste. Thomas had lost his football, lost The Game, lost all credibility. If he had played ten Hall of Fame seasons, then written the book he did with *Sports Illustrated* football expert Paul Zimmerman in 1988, his perceptions would have shocked Cowboy fans and perhaps rocked the organization. But by then he was the boy who cried "plastic." He was written off as a "doper" because of his bizarre behavior and a 1972 conviction for marijuana possession (later erased by pardon). He was dismissed by those in the organization as "a very troubled young man." A weirdo. Another poor black kid who let fame go to his empty head.

Duane Thomas and the Fall of America's Team hit Dallas in 1988 with all the impact of a new telephone book. I couldn't bring myself to read it for six months. Duane Thomas was very old news. I heard not a word about the book on any of the three Dallas–Fort Worth talk shows. It just faded away, as Thomas had after Super Bowl VI.

Only now do I realize how accurately Thomas saw the Cowboy organization in 1972. His book includes occasional journal entries from his playing days. Thomas wrote, "Tex Schramm: A horse-trading mentality. Big ego. His own sports show. Conservative dresser. P.R. specialist . . . A closet racist. Crusty.

"Gil Brandt: . . . Has the mentality of a street pimp. No integrity and no alliance to anything but power and money. Tex's hatchet man. Supplier of vices . . . Excellent negotiator. Very shrewd and cunning with in-depth knowledge of each player. A pro. A liar.

"Tom Landry: . . . An illusionist who used Christianity for his own vanity, greed, and power. A John Birch mentality. Used the computer to create Landry's Humanoids and recruited predominantly Southern players, both black and white, to keep separation active and maintain total control. Large ego. White supremacist mentality. His philosophy was intimidation, intimidation, intimidation, of the mind and body."

Much truth there. But now, it comes off as a bitter cheap shot. Now, probably, most fans view Thomas as another of the many Cowboy stars who had it all and blew it.

Thomas the first-round choice was handsome, light-skinned, intelligent, well-spoken—and, fire up the P.R. machine, he grew up a few blocks from the Cotton Bowl! Was Thomas ever in tall cotton. In he sauntered to a team that had nineteen active All-Pros—past, present, or future. The Cowboys had six future members of the Hall of Fame. From the ghetto to Super Bowl City. Was Duane Thomas not blessed? Here was a six-foot-two, 230-pound poet in motion.

Perhaps it was ominous that his father once ran a funeral home near the Cotton Bowl.

Thomas just couldn't seem to live with playing a game that made Landry-Schramm-Brandt filthy rich and famous. He couldn't abide the Roman notion that he was running through Lions for the vicarious pleasure of white "Christians" who were being served by black bartenders up in their luxury suites. Yes, on the 1971 Sunday that Murchison unveiled "the best stadium money can buy," Texas Stadium in Irving, Thomas scored the first touchdown on a fifty-six-yard run. Yes, Thomas had gone uptown, over the Berlin Wall along the Trinity. Murchison, by moving and raising ticket prices, had made it clear to black fans that this was basically a private party. And Thomas was providing the entertainment.

In return, of course, Thomas was making more money than he ever thought he would. He was testing his talent against the very best. He was worshiped by hundreds of thousands of fans, black and white. He was on top of both worlds, but he couldn't seem to live in both. So he retreated into his own private sensory-deprivation tank of silence. On planes and in meetings he often rolled a stocking cap down completely over his face. He saw no evil. He heard only the game plan. He lived only for kickoffs. He quit speaking to reporters, teammates, coaches—anyone associated with the Organization.

The less he said, the more national attention he drew to himself. The P.R. machine was running amok with the Dallas Cowboy Who Said Nothing. Thomas wrote in his journal: "How could this nappy-haired little nigger from Dallas, Texas, have this type of impact on these tyrants, these giants? . . . I said, God almighty, I don't believe it was happening to me, but it was."

Thomas had thrown Thomas Wade Landry for a loss. For Landry, Thomas was a one-man Watts riot. He was the first of many black stars who would openly defy Landry's rule. Pro Bowl cornerback Everson Walls, whose rookie year was 1981, would tell Thomas, "You paved the way for a lot of us."

Landry's conclusion: "I made a mistake having one set of rules for the team and one for Duane."

Before the '71 season Landry traded Thomas to New England, but Thomas immediately clashed with coach John Mazur. After five days New England canceled the trade and claimed Thomas had flunked his physical. The league office ruled Thomas had to return to Dallas.

And Thomas helped Landry return to the Super Bowl by playing beautiful football—move-over-Jim-Brown football. As he told me that night in L.A., "Tony Dorsett couldn't carry my jock."

As some two thousand media people stormed New Orleans for Super Week, Thomas sat silently through interview sessions. Through dozens of questions Thomas was the riddle of the sphinx. The world was his stage, and he stared back at the cameras, seemingly amused by the national stir he was causing. It was as if he were sticking Super Bowl hype right up North Dallas's upturned nose.

This time he didn't fumble. He gained ninety-five yards on nineteen carries as Dallas finally won a big one 24–3 over Miami. Paul Zimmerman says a *Sport* magazine editor overruled the MVP vote by sportswriters, who overwhelmingly selected Thomas. The magazine, says Zimmerman, couldn't be sure Thomas would show up in New York to accept his award (a car) and say a few words to generate publicity for *Sport* and its sponsors. The MVP went to Staubach, who was twelve of nineteen for 119 yards and two TDs.

Thomas, with actor/advisor Jim Brown looking over his shoulder, then unnerved CBS's Brookshier during a locker room interview. Brookshier asked, "Are you really that fast?" Thomas: "Evidently."

Thomas was traded to San Diego, which traded him to Washington. He tried Hawaii of the WFL, which soon folded. Landry agreed to give him a second chance in the spring of 1976, but he had lost too much weight and explosion, perhaps running too much long distance, another of his escapes. He was cut in training camp. He failed in his 1978 tryout with Green Bay.

But he couldn't keep from crawling back to the Cowboy organization. Brandt got him a job as a maître d'. Schramm got him a small part in *Cowboys Cheerleaders II* as the boyfriend of a Cheerleader. Yes, Schramm finally helped turn him into an actor. What a power trip this must have been for Brandt and Schramm, finding work for the ex-star who had to sell his Super Bowl ring.

What if, in protest, Thomas had quit football after the Super Bowl victory? Think of the impact Thomas might have had by telling Brookshier he was retiring because he no longer could live with the Cowboys' closet racism, the pimping, the hypocritical Christianity. What if he had returned to his old neighborhood, found a job the way most of his friends had to, and played sandlot football for the pure joy of it? No one forced him to play pro football. What if he had started running marathons simply for the personal achievement? What if he had coached and counseled kids who were growing up just as he had?

Or was Thomas more like Landry-Schramm-Brandt than he could bear to admit? Was Thomas a plastic man, too?

In 1983 he called to see if I wanted to buy some insurance. He said he had been in Nigeria trying to put in fast-food fried chicken franchises. But his partner, he said, had contracted malaria. The last I heard, Thomas was back in L.A. trying to start over again.

Duane Thomas's motel roommate when he first hit Dallas as a rookie was Pat Toomay. They were paired alphabetically, not by choice. In fact, they clashed over $30 of phone calls to West Texas that Thomas claimed not to have made. Thomas and Toomay were as different as Watts and Haight-Ashbury. Toomay would pose a subtle new threat to Landry and his "humanoids." By Landry's standards, Toomay was a '60s flower child, a bearded math major from Vanderbilt who hated wearing a tie.

Toomay would ask some Cowboys, "Why are you doing this shit?"

Toomay was a classic Brandt "find"—a six-foot-six high school basketball star who had been recruited by Vandy as a quarterback. What a Draft Day story Brandt could tell. By the end of Toomay's freshman year he was playing safety. Then, as he matured to 225 pounds—"I never touched a weight"—he was playing linebacker, then standup defensive end. Imagine a former Commodore quarterback sacking quarterbacks for the Cowboys. Toomay did it mostly with quickness—mental and physical. Imagine a killer pacifist. Could Brandt find 'em or what?

"They knew I could run," Toomay says, "and they took me in the sixth round, where they historically had hit on guys. D. D. [Lewis], Blaine [Nye], Rayfield [Wright], Walt Garrison, Bob Hayes—all of 'em were right along in there. Gil had sent me his full-color brochure, 'Life with the Cowboys,' and there was Calvin Hill by the Divinity School at SMU, with the Dallas skyline in the background, and I thought, 'Goddamn, this place looks great.' Gil came with Anne [his wife] to sign me at the Holiday Inn Vanderbilt, and I asked my linebacker coach if I needed an agent. He said, 'No, these are good people.' Then he said, 'By the way, ask Gil when I'm going to get that suit in the mail from [Dallas-based] Haggar.' I should have put two and two together. I told Gil, 'I trust you.' Twelve years later I find out I was the lowest paid defensive lineman in the NFL by a factor of two.

"But hey, after I had made the team, Gil made sure I flunked my [military] draft physical. I had 'high blood pressure' for three days straight. Gil gave me a wry smile and said, 'It's funny how all the guys we like fail their draft physicals.' "

Funny, but Toomay would become Landry's pass-rushing specialist for two Super Bowl teams and two final-four teams. Funnier still, Toomay's father is a retired Air Force officer and engineer. Remind you of anyone? Toomay's father is even mistaken for Landry in airports, so maybe Toomay was less intimidated by Landry because he'd "grown up with him."

Toomay was a gridiron oxymoron, a gentle bear. He read existential philosophy; he dipped snuff. On the side Toomay managed the career of a progressive C&W singer, Ray Wylie Hubbard (and his Cowboy Twinkies), whose one big hit, "Up Against the Wall Redneck Mother," became Schramm's public-address theme song after Cowboy touchdowns. Toomay wrote his own "Life with the Cowboys," a tragicomic gem called *The Crunch*. Toomay went on to play for the Buffalo Bills and Oakland Raiders before settling in Dallas to write a novel, *On Any Given Sunday*, a faith-shaker about NFL game-fixing.

Unlike Thomas, Toomay may have been the most quoted player

in NFL history. I don't know a veteran sportswriter in the country who didn't interview Toomay at least once by phone. At the *Los Angeles Times* when I was assigned an in-depth piece on, say, what Freud would have thought of the Super Bowl, editors always would add, "Call Pat Toomay. He'll be great on this."

Toomay was a rare star who could step back and laugh at himself and his game. Laugh with intellect and wit. Cowboys did not laugh at football. Here was another Cowboy too smart for Landry's own good.

Allow Toomay to put 1970 to 1974 into wry perspective:

> I had hair down to my shoulders, and they assumed I was on dope. The irony was, I was the only one who wasn't. All their "character" guys—their Southern good ol' boys—were experimenting with pot. But Ernie Stautner [the defensive line coach] gave *me* the lecture about how marijuana leaves a residue on the brain. He was talking to the wrong guy.
>
> Drug use was prevalent because of the way we were treated behind closed doors versus the way we were treated out in public. There just wasn't that much money then [Toomay made $21,000 in his fourth year]. I mean, Lee Roy Jordan didn't make $100,000 until his [fourteenth and] last season. For, say, $250,000 you can take any shit anybody wants to dish out. But when you're barely making more than you could on the outside, and they're telling you, "You should be happy with that because we're going to make you somebody," well, it's tough. Inside [the locker room] we were treated with disdain and disrespect and cynicism. There was this constant atmosphere of fear, of losing your job. You have a mortgage and a family, and you're not really that far from having a middle-class income. You're at risk. You're sweating it. Then you go out on the street, and you're treated like this incredible fucking hero. You say, "Who am I?" Drugs became the mediator between the two worlds. That was one way to anesthetize yourself. I think Bob Hayes [convicted in 1979 of trafficking in narcotics; later pardoned] was an example of that. "Who am I?" . . . One time Schramm was talking to the team and actually called us his "product." . . . Everything with Landry was image. The image defined the person. He said, "Roger is the kind of image we want in professional football." He didn't say the kind of person.

The image, says Toomay, ended as the day-after game film began. The entire team jammed into the sweatbox meeting room for the dreaded sessions. While some teams broke into groups for film critiques by position coaches, Landry required every player to sit through every play and replay. This, of course, magnified the humiliation when Landry singled out a mistake. Sitting in the dark, a guilty player could feel fifty-odd pairs of eyes on him. Talk about peer pressure. Landry didn't have to raise his voice. All he had to do was point out one false step, one stupid read, one missed block or tackle—and run the film back two or three times. Landry let the projector rant and rave, rant and rave.

"The fixing of Christian guilt," Toomay calls the sessions. "Guys actually took downers to get through the entire film. I'd sit in the back next to Walt Garrison, and I couldn't believe the great recall he had of the game. He'd say, 'Uh, oh, I'm about to get reamed for this.' . . . Sometimes it could be even worse after we had won big. We all wore those gray T-shirts, and if you'd wanted to know who'd played well and who hadn't, you could have watched us file out afterwards and seen who had the biggest sweat stains under his arm."

After one session, Toomay remembers, All-Pro guard John Niland's T-shirt looked as if he had just played a game. For Niland, from Amityville, New York, it must have been horror. "Yeah, Tom really got a bee in his bonnet for Niland. I think he wanted to move in Blaine Nye [for Niland]. So this one session was just unmerciful. Tom just kept picking out things, picking out things, and Niland was sinking lower and lower. Tom just went on and on in that relentless drone. I'm not saying Niland played well. It was just the relentlessness of it.

"In Oakland [where Toomay finished out his career], if we won, we celebrated. Nobody really cared about the films even if we won by only two points over Kansas City, the worst team in the division. Victories are hard to come by. So we watched the films in our position groups, and we were treated with an acute sensitivity. The criticism was nonspecific, like, 'Some of you guys are doing this.' Sometimes we'd laugh and say, 'Come on, name names.' "

In Dallas, names always were named.

"You lived for Tom to call you a 'pro' [in front of the team]," Toomay recalls. "That meant you would play when you were hurt. You would take pills, injections, whatever it took. You had to learn not to feel pain. Your body had to become something that wasn't part of you, like a piece of furniture. So you saw guys getting hooked on Demerol [a painkiller]. You saw guys going on this incredible

odyssey of injuries through the season. You were amazed a guy like
Walt Garrison was still alive. He played the NFC championship
game in '70 with back spasms, a sprained knee, sprained ankle, and
fractured clavicle, and had to be carried off the field. But he still ran
for fifty yards and caught a couple of key passes. He was the ultimate
'pro.' It was like, you got to heaven if you played with pain.

"Then you started hearing all the rumors about Gil, how he ran
hookers for coaches at the College All-Star Game. You wondered
how Tom could let this go on and have a moral sense. Well, he
doesn't."

To keep his sanity, Toomay bonded with unCowboys Blaine
Nye and Larry Cole. The three formed what they called the Zero
Club, in mock protest of all the pretty-boy Cowboys. Toomay says of
their first outing on a camp night off: "It was an eventful evening.
The movie was *How to Frame a Figg*, starring Don Knotts. Cole
farted in the middle of it. We walked home."

This is the way Pat Toomay anesthetized himself against Tom
Landry.

Niland didn't cope so successfully. "He took mescaline or something and saw God," Toomay says of a 1973 incident, "and he went
up and down the street banging on doors." Brandt said it took six
officers to subdue Niland, who had walked barefoot for nearly three
miles from Parkland Hospital. "He was on some substance," Brandt
told reporters. Brandt says Niland wound up banging on the door of
a rabbi, a big Cowboy fan who immediately recognized him and
called the police.

Niland, who was active in the Fellowship of Christian Athletes,
wound up doing time for making false statements on a loan appli-
cation.

Toomay was one of the normal guys on this team. He jumped
for big bucks in 1974 to the WFL's Birmingham Americans
($150,000 the first year, compared to an offer of $60,000 from
Brandt). He finally found an NFL home among the castoffs and
misfits taken in by the Oakland Raiders. Toomay says, "Not one
of those guys could have played in Dallas. Stabler, Biletnikoff,
Branch, Upshaw, Casper—no way. [Coach John] Madden would
come by your locker before practice and sit down and talk about
something on the front page, a current event. You actually felt
human."

Yet Toomay the writer still makes his home in Dallas. He says he isn't sure why. The school roots of his two sons? Or is it that he, like so many ex-Cowboys, can't quite tear himself away from the fame? Didn't he earn it with knee operations that now keep him from playing his beloved basketball or from jogging? Doesn't a part of him still want to be treated as "some kind of incredible fucking hero"?

Toomay still calls Dallas "the home of the anti-Christ." He says, "There's really no reason for this city to be here, so people end up living in their imaginations. This was the perfect seed bed for what Schramm was trying to do."

But if you consider Toomay some sort of hippie malcontent, consider this: The last thing Landry said to him in 1974 was, "You're a pro." Funny, but the players who criticized the Cowboys—the ones written off as flakes—usually were the most perceptive.

During his rookie year, the fall of 1970, Toomay and his wife Becky were invited to several get-togethers at Gil Brandt's home. The first night, Toomay absently sat back in a chair—and nearly squashed owner Clint Murchison. "I couldn't believe it," Toomay says. "He was like a mouse."

Toomay and his wife began to wonder why Murchison would materialize unaccompanied at a rookie party. As Becky hit it off with Brandt's wife, Anne, the Toomays began to understand. Becky sometimes watched the televised away games with Anne.

Toomay says, "The word was that Clint met Anne [who was from Norman, Oklahoma] when he went to a quarry in Oklahoma to get some special stones for his dream house."

Becky says, "The way I understood it, Anne came to Dallas because of Clint. She was very attractive, a very good dresser, very clever. When she realized she was just going to be another one of Clint's girlfriends, she married Gil [on January 31, 1970]. But you could tell she wasn't happy."

Apparently, Murchison continued to pursue Mrs. Brandt for two more years. "It was obvious," Toomay says, "why Clint came to the parties." Finally, Murchison's wife Jane sued him for divorce in the fall of 1972, citing his flagrant infidelity. When the divorce was final on January 3, 1973, Clint reportedly gave Jane $10 million cash and a five-story mansion on New York's Sutton Place that once belonged to Aristotle Onassis.

Seventeen months after Murchison was divorced, Gil and Anne Brandt were divorced, on July 30, 1974. Did Brandt see what was going on? All Bedford Wynne would say was, "Gil was always very eager to please Clint."

About ten months later Anne became Mrs. Clint Murchison. She was in her mid-thirties. What a rise for a woman born in poverty who married at seventeen, had two children, was divorced at twenty, remarried, and was divorced again at twenty-one. But Anne wasn't the typical blonde bimbo on Murchison's lists. With short, stylish brown hair, Anne was "handsome" pretty. Anne was more assertive and analytical than soft and cuddly. Anne even knew football.

Murchison's mother, who died when he was an infant, was named Anne.

During the time before Anne Brandt became Anne Murchison, there were reports that Gil might leave the organization, perhaps for a job with the Atlanta Falcons. Bum Bright, a friend of Murchison's who bought the team from him in 1984, says Murchison asked that he "take care of" Brandt because of an arrangement Brandt and Murchison had involving Anne.

"That's the way I understood it," Bright says. Brandt was to have a job and expense account security as long as Bright owned the Cowboys.

Schramm says he had no knowledge of any such arrangement. That's difficult to believe only because I heard about "the deal" so often from people who worked for Schramm. Several insiders say Schramm was tormented by why Landry was so protective of Brandt through so many poor drafts in the '80s. Was it out of loyalty to Brandt and Murchison? Was Landry at least vaguely aware of their arrangement? Surely he wasn't so focused that he didn't notice Mrs. Brandt was suddenly sitting with Murchison on team charters.

I wasn't able to ask Landry if he was aware of Brandt's job security. Landry wouldn't be interviewed for this book because, he said, he was doing his own book. Brandt wouldn't be interviewed because, he said, he might do a book.

But the odds are, Landry would have given the same sort of answer he would when I'd ask about Brandt's ethics on other occasions. "Gosh, I'm too busy to try to keep up with that Gil," Landry would say with a chuckle.

Shortly before Anne and Clint were married, Brandt provided

Landry with the inside info for Brandt's greatest draft—and last hurrah. In 1975 the Cowboys hit on a "Dirty Dozen" rookies that included Randy White, Thomas Henderson, Bob Breunig, and Herb Scott. From 1976 on the Cowboys drafted as if there were a plague on their house. No franchise made worse picks and had worse luck.

Duane Thomas on Landry's first championship team: "There was a level of talent that produced success, even though conditions were socially primitive. But once the talent slips on a team like that, there's no backlog of love to fall back on."

7

I DIDN'T personally experience the competitor in Roger Staubach until the fall after he retired. That year I occasionally jogged and played basketball with Pat Toomay at the Aerobics Center, *the* place to work out in North Dallas. A one-mile track encircles the landscaped grounds (including duck pond) of this state-of-the-heart facility. Lots of Cowboys and ex-Cowboys worked out at the Aerobics Center—at no charge, of course. Staubach often was on display, though he may have insisted on paying. I was welcomed because I wrote about the Cowboys.

One afternoon I found myself in a pickup basketball game with Staubach. It was Toomay and I on one team, Staubach on the other. I stumbled momentarily into the "Twilight Zone" and made nearly every shot I threw up for three games. By the way, I'm five-feet-eleven and 155 pounds and have severe white man's disease: I can jump only in checkers. In basketball I shoot lots of twenty-foot set shots. On this day they became twenty-five footers that had Staubach saying, "When are you going to miss?"

We had the better team and won all three games. Staubach

acted quite sportsmanlike. He told me, "That's the hottest I've ever seen anybody." I was honored and then returned to the real world.

That was a Wednesday, as I recall. On Friday, Staubach tried to arrange a rematch—Toomay and I versus Staubach and a partner of his choosing, Cliff Harris. Harris, the former All-Pro safety known as Crash, was, like Staubach, in his first year of retirement. Harris called Toomay to see if he could play basketball—no mention of me or a rematch—but Toomay couldn't make it. I had jogged by myself at the Aerobics Center and was preparing to leave when Staubach and Harris asked me to play.

I thought it was an all-comers game of four on four, but a friend of theirs materialized—my partner, I realized—and Staubach said, "Let's go." Two on two, full court, Harris guarding me. Harris had been steamed over a column I'd written on him the season before. I quickly discovered Harris played basketball pretty much the way he played football. Each time I drove to the basket, I got Crashed. If it had been a real game, Harris might have fouled out in the first quarter.

I found myself in the "Twilight Zone" again for a different reason. I was in a daze. What was going on?

Staubach was going at it as if this were Super Sunday. He was diving into spectators for loose balls, elbowing for rebound position, berating himself after his few misses. At thirty-nine he wasn't exceptionally quick, but he had a nice fifteen-foot jumpshot. They killed us all three games. I was just thankful to be alive and walking. After this game Landry would have called me a "pro."

When I called Toomay to tell him what happened, he was mad enough to go looking for Staubach and Harris. He said something like, "This is sick. Those guys just don't know how to rejoin society once Tom tells them they can't play anymore." He also said, "Roger just can't stand to lose."

There. That's it. That's the story of Staubach's Cowboys, the ones who became America's Team. Really, they weren't Landry's as much as they were his quarterback's.

A former team official says, "Roger, Tom, Tex, and Gil have one thing in common—all of them are poor sports. None of them could stand to lose or take one ounce of criticism. All of them had huge egos. Roger could be a big baby.

"But Roger was their catalyst. Because he wanted to be a goody two-shoes, some people thought he was a bit of a wuss. But what most people don't understand is that if Roger had gone into boxing, he would have been the heavyweight champion. He played at six-feet-two, 205, and God never made one any tougher."

You want validation from an ex-star who was anything but a goody two-shoes? From Hollywood Henderson, who fought his way up out of the ghetto? Henderson says, "Roger is the most fascinating competitor I've ever known. There's a layer of mad in Roger. If I were in a fight in an alley in the middle of Harlem, he's the one guy I'd want at my back. I'm truly glad Clint Longley walked out of the room [after sucker-punching Staubach during a '76 training camp dispute]. He would have been killed."

Staubach was no wuss. Teammates watched him take more than his share of large-needle cortisone injections.

But like Thomas Wade Landry, Roger Thomas Staubach had an "altar ego." Off the field he was a Catholic who believed fiercely in doing good works and remaining faithful to wife Marianne. A front-office source says, "Roger would drink a beer. He'd look at a pretty woman, but he wouldn't pursue it."

But during games he pursued victory the way so many others in the organization did pretty women. During battle Staubach could cuss like a, well, sailor—even the f-word. Recently, as Staubach sat in a Schramm-like office of the North Dallas real estate company he owns, he told me, "I've always been fairly determined in business, but as an athlete I was *not* the same person. I can compete in perseverance and intensity with anybody. Off the field I'm a family man—more even keel. But in the athletic environment you just have to realize these guys are out there to hurt you and take something from you."

Staubach says he still misses playing football. In fact, he wishes he had played "five more years." Perhaps he would have if Landry had tried to talk him out of retiring.

At forty-eight, save for his combed-back waves of graying hair, Staubach still looks fit enough to play. After Staubach dominated a 1989 flag-football game against ex-Redskins, his soulmate Cowboy receiver, Drew Pearson, said, "I promise you, Roger still throws with at least as much velocity as he ever did. He probably could still be bringing the Cowboys from behind today."

*   *   *

Miracle Number 1: "It all started there," Staubach says. December 23, 1972, at San Francisco's Candlestick Park, where it all would end for America's Team nine seasons later. In the same end zone in which 49er Dwight Clark would make The Catch that kept the '81 Cowboys from the Super Bowl, Staubach completed Comeback I. Even more amazing than the final score was that it didn't secure a starting job for Staubach.

A brief digression: Even as the Cowboys rolled toward a 14–3 record and Super Bowl championship the season before, Landry couldn't decide between Staubach and Craig Morton. Staubach started the first three games and the Cowboys were 2–1. In the fourth game, on Monday night against the New York Giants, the Cowboys led 13–6 at the half when Landry pulled Staubach. When Landry tried to explain to Staubach after the game (Cowboys 20–13), Staubach told him, "Coach, don't say anything. Whatever you say, you'll never understand me. What you just did to me out there was not called for."

Those words would echo ominously through the next eight great seasons. Personal opinion: Landry resented the growing credit Staubach received for saving so many days.

That Super season, 1971, Landry even resorted to alternating Staubach and Morton every other play for a game in Chicago. "Shocker of shockers," Staubach called it. Bears linebacker Doug Buffone said, "I think Landry's cracking." Mount Landry cracking?

Once Landry settled on Staubach, the '71 Cowboys won ten straight, including the Super Bowl. But the following preseason, Roger the Dodger tore up a shoulder scrambling against the Rams and missed the regular season. The Cowboys went 10–4 behind Morton but lost their final game at home to the Giants 23–3. Not a good sign. In their first-round playoff game at San Francisco, they trailed 28–13 with 1:48 left in the third quarter when Landry replaced Morton with Staubach. Staubach was rusty and off-target. He threw incompletions. He was sacked. He fumbled. San Francisco's Bruce Gossett missed a thirty-two-yard field goal that would have made it 31–13.

Then, with six minutes left and 49er linebacker Dave Wilcox yelling at Staubach, "How does it feel to lose?" it started. Comeback I. In the hurry-up offense Staubach was able to call many of his own plays. Landry, who later admitted "I thought we'd lost," was reduced to a spectator.

Staubach was winging it. No more robot QB. With just under a minute left, trailing 28–23 at the 49er 10-yard line, Staubach called "62 Wing Sideline," for Billy Parks. But as the Cowboys broke the huddle, Staubach said to Ron Sellers, "Just run a hook inside and be alert." Staubach was all but making up plays in the backyard.

The 49ers came with a max blitz. "I didn't have time to look for Parks," Staubach says. But he fired quickly to Sellers. Final: Cowboys 30–28. Earlier that afternoon Pittsburgh had beaten Oakland with the Immaculate Reception catch by Franco Harris. But this had been equally miraculous. And on the twenty-third day the Cowboys rose from the dead.

Staubach says, "That game set a precedent for the Cowboys. No matter how badly we played for three quarters, we knew anything was possible for us. And other teams knew it, too."

But no way was Landry about to put an entire game in Staubach's hands. The following week Landry reasserted himself with a new passing-down package for the Redskins. Staubach says, "This confused me and the receivers." Staubach didn't play well. Washington did. The Cowboys were eliminated, 26–3.

Asked why he stuck with Staubach, Landry reacted with one of the inscrutable responses that would plague me for ten years: "I left Roger in because we didn't move the ball at all. If we had been moving the ball but having the breaks go against us, I would have put Morton in." Huh? These explanations were seldom questioned by fans or writers because they came down from Mount Landry. Other media questioners around me would nod in awe as Landry spoke, as if he knew something we'd never comprehend. The Image was beyond question. Landry could justify just about any decision with convoluted doubletalk. It sounded good until you thought about it. Huh?

The only player who openly questioned Landry about his tactical decisions was Staubach. Now, he says, "I always wanted to call the plays because I would have been a very good player to control things on the field. I was not a brilliant reader of defenses. Craig was much more in the mold of what Coach Landry wanted at quarterback, and Danny [White, Staubach's successor] was much more of a scholar of the game. The coaches would ask me to get up at the blackboard and show a blocking scheme, and I'd kid around and drive 'em crazy. I just knew *instinctively*."

"If we'd had an offensive coordinator calling the plays who worked closely with the quarterbacks all week, that would have been different. But Coach Landry controlled everything, and he and I didn't really have any dialogue until Saturday night when he'd call me up to go over the game plan."

Even after Miracle Number 1 in San Francisco, Staubach wasn't sure he wanted to play for Landry. Through the next preseason he continued to split time with Morton. Staubach actually was booed by the Morton lovers during the final exhibition game at Texas Stadium. For Staubach, it took giving Landry an ultimatum to be given the starting job. Staubach told Landry that if he wasn't going to be the starting quarterback—and preferably call the plays—he'd like to be traded, preferably to Atlanta. In 1973 the Falcons were a talented young team without an established quarterback.

Landry started Staubach. But four weeks into the season Landry replaced him midway through a game at Washington. Staubach left with leg cramps. The Cowboys led 7–0. Landry stuck with Morton as the Cowboys lost 14–7. Staubach says his leg felt fine after a few minutes. When it came to Staubach, Landry remained a Doubting Thomas.

Staubach says, "Some people were saying Coach Landry favored me because we were very active in the Fellowship of Christian Athletes. Coach Landry had nothing to do with my joining the FCA." On the surface Staubach is saying he wasn't a religious phony who joined FCA to win favor from Landry. But between the lines he's saying, "Hey, Landry didn't favor me, and he wouldn't have favored me if I'd been the Apostle Paul."

Yet Landry did finally give in and allow Staubach to call his own plays for the first eleven games of 1973. Staubach says, "We were leading the NFL in offense when we lost 14–7 to Miami on Thanksgiving. I had called a goal line play on third-and-one at their 9. Coach Landry thought I should have called a short-yardage play. He called me in the next day and said, 'Roger, [because] your mother's dying of cancer and you've got too much on your mind, I'm going to call the plays again.'"

Landry would, anyway, until all was nearly lost.

Drew Pearson grew up "white" in South River, New Jersey. "It was called Little Poland," he says. "My teammates called me Drewski.

I didn't even know I was black until I ventured out to Oklahoma [to attend Tulsa University]."

For two seasons in high school Pearson caught the passes of Joe Theismann, who went on to Notre Dame, Redskin, and microphone fame. But when Theismann left South River, Pearson became the star QB. He chose Tulsa over Nebraska because Tulsa also offered a nationally ranked baseball program. But Pearson stuck to football. He made second-team All-Missouri Valley as a sophomore, but the team wasn't winning. So Pearson moved back to receiver, where about all he could do was make catches.

Cowboy scout Ron Meyer, who would coach New England and Indianapolis, timed Pearson at 4.6 in the forty-yard dash. The Cowboys wanted their *linemen* to run 4.6. Pearson's dimensions—six-feet-one, 160 pounds—gave the computer indigestion.

"What Drew had," says Staubach, "was the biggest heart I've ever seen."

Pearson sat through seventeen rounds of the NFL draft—452 players—without getting a call. Cowboy scout Bob Griffin called the next day to see if Pearson would sign a free-agent deal. "After being dejected and rejected," Pearson says, "it was like hearing the voice of God." The Cowboys offered $14,500 for the first season and a $150 signing bonus, Pearson says. Pittsburgh offered $18,000 and $1,500 to sign. "But my coach, F. A. Dry, told me it wasn't the money that mattered but the opportunity to play with the best."

Gil Brandt was good buddies with Dry. Did Dry owe Brandt a favor? "Knowing Gil," says Pearson, "I wouldn't put it past him."

At his first minicamp Pearson roomed with the Cowboys' second-round pick, receiver Golden Richards from Hawaii. "I thought, 'What is this Golden shit?' " says Pearson. "Only the Cowboys would have a guy named Golden." Goldens ruled in Dallas. Pearson worked on a loading dock at night and worked out at the Cowboy practice field in the summer mornings. The veterans were on vacation—all but Staubach, who needed someone crazy enough to catch his obsessive-compulsive passes in the killer heat.

Pearson says, "I was able to spend six to eight hours a day with Roger. I was in awe. I was thinking, 'Why would Roger Staubach do this for *me*?' But he liked my work ethic. I was married then, working at night, going up against the odds. That's what Roger's all about. We developed a really good rapport. He even went in and asked Gil to give me a little more money. Gil gave me a check for $500, which seemed like a lot then.

"I also was lucky the Cowboys had just acquired Otto Stowe [a wide receiver from Miami, for Ron Sellers and a second-round choice]. Otto had played with Paul Warfield, and he really taught me a lot. What a blessing. [Mike] Ditka was receivers coach, and he didn't know shit about wide receiver. He was a tight end."

Staubach didn't know much about precise route-running, either, but he knew what felt right. "What you have to remember about Drew," says Staubach, "is that he was a quarterback. Drew had a feel for how to beat coverages just like I did. A lot of times we were almost better off playing schoolyard ball."

The rapport first manifested itself in the final regular season game of 1973 in St. Louis. Pearson, no bashful rookie, told Staubach he could get open by breaking off his route in a seam of the Cardinals' zone. So Staubach revised a play sent in by Landry. Pearson says: "I told Roger, 'If it's not there, don't throw it.' I couldn't *believe* he threw it. It was almost over my head. I got people drilling me from all sides, and I go up and the ball's traveling so fast it nearly bends me backward. But I hung on. That solidified our confidence in each other. Roger had the arm to just defy double coverage, and he knew I'd protect him from interceptions by going up to get the ball no matter how much punishment I had to take.

"When I got back to the sideline, Coach Landry came over and congratulated me."

Several similar reactions by Landry would frustrate the hell out of (or into) Staubach. When Staubach's impromptu changes resulted in big plays, Landry wouldn't congratulate the quarterback. He wouldn't even ask Staubach to replay his thinking so Landry could see what his quarterback saw. Staubach says, "Sometimes we'd be watching the films, and he'd say, 'Now Drew, you were supposed to run such-and-such a route. Why did you do this?' Drew would say, 'Well, Roger told me . . .' And Coach Landry would just nod and go on."

The following Sunday in a first-round playoff game against the Rams, Staubach and Pearson found the magic wavelength again. A 17–0 Cowboy lead had dissolved to 17–16. Cowboys, third-and-fourteen at their 17. Texas Stadium, going fickle with silence. Landry sent in a deep sideline pass to Bob Hayes. Pearson was supposed to run a turn-in route. Earlier, on the same play, Staubach had changed Pearson's route from a turn-in to a post (running deep toward the goalpost). Staubach hadn't thrown to him, but Pearson had let Staubach know he was open. This time Staubach told Pearson to run the post again.

Pearson: "The Rams had all the momentum, and remember, Roger was taking a chance on a rookie. He had just been sacked, and he told the line to give him max protection. I took off on the post and was double-covered by Eddie McMillan and Steve Preece. No way should Roger have thrown it, but here it came. The defensive backs ran into each other, and I was gone for an eighty-three-yard touchdown. The stadium exploded. Tom was *shocked*. That was the backbreaker. We won 27–16."

After the 1973 season the Cowboys crumbled with contract revolt. Pat Toomay, Craig Morton, Otto Stowe, Calvin Hill, D. D. Lewis, Jethro Pugh, Rayfield Wright, and Mike Montgomery signed future contracts with the WFL. Only Hill would jump leagues. But the damage was done to what morale Landry had left.

Schramm had become a hero—a role model, even—for Dallas–Fort Worth businessmen. Some would have given their right ventricle to be Schramm. He controlled the stars they wanted to be. He was CEO for Dallas Cowboys Football Inc. What orgasmic power.

Schramm defended his salary structure with, "We don't have any real high-paid guys. But on the average we pay as well as anyone in the league."

By 1973 Lee Roy Jordan had heard enough of that stuff. He figured he had the organization over an oil barrel, and this time he wasn't backing down. Schramm could convince the writers who drank with him that other contract impasses were forced by ungrateful fools. But up against Jordan, Schramm was defenseless. Jordan was one of the most unselfish, dedicated leaders the game had known. He was Bear Bryant's favorite—210 pounds of every cliché ever bestowed on a player. Jordan was what football was all about. Jordan was the Staubach of the Cowboy defense. If Lee Roy Jordan held out for a better contract, the media and fans finally would say, "Wait a second, Tex."

Staubach and Jordan were roommates. Jordan says, "We both loved third downs. I loved to call on the guys in the huddle. 'You, Larry Cole, it's your turn to make a play.' I used to go from man to man in the locker room and motivate them. Tom was a genius with the Xs and Os, but he wasn't a motivator. . . . But here I was after eleven seasons (and four Pro Bowls) making around $50,000. I mean, Bob Lilly never made $100,000. That's the crime of the century.

Nobody paid lower than the Cowboys did. Nobody. Roger never made any money, either. Roger loved to play and he'd sign quick. I'd say, 'You're the reason I can't get a raise, son. You are at the top of the scale.' Of course, Roger would make more off the field than the rest of us could."

In cold-war negotiations Brandt would sell Cowboys on the financial advantage of living in Dallas. He flashed statistics that ranked the city low in only one category: cost of living. He told them their earning power didn't really begin in Dallas until after they retired from football and cashed in on lifelong hero worship. But by 1974 Jordan demanded to negotiate directly with Schramm.

"I didn't even have an agent," Jordan says. "I told Mr. Schramm, 'My little ol' country ass from Excel, Alabama, is thinking all this up on his own.' In our last meeting before training camp he just gave me this little backhand wave, like he didn't want to hear any more. That was the deepest I ever was hurt in my life. I decided to have the best camp I'd ever had, which I did. Then the week before the season, when I saw they'd cut another middle linebacker, I said, 'Well, they just made my decision.' I missed the meeting that day. I'd never even been late to a meeting. Mr. Schramm called and said, 'I can't believe you're the type of player who'd do this kind of negotiating.' I said, 'You *made* me this type of player.' "

Jordan "won." Schramm gave Jordan his $100,000, but not until the final year (1976) of a new contract. Jordan even paid for that. For twelve years Schramm refused to enshrine Jordan in the Cowboys' Ring of Honor, where he obviously belonged. Talk about a sore loser. Jordan even went to Schramm's office in 1988 to "bury the hatchet" and ask if Schramm was keeping him out of the Ring because he hadn't been great enough. Schramm certainly took his pound of flesh, out of Jordan's heart.

Jordan says, "If you evaluate me on pure ability, I wasn't a Lilly or Staubach or Mel Renfro. If that was Mr. Schramm's criterion, fine. But if you look at my contributions, I belong with those guys."

Only after Schramm had been deposed did new owner Jerry Jones enshrine Jordan in 1989.

Where was Landry all those years? Wouldn't he have stood up for a player who gave him so much? "Well," says Jordan, "I think Coach Landry understood why I held out, but he just never got involved in the business side. That was Mr. Schramm's domain."

*   *   *

Miracle Number 2: This one fell from the heavens in 1975.

In 1974, torn by contract dissension, the Cowboys went 8–6 and missed the playoffs. In fact, they would have finished 7–7 if Drew Pearson hadn't changed a route sent in by Landry late in a Thanksgiving game against Washington. Staubach had been literally knocked out and replaced by a rookie from Abilene Christian named Clint Longley. Dallas trailed 23–17 with twenty-three seconds left. Pearson told Longley to forget the play called, he was going deep. Fifty-yard TD pass. Dallas 24–23.

So the Cowboys' Rome probably would have fallen by 1975 if not for the "Dirty Dozen" draft upon which Gil Brandt made his national reputation. Twelve rookies made the team. Nine would become starters. Five would make the Pro Bowl team. Has there ever been a better NFL draft? Landry's hat had to be off to Brandt.

Still, 1975 belonged to Staubach and Pearson. Imagine: Staubach's only dependable receiver was a free agent from Tulsa who wasn't very fast. But assistant coach Ditka suggested putting Staubach five yards back of the center in the old "spread" or Shotgun formation, allowing a second longer to throw. Assistant coach Dan Reeves pushed for the change. Landry had the courage to try it. The Shotgun was first used by the 49ers in the late '50s, but Landry's Cowboys were about to reinvent it and make it their offensive trademark.

The Cowboys slipped into the playoffs at 10–4 and were sentenced to a first-round playoff game in ice-bound Minnesota, on a day unfit for man or Viking.

The Cowboys trailed 14–10, with forty-four seconds left. Fourth-and-sixteen from their 25-yard line. Pearson says, "I was pissed off because I hadn't caught a pass all day. Tom just felt the flanker wasn't going to catch any passes against Minnesota. But Roger finally turned to me and said, 'Drew, whatcha got?' I said, 'Let's try a post corner.' That's where Roger pumps like I'm running a post, then I break back to the corner. Nate Wright [the cornerback who had covered Pearson all game] took Roger's fake just enough, and Roger really drilled it in on the sideline. My feeling was, 'If the son of a bitch is anywhere near in bounds, I will catch it.' I did and went sliding along the ice that was out of bounds. That's when one of the security guards kicked me. But I looked back and the ref was signaling that my feet were in bounds, so we had a first down [at the 50]. Landry will tell you to this day he thought the game was over."

Pearson hustled back to the huddle and told Roger he was "totally exhausted." So Staubach tried throwing to the other side, to Preston Pearson—incomplete. Twenty-four seconds remained. Pearson: "Rog says, 'Drew, you got to go now. What can you get 'em on?' I thought of the route we beat Washington with on Thanksgiving, where I fake the sixteen (down and across), the bread-and-butter route everybody knows we run, then I go deep. Roger said he'd give me a big pump [fake] at fifteen yards."

Staubach: "Coach Landry wanted to go with the sixteen route, but if Drew catches it [and is tackled], the game's over because we don't have any time-outs left."

Pearson: "So Wright has me man-to-man outside, knowing he has help in the middle. He bites for the pump, and when I come out of my fake, Wright and I are neck and neck. He's not a fast guy, so I'm thinking if Roger just lays it out there, I've got that extra burst. But when I looked back . . ."

Staubach has underthrown the pass by ten yards. This was partly because he had made such an exaggerated fake, which had caused safety Paul Krausse to take one false step. Krausse couldn't recover in time to help Wright. Pearson: "I really put on the brakes and turned back for the ball. Everybody said I pushed Wright, but as I turned inside to him, I was just trying to get my hands free. Maybe I put one hand on him, but I didn't push him. My hands were frozen because it was below zero and I wasn't wearing gloves, so I really couldn't feel anything. The ball hit my left hand first, and I thought I'd dropped it. I thought, 'Damn.' But the ball just kind of stuck between my right elbow and hip. I never wore any stickum on my hands or jersey, so I still don't know how it happened, but I took a couple of steps backward [into the end zone] and realized I still had the ball. I was as stunned as everybody else. I had to run past the Vikings' bench to get to ours [they were on the same side of the field] so I started to see the dejection on their faces. They were yelling, 'Cheat! Cheat! You pushed!' But I said to hell with that, we got it in the bank."

Dallas 17, Minnesota 14.

The pass became known as the Hail Mary—the standard by which all last-second prayers would be measured. Yes, an underthrown fifty-yarder would be voted in 1987 by *Dallas Times Herald* readers as the greatest play in Cowboy history. The Hail Mary would set in stone the images of Staubach as God's Quarterback and Landry as God's Coach. It also would convince a growing cult of Cowboy haters that Dallas was the luckiest team in world history.

"That one play," says Staubach, "would make our next four years."

I once had an enlightening and humbling discussion with a woman who grew up in North Dallas, a lifelong Cowboy fan. She attended *the* private school for girls, Hockaday, and graduated from Vanderbilt. She worshiped faithfully at Staubach's church, St. Rita's.

I told her I didn't really understand the difference between Landry's religion—my religion—and Staubach's. I told her I was raised blindly Protestant in Oklahoma City and didn't understand the difference between Christians and Catholics. I had made my first self-righteous mistake.

"There's no difference between Christians and Catholics," she said, offended. "Catholics *are* Christians, but there are a few fundamental differences between Protestants and Catholics. Catholics are taught that you get to heaven by doing good works and helping others. Protestants say that you ask God into your heart and give yourself to Him, and you automatically go to heaven. By God's grace alone, a Protestant is saved. Catholics are taught that you have to confess your sins and do penance. Protestants believe in going out and trying to convert people from other faiths to their faith because they see it as the one and only faith. But we aren't taught it's our duty to go out and claim other people for Catholicism. We do have missionaries in other countries working with people who don't have a faith to begin with—helping the heathens know God—but we aren't taught to believe that people in other faiths are going to hell."

She was right. I was led to believe Catholics were going to hell.

She continued, "We also believe that because Mary conceived and bore a child through immaculate conception, she should be reverenced as the Holy Mother. Protestants don't believe Mary or any of our saints should be worshiped because only Jesus and God the Holy Spirit should have that distinction. Protestants consider worshiping Mary to be idol worship."

So what, I asked, is a Hail Mary? She said, "It's a prayer that's part of the Rosary. To say a Rosary, you say one Our Father, ten Hail

Marys, and one Glory Be to the Father, then repeat that five times. A Hail Mary goes, 'Hail Mary, full of grace, the Lord is with thee. Blessed art thou amongst women, and blessed is the fruit of thy womb, Jesus. Holy Mary, Mother of God, pray for us sinners now and at the hour of our death. Amen.' "

She said an entire Hail Mary in far less time than it took Staubach to throw one.

Okay, I said, but why was I given the feeling as a child that Catholics could be wilder than "Christians" because Catholics could sin, wipe their slate clean at confession, then sin some more? She said, "We're taught that you can lie to the priest, but you can't lie to God. You cannot have knowledge in your heart that, once you've been forgiven, you'll go right out and sin some more."

This discussion opened my eyes as I reread a passage in Staubach's mid-'70s book, *First Down, Lifetime to Go.* He says,

> I've been asked many times about my Christian faith. Today people like to categorize you as a liberal, conservative, moderate, radical, or fundamentalist in Christianity as well as politics. But I have to say I'm not sure about my category as a Christian.
>
> I do know this: I believe in Jesus Christ as the son of God. . . . He is my Lord, and I believe He loves all with a constant and intense love. I believe in the Bible as His Word, but I am very concerned when fellow Christians start using it so strictly, allowing little interpretation to judge the worthiness and the chance of salvation of all other people. It disturbs me when the fundamentalist Christian says the Jewish person is not saved because of ignoring Christ. I believe that all people have a chance for salvation, based on their own situation and God's all-fair judgment. . . . I hope the years ahead will find many people taking a broader view of religion. I believe they have taken a narrow view partly because they distrusted our humanity. I don't think things on this earth are evil. We can make them so, or misuse them, but . . . I can't see how drinking, eating, dancing, and enjoying the things of this earth can be wrong. So many people make religion seem like a "shall not" religion. I believe religion is a "do" religion, a religion of love, so I welcome the disappearance of the overoccupation with sin and the greater accent on loving, caring, and doing for others. There are some who say that if you have a beer or a glass of wine occasionally, that you're not a Christian. That is ridiculous. Christianity is just living and enjoying the fruits of this life in moderation according to Christ's example. And it isn't wrong to have some money as long as you use it properly and don't let it possess you.
>
> If you allow Christianity to encompass every phase of your life

you can live it to the fullest. It can't just be part of your portfolio, like your investments. You must have it in your business life, your political life, your social life. You can't just bring it out at what seems like an opportune time. Christianity as a crutch just doesn't work.

Courageous words when you consider the famed faith of Staubach's coach.

Recently, I asked Staubach if he thought Landry, as a Christian, should have coexisted in business with Schramm, Brandt, and Murchison. Carefully, Staubach said, "I wouldn't want my number-one person [in the Staubach Companies, with offices in Dallas, Washington, D.C., Los Angeles, and Atlanta] out there being a real dog [morally and ethically] all over the country. I wouldn't allow that. That really bothers me."

But Staubach hastened to add, "Landry was a great football coach. You can pick on his weaknesses, but you have to look at history. Over a long period, what he did was pretty darn special."

You can pick on Staubach's weaknesses, too. Dallas has been very, very good to him. He has done lots of business with lots of wealthy people who cling to the image of Landry and Staubach, the father and son. Staubach is too smart to criticize Landry publicly for much beyond play-calling. Staubach often uses play-calling jokes as part of his after-dinner speeches or introductions of Landry. He knows most fans treat his frustration as a long-running gag, an inside joke, one Smothers brother saying, "Mom liked you best."

But this was no joke.

Though Staubach admits he has no close relationship with Landry, Staubach says he knows "what I meant to him." But does he? Pat Toomay says, "Roger is fooling himself if he actually believes Tom felt anything for him at all. Tom is incapable of relationships." For sure, Staubach still hasn't quite come to grips with why, on his way to the Hall of Fame, he never was entrusted with the play-calling. A childish peeve? No; for Landry, choosing the play was like choosing the words for the classic he was writing. Staubach was only supposed to type, not edit. For Landry, choosing the play was his way of playing quarterback forever. This was the ultimate challenge and control. Landry's letting a veteran quarterback call plays was like Einstein or Mozart or Picasso *collaborating*. To paraphrase Blaine Nye, it wasn't whether the Cowboys won or lost but who got the *credit*. Winning wasn't everything to Landry, credit was.

And so, a decade after retiring, Roger Staubach fights bitterness over why the ultimate father-figure coach never let him drive. But he must be careful about what he says. Staubach says he might run for political office. He has enough trouble in Dallas living up to his own image.

From time to time Staubach has been accused by real estate competitors of using cutthroat or unethical tactics. He says some people are jealous of him because they think he prospers on name alone. "We work darn hard," he says. "And it hasn't all been a bed of roses. What's happened to the market in Dallas has been a tragedy. I'm the only one left standing in a lot of the deals I was in."

But is Staubach a "different person" in business the way he was in football? Sometimes, perhaps. But Christianity is as large a part of Staubach's portfolio as perhaps any Dallasite's. He does many "good works." He would improve his net worth considerably if he called in his "loans" to ex-teammates. Several say he has given thousands to struggling buddies. He dedicates more than his share of time (and probably money) to charity and the FCA. If he weren't expected to be a saint, even more people would consider him one. One thing about Staubach: I never heard one of his teammates accuse him of turning religious only when necessary.

Somehow it's fitting that the greatest play in Landry's career was named after a saint worshiped only by Catholics.

After the Hail Mary, Staubach's '75 Cowboys upset the Rams 37–7 in Los Angeles. Yes, they were back in the Super Bowl again, in Miami. The Cowboys wouldn't go away. It was God's Quarterback and a "Dirty Dozen" rookies against the big, bad Steelers. Goldilocks versus the Three Dozen Bears. The Cowboys lost 21–17, but Staubach was heaving potential Hail Marys as time ran out.

The Rams returned the favor in the '76 playoffs. At Texas Stadium, behind a gimp-kneed NFL rookie named Pat Haden, the Rams stunned the Cowboys 14–12.

But the following season, the 14–2 Cowboys rode their Doomsday defense all the way to New Orleans for Super Bowl XII. The opponent, Denver, was quarterbacked by Staubach's old rival Craig Morton. Morton would have admired Staubach's courage on the game-breaking play.

The Cowboys led 13–3 in the third quarter. In hustled the play messenger, Butch Johnson, a second-year receiver out of Cal Riverside. Johnson says, "The play was supposed to go to [tight end] Billy Joe DuPree. I was supposed to go down seventeen yards and cross. But Roger told me to run a post. I said, 'Roger, are you sure?' I mean, in a game like that, you just don't want to make any mistakes. Roger said, 'Run the post.' I said [in an if-you-say-so tone], 'Okay, I'll run the post.' "

Staubach says, "I remembered from watching film that their safety, Bernard Jackson, would cheat in the middle. So I whispered to Butch to change his route—*whispered*. If I had called '83-Y-post' in the huddle, everybody would have said, 'Hey, Roger's going against the coach.' "

The result was a LeRoy Nieman painting. Literally. The original, a wedding present from his wife, hangs in Butch Johnson's home.

Perhaps Johnson had the courage of Staubach's conviction. He ran the sweetest post since Emily. He left his feet, did his outstretched Superman imitation as he flew over the goal line, snared the nearly overthrown bomb with nothing but fingertips, inches above the carpet, twisted his elbows away at impact, and clutched the ball to his chest as he hit shoulder first. Pretty as a picture: a forty-five-yard TD pass. Dallas 20–3. Pass the Morton Salt, the Broncos were done.

Staubach says, "Coach Landry ran right over to Butch. He never once said a word to me. He was curious, but he wasn't going to ask me."

Miracle Number 3: The final regular-season game of Staubach's final season, 1979. Redskins at Cowboys for the NFC East title. Another rivals revival. This time the Redskins were showing up the Cowboys in their very own sanctuary. Redskins 34–21, with about three minutes left.

One of the Redskin linemen made the mistake of saying something to Staubach like, "How's your milkshake gonna taste tonight?" This was like the Three Stooges episode in which they go berserk when anyone says, "Niagara Falls." You did not say "Niagara Falls" to Staubach until the clock had run out.

Berserk: With forty-five seconds left, the Cowboys were at the Redskins' 8-yard line. A Staubach touchdown pass at 2:20 had cut the margin to 34–28. Staubach says, "Same thing as happened with Butch in the Super Bowl happened with Tony Hill. The play was supposed to be a 13 pass to Billy Joe DuPree. Tony's job was to do nothing, but I leaned over and said, 'Tony, if they blitz, run a quick streak.'"

They blitzed: Dallas 35, Washington 34. I didn't have the heart to ask Staubach if Landry congratulated Tony Hill.

Miracle Number 4: Reunion Arena, downtown Dallas, September 1985. I had agreed to play sitting duck in a $50-per-throw dunk tank at a charity sports carnival. Above a vat of freezing water I teetered on a bar connected to a small red target. A direct hit released the bar, and I went twenty thousand leagues under.

Naturally, several Cowboys lined up with fistfuls of dollars. They were going to *prove* I was all wet. From about forty feet away they were to throw baseballs at a target that couldn't have been much bigger than a softball. At first, as they wound up, I held my nose for baptism, but as ball after ball thudded shamefully off the tarp behind me, I held my nose to mock these rag-armed Magoos. The most embarrassing of all was the starting quarterback, another "next Staubach," Gary Hogeboom. He must have thrown $300 down the drain as a growing crowd of around five hundred hooted.

One spectator was ol' Number 12, Staubach, in sport coat and long-sleeve shirt. Off came the sport coat. Out came the wallet. Up he stepped. I might as well have yelled, "Niagara Falls." I had seen that look before: the Glaze. He will beat you or die. Still, how could he throw accurately in a starched white long-sleeve button-down? It restricts you as you draw back and as you follow through. But as Staubach followed through, I heard no thud. I yelled, "That's incredi—glub glub."

True story: On his first throw, another Hail Mary. Hail, Roger.

As I sat in his office not long ago, I imagined Staubach in Landry's office in 1980. Did the conversation go the way Don Meredith's last harrumph went? I was struck by the second thoughts that still linger from Staubach's final session with Landry.

"I wish I'd played another five years," he said, then added, "but the concussions were definitely an issue. I'd had so many."

Yes, after eleven pro seasons, the thirty-eight-year-old Staubach seemed to be more and more susceptible to concussions. With a wife and five children, Staubach certainly didn't want to be wheeled out of football with a cauliflower brain. Staubach said, "A doctor in New York said the concussions were cumulative and that there was some change in my reflexes from my left to right side. But a doctor in Dallas felt that everything was fine, just that there was some concern there had been so many. Of course, I wanted to be able to make my own [retirement] decision and not have some coach knock on my door. . . . Yet I missed it a heckuva lot more than I realized I would."

In the spring of 1980 Staubach met with Landry and asked the question every Cowboy wanted to ask: Are you happy with my performance? "Tom said I was playing at a level that I should continue to play."

Well, gosh, Staubach told Landry, he was wrestling with this concussion deal. It certainly sounds as if Staubach wanted Landry to say, "Rog, you and I have been a great team for a lotta great years. Why not chance it for one or two more?" After all, Landry always told his team, "Injuries are just part of the bi'ness."

Instead, Staubach got the old "Well, if you think it's that serious, you should go ahead and retire."

Awkward silence.

Then: "Coach, would you let me call the plays?"

Dead silence.

Staubach says, "He didn't say anything. He knew I was kidding. He knew I'd already thought my decision through and that I wasn't negotiating."

But did Landry? Staubach doesn't sound convincing. So he retired. Or maybe he was retired. "Tex called to talk me out of it but, heck, Coach Landry and I already had agreed." For the first and last time?

8

WEDNESDAY, JANUARY 17, 1979. Bahia Mar Hotel, on the South Florida beach. Hollywood Henderson had gone from Hollywood, California—where he personally had finished off Pat Haden's Rams in the NFC Championship Game—to Hollywood, Florida, near where the Cowboys were quartered for Super Bowl XIII. What an appropriate number for this game.

Ten days earlier Thomas "Hollywood" Henderson had returned an interception for the exclamation-point touchdown of Cowboys 28, Rams 0. Henderson celebrated by dunking the football over the goal-post crossbar. In your pretty face, Hollywood. Hollywood had arrived. His limo stretched all the way to the Super Bowl in Miami. All the country was his stage.

I wanted to talk to Henderson before the buses arrived at the Bahia Mar, another of the gaudy dowager hotels along the beach strip. Soon, reporters would swarm like the love bugs that splatter South Florida windshields. A thousand or more were on their way from the NFL headquarters hotel in Miami. Every city in America would be represented by at least one writer or broadcaster. And from what I'd heard, most of them wanted to interview Hollywood.

It was another sticky, gusty *Body Heat* day. Sweating, I caught Henderson as he walked out of his room. "Skip Bayless!" he said. "What do you think of me now, Skip Bayless?"

I'd been writing in Dallas for only four months. The hottest of many blue-flame Cowboy topics was Henderson. I'd mentioned in a column that Henderson might have his hands (or mouth) full against New England's All-Pro tight end Russ Francis. But no, even Tom Landry had complimented Henderson in the day-after film session. "Tom even called me a pro," Henderson had told me.

Henderson was playing with pain, all right—emotional pain. But I didn't know that then. I had written a mock apology to Henderson, concluding, "Forget Ali. You are the greatest." The next day Henderson was named to the Pro Bowl squad. Now, he says, "Tex Schramm came up to me at practice and whispered, 'You've made the Pro Bowl, but don't make a big deal of it. Be discreet.' That in a nutshell was the Dallas Cowboys. They wanted to have the power. But all of a sudden I had the power because the rest of the NFL [players vote for the Pro Bowl] had said I was the best. I started jumping around the practice field screaming, 'I made it! I made it!' I looked back over my shoulder and grinned at Tex. He was over there going, 'Dammit. Fuck. Shit.' "

Even Roger Staubach says, "Thomas Henderson had Hall of Fame talent." Henderson was Gil Brandt's greatest discovery—his best and last. Henderson was a linebacker from tiny Langston College, outside Oklahoma City. When Brandt fed Henderson's data into the computer, it must have responded, "Not of human race." Henderson: six-feet-two, 220. Could run with most halfbacks. Had NBA quickness and leaping ability. Had the agility of a gymnast. Could match bench presses with most linemen, yet didn't lift weights. Could match IQ and wit with Ivy Leaguers, yet his classroom had been the streets.

"He could be so clever and charming," Schramm said.

And God said, "Let there be Hollywood." The bearded Henderson even was leading-man handsome. "Thomas," says Butch Johnson, "could have been our first bona fide superstar, a *super* superstar. He was good-looking, physical, durable, a risk-taker. When he walked into a room, people turned to look."

Here was one mean mother (raised without a father) who appeared to be the perfect "son" for Landry. Henderson was deeply

insecure—"deeply shame-based," he says, "and trying desperately
to hide it." His mother had shot his father, badly wounding him.
Henderson had grown up frequently "smelling like urine," he says.
Surely he would fear and respect Tom Landry and fall in Flex step.
Surely he was poor and smart enough to be a good, grateful Cow-
boy.

Yes, here was a black star who could even dazzle the white
media. Henderson would keep writers (and opponents) in stitches.
This was no Duane Thomas. Thomas Henderson couldn't stop smiling and talking unless he stopped breathing.

Brandt recommended that Landry take Henderson with the
Cowboys' second pick in the first round—the eighteenth pick in the
1975 draft. Brandt would mount this diamond in the rough on yet
another Super Bowl ring.

And here was Henderson four seasons later, crashing like high
tide upon Super Bowl City. He even had adopted a nickname, a
public alter ego. As we walked toward the ballroom interview session, he said, "Do you realize 'Hollywood' is on the cover of *Time*
and *Newsweek?* Do you realize 'Hollywood' is a bigger story than
the fucking Shah of Iran? Think about that. Reporters have come
from all over the world to talk to me, Thomas 'Hollywood' Henderson. You just watch what I do in this interview. I'll be more
famous than Landry, Schramm, or Brandt. They can't stop me. By
tomorrow people will be talking about me *all over the world."*

Yes, Henderson was perhaps the first player shrewd enough to
use this awesome P.R. platform for self-promotion. Schramm and
Pete Rozelle had created a Super Bowl Week that generated millions' worth of publicity. Brilliant setup: The NFL required its Super opponents to arrive on Monday before the game, then made all
players and coaches available for interview sessions on Tuesday,
Wednesday, and Thursday (along with breakfast or lunch for the
media), capped off by one more coaches' press conference on Friday. Stories were as plentiful as free sweet rolls; good stories were
scarce. Some newspaper guys hustled for creative angles; many ordered Rozelle's room service.

Usually, the best quotes to come out of most Super Weeks
were: "We have to establish our running game," or the dreaded
"The key will be turnovers." Most players and coaches graduated
from the Bear Bryant School of Journalism: The less said to reporters, the better. Offering anything more than bare-minimum clichés,

they believed, could result in spilling secrets, enraging and moti-
vating the other team, or sounding like a publicity hound to teammates.

But as long as most newspapermen had early, daily access to
the stars and coaches, they were happy. The game almost always
was staged in a resort setting, so easy work days could lead to deeper
tans and longer nights. There were nightly parties, courtesy cars,
racetrack outings, a cruise, golf and tennis tournaments. Sure, we
young-gun columnists complained constantly about the "pack" journalism and dull interviews, but most of us would have threatened to
quit if our editors hadn't sent us. For media stars, the Super Bowl
had become the place to be, just as Schramm had planned. Even
without a local team in the game, some newspapers routinely sent
five or six staffers, who had to justify their privileged presence by
doing two or three stories a day. Newspapers could justify running
pages of nonstories because the Super Bowl was watched by just
about everyone but blind communists. Through the '70s our week-
long nuclear buildups had helped make Super Sunday a new national holiday.

Henderson was about to take outrageous advantage of the
NFL's publicity machine. The only thing the NFL couldn't supply
was what we in the business called "a great talker." We could com-
pose literature about All-Pros with nothing to say, and our editors
would ask by phone, "Isn't anything happening down there?" Or we
could bang out quote-laden pieces on backup tackles who offered
amusing "inside" stories, and editors would call to say, "Hey, great
stuff."

Thomas Henderson all but typed for us. His interview horde
grew so large that it had to be moved from one ballroom (where each
Cowboy starter had a table to himself) to another, where we'd just
finished interviewing Landry during breakfast. Yes, Thomas was
suddenly as big as Tom. Start the presses.

Henderson instantly became a household name spewing household quotes. The most legendary: "Terry Bradshaw is so dumb he
couldn't spell cat if you spotted him the 'c' and the 'a.' " Bradshaw
happened to be the quarterback for the opposition, the Pittsburgh
Steelers. A linebacker on one Super Bowl team simply did not call
the star quarterback on the other team "dumb."

Then again, this linebacker had just breakfasted on cocaine.
Henderson, like the organization he played for, could put up a

great front. It was as if the entire organization's lust, thirst, vanity, and insecurity had been concentrated in one beautiful specimen. Here was Landry-Schramm-Brandt's worst nightmare, grinning back at them in the gilded mirror. He even had a gold star in his front tooth. Here was hell on wheels.

Like the Cowboys, Henderson was innovative right down to his "high." Schramm and Murchison could have their crusty old J&B. Among pro athletes, Henderson was ahead of his time. He did coke when a lot of us still thought it was a soft drink. Not only that, he free-based cocaine before I'd even gotten over seeing four or five Cowboys (Henderson among them) smoke cigarettes in the locker room. For America's Team, Henderson was a binging harbinger. He was the rise and the fall.

A source close to Schramm says, "Thomas Henderson dramatically changed sports history. When he arrived on the scene in '75, there weren't any Thomas Hendersons. Now these self-promoters are running around all over sports, from Brian Bosworth to Deion Sanders. Thomas could talk shit and back it up with extraordinary talent.

"He epitomized the Cowboy organization at its peak in 1979. He could party all night and still be the best at his position. He was a microcosm of the whole picture. At their zenith the Cowboys were the very best. So was Thomas. But when he and the Cowboys were at their peak, the entire country had to put up with so much shit from them that the new regime is still paying for it.

"My God, Thomas Henderson fell all the way to sodomizing a girl in a wheelchair [a sixteen-year-old paraplegic accused Henderson of forced oral copulation; he was convicted of sexual battery] and doing time in prison [two and a half years]. He was a symbol. Tex would never admit that, but he was."

During that morning's interview Henderson gave me a little wink. Yes, I wrote a column about him that afternoon. Okay, I wrote another about him later in the week. And you're right, I predicted the Cowboys would beat the Steelers, something like 24–21. I was blinded. I believed the Cowboys would become the team of the '70s *and* '80s.

Landry's main problem with Thomas Henderson was that Hollywood wasn't blinded. He wasn't a Cowboy fan. He wasn't even much of a football fan. He didn't know enough to be in awe. He hadn't watched enough Cowboy games on TV and allowed the image of Mount Landry to loom in his living room and psyche. Henderson says, "It just never occurred to me that Tom Landry was any big deal. He isn't. He's just a nice man who needs to read *Dianetics*. It always amazed me the amount of talent I played with that was *afraid* of Tom Landry and the Cowboys.

"So they gave me number 56 and I said, 'What a boring number.' I saw we were going to be on TV more than anybody. I said, what the hell, I came from a braggadocio neighborhood where everyone thrived on one-upsmanship. It never occurred to me to step in line and be a good boy. Everybody said, 'Man, he's raising hell.' But I was just being myself. I've never been afraid to say what I think is the truth, to let my perceptions flow.

"So I made 56 a popular number. Lawrence Taylor came up to me one time at a fight in Atlantic City and said, 'Man, you're the reason I wear 56.' In team sports I was the first one to show everyone it was okay to say you were great."

He may have been the first player. But several in his front office were a year or two ahead of him.

That Sunday at the Orange Bowl, Bradshaw completed seventeen of thirty for 318 yards and four touchdowns. Pittsburgh won 35–31. Cowboy fans had the usual thirty-one excuses—mainly an iffy interference call on cornerback Benny Barnes and a TD lob from Staubach dropped by a wide-open Jackie Smith. But the truth was, the Cowboy defense simply wasn't good enough. The game didn't seem four-point close. A Bradshaw-to-Swann TD made it 35–17 with 6:51 left.

Ironically, the "Li'l Abner" who couldn't spell cat was the first to spell doom for Dallas's Doomsday defense. Bradshaw had read Landry's Flex as if it were by Dell.

Years later Bradshaw told me, "Shoot, there was no big mystery about how to beat the Flex. You threw on first down. The corners were almost always man-to-man on first down because the Flex was geared to stop the run. I almost felt sorry for their cornerbacks. I had Lynn Swann and John Stallworth out there, and all I had to do was throw it and they'd go get it."

In Super XIII, Bradshaw threw half his passes (fifteen) on first down, completing nine, two for TDs. He continued: "You see, the rules had changed, and holding was all but legalized. So it negated a lot of their quickness in their pass rush. They just couldn't get the pressure they had the year before (in Super XII, when defensive linemen Harvey Martin and Randy White were co-MVPs against Denver). We had such strong, massive linemen, and they weren't spooked by the Flex. On running plays we just tried to blow the Cowboys off the ball."

The rules changes were turning pass-rushing end Harvey "Too Mean" Martin into more of Harvey the invisible rabbit. His league-leading twenty-three quarterback sacks in 1977 had fallen to sixteen in '78 and would bottom out at ten in '79. At 260 pounds Martin simply had outquicked left tackles in '77 when he was the Associated Press NFL player of the year. But Martin was not terribly strong. Despite his Too Mean image—"I didn't start that," he told me, "that was a P.R. gimmick"—Martin had grown up in South Dallas as something of a mama's boy. Thomas Henderson says, "Harvey is not someone I'd want at my back in an alley fight." Once Harvey could be legally latched onto by blockers, he often couldn't fight free. The Steelers were the first to "Martinize" Harvey.

The Steelers were the first to expose Landry's great and powerful scheme as mostly smoke and neon—as the ex-Flex.

A great thought from psychologist Don Beck and his partners on Landry, who collects classic cars: "Tom built a great '63 Buick, but it just wasn't in his nature to change."

The next week I found myself in Los Angeles, across a hotel coffee shop table from "Butch and Sundance." Sidekicks Cliff Harris and Charlie Waters, the Cowboys' All-Pro safeties, were known among writers as great talkers. You went to Hollywood for the funny or controversial quotes. Cliff and Charlie provided the clever perspective and analysis. These two could talk Xs and Os as if they were neutrons and protons. They could make the Flex seem like something Thrush or Spectre was trying to duplicate. They knew how to play the media game the way management wanted it played. They were "good guys" who sold high-Tex football as if it were a religious crusade. In return, Landry-Schramm-Brandt immortalized Harris and Waters for interviewers who had All-Pro votes. This is how the System worked.

In Dallas, Harris and Waters probably were the two most popular Cowboys. Staubach you worshiped; Harris and Waters became
part of your family. It was as if they were still playing high school
football.

But beneath the Tom and Huck image I soon found two tor-
tured mortals who love-hated their jobs. Harris and Waters were
fueled by fear. They believed the same organization that made them
could break them. No Cowboys I knew were any more afraid of Tom
Landry than these two. "The Man," they called Landry.

Neither Harris nor Waters came to the Cowboys a sure star, or
even a starter. Even as all-stars they still treated games as "Big
Brother is filming you." Harris, the balding one with the handlebar
mustache, wide shoulders, thin waist, and skinny legs, was the
highly publicized free-agent find from Ouachita Baptist in Arkansas.
Crash Harris was known for hurling himself at ball carriers with no
regard for life after football. His goal from the start had been to "be
somebody." Among teammates the psycho-eyed Harris was known
as a guy who would take just about any pill or injection to help him
be somebody.

Waters was the deep-thinking poster boy from the deep South.
At Clemson he had played quarterback and receiver, but the Cowboys made him a cornerback, then a "coach-on-the-field" safety.
Waters did Oriental painting. He could discuss Buddhist philosophy. And he worshiped at the base of Mount Landry. Waters might
have given his life for Landry, and nearly did. I haven't known an
athlete more dedicated to suffering than Waters, who underwent
major operations on his knees, shoulders, and arm. Waters took
kamikaze pride in going under the knife for The Man. After one
surgery, he said, he went through a second hell breaking himself of
a painkiller addiction.

As a long-haired rookie, Waters often gave his body to Greenville Avenue's nightlife. But after marrying Rosie, an actress/model,
Waters had gotten religion—Flexology.

Or so I thought. Terry Bradshaw's record-breaking Super Bowl
had shaken Waters's faith. Harris's, too. They were in L.A. to prepare for the Pro Bowl, but their psyches were still in Miami. They
surprised me by encouraging me to write a column about what was
wrong with the Flex. They shared their deepest, darkest criticisms—
the same I would hear from Bradshaw—but asked that I not use
their names in the column. Harris said, "Our ass will be grass if the
coaches find out where this came from."

But: "Hey, after a while, any great NFL defensive alignment that doesn't change will be overcome and annihilated."

Was I listening to sore losers or voices of reason? I leaned toward the latter. I wrote the column. I don't remember getting much reader reaction. In Dallas, who would believe Cowboy "insiders" were doubting the Flex? No doubt it was coincidence that, before the next training camp, Landry mentioned something about experimenting with "some 3-4" (a four-linebacker alignment based more on chasing the ball). This was to become Landry's annual summer smokescreen. This sent a message to fans—and to Schramm, the innovator—that Landry was changing with the times. But always, by Opening Sunday, the Cowboys were in nothing but Flex.

As the Genius, Landry's image was of lab rats and bubbling test tubes. Yet he was experimental only on offense. His offensive *concept* hadn't changed since the early '60s. He wasn't an innovator the way, say, San Francisco coach Bill Walsh was. But Landry was fascinated with trick plays—"exotics"—for which he would set up a defense and exploit its animal instincts. Landry's exotics became his offensive claim to fame.

After Super Bowl XII several Cowboys also complained about Landry's trick plays. On the Cowboys' opening drive, the line had opened repeated holes for Tony Dorsett when Landry called a flanker reverse pass, thrown by Drew Pearson. Pearson fumbled the exchange. The Cowboys lost an opportunity to score first in what became a scoring battle. Had Landry's ego gotten the best of him? Naturally, if the play had gone for a TD, players would have shaken their heads and said, "Landry's amazing." Ditto, millions of viewers.

Instead, Harris said, "We need to get back to just playing football."

For the next nine seasons I would hear the same off-the-record words from Cowboy after Cowboy—who came and went. Only the Flex remained.

The first day of my first visit to Cowboy camp in Thousand Oaks, California, I wandered into Gil Brandt's dorm-room office and left with a must-write column. Out of the metallic-blue, Brandt hinted that Cliff Harris, who had been voted to five straight Pro Bowls, might lose his job to Randy Hughes, a bigger, faster, computer-chosen athlete from Oklahoma. Brandt spoke with the authority of a head coach.

Had Brandt found out Harris had criticized the Flex to me? Was this punishment for his disloyalty? Or was this the way the Cowboys motivated a nine-year starter?

Harris kept his job that season and again was voted to the Pro Bowl. Then he stunned and impressed me by retiring at age thirty-one. I thought, "Well, he got them before they got him." Or did he?

Later, Harris told Paul Zimmerman of *Sports Illustrated*, "Tom Landry knows the System, and when the end is nigh, he can be a cold-blooded son of a gun. The System worked on insecurity. I never knew whether I was going to be back, even in my All-Pro years."

That summer I played golf several times with Brandt at camp and in his annual two-day tournament for college coaches at Las Colinas Country Club in Dallas. All the big-name governorlike coaches came to Dallas each June for the College Football Association convention and blowout. Why was it always in Dallas? Probably because of Brandt's budgetless hospitality. The event's highlight was Brandt's prize-laden golf/tennis tournament, followed by a party at the Stadium Club at Texas Stadium for coaches, media, and wives.

Brandt always had two or three rising-star coaches for whom he really rolled out the magic carpet. Brandt's "boys," they were called. Brandt loved to say he got them jobs up their ladders to national championships. One of Brandt's "boys" was Jimmy Johnson, who was at Oklahoma State. Brandt would take credit for getting Johnson a promotion to the University of Miami in 1984 (Johnson was named UM coach during Brandt's golf tournament). At a later tournament Johnson's wife, Linda Kay, won a drawing for a flight to Spain. A source close to Brandt says, "Gil rigged the drawing for Linda Kay. I saw him holding her ticket in his hand before he drew."

Brandt always included me in his coaches-tournament foursome. I'm sure it was, "I'll scratch your back(swing) if you'll scratch mine in print." I didn't always glorify him in columns, but I did love being around him. On one tee he'd tell me how a star running back at Texas was gay. On another he'd tell me the key to the Cowboys' success was building with character.

One June I played with Brandt, Jackie Sherrill (then at Pitt), and John Mackovic (then at Wake Forest). Though it was a "scramble" format, Mackovic would have shot four or five under par on his own ball. Our foursome won the tournament. Brandt leaned over and said, "This guy reminds me of a young Tom Landry."

The next year Mackovic was Landry's quarterback coach. Landry listened to Brandt.

That August I was surprised to hear Charlie Waters being openly hostile to Brandt. "It's always good to see you, Gil," Waters said in a sarcastic stage voice intended for teammates. Brandt, who seemed intimidated by players in groups, walked away as if he didn't hear. Waters and Brandt were embroiled in a contract battle.

A front-office source says, "Gil could be a real bastard because he loved to impress Tex and Clint by coming in under budget. But Tom set the salary structure by ranking the players for Gil and Tex. He just let them do his dirty work."

That Saturday night in Seattle's Kingdome, Waters caught a cleat in a carpet seam, wrecked his knee, and was lost for the season. Two days later Waters went under the knife at the clinic of longtime team doctor Marvin Knight, an hour's drive from Dallas in Muenster. Many players feared Knight, whom they called "ol' Shaky." A gruff coot, Knight dressed for games in cowboy hat, business suit, and cowboy boots. He chain-smoked on the sidelines. Knight was said to be close to Murchison and Schramm.

The day after his surgery, Waters called me at home. As he drifted in and out on Demerol, he said he was thinking about putting "snakes in Gil Brandt's hot tub." Then he apologized profusely for ever doubting the Flex. "The Flex," he said, "will overcome."

That season Waters observed games from the press box. He continued to doubt. He worked up his courage and went in to see Landry. He told *Sports Illustrated's* Zimmerman, "I was firmly convinced we should go to the 3–4 defense. We had to get our linebackers off the trolley tracks, give them more flexibility. I thought Coach Landry would welcome the idea of an older veteran coming in to offer ideas to help the team. Well, I got all wrapped up in my little speech, and then I took a look at Coach Landry. His eyes were cold and steely, his jaw muscles were tight. He was staring off into space, waiting for me to finish. Right then I knew I'd done the wrong thing. I'd tampered with something that was his, that was special to him. Our relationship was never the same after that."

After Waters's final season he applied for the assistant's position vacated by Mike Ditka, receivers coach. "I thought I was perfect," Waters told the *Dallas Times Herald*. "But Coach Landry made me take a psychological test, which seemed ridiculous. Didn't he know me after twelve years?" Landry offered Waters special-teams coach, the lowest rung, at a minimal $30,000. "I thought it was a slap," says Waters, who now coaches defensive backs for Dan Reeves in Denver. So much for dying for The Man's cause.

The '79 Cowboys were 7–1 heading to Pittsburgh for a Super Bowl rematch. By then it was official: America had a Team. "By mid-'79," says Thomas Henderson, "the America's Team concept had swept the country. It was mostly because of Tom Landry and his Christianity that the masses identified with the organization. That was the catalyst. But then came Tex Schramm's genius of promoting America's Team so that every patriot from places like Butte, Montana, stationed around the world would say, 'That's *my* team.' "

Says ex-linebacker D. D. Lewis, "What amazed me was that it was almost like we had *won* the Super Bowl. I still run into people who think we were the team of the '70s, that we kept beating Pittsburgh."

By the time the Cowboys reached the locker room at Pittsburgh, Hollywood Henderson was about to topple off the edge of this awesome platform. That week he had a "cold" and couldn't practice. As Henderson changed into his armor for the game, Landry walked up and told him Mike Hegman would start in his place.

Henderson says, "I said to him, 'How dare you have double standards for Thomas and the team.' He always told us a starter couldn't lose his job because of injury or illness. The trainer had told me to take a day off. I had a bad cold, though I wasn't sure if it was a cold or a cocaine hangover.

"Landry walked away and I said, 'Fuck you!' I followed him back to the coaches' dressing room and said, 'Coach Landry, if I don't start today, then I'm not playing the rest of the season.' I went back, took my goddamn pants off, and just sat there in my jock. The whole team saw what was going on. No one had ever stood up to him like that. I said, 'Okay, big boy, put on your hat and go on out on the field without me.'

"He came back and said he had checked with the trainer and

that it was okay for me to start. He said, in effect, 'You win.' That set the stage for Tom Landry to fire me."

Henderson "won," but the Cowboys lost 14–3.

D. D. Lewis (Dwight Douglas, after Dwight Eisenhower and Douglas MacArthur) was the last of the Southern good ol' Cowboys. He grew up poor and troubled as one of fourteen children in Knoxville, Tennessee. At Mississippi State he was the Southeastern Conference player of the year in 1967. At around 210 pounds, he was an undersized overachiever. He smoked, drank, and kicked butt.

But fittingly, Lewis played weak-side linebacker for the Cowboys. Come contract time he was a pushover. Lewis even called rookies for Brandt and told them money wasn't as important as the opportunity to play for the Cowboys.

"I was scared," Lewis says. "I saw a great cartoon once of a Cadillac facade on the front of a beat-up Volkswagen. The caption was, 'Cowboy salaries.' "

So here came a strong-side linebacker, Thomas Henderson, flashing gold and money. "I liked Thomas at first," Lewis says. "But I saw him teaching guys how to play the media. He'd say some stupid BS and the press would jump all over it. Then I'd see him asleep in meetings, and I felt like he was stealing [playoff] money from me.

"He was from the streets, from the poor side just like me. And the sucker had no humility at all. Thomas talked to Ed Jones like he was a nigger. He'd tell Ed, 'I know everything about gold.' Big fucking deal. Thomas had pulled up that training camp in a limo, and he was broke, bumming weed [cigarettes] off everybody. It just rubbed me the wrong way. I didn't handle it right.

"I mean, this guy had unbelievable talent. There might have been some jealousy on my part."

Soon after the loss in Pittsburgh, Lewis and Henderson found themselves alone in the shower after practice. Here was a clash for the Cowboy ages: '60s die-for-the-cause versus "me" generation. Don't-ask-why versus why-the-fuck? Rebel flag versus black rebel.

Henderson: "I stood in the shower and said, 'I will beat your white prejudiced fucking ass right here, motherfucker.' I called him a goddamned alcoholic. He was, too, but he just wasn't ready to hear it."

Lewis: "I should have jumped on him and punched him out. But after a while he walked out of the shower. I got madder and madder. Once I decided to go after him, he had dressed and gone."

On Sunday, November 18, the Cowboys lost 34–20 at Washington. The Redskins even rubbed it in with a last-second field goal. Afterward, Drew Pearson told me, "Man, all this America's Team shit is killing us. That's all we heard all day from the Redskins: 'Whose team are you now, motherfuckers?' "

As the game ended, CBS cameras focused on Thomas Henderson, who was cutting up on the sidelines. That was it.

"When Tom fired me," Henderson says, "he mentioned his inability to understand what was going on. But I guarantee you, Gil Brandt with all his police connections and undercover people all over Dallas—he knew as early as 1977. He'd say to me, 'I understand you're hanging around with some shady characters.' It was a very uncomfortable situation for the Cowboys. They never figured I'd be the first athlete to go public with his cocaine addiction.

"But by late '79, I was done. You can fake it [financially] in Dallas for about five years . If you're a Cowboy, you can sit down and have a drink with a guy, and he'll loan you a thousand. It's a wide town, so you can find another hot bar and another guy who'll loan you two thousand. It's like that porno flick, *Debbie Does Dallas* [about a Cowboy-like cheerleader]. Well, a lot of Cowboys were doing Dallas, too.

"But the main reason Tom fired me was to try to show the team he had control. The truth was, he never really had control. He was just a guy who made everybody think he had control. You know what the title of your book should be? *Tom Landry and All that Never Was.*"

Two games later New Jersey's own Drew Pearson caught a touchdown pass against the "New Jersey" Giants ("I loved to talk trash with those guys") and was a little too eager to spike the ball. As he planted, his knee buckled. Roger Staubach says, "People didn't realize how much we missed Drew the rest of the year, especially against the Rams."

In a divisional playoff game at Texas Stadium, Vince Ferragamo's Rams eliminated Staubach's Cowboys 21–19. Staubach completed his final pass—unintentionally and illegally—to offensive lineman Herb Scott. A Hail Mary Poppins? It wasn't supposed to end that way. Three months later, Staubach retired.

D. D. Lewis didn't retire until after the 1981 season, his fourteenth. After fourteen years of suspended adolescence—of Father Tom telling him where and when—Lewis was on his own. Lewis was lost. Lewis drank more and more. In his condition, Lewis chose the wrong second career—making appearances and commercials for Miller Lite. His marriage, like some of his drinks, was on the rocks.

One night Lewis was driving back to Dallas from Shreveport as if he were bound for hell. He was too drunk to remember how fast he was going. Real fast. As his car left the road, hurtling into the blackness, Lewis blacked out. He awoke the next morning in the middle of a miraculously level, unobstructed field. He needed a tow truck but not an ambulance. He says, "I honestly don't know how I survived."

Hung over and humiliated, he walked up the road to a service station. Just then a busload of football fans pulled in. One recognized Lewis. Suddenly, he was signing autographs. He was D. D. Lewis of the Dallas Cowboys again. He was a TV image. He was immortal.

Or had he died and gone to hell?

Soon D. D. Lewis joined Alcoholics Anonymous, where one motto is "Check your bullshit at the door." The meetings were so humbling for Lewis that at one point he considered growing his hair into a ponytail and becoming a carpenter. Imagine: Number 50 a ponytailed carpenter.

Today, remarried, Lewis appears to be living happily ever after as a salesman for an old friend's fertilizer company. Now, he sells the stuff instead of hiding behind it. Now, his words help work some minor miracles in AA.

But as Lewis began his recovery, one man he had come to grips with was The Man, Landry. "Really," Lewis says, "Staubach and Bob Breunig and the team Bible study affected me more religiously than anything Tom did. Now, I certainly respected him for *his* faith. Here was a guy who could walk the walk. But I thought I couldn't look at a woman or have any sinful thoughts. Hell, that way I might as well not leave the house. I was condemned from the get-go. I had to learn that God still loves you. We're human beings. We're going to make mistakes."

I asked Lewis if he thinks Landry looks at pretty women. "I think he doesn't. I'm so glad I don't have to live that way."

Not long ago Thomas Henderson sat among autograph seekers in the lobby of a North Dallas hotel. He had returned for his sixth "birthday" party.

"I've been sober for six years," said Henderson. Like Lewis, he found life through Alcoholics Anonymous and similar programs. Prison behind him, he has become an evangelist—something like his old coach. Imagine: Thomas Henderson as a role model. Or "hope model," as he says. Henderson tours the country giving his "Hope After Dope" speech. I've heard it. I was prepared to scoff, but it hits the way Henderson once did. Henderson's greatest gift turned out to be gab.

Maybe there was purpose to his premature fall. "If I can recover," Henderson says, "anybody can."

Henderson told me the story of a day he spoke at Brookhaven Hospital in Dallas. Of all people, up walked D. D. Lewis, who had heard Henderson would be there and had made a special trip. "He told me he was sorry for everything that happened," Henderson says. "He told me he was wrong. Then he gave me a big hug. Man, I got tears in my eyes."

9

BY 1980 Tom Landry was as recognizable as perhaps any figure in America. His Cowboys had made the playoffs fourteen of the previous fifteen seasons. They had played in NFL title games in '66 and '67 and in five of the last ten Super Bowls. That's a lot of newspaper stories and TV closeups. When you thought of pro football, you thought of Landry, whether you loved or loathed his Cowboys.

He was always there.

His visibility/credibility quotient had to be as high as any American leader's, in or out of Washington. Landry was the best of two religions, Christianity and football. You didn't have to like football to be fascinated by the Man in the Hat. Who was he? God's right-hand man? Or a cold, calculating genius? Was Tom Landry literally a maker of men—of robostars? Millions of Americans had an opinion. Millions spent Sunday afternoons in the presence of Landry's image on their living-room TV.

The columnist who surely has written the most words on Landry, legendary Blackie Sherrod of the *Dallas Morning News*, writes, "The single most powerful influence on our lives for the last half-century has been television. . . . Television, not principles or platforms, elects the nation's leaders." Landry's principles and platforms didn't matter as much as the way he came across on TV. Landry, in hat and suit, was blessed with an overpowering TV presence. It was nothing he said or did. It certainly wasn't charisma or charm, facial or body language. Landry was a master of underacting. He seldom changed expressions or posture. He was a living monument. He struck a twenty-nine-year pose that could turn a portable TV into a theater screen. Landry, backdropped by Schramm's Cowboy kingdom, projected strength and wisdom as only a Cecil B. DeMille epic could. Could even Charlton Heston have done Landry's role justice?

For many Christians, watching Landry became an extension of the Sunday church service. Landry was the strong, silent type of evangelist. His weekly message: God and the Cowboys are still good. While Catholics everywhere pulled for Notre Dame, all faiths pulled for Landry.

And by 1980 Landry was pulled in all directions. Tom Landry, whose coaching weakness was communication and motivation, was asked to speak to groups all over the country. "The volume of requests is incredible," said one of his two secretaries, Barbara Goodman. "He could speak every day or night, if he had the time." Church groups, civic groups, sports groups. Prayer breakfasts, business luncheons, athletic banquets. Commencements, dedications, conventions—how about Tom Landry? What finer man was there in America than Tom Landry? As sports were "going to hell" for many fans, Landry became a last hope. Who else was there? Billy Martin? Bobby Knight? As athletes' salaries and NBA leapers rose out of sight, as baseball and football were dominated more and more by roll-your-eyes models, the masses clung to Landry. His virtue endured.

Fellowship of Christian Athletes "huddle groups" at high schools all over America wanted Landry. The Billy Graham Crusade wanted Landry. Sinners listened to Graham because they needed to. They listened to Landry because they wanted to. Before them was a great Christian *who coached the Dallas Cowboys*. Lord, what a combination.

Perhaps Gil Brandt said it best: "I believe people across the country see Tom on TV and they sense the qualities America was built on—dedication, strength, truth, and honesty."

Of course, Landry could have slowed the speaking requests by saying sorry, coaching just took too much of his time. But as he spread God's word, word spread that Landry would speak just about anywhere during the off-season. Business-oriented groups would pay him top dollar for a celebrity speaker—up to $15,000 or so. But for Christian functions Landry often spoke for no more than travel expenses, if that. After he became a Christian in 1959, he says, he started looking for a platform to tell others of his faith. Schramm had helped provide him with one of America's loftiest stages. Who would have believed Landry could have such national impact from Dallas? Yet he and Schramm helped turn Dallas into a "third coast," as it's called. God's power?

Schramm, of course, loved for Landry to spread Schramm's word: *Cowboy*. People who saw Landry speak in California or New York were more likely to watch the Cowboys on TV or buy Cowboy T-shirts or hats. But more and more in the early '80s Schramm appeared concerned about the amount of predraft time Landry spent out of the office. While Philadelphia coach Dick Vermeil and Washington coach Joe Gibbs often slept in their offices, Landry was sleeping in hotels throughout the country. By 1980 you'd have thought Landry at least would confine his engagements to larger groups. But no request was too small for God's Coach.

That year I was surprised to hear that Landry had agreed to speak at Bethany Nazarene College on the outskirts of my hometown, Oklahoma City. My best friend's father, who worked for the Billy Graham Crusade, had Landry over for dinner. Think of the time commitment: the travel, the glad-handing, the two-hour function, the dinner.

That year Landry also accepted a request from Chuck Bowman, a national FCA leader based in Oklahoma City, to speak to about one hundred junior high kids in Ardmore, Oklahoma. Ardmore! "He stood there and signed autographs for three hours," Bowman says. "The man will just do anything for FCA. At a time when FCA was about to stagger and fall, Coach Landry put new fuel in its tank. I doubt Bud Wilkinson could have done that, and I worship the man [Bowman played under Wilkinson at Oklahoma]. Bud's faith, though strong, wasn't respected like Landry's. It took a man who walks his talk. We had to have Coach Landry for his credibility."

At Bowman's request, Landry brought along ex-Oklahoma star and Cowboy safety Randy Hughes to Ardmore. Bowman says,

"Coach Landry told the group that Randy was one of the best line-backers he'd ever had, but of course, everybody knew Randy was a safety. Afterward, Randy told me, 'I doubt he even knows my name.' He said he and Coach Landry had sat next to each other on the plane and that Coach Landry hadn't said a word the whole way. Coach Landry was committed to not being partial to any one player, so he stayed aloof. But this is a man who has put his arm around me as we've walked down the street.

"He's a totally opposite person from what most people in America think. On TV he looked like the coldest man on the face of the earth, but one on one he has a warm heart. And in front of an audience he's totally different. It's not like he's in front of his team. He's a tremendous public speaker. I promise you, he could get $15,000 a night every night if he wanted. I get two or three calls a week for him—civic clubs, charities, nonprofit groups that want to raise funds. He's the most sought-after person you can get. And if he's not available, they want Roger Staubach. Yet Coach Landry has even agreed to go to a little town called Woodward [Oklahoma] for me, and they'll get kids from small high schools in Texas and Colorado and we'll have twenty-five hundred.

"I just think it's Coach Landry aura—he's a man you want to understand and know. People always walk out and say, 'Boy, he's different from what we thought.' "

FCA was saved financially by a program called Tom Landry Associates. A $10,000 gift allows an Associate to attend an annual gathering and rub faiths with Landry. Last year there were more than one hundred Associates—and "four or five" Lifetime Landrys, says Bowman, who give a one-time gift of $100,000. "We bring in the men and their wives, and it's like a little piece of heaven. It's one of those evenings you dream about. They're held spellbound by Coach Landry's comments. He speaks of the FCA as if it's his creation. He says it gave him hope and kept him humble.

"Without him the FCA ministry nationwide would really struggle financially. We're here in the Bible Belt, but back East, they don't know FCA from PTA. But because of Tom Landry, we can go into New York or L.A. and draw a crowd."

Landry has drawn a crowd in twenty-three cities for the Billy Graham Crusade, which calls upon him once or twice a year. He's paid a "token" $500, says Charlie Riggs, a Graham staffer of thirty-eight years who coordinates Landry's appearances. Landry's involvement began, appropriately enough, just before that Dallas Palace, that House of Greed, Texas Stadium, opened in 1971. He served as chairman when the Graham Crusade made a two-week stop in Dallas. Texas Stadium wasn't quite ready, but thanks to Landry's influence an unpaved, muddy parking lot was covered with plywood. The Graham Crusade baptized Texas Stadium.

"We averaged forty-six thousand a night," says Riggs, "and Tom was there every night. I've had him speak to our lay groups [businessmen who help support Crusades financially] in, gosh, Chicago, St. Louis, Tacoma, Anaheim, Little Rock. . . . The Cowboys truly were America's Team. There's not a place in the country where people wouldn't come out to see Tom. The women and children were crazy about him, too. In Rochester his group got so large we had to move to a dome that seated over five thousand. He'll get the guys laughing hysterically one minute, then he'll hit 'em with a punch line: 'The Apostle Paul says to be a winner you must fight the good fight.' Then another joke, then he hits 'em again. Tom's just an outstanding communicator. He never fails to deliver the goods.

"One time in Asheville, he was so sick he could barely speak. But he still tried, and his voice kept cracking to where half the people couldn't even understand him. Then wham! His voice kicked back in and he was incredible. You almost have to believe God's anointings are on the guy.

"He is unashamed to stand up and give his testimony for God. He's one of the best things that ever happened to our lay work. He's certainly as popular as any speaker we've ever had."

Billy Graham on Landry: "I have known Tom Landry for about thirty years and consider him one of the greatest Christian gentlemen I've ever known. . . . He is like a John the Baptist to me. In football I consider him the greatest coach in American history. As long as they play a game called football, he will be remembered and honored. . . . When we opened Texas Stadium, Clint Murchison said our organization showed him how the traffic should flow. As a result he gave us $100,000 for the Crusade. I feel that I had a small part in Texas Stadium and certainly hope it will be called Tom Landry Stadium."

High praise indeed. Yet Landry never grew too big for Dallas. The most powerful religious figure in Dallas, First Baptist pastor W. A. Criswell, says, "Being a pastor, I cannot help but be sensitive to the Christian commitment of men in public places. This is the attribute that so impresses me about Coach Landry. He is ever the faithful and worthy Christian. We have had him in our church many times. I have been with him personally on many occasions. Always he is the soul of Christian excellence. God be praised for his wonderful influence forever."

Donnie Snyder, Dallas area director of FCA, adds only a hint of perspective about Landry the speaker, saying, "Coach Landry wouldn't be categorized as a great orator, but he's very captivating. I've seen him keep everyone on the edge of their seats, whether they're high school students or businessmen with a net worth of over a million dollars. He's not an emotional speaker. He just comes across with tremendous sincerity. His tremendous consistency in his life is what moves you. He doesn't need to be emotional. He has affected literally thousands of lives. I get letters all the time from people who have been deeply affected by him. Coach Landry has talked about how he's gotten weary and worn out and then he receives a letter from someone who says he [Landry] has helped change his life and it makes it all worthwhile. He used the success of the Cowboys in the right way. But then, his success was an offshoot of his Christian faith."

And only the success of the Cowboys made Landry a soul-winning speaker. Forgive my devil's advocate view, but if Landry weren't "Coach Landry of the Cowboys," his delivery would be average at best. I've heard him a couple of times and studied several tapes, including the most requested tape offered by the FCA— Landry's '88 address to the first national FCA conference, in Kansas City. He appears nervous. He says "you know" a lot. He wears glasses and reads much of his speech. He often stumbles over or mispronounces words. Follow is "foller." Perspiration comes out "prehspiration." He says "Garden of Even." His slight speech impediment persists.

Yet perhaps that's all part of Landry's evangelical impact. Suddenly, the Great Stoneface TV image has materialized before a group as "prehspirin'" flesh and blood. He is fallible and humble. He pokes fun at himself and his teams. Here is the Man in the Hat, hatless. He seems bald to the core. You begin to feel genuine emotion from him the final ten minutes of his testimony. Voice rising, speaking faster, he quotes scripture from memory. He opens up, reaches out, touches hearts. Here is Tom Landry saying very simply that America is going straight to hell unless we "run the race set before us by Jesus."

Saying it with a sincerity he couldn't quite summon for his teams.

If anything ever appeared to bother Landry, it was the one image that captivated America—his sideline TV closeups. Stoneface was quick to say that wasn't the real Landry. Fighting irritation, he said, "People based their judgments just on what they saw on the sideline. The way I trained myself to concentrate, I blanked everything else out. You can't show emotion. I trained myself from watching Ben Hogan. He never let his concentration break. I couldn't react emotionally to big plays because I had to be thinking of the next one. To be the best you can be in sports is a matter of blocking out all distractions, positive or negative. If you show emotion in competition even for a second, you'll be ineffective."

Perhaps Landry was uncomfortable with the troubling dichotomy his image presented to Christians. Landry said, "You can tell a Christian just by the glow on his or her face. They don't have to tell you they're a Christian. You just know it." Yet some fans—and most of Landry's players—didn't immediately sense he was a Christian. During football ("bi'ness") hours, Landry didn't often glow.

Perhaps that's one reason Landry, away from football, went out of his way to show his "fun" side. During speeches he told old jokes set in a Cowboy context. They were even funnier because Stoneface was telling them. Stories like: "We were so bad our first year in 1960 that some guys didn't even want to touch the ball. The Bears came to Dallas and beat us, and [Bear coach] George Halas told me they knew every play we were going to run. I said, 'That's impossible. How could you know that?' And he said, 'Every time you broke the huddle, three guys would be laughing like heck and one would be white as a ghost.'"

The resulting guffaws said, "Hey, ol' Tom really can be funny."

His wife Alicia once told me, "I wish people could see the Tommy I see. He can really be fun." She also said, "Away from the field, he's warm and understanding. He always has been better with our children than I have because he keeps calm and has a great understanding." Tom Landry, "Father Knows Best"? It was hard not to believe Alicia, who seemed such a fun person. She radiated. She laughed, even at herself. Yet she constantly told interviewers what a nice person her husband was, as if we needed reminding.

After a while I wondered if she were trying to convince herself. Was it because she didn't know the "heartless coach" she sometimes read about? Did she see only the altar ego? Did she worry about how her husband's image affected hers?

Alicia seemed to enjoy being Mrs. Tom Landry, North Dallas socialite. And according to many Cowboys, Landry enjoyed being Himself, the celebrity coach. Perhaps Landry had some "Hollywood" in him. In 1983, with Alicia's encouragement, he surely surprised some fans by doing an American Express commercial: "You don't know me, but I'm the most famous cowboy in Texas. . . ." Landry, dressed in long-rider cowboy garb, stood in an Old West saloon. He concludes, "You never know when you'll be surrounded by . . . Redskins." And, as he's surrounded by Redskin football players, he warily says, "Howdy."

This opened the locker room door for Dallas-area TV reporters to dare to have fun with Landry. Says former KXAS-TV reporter Mike Fernandez, "One year I wanted to do a light story giving Landry a hair dryer for his birthday. Producers and other reporters at the station said absolutely not. But I had a feeling he'd go along with it, and he did. In fact, when I gave him the hair dryer on camera, he had a funny line. He said, 'And I wanted a curling iron.' Everybody at the station was shocked. I don't think any coach in football would go along with the things Landry did. He'd do just about anything. Bill Parcells, Joe Gibbs, Don Shula—none of those guys would do that stuff. They would have said it made 'em look silly or stupid."

For another Dallas TV station Landry ducked into a phone booth as if he were changing into Superman attire. Landry went along with an April Fools ruse—Cowboys Trade for Draft Rights to John Elway—that created switchboard hysteria. Landry often did goofy bits to help promote radio stations, things like: *Hi, I'm Tom Landry, and even I listen to K-Rock.*

Was this Landry trying to show Christians he can glow? Or was this Landry the Dallas businessman trying to spread his fame so he could cash in the way so many of his players and business partners were? Would Billy Graham make an American Express commercial? Landry began to advertise for many products and companies. Though Landry didn't advertise it, making lots of money did seem important to him. He invested heavily in drilling projects with his oil-man son Tom Jr. He sat on the board of a Dallas corporation. The

Landrys had getaway homes in Austin and Palm Springs. Landry flew his own plane.

Certainly, by age fifty-five in 1980, Landry had earned the right to build a retirement fortune if he chose. But the question was: How could he possibly juggle his religious, business, and football commitments without the latter suffering? How could he devote the fewest year-round hours to football of any NFL coach and continue winning? The answer, of course, was that he couldn't.

When Landry spoke to groups in the early '80s, was he promoting himself as well as his Lord? Did he envision a second $20,000-a-pop career as an after-dinner speaker, a commercial-maker, politician, even an actor? Yes, Landry says he's interested in doing some acting. Lately Landry went even a little more "Hollywood" in a commercial for Quality International motels. A suitcase lying on a motel room bed opens and up pops Landry, guitar in hand. In a fingernails-on-chalkboard twang, he sings, "Mamas, don't let your babies grow up to be . . . Redskins." Does this make Landry seem more human when he delivers his testimony for God?

Maybe so. For sure, Landry was as skilled an image-maker as Schramm. I constantly was surprised by how concerned Landry was with the way he was portrayed in the papers. He often grinned and said, "Aw, I don't have time to read what y'all write." But indications were that he read every discouraging word. Assistants said Landry often remarked about how his moves "came off" in print. Some assistants were reprimanded by Landry for what they said to reporters. Ex-assistant Paul Hackett said, "We had to be concerned constantly with how we were perceived through the newspapers."

Landry dedicated more time to that perception than perhaps any NFL coach. Among writers, locally and nationally, Landry was considered a saint because he promptly returned phone calls and because he answered questions with civility after losses. He wasn't an entertaining interview, in the Texas tradition of Bum Phillips or Darrell Royal. No spontaneous wit or "Lonesome Dove" wisdom. Landry often talked around the question. But the key was, he *talked*. During the season some coaches won't return media calls, and if they do, it's after a writer's deadline. Some coaches will end an interview with the first tough question. After losses, some coaches will try to intimidate or humiliate a questioner. Many coaches, if criticized in print, will criticize the writer face-to-face, even threaten him physically or try to show him up in front of the team. Not Landry.

Day or night, home or away, weekdays or weekends, Landry would give a reporter ten solid minutes, minimum. You could get him in his office, at home, or in his hotel room. No coach ever has been more accessible. No matter how small your paper's circulation or how distant your city, Landry would call you back.

Not once did Landry say one word to me about anything I had written, pro or con. And in the end, my prose often was con. Still, he called back. He talked.

Nearly every longtime pro football writer, from New York to L.A., has a story about how Tom Landry called him back at home. Maybe his wife answered and said, "Honey, it's T-T-Tom L-L-Landry!" One pleasant call to one cynical writer in one faraway city would make for Landry a fan for life. How could you portray Landry as cold and calculating after he was so nice to you on the phone? How could the important Dallas writers criticize Landry when, in front of their peers at press conferences, he always called each one by his first name? This had a powerful effect. It made a writer feel "close" to Landry. It made him feel that ol' Tom had so much respect for his stature and understanding of football that he prefaced each answer with the writer's first name.

Sure, Landry was nice to media people because he had a nice side. But he had another side he didn't want probed or criticized.

By the early '80s I was considered a devil worshiper by some readers for asking Landry, "Does it concern you that your games are played on the Sabbath?" His answer: "I can't control that. It's just part of the bi'ness we're in." I asked, "As a Christian, does the increasing violence of pro football concern you?" His answer, "Well, to a certain extent, sure. But it's just part of this bi'ness. What are you gonna do?"

Landry could say just about anything without anyone saying, "Wait a second." As Staubach was enshrined in the Pro Football Hall of Fame, Landry told the audience, "He had a Navy haircut and a gung-ho attitude. It didn't take long to make a believer out of me." It didn't? That had to be news to Staubach. Of course, by then Landry could have said, "The Cowboys are a nonprofit organization dedicated to the FCA," and many Americans would have nodded and said, "What a guy."

Most people saw and heard only greatness in Landry. Off camera this sometimes seemed to steam Tex Schramm. For his books on Landry and Schramm, former Cowboy beat writer Bob St. John asked Landry what he thought of Schramm. Landry said, "We have no relationship outside of football, but we have been able to work together successfully. Tex is obsessed with the NFL and with the Cowboys winning. Because of this, his whole life pattern is turned in that direction. . . . I look at things differently because I'm a Christian and under God's command. Winning or losing a football game doesn't have that lingering effect on me because of this. If my life depended on the Cowboys winning or being successful, I'm sure I'd get outraged just like Tex does. Your priorities cause you to act a certain way.

"Tex has extremely strong feelings and is very outspoken about the way he feels regarding our place in history. It doesn't mean that much to me. People are always asking me how I want to be remembered, and honestly, I have no feelings about that whatsoever. I enjoy the challenge and I enjoy seeing young men become successful, and, if I can, help them in that direction."

Schramm's legendary fits of profanity? "Sure, I'm a Christian and it bothers me. But I could say that about a lot of players, too. But being around Tex, I know it's just part of his speech pattern, not meant to be taken literally much of the time. That's the pattern of speech in much of our society today. People often don't know what they're saying, what the words mean. It's just a way for them to express themselves."

Is ex-"malcontent" Butch Johnson, a bright man who owns a car dealership in Denver, imagining things when he says, "Tom knew exactly how to play the camera angles during games. He'd turn away and say under his breath, 'Goddamn it.'" Is this one reason Schramm indicated to staffers that Landry could be holier-than-thou?

Landry, on Schramm, to St. John: "God is forgiving and everybody has the potential of going to heaven. He has to be, for somebody like me to have a chance. When Jesus was on earth, He didn't associate with believers but with sinners. Now, I'm not saying I do that. I'm just saying that as a Christian you have to be open to any person, regardless of whether they have religious beliefs or not, because they have the possibility of becoming Christians."

Was Landry rationalizing that his sin-sational organization

needed his influence? If so, why did he allow Schramm to create the Vegas-style Cheerleaders and use seductive centerfoldlike poses of them to help sell the team's weekly newspaper? Landry told me, "That's Tex's area. But I'd like to see a little more wholesome image." Landry quietly voiced his displeasure to Russ Russell, who shot the pictures for the *Cowboys Weekly*. But Landry never made a stand with Schramm.

By the early '80s I sometimes wondered why Landry the Christian didn't walk away from football. What a classy statement he could have made. If making history truly meant nothing to him, what was left to prove? In a 1980 interview Landry waxed sheepishly humble and said, "Gosh, I've survived two decades and that's more than my allotment. I'm on borrowed time now."

After Clint Murchison gave Landry a $2 million bonus in 1983, how much more money did he desire from coaching? Why not become a full-time evangelist and entrepreneur? Couldn't he sense the decay in his talent and schemes? The moral decay in his organization? Landry never said his NFL purpose was to preach or proselytize to his business partners or players. He was careful not to force his faith on those he worked with. So if Landry's Christian influence helped Schramm and Brandt, it only was to operate as Jim Bakker types—as Tom Landry Associates who believed a sucker was reborn every minute.

Asked who would replace Landry, Brandt said, "It's tough to replace God."

Had Landry the coach become addicted to his adulation? Dallas worshiped its heroes as if they were gods. For Dallas, Landry was the ultimate status symbol, its greatest claim to fame. As an armchair shrink, I sometimes wondered if Landry were suffering from delusions of grandeur—not so much his but his millions of fans'. If, every day, you read and heard that you were God's Coach, wouldn't you start believing you were infallible? If you were just a guy from Mission who nearly became an insurance salesman, and suddenly Billy Graham was calling you his "John the Baptist," wouldn't it be easy to lose sight of who you were?

Did Landry believe his God—who had saved him from bomber crashes and directed him to the Cowboys—would keep making him a winner? In his heart of hearts, did Landry believe that the more he spread God's word, the more his team would win?

Or was Landry simply too proud and egotistical to give up being a "genius" coach?

Was he prepared to subject himself to more and more intelligent players who weren't afraid to ask why?

Listen again to ex-safety Dextor Clinkscale, a Christian and an '80s team leader cited by Landry for his intelligence. Clinkscale says, "By 1980 we were through with the great and wonderful '70s. Roger was gone. Players were starting to understand that P.R. could be used for personal gain as well as management gain. They were realizing that if you just blindly played your technique you could wind up in surgery the way so many of the '70s Cowboys did—that there were ways to preserve yourself. Players were saying, 'What is Tom *doing?* Why is he keeping all these old coaches around him?' We were getting negativity from the outside just like the Raiders got—other teams hating us. But unlike the Raiders, we had negativity within, too. The Raiders' management told them, 'Be on time for practice and let's win the game.' We were told, 'Be on time, keep your fingernails clean, and wipe your feet on the mat before you enter this rinky-dink practice field.' "

So by the '80s, could Landry be a Christian coach? Clinkscale:

Can a corporate CEO be a Christian? A Donald Trump? I suppose it can be done, but the nature of the sport is so violent that it takes you back to Roman times. We weren't people. We were gladiators. Is it Christian for me to want to blast the crap out of somebody for the pleasure of those in the stands? It's not the same as, say, hitting a tennis ball with the same type of fury. The only thing we didn't do was kill each other, though we sometimes caused paralysis. At my last NFLPA meeting [Clinkscale was the Players Association representative for the Cowboys] we discussed how the average life expectancy for an ex-NFL player is around fifty-two or fifty-three. You're doing so much banging of the brain and tearing of the limbs and damaging of the organs, and who knows what cancers you were causing when you ingested all the things they wanted you to ingest. For example, Coach Landry was down on [wide receiver] Doug Donley because he wouldn't take an injection and play with pain. I told Donley, "Don't take one. Don't worry about it." He took one, anyway.

In my dealings with all the people I met in Dallas, the one I don't know as a person is Tom Landry. There are certain people, if they don't tell you they're a Christian, you just know it by the way they act, even in their business. But *he* was just a football coach, and whatever went along with that. In his dealings with players, they often called him a liar—a Zeus, a mythological god, a *false* god. But to me he was a coach with no exceptions, a coach whose strengths were very exaggerated. You know, sometimes I wished I had just walked up to him at rookie orientation and introduced myself and gone on back home and held on to my image of him.

For years people on TV said Jim Bakker was a Christian, but his friends knew he didn't always do Christian things. But just looking at TV I presumed Tom Landry was a Christian because Pat Summerall and John Madden were always talking about his relationship with Jesus Christ. As players, what was said on TV and written in the papers was all we knew. He was that detached from us. When I'd hear people say what a great Christian speaker Coach Landry was, I'd think, "Man, I wish he'd talk to us like that." Maybe that's what was missing.

Among players, Landry's '70s response to that criticism was getting older than the King James version: "If you get close to players, you allow them to enhance their weaknesses. My job is to get players to do what they don't want to do."

To die for his cause? As the '80s began, Landry was about to be openly challenged. No more Staubach—no more leader, buffer, miracle-maker. The good-ol'-boy white players and "good nigger" blacks—the compliant cogs—were dying out. Landry soon would lose his creative motivators, assistants Dan Reeves and Mike Ditka. Landry alone would have to face the team-wrecking issues of antiquated systems, fair pay, racial tension, cocaine/alcohol/steroid abuse, and lust run amok.

Landry often would fail and flail. He would spread blame as he did God's word. Sometimes I would think, "If only he had retired on top in 1980."

Yet, as I reviewed the tape of Landry's '88 FCA address, parts of it meant more to me because of his coaching collapse. On the tape he reads one of his favorite quotes, from Harry Truman: "The way you endure that which you must endure is more important than the crisis itself." And it certainly was startling to hear him say, "We have a tremendous challenge in FCA to overcome a devastating problem with alcohol, drugs, and sexual permissiveness. I don't know whether God let this go to give us a chance to see if we're up to the challenge. But I guarantee you we have the best chance today in FCA to do something about it."

Landry's organization was all but fueled by alcohol, drugs, and sexual permissiveness. Was crusading against these evils through FCA Landry's way to atone?

He concludes, emotion rising, "We must get on the campuses of every high school and junior high with an alternate life-style—to say, hey, there's another way, and a better way, for you."

Was there a better way for Landry to become what he is today? When Landry was fired in 1989, Billy Graham aide Charlie Riggs wrote Landry a note, saying, "God has prepared you through the Dallas Cowboys for your greatest ministry—to share your faith with the world. Now you can have some of the best times of your life."

But first Landry suffered. He was overwhelmed. He compromised.

Did the end justify all? You make the call.

10

THE SPRING sun was disappearing in a yellow-orange blaze. The evening breeze was gentle and peaceful. The flowers and crickets had come back to life outside Danny White's two-story home, which was far removed from anything "Dallas." White lived almost out in the country, in Wylie, near a fishing pond, a thirty- or forty-minute drive north of the Cowboys' practice field in North Dallas. There were a few other nice homes near White's, but they were up the road a piece. White wanted to give his wife Jo Lynn and their three children a life away from Dallas Cowboy football. After practices and games, White took flight.

It was May 1980. Roger Staubach had retired, saying, "The Cowboys won't miss a beat without me. Danny White is a great quarterback."

Staubach's humility and blessing only increased White's plight. After four seasons of backing up Captain America, White now was expected to become Staubach. After four fairly quiet years out in the P.R. boondocks, White's life was about to belong to every Cowboy fan. Dallas was about to have White for breakfast, lunch, and Sunday dinner. Perhaps no position in sports was more scrutinized and criticized than the Cowboy quarterback was in Dallas through the 1980s. White was about to feel white-hot heat few athletes ever have.

It's doubtful even Staubach could have followed Staubach. In the early '70s Staubach didn't take over the NFL's most loved/hated team performing before the world's most spoiled fans. White did, in 1980.

That perfect spring evening I had driven out to Wylie to interview White about how his life had already changed. As he walked me back out to my car, he paused near a small vegetable garden. "That's my garden," he said. "You never know when you might need it. There could be a war, a famine . . ."

White would need his garden many times through the next eight seasons. His coach would need emergency rations, too. If ever Tom Landry had a soft spot for a player, it was Danny White. Landry sometimes referred to Danny as Dan. That was Landry: formalizing a nickname into a pet name. Dan White was Landry's kind of quarterback. He had a coach's mind—the perfect extension of Landry's. He had a much deeper grasp of the offense than Meredith or Staubach ever did. White hadn't made a single wave as a four-year backup, and he didn't rock Landry's boat as the starter. He didn't question game plans to the media or privately to Landry. He all but left polished apples on Landry's lectern. Landry rewarded that loyalty with stubborn loyalty. Landry would stick with White through thin and thinner. White, like Landry, was a company man. White, like Landry, was a terrific punter. White was a Landrylike competitor.

White was like a son or maybe grandson to Landry. Oh, how Landry wanted White to show the world he could play in Staubach's league. What tormented Landry was that White clearly was a more productive and efficient quarterback than Saint Roger. White's first season as starter was the greatest season for Landry's offense. The Cowboys led the league in scoring and set team records for points and touchdowns. White's twenty-eight TD passes broke by one Staubach's club record, set the season before. No doubt White moved the team better than Staubach. He almost always was heady and steady. White made all kinds of nice plays.

But Staubach made *the* play. It was as simple as that: Wilford Daniel White couldn't make the Hall of Fame play. His Hail Mary often turned into a Hell No. If you measure White by normal NFL standards, he was a very good quarterback. Measure him by Staubach's, and he lost three straight last-step-to-the-Super-Bowl games. In Dallas in the early '80s that made you a loser, son.

Number 11 was at his worst when he tried to force a throw, to will victory the way Number 12 did. White often took even greater risks than Staubach. But White didn't have Staubach's arm or magic. White had derring-don't. White had a flair for the disastrously dramatic—the interception returned for the game-breaking touchdown, the sacked fumble near his goal line. The Master of Disaster, I nicknamed him in 1983, and it stuck. Danny White could turn quickly into Danny Black, in the clutch and in the locker room.

While Staubach could unite and ignite teammates—especially blacks—White could turn them off and against him. The team had trusted Staubach as a leader and performer. Staubach didn't just *say* he was faithful to his wife or that he did unto others; he was and did. He didn't just *tell* the media that winning was more important to him than personal glory or financial gain; he proved it.

White never won his team's trust. No matter how many great "reads" and accurate throws he made, too many teammates feared his worst-case interceptions or fumbles. For White, throwing a pass through the eye of a needle would have been easier than getting to Cowboy heaven. Oh, he didn't make fatal mistakes every week or even every playoff game. But by Staubach standards, it seemed that way. White had good games lost in tragic endings. Staubach's poor games were remembered only as miraculous comebacks.

Following Staubach, White could manage only a locker room reputation as a coach's and GM's pet. He was known as Tom Jr. or Tex Jr. Landry, in fact, helped split the team racially by testifying for his quarterback. White wound up in court after striking a 205-pound high school football player. The seventeen-year-old said White punched him in the nose. White said he used the back of his hand "to enforce my comments." The kid, said White, had driven recklessly, endangering the lives of White and his three children, who were riding in White's van. At a stop light White got out of his van and after an angry exchange struck the kid through the window of his car. "My comments," said White, "got no reaction whatsoever."

Landry testified, "Under the same type of stress situation that Danny was under, I might do the same thing." He would? Instead of turning the other cheek, Landry would smack a seventeen-year-old's? Landry's words alone probably would have cleared White. The jury ruled in White's favor.

Yet Landry and Schramm reprimanded a contingent of black (and a few white) players for missing part of a work day to testify as character witnesses for Ron Springs, a black tailback respected as a "gamer" who made clutch plays. Springs was considered a malcontent by management because he was an outspoken resident of "the ghetto," an area of lockers populated mostly by blacks. Springs could do hilarious dramatizations of Martin Luther King's "I have a dream" speech, and perhaps management feared just how far he would lead a Tony Dorsett or Everson Walls, who looked up to him. Springs was nicknamed "Idi" because he looked something like Idi Amin. He had football wisdom. He knew how to win. But he could act foolishly away from football.

He was charged with assaulting a female police officer during an altercation in a top-dollar topless bar called the Million Dollar Saloon, where many Dallas jocks went to see and be seen. Several witnesses testified that Springs hit the officer "by accident." He was found guilty of resisting arrest and given a probated sentence and fine.

Afterward Springs said there "isn't a plane fast enough to get me out of Dallas." He finished his career in Tampa Bay. Later, when I asked Dallas native Walls where Springs was living, he said, "He moved to Cleveland [Springs had played at Ohio State]. He wanted to start a business. You know a black can't make it as a small-business man in Dallas."

In Landry's eyes, probably, the Springs and White incidents were apples and oranges, rotten and ripe. But to many black players, the reprimand and perceived double standard ate away at their trust of their coach and quarterback.

White's leadership credibility may have been ruined for good during the 1982 players' strike. First, he blasted the owners, saying, "They can't be trusted." Then, as the strike wore on, White met with Tex Schramm, a leader of the owners, and told reporters he thought he and Schramm had come up with a strike-breaking compromise. Ed Garvey, negotiating for the Players Association, openly scoffed at White, saying, "I understand Schramm is negotiating with Danny White. If they resolve all the issues, is that binding?" White wasn't even the Cowboys' player representative; Robert Newhouse was. Newhouse had flown to Washington for an NFLPA strategy session. White flew to Washington and was allowed to sit in. White later was accused by teammates of walking straight out of that meeting, calling Schramm, and divulging inside information in the name of settling the strike. Many Cowboys were furious with White for allegedly jeopardizing a cause for which they had sacrificed nearly eight weeks of salary. But black Cowboys were especially resentful. To them it appeared Danny "Too" White had stepped in because he thought Newhouse, who is black, couldn't handle the job. Newhouse had been "shown up."

Word around the locker room was that White had sold out to management in return for contract favors. White vehemently denied all charges, but the damage was done. He wasn't a tackle or a linebacker, he was the quarterback. Big Brother was *quarterbacking* them. Philadelphia linebacker John Bunting, a member of the NFLPA executive committee, said, "It's going to take Danny White a long time to get respect from the rank-and-file membership of the union."

A marked team had a marked quarterback. And White was going to fill Staubach's winged cleats?

Via minicams, White projected a "nice young man" image, but several teammates questioned whether White, a Mormon, was as religious as he said in interviews or if he measured up to his 1982 Dallas Father of the Year award. They wondered if he was a national Boy Scout leader "for show." They even talked about his "spooky" eyes, which appeared to reflect in bright lights almost like a cat's. One eye sometimes seemed to wander. A telltale eye?

Some teammates thought White spent far too much time on his many business ventures. White, they said, was mostly in it for White. Staubach's one-for-all Cowboys were becoming every man for himself.

Given all this, maybe White didn't have a prayer. Says Butch Johnson, "We became a team of stars. Everybody went on his own image campaign."

But oh, what stars the 1980 team had. White was surrounded by an embarrassment of prime-timers in their prime. By veterans who had learned and made peace with Landry's systems. By receivers Butch Johnson, Drew Pearson, Tony Hill, Billy Joe DuPree, Doug Cosbie, Preston Pearson, and Ron Springs. By tailback Tony Dorsett and fullback Robert Newhouse. By Pro Bowlers Pat Donovan and Herb Scott in the offensive line.

The defensive line—a Doomsday II of Ed Jones, Randy White, John Dutton, and Harvey Martin—remained one of football's most feared. Cowboy Mystique was at its Transylvanian peak. "Sometimes," Charlie Waters said, "it does seem like we could just throw our starred helmets out there and the other team would fold up."

So, even without Staubach, it was no upset when the Cowboys blew out the Rams 34–13 in a wild-card playoff game at Texas Stadium. But a week later the Falcons were well on their way to upsetting the Cowboys in Atlanta. The Falcons led 24–10 after three quarters, and 27–17 with under four minutes left. Twice White plugged into the Hail Mary connection, finding Drew Pearson for touchdowns from twenty-three and fourteen yards, the latter with forty-two seconds left. Cowboys 30–27. Roger who?

My editor called the press box in Atlanta and said, "I hope you're going to write that Danny White has proven he's better than Staubach."

Gosh, I said, maybe we should wait a week or two.

Unfortunately for White, that minor miracle was his first and last. The following Sunday in Philadelphia, in thirty-below windchill, the small-handed White couldn't seem to get a grip on the ball or the Eagles. White went twelve of thirty-one for 127 yards. He was intercepted once and fumbled once, at the Cowboy 11-yard line. The Eagles were Super Bowl-bound, 20–7. As Eagles coach Dick Vermeil said, "Everything I do all year is geared to beating Dallas." Yes, Vermeil would "burn out" prematurely, but that year Vermeil and his staff outworked and outmotivated Landry and his. That blue-collar Philly team simply out-emotioned the Metallic Blue. Said Eagles kicker Tony Franklin, a native of Fort Worth, "You cannot believe how much this team and this city hate the Dallas Cowboys. There was simply no way we were going to lose this game."

You wonder if even Staubach, following himself, could have found a way that day. Curious, wasn't it, that Tom Landry, one of America's most beloved figures, coached its most resented team.

By the early '80s the "America's Team" distinction had sonic-boomeranged. The mirror had cracked. White captured the crumbling essence: "We all benefit from being America's Team and Dallas Cowboys [in marketability], but we pay for it on Sundays." This

1981 Charlie Waters quote easily could have been construed as typical Cowboy whining: "It was bad enough without the 'America's Team' thing. Every team already hates us because we always win. I'm not asking for a cruise when we go out there. I'm just asking them not to hate us. No matter who we play, we seem to get the best performances out of everybody [opponents]."

That quote spoke columns—critical newspaper columns in rival cities—about why the Cowboys were despised. Waters said, ". . . because we always win." But the Cowboys didn't always win. The Steelers had won four Super Bowls in the '70s, including two against the Cowboys. With help from Landry-Schramm-Brandt the Cowboys had brainwashed themselves into believing they won every game. The refs could steal victory from them or it could be too cold to play high-tech football or a star or two could be hurt, but the Cowboys always won. The Bible tells us so.

That arrogance inspired another Cowboy first: *The Semi-Official Dallas Cowboys Haters' Handbook*, which sold as briskly as head-bobbing Cowboy dolls. Imagine: an entire book for people who didn't like the Cowboys.

Imagine the near-riots Schramm caused in rival cities with these Texisms: "We lead and others seem to follow." And: "I like the attitude of Babe Ruth, pointing to the stands, then doing it." And: "Many members of the national media want us to lose, but they sure don't want us to go away." And: "It's one thing to win a lot of football games. It's another to win them in an aura that reeks of class." And: "I get very upset when people call us arrogant. I just don't see it." Would the NFL's parity-based system of reverse-order drafting and scheduling undermine a dynasty? Schramm: "You can't legislate intelligence."

Would you believe Schramm redesigned the Cowboy uniforms after videotaping a male model at Texas Stadium to see exactly how they'd look on TV? Yes, you would. Schramm rejected forty different shades before selecting his fantasy blue. Schramm put numbers on the hips of new pants because "if Calvin can put his name on the pockets, we can put our numbers on the hip." The pants were fashioned of a material that "has greater light reflectivity, which gives it that true silver glow." Tony Dorsett's initial response? "They kinda look like ladies' satin pants."

This response came from Joe Gordon, P.R. director of the Steelers: "The Cowboys seem to be really hung up on image, whereas the

Steelers are more concerned with the end result, which is winning. . . . The constant hype? We feel we're past that level."

Landry said, "I'm sure teams like Pittsburgh and L.A. resent
the 'America's Team' thing. If I was on another team, I'd resent it,
too. But we'll live with it."

Why didn't Landry tell Schramm to put a cork in the self-
celebrating? Okay, that was "Tex's area," but it was drastically af-
fecting Landry's. The truth was, Landry's superiority complex
rivaled Schramm's. Pat Toomay told *Sports Illustrated* of a talk
Landry gave the team in 1973. "He said, 'I can now walk down the
street in New York and I'm recognized.' Blaine Nye looked at me
and said, 'What are we shooting for next, Europe?' "

Gil Brandt may have been shooting for the world. Brandt was
so powerful that he was able to move the annual photo session
blowout for the *Playboy* preseason All-America team (chosen mostly
by Brandt) to Dallas, where he and his lab assistants could have
more time to focus their microscopes. The Redskins and Eagles filed
formal complaints with the league office, alleging Brandt had ad-
ministered, in violation of NFL rules, an electronic hand-eye coor-
dination test to potential draftees. The league office investigated and
said there was no violation . . . which sparked new accusations that
Schramm ran the league office.

Then-Cardinal quarterback Neil Lomax told me this story:
"When I was in Dallas before the draft, Gil and I really became
buddies, I thought. He let me take his car, and I met his family and
had these nice dinners with him. He told me, 'If you're still there
when our turn comes, we'll take you.' So I shared a lot of myself with
him, and I agreed to take one of these psychological-type tests,
which I'd been told was against the rules.

"Well, I was still there when the Cowboys' turn came, and they
didn't take me [opting for offensive lineman Howard Richards]. I
had to wonder if Gil had compiled all that information on me just to
use to the Cowboys' advantage when they played against me."

As he traveled, Brandt was treated with nearly as much awe as
evangelist Landry. When Gil Brandt of the Dallas Cowboys visited
a school, he almost always was given special access to the players and
VIP press box treatment during games. How many other scouts
emerged from limos? Brandt did. Brandt knew and saw all. Brandt
was Captain Computer. Brandt said, "You know, everyone laughed
at us when we first started using computers. Now everyone else uses

them, too. The computer gives us an edge—just a little edge, a 5 to 10 percent advantage."

Brandt loved to tell writers in New York and L.A. about how the Cowboys' computer system was created originally by a shy little man from Aligarh, India, named Salam Qureishi. Salam, said Brandt, chuckling, "didn't know whether a football was full of air or feathers." Oh, those Wowboys.

They actually programmed a computer to rank draftees. A prospect was given a number grade by scouts in a number of areas. For example, a prospect might be graded high in "coachability" but low in "explosion." His cumulative score would tell Brandt and Landry how he measured against thousands of potential cogs. Yet many fans were led to believe the Cowboy Computer ran the organization the way Hal, the on-board computer, took over the spaceship in *2001: A Space Odyssey*. The image: On Draft Day the Computer summoned Brandt and said, "Howard Richards."

Of course, the reality was that a computer was only as all-knowing as the scouts who fed it. As Bear GM Jim Finks said, "I don't know if the Cowboys actually were the first to use a computer, but they were definitely the first to brag about it."

I don't know if Brandt was the first to snooker struggling franchises out of future draft choices. But he and Schramm definitely were the first to brag about it.

By the late '70s, with the draft moved back four months to around May 1, Brandt was losing his edge and touch. Now every team had the time and spent the money to find and evaluate Death Valley State's John Dough, who ran a 4.2 40. No longer was Brandt a kid in his own candy store. Now all teams lined up at the same counter, and Brandt was left reaching for (Milk) Duds. No more secrets. Like everyone else, Brandt was forced to sense hidden stardom in a Top 50 draftee who might or might not be worth a first-round choice. Brandt was about to be exposed as no more than an info-gathering Draftnik.

But for a while Brandt beat the system by beating gullible GMs out of their top draft choices. Ed Jones was made possible in 1974 by Houston, which gave its choice for used cars Tody Smith and Billy Parks. Randy White came courtesy of the Giants in 1975, for Craig Morton. And Tony Dorsett was a gift from Seattle in 1977, for the Cowboys' late first-round choice and three seconds. Oh, did Brandt and Schramm ever expand their chests and egos over the rape of

Seattle. The Seahawk franchise may still have been trying to get even in 1988 when it traded left tackle Ron Essink to the Cowboys, who were desperate for a left tackle. The Cowboys gave Seattle a fifth-round choice, no small price. Essink played briefly in one exhibition game, walked in the next morning, and retired. The league office ruled that Seattle could keep the fifth-round pick. A setup? Did Seattle know he had decided to retire and asked him to play one last little game? Knowing Brandt, I wouldn't put it past Seattle.

In 1982 Brandt said, "You know, it's extremely hard for us to make a trade anymore. We used to pick up draft choices from lots of teams, but now they're all trying to do the same thing."

What Brandt didn't say, or acknowledge, was that many teams wouldn't even return his calls. Says Cowboy scout John Wooten, "There was just too much animosity for us to even talk trade with lots of teams." Where was Landry?

"That's Gil's area," Landry said.

What did Billy Graham Crusaders or FCA faithful think if they saw the 1982 story in *Sports Illustrated*, "Dallas Can Have 'Em"? Subtitle: "The Cowboys may be hot stuff in Big D, but in the rest of the country America's Team seems to have attracted a multitude of haters turned off by its attitude, image, and success." Writer Paul Zimmerman opened with this exchange: " 'Who's the most hated team in the NFL?' Raider owner Al Davis asks. 'The Raiders,' you answer. 'Wrong,' says Davis. 'We're the second-most. We'll never catch the Cowboys.' "

Selected passages: Former 49ers quarterback John Brodie said, "The Cowboys invalidate the thing they promote the most and the thing they have the least of, and that's class."

Mike Manuche, New York restaurateur: "In the old days they had stand-up guys, Lilly, Renfro, Garrison. Now it seems like they're all a bunch of moaners."

CBS announcer Tom Brookshier: "Dallas fans never feel the Cowboys have lost a game. It's always that the referees screwed 'em or the Good Lord looked the other way or something. It's the toughest place to broadcast a game. Sagebrush, U.S.A. Their fans don't know football, they just know something's wrong if the Cowboys aren't winning by two TDs. . . . You do a game in Detroit, say, the people there have seen a little football. You can't BS 'em. But try to tell the truth in Dallas, and you'll find some frozen hemlock in your nachos."

CBS announcer John Madden: "The thing I hate about doing one of their games is that they lead the league in lobbies. Normally, there'll be thirty or forty people milling around the lobby where a team's staying. When the Cowboys are in a hotel, it'll be more like five hundred. You can't even get in the damn dining room. You have to call room service."

Beano Cook, then with CBS, to Schramm: "You're one of the two most efficient organizations in the twentieth century." The other? "The Third Reich."

Finally, more from Al Davis: "The Cowboys are wired to the league office, everyone knows that. And you can bet every game official knows that, too. If there's one team that's going to get a break, it's Dallas—on the calls, on the scheduling, on the Competition Committee."

Lord, even Al Davis, the NFL's Darth Raider, was painting the Cowboys black. Sometimes I was, too, while picking the hemlock from my nachos.

In 1981 I wrote a column in which I didn't exactly treat the Cowboy Cheerleaders as Dallas debutantes. I hinted these girls were being taken for a ride by a well-known stranger, Tex Schramm.

The column was inspired by a tip and by a flip comment from Charlie Waters, the Flex's sex symbol.

First, I received an anonymous phone tip from a guy who said he worked at Texas Stadium. He claimed some sort of peephole had been built into the Cheerleaders' dressing room at Texas Stadium. I asked around but couldn't find a stadium official who did anything but laugh at the notion. Only recently, reading Jane Wolfe's book, *The Murchisons*, did I run across a little revelation that made me wonder if I should have more doggedly pursued the 1981 tip. Wolfe writes: "After leasing space to a health club, Clint [Murchison] built a one-way mirror into the women's dressing room and invited his buddies to come by and watch the women undress."

Hmmm.

But Waters' comment definitely opened my eyes. He said, "Most football teams have cheerleaders. Our Cheerleaders just happen to have a football team."

The Cheerleaders were that big, internationally. They made TV movies and "Love Boat" appearances and performed all over the world. This had to be P. T. Schramm's greatest achievement. He was selling the world on "wholesome" sleaze. Innocent Texas beauties who thought they had won a Miss America's Team contest were all but dancing in Schramm's Million Dollar Saloon. These All-American girls were actually all-binocular. Adjusting his field glasses, the husband could say to his wife, "Don't bother me now, honey, I'm focusing on the tight end."

Right. Even in the '80s the Cheerleaders wore seriously '70s halter tops of silvery blue that covered just barely enough but left the midriff bare all the way down to white hot pants. The white go-go boots gave the costume that Vegas showgirl touch. "A touch of class," Schramm called the Cheerleaders. Some of his red-blooded male fans dropped the "c" and "l."

The Cheerleaders practiced for hours. But not once did I hear any fan say, "What a terrific routine." The Cheerleaders could really shake those, uh, pom-poms. But they did not lead cheers. Not once did I see them do, "Two bits, four bits, six bits a dollar, all for the Cowboys, stand up and holler." Besides, how many Cowboy fans would have stood up and hollered?

The Leerleaders, I called them.

And they were as important as Landry and Staubach to the national impact of America's Team. The Cheerleaders sent a subliminal message to pro football lovers: You can have your cheesecake and drink beer, too. Schramm's scam: Wrap showgirls around helmeted gladiators and watch the TV ratings rise.

But did he simply hire girls who looked vaguely "nasty," as the Raiders and Eagles did? Those squads led the league in cleavage and mascara. Those women seemed to accept that their role was simply to shimmy and lean toward the crowd. No, Schramm sold Texas girls on what an honor it was to represent their team, state, and country. After a while you would have believed Florence Nightingale and Madame Curie had been Cheerleaders.

After I wrote my column I received an impassioned letter from one of Schramm's maidens of honor. I withhold this Cheerleader's name as a public service to her. In part, it said, "Every girl in Texas dreams of being a Dallas Cowboy Cheerleader. The proudest day of my life was when I made the squad. If you could feel what it feels like to be performing on the field at Texas Stadium, you would be ashamed of the trash you have written. The Cheerleaders are tasteful and wholesome and we work many, many hours. People love us wherever we go. We have become an American institution just like Coach Landry and the Cowboys. We spread 'cheer.' We visit hospitals and our troops overseas. If you'll check your press guide [yes, the Cheerleaders and their occupations were listed], you'll find that every Cheerleader is an upstanding, intelligent member of the community. I am living every girl's dream, Mr. Bayless, and failures like you are just jealous."

I wish this upstanding, intelligent woman could have sat in on the meetings when Schramm first fantasized about his Cheerleaders concept. A source says, "Tex knew some people would be adamantly opposed. Tom was never consulted. But Tex talked about how, when a network telecast went to commercial, the camera usually looked for a quick shot of a 'honey' in the stands. So Tex said, 'Instead, the camera will spend five seconds on one of our girls on the sideline,' which is exactly what started happening. Tex said, 'That's how we'll build our image.'

"Remember, the late '70s were an era of the Farrah Fawcett posters, with the nipples showing through the suit. So Tex and Gil were the first guys to say, 'We're going to do a sexy poster, too.' They did a 'team picture' of the Cheerleaders and Gil sent thousands of 'em all over the country. Their goal was to get a Cheerleader poster up in every locker room of every college in the country, including NAIA and Division II. They wanted it tasteful, but with cleavage and asses. They wanted it provocative. They succeeded in blanketing the country with that poster."

Listen, dear Cheerleader, to current Cowboy P.R. director Greg Aiello: "The word Tex said most was 'unique.' And he really focused on the Cheerleaders. . . . The typical notion of cheerleaders was leading cheers. But obviously, half the big deal of looking at cheerleaders was that they were the prettiest girls. So Tex said, okay, let's put 'em in sexy costumes. Let's turn 'em into showgirls.

"So there were a whole lot of ways to like the Cowboys. If you were religious, you could like Tom and tune out Tex and the Hollywood stuff. If you liked Cheerleaders and flashy uniforms, you could tune out Tom."

Or, if you were only outwardly religious, you could quietly focus your binoculars on the "tight end." Yet Schramm wasn't even outwardly religious. As it says on page three of his authorized biography, *Tex!*: "Connie [Schramm's secretary] is a mature, attractive woman, as Schramm would have his secretaries be, as he would have women in general be. Schramm does not try to temper nor, certainly, hide his affection for attractive women. This is personified in many ways, such as his interest in Cowboy Cheerleaders and his friendship with former Miss America Phyllis George. He can be very egotistical and, certainly, is vain."

For years I heard stories from Cowboy staffers and media followers about Schramm and Suzanne Mitchell, a secretary of Schramm's who became director of the Cheerleaders. Over twelve years, I heard three of Schramm's P.R. men mention his relationship with Mitchell several times, as did three front-office secretaries, a scout, numerous players, and many of the newspaper, TV, and radio guys close to Schramm. I also heard for years at training camp about a California woman Schramm knew. Numerous times on the sidelines at morning practice, I heard morning-after stories from media people who had been out with Schramm's party the night before. The stories about Suzanne Mitchell and about the California woman became part of Cowboy lore, so I was never quite sure where the facts stopped and the fiction began. With P. T. Schramm, you never knew. For all I knew, Schramm allowed the stories to grow along with his mystique. Just as Brandt seemed to like college coaches to believe he could provide them with just about anything, perhaps Schramm promoted his macho legend. Perhaps it was no more than winking locker-room talk, exaggerated boasts. For sure, the stories deepened the respect for Schramm among some of my colleagues who considered Texas E. a real man's man.

A staffer who worked closely with Schramm for several years and who knows Mitchell well says, "It [Tex and Suzanne] was always a rumor around the office. But there was never anything to say definitively they were. Suzanne was a very bright business person, and she became his right-hand woman. She wasn't afraid to speak her mind and challenge him, and he was attracted to that. She even finalized the player contracts—you know, dotted the i's and crossed the t's. She conducted a lot of Tex's personal business. She was present at every staff meeting. Sometimes when something happened [a team crisis], she'd go in Tex's office and lock the door and be in there for hours, so people wondered. But she was like his Rock of Gibraltar.

"But she would often voluntarily talk about it [the rumors] like it really bothered her. She'd be so defensive about it that it made you wonder."

Frankly, the Tex-Suzanne rumors became pretty routine stuff
in the torrid context of so many other internal affairs I began to see
or hear about. "The Cowboys had the most incestuous front office in
the NFL," says a writer who has covered the Cowboys and the NFL
for twelve years. No doubt every NFL team—every corporation—
has its share of similar situations. But it was hard for me to get used
to seeing all this "Bob and Carol and Ted and Dallas" within Tom
Landry's organization. One secretary was known for her parking
garage liaisons with a high-ranking team official. Another secretary
was juggling affairs with a scout, a running back, and a safety. Two
married staffers had affairs with training camp secretaries. On and
on it went. While most Landry fans probably thought the Cowboy
offices to be something of an all-business monastery, they were
something else. Cowboy staffers worked and played hard.

In the later '80s, Cowboy owner Bum Bright began to hear the
stories about Schramm and Mitchell and Schramm and the woman
in California. Bright did not approve. But he says, "I hear about
these banks [in downtown Dallas] where just about everybody on
the board has something on the side and often get the women jobs
right there in the banks. I guess it's just the way things are. As long
as the personal doesn't get in the way of the professional, what are
you going to do?" All Bright knew for sure about Mitchell was that
she kept many important Cowboy documents locked in her desk and
that Schramm once talked to him about a home loan for Mitchell.

In the early '80s, Mitchell had longish, straight, bleached hair,
wore sultry makeup, and had the body of a Cheerleader. Schramm,
perhaps, had made her dream come true when he made her director
of the Cheerleaders. For sure, she became famous from the many
newspaper, magazine, and TV stories done about her and her girls.
She must have felt like the most powerful woman in Texas. Suzanne
told Sports Illustrated, "I run it as a little football club. We have our
training camp, our tryout, our cuts. We study films, and we have
three or four hours of training—rehearsals—every night. This past
spring we had close to two thousand girls audition. . . . I understand that where little girls used to dream of being Miss America,
now they dream of becoming a cheerleader for the Cowboys instead."

Suzanne even ran a Little Miss Dallas Cowboys Cheerleader
contest, which annually attracted around forty thousand entrants.
Only in Texas. There was a line of Cheerleaders outfits for children,

along with costume jewelry, coloring books, trading cards, and a Cheerleaders book called *Decade of Dreams.*

Cheerleaders probably felt overpaid at $15 a game.

Only when the Cheerleaders appeared outside Texas did they occasionally draw protest. Once, trying to boost sagging attendance, athletic department officials at Fresno State invited the Cheerleaders to perform at halftime of the Fresno State–Weber State game. A member of the FSU faculty, unfortunately named Rhita Flake, gathered one hundred signatures from faculty members protesting the Cheerleaders' visit. Flake said, "Their primary function is apparently to provide sexually aggressive entertainment for male sports fans. We believe this is demeaning to women and a counterproductive use of university resources."

Suzanne Mitchell actually told the *Dallas Morning News:* "Obviously, they are not fully abreast of the facts. . . . The first thing I'd like to ask her is what has *she* ever done for her country? [The Cheerleaders had visited military bases in Korea each of the last three Christmases.] We helicoptered into the DMZ in weather twenty below. I'd like to ask her what's so suggestive about wearing helmets and flak jackets." Suzanne said nothing "suggestive" was planned for the FSU halftime. "Just two country-and-western numbers, and we're closing with Neil Diamond's 'America.'"

When the Cheerleaders appeared at Kent State, known for a tragic protest, female students toted GO HOME! signs. But beside them, frat members held up signs that said, DON'T YOU DARE!

Schramm must have loved it.

She was a neon vision of Greenville Avenue. She was the top-heavy embodiment of Cafe Dallas, where the sexiest women in Dallas hung out, literally. She was a member of the Cowboy "family." While having a high-voltage, on-off affair with a prominent married assistant coach, mostly in road hotels, she was seeing a rookie wide receiver and a TV sportscaster who traveled with the team. One pre-game night in San Francisco, she felt understandably abused and confused and tried to drown herself in hospitality suite booze. I ran into her around midnight in the lobby of the team hotel, the St. Francis, and we stood by the elevators and talked for a few minutes. I asked why she put herself through all this.

I was so amazed by her answer that I soon returned to my room and jotted it down, for future reference. She said, "There's just something about this team that makes a woman lose her head. It seems like they only draft beautiful guys. They wear the sexiest uniforms. It's like this incredible power fuck.

"And it's weird, but you don't feel so guilty about it because of Tom. Tom makes it okay—you know, being such a Christian and all."

What a concept: God looked the other way for God's Team. Under Landry, all sins were waived? This was an offshoot of the attitude on team flights. Often I heard, "We don't have to worry about this plane going down. Not with Landry on it."

I wondered if Don Smerek felt bulletproof one night outside Cafe Dallas, a backgammon disco in a shopping plaza along Greenville Avenue. People did not line up at this cafe for chicken-fried steak. Other than tarts, no food was served. I waited through the block-long line just once, while watching several Cowboys being ushered right in—even a backup defensive end like Smerek. Once inside it was all reverberating hormones. After a 1981 night in Cafe Dallas, about 2 A.M., Smerek's adrenaline got the best of him as he grew impatient with another driver in a parking lot jam. Smerek got out of the car he was riding in and, according to witnesses, started kicking the door of the other car.

The driver shot Smerek in the chest with a .32-caliber revolver, seriously wounding him. The bullet passed through Smerek's back.

A small vial of white powder was found in Smerek's shirt, but police said no charges would be filed, even if it was cocaine, because the shirt had been removed from Smerek and could have been tampered with. A grand jury decided not to indict the man who shot Smerek, on grounds of self-defense. Schramm soon defended Smerek, saying tests hadn't proven the substance to be cocaine. "Hell, he might like sugar," Schramm said. "He might be a diabetic. . . . It's unfair to come out and say 'drugs in sports.' When you say Cowboys, they're some of the finest young men in our community."

Yet it seemed that every other day another Cowboy was arrested for alleged DWI, rape, assault, bankruptcy. Mike Hegman, a Greenville Avenue regular, was charged with forging twenty-seven checks worth $10,534 from his roommate's bank account. After Staubach and other teammates helped Hegman repay the money, Hegman got off with unsupervised probation. But popular Pro Bowl placekicker Rafael Septien, a professed Christian married to a woman who occasionally sang "God Bless America" before Maverick games, wasn't so fortunate. He pleaded guilty to indecency with a child (age ten) and was placed on probation for ten years and ordered to undergo psychiatric treatment—a stunningly sad fall.

Was Landry's team as wild after hours as the Raiders were reputed to be, or did it just seem that way? Several players, including Septien, accused the Cowboys of withholding injury information from them, but wasn't that the way lots of NFL teams did business? Wasn't it easier to be overly critical of the Cowboys because Tom Landry oversaw the organization?

In a joint suit ex-Cowboys Mike Gaechter, Willie Townes, and Leon Donohue sued the Cowboys for misleading them about the extent of injuries. The jury ruled 10–2 in favor of the team. Pettis Norman, who played for the Cowboys from 1962 to 1970, finished his career in San Diego, where he sued Charger doctors for malpractice. But in testimony on behalf of the Charger doctors, Cowboy doctor John Gunn said his examinations had shown 25 percent permanent disability in both of Norman's knees as early as 1963. "I was absolutely shocked," says Norman, now a community leader in Dallas. He attempted to sue the Cowboys, he says, but the case was dismissed on procedural grounds.

Norman says he isn't bitter but "I just wish I'd been able to make my own decision whether or not to go on playing after '63. I'm not sure what I'd have done if I'd known. But I'd told myself when I finished playing I'd learn to snow ski, and I can't do that now. I was a good tennis player in high school. I can't do that now."

Septien told reporters after the 1981 season that doctors and trainers told him to keep kicking with a "pulled groin," which actually was a hernia that required surgery. When questioned, Landry readily admitted the doctors had made him aware early in the season that Septien had a hernia. "The doctors said it was something that could be handled after the season," Landry said. "In that case, you go ahead and let him play. If you tell him, he worries and doesn't kick well. We just didn't tell him. So he went on—he went all the way to the Pro Bowl. . . . If I had it to do again, I'd do the same thing."

Yes, kickers have fragile psyches, and Septien's confidence and concentration might have been cracked if he'd been told he was snapping his torso into kickoffs and fifty-yard field goals with a hernia. But again, the choice wasn't Septien's. Landry made the decision for him based on what was best for the team and perhaps for Septien's stardom. Did this treatment by a coach Septien once considered "like a god" contribute to Septien's religious disillusionment or downfall?

I wouldn't have thought twice about Ed "Too Tall" Jones's behavior if I hadn't heard CBS announcers consistently refer to him as "one of the finest men in the game." For sure, he often appeared on the Dallas charity circuit—to the hoots of teammates, who figured he was trying to meet some "new white pussy." Teammates respectfully referred to Jones as "the world's greatest lover." Yes, the most towering symbol of Cowboy Mystique, the six-foot-nine giant with the most fitting nickname in sports, was called Big Ed in the locker room.

Dextor Clinkscale, who played on the strong side of the Flex with Jones, says, "Ed was the Kareem of football, in terms of talent, size, durability, and longevity. People always looked at him and wondered what he could do if he really tried. But he was an excellent technician who knew how to avoid injuries. He was never a great worker, but man was he a great womanizer. Even at six-nine, he thought he had the dexterity of a Spud Webb. He wasn't ashamed of his size; he was proud of it. He wasn't at all a drug offender, but he had the all-time libido that just kept him *out there*. He was always sitting at the bar, trying to persuade some young lady to go back to his place with him [Jones has always been a bachelor]. His home was very neat. I never heard a girl say he was anything but a nice guy. It's just that he loves sex and the girls in Dallas do, too."

Thomas Henderson, who wrote of orgies he shared with Jones, says, "He was a prime example of a man who would do exactly what Tom said and never make any waves. He had it too good in Dallas. That's why he's lasted all these years [fifteen]. Every year a new crop [of girls] becomes legal."

That, at least, may have been part of Jones's motivation. A man so feared on the field always seemed so fearful when questioned by reporters about anything beyond the weather. It was as if he just wanted to do his job as well as he could, preserve his status and image, and slip into the night. Jones never seemed to get too caught up in winning or losing.

I always was amazed to hear that a man so tight-lipped and straight-faced around the media annually hosted the "party of the century"—Ed Jones's Memorial Day Party. It began with softball, a live band, and catered food in Jones's giant backyard off Marsh Lane in North Dallas. It escalated into musical beds. Women who were "available" were given gray Cowboy shorts and half T-shirts. The Grays, they were called. Grays didn't require much wooing. Clink-scale says, "The party was mostly black players and a whole host of unattended girls, more of them white. A white girl could overcome race with status. Status gave a lot of black Cowboys white pussy. After a while, every room in the house was in use."

Big Ed managed to confine his headlines to the sports pages on all but a few occasions. There was a DWI in which the arresting officer said he had to chase Jones's Mercedes through "four near-accidents." There was a nurse who accused Jones of mounting her after she had fallen asleep—imagine waking to that—but she decided not to prosecute. And Jones and a female companion were arrested in a nightclub parking lot when police officers investigated "public lewdness" and the woman became abusive. Was she upset by the interruption? No charges were filed.

Cowboys will be Cowboys.

Bedford Wynne finally gave up the day before Thanksgiving, 1981. He had no choice, really. "I was living a great life," he said, "but I was dying a little more each day." Wynne—part owner of the Cowboys, best buddy of Clint Murchison, drinking buddy of Tex Schramm, hero of J. R. Ewings throughout North Dallas—had partied his way through sixteen straight winning seasons. "I had gambled and drank away all my money," he said. "Too much chasing [women], too. I told my doctor I needed help, and he arranged for me to go to Hazelden [Foundation clinic in Minneapolis]. I was supposed to leave that day, but I said no, I've got to be with Tom tomorrow [the Cowboys were playing the Bears]. I have no idea why I thought that. I hadn't said a word to Tom in fifteen years, or he to me.

"Well, I'd lost my [Texas Stadium] box, but I went to the game and had a farewell drink in everybody else's box. I wound up down on the sideline at the end of the game. Dr. Knight said something to me about how he hated that they'd put those white lines around the bench restricting him from smoking. Then he looked at me and said, 'But if I lit a cigarette right now, you've got so much alcohol in you, this whole place might blow.' "

It nearly blew as a last-second Bears field goal just missed. Cowboys 10–9. Bedford Wynne sank to his knees, but not to give thanks. "I couldn't even walk," he said. "Dr. Knight took me by one arm and D. D. Lewis took me by the other, and they helped me up off the field and up the tunnel [toward the locker room and parking lot]."

Mr. Hospitality Suite had ordered his last bullshot. His bottle was empty. And so, in many ways, was the entire organization's.

Sunday morning, January 10, 1982. St. Francis Hotel, San Francisco. From about the fortieth floor I stepped onto one of those glass *High Anxiety* elevators. Already aboard was defensive tackle Larry Bethea.

"Well," I said, trying to sound cheerful, "this is it."

"This is it," Bethea said. "If I don't do it today, I may never do it."

We were about four hours away from the NFC Championship game at Candlestick Park. Cowboys versus 49ers. Starting defensive tackle John Dutton was hurt. Bethea would get another shot, perhaps his last. After four seasons the Cowboys were still waiting for Bethea to live up to Gil Brandt's reputation. He was Brandt's top recommendation in 1978, the final player picked in the first round. Ah, yes, another Brandt "find"—a choice that stunned the writers gathered at Draft Central in the Cowboys' eleventh-floor offices. Brandt had to spell Bethea's name for them. Brandt sniffed and said, "All the books list him at six-four, 230, but he'll go six-five, 255. I've already got him lifting weights. You see, he played tight end as a freshman. When he moved inside [to defensive tackle], the team was on probation and losing. That cuts down on your incentive. Then when he was a senior, he woke up and saw he had a chance to make some money playing football. . . . He's a good football player. He just didn't get noticed."

By the time Bethea landed in Dallas that Draft Day afternoon, reporters and photographers would have believed he flew in without a plane. The Cowboys were one of the first NFL teams to fly in their first-round choice on Draft Day to maximize his media exposure. Behold: more "Doomsday."

Four years later Bethea still was trying to live up. *He* hadn't picked himself too high; Brandt had.

Since Brandt had become the Draftmaster, Bethea was his first major miss. The Flex hexed Bethea, who couldn't seem to bury his ball-chasing instincts. The computer failed to probe his heart, which was big but soft. "A 255-pound sack of sugar," I called Bethea in a column. Nice athlete. No football player.

Bethea would be followed through the 1980s by Brandt specials who always made Cowboy fans say, "Who?" Again and again Brandt reached for guys who could do just about everything but play football: Second-rounder Aaron Mitchell in '79, Howard Richards (first) and Doug Donley (second) in '81, Rod Hill (first) and Jeff Rohrer (second) in '82, Kevin Brooks (first) and Jessie Penn (second) in '85.

Jim Jeffcoat (first, '83) became a starter but not a star. Victor Scott (second, '84) was a potential star whose career was damaged by two league suspensions for substance abuse. When Brandt didn't miss, lightning didn't either. It almost seemed like God's Team of the '70s was experiencing His wrath. Robert Shaw (first, '79) wrecked his knee after two seasons. Billy Cannon (first, '84) soon suffered a neck injury and had to quit. Mike Sherrard (first, '86) twice broke the same leg while running and played just one Cowboy season. Landry quickly gave up on Todd Christiansen (second, '78) and Mike Walter (second, '83); Christiansen became a Pro Bowl star with the Raiders, Walter a steady starter for the 49ers.

When you remember this franchise traded its first and second choice in 1980 for John Dutton, you realize the Cowboys played the '80s with almost no fresh bullets. It was mostly Landry's System versus the world, and the world began to win.

John Wooten, the fifteen-year Cowboy scout who finally replaced Brandt in 1989, says, "All those conversions [picks who became stars] in the '70s came under the 'best-athlete-available' category. I credit Gil for all those. But by the late '70s, the game was changing to physical, kick-your-butt football, and we kept going for the 'best athlete.' One of our scouts was very against taking Bethea, but Gil liked him. I think Bethea had made two plays in his entire career at Michigan State.

"Our image just ate us up. I pray I'll never be afraid to deal with something because of image."

Image ate Larry Bethea alive.

Dennis Thurman (eleventh round) was the only other choice to last from the '78 draft. Thurman and Bethea roomed together. Thurman, from L.A. and Southern Cal, came to know a Bethea who was brought up on the Bible and hadn't used drugs. Thurman says, "He was so gentle. He had a sensitivity that surprised you because most big guys are afraid to let you see that side. Everything had come so easily for him, and suddenly he was the Cowboys' first-round pick and he was failing. At night he'd ask me, 'Man, am I just not good enough?' He just couldn't get the hang of the Flex.

"He was feeling so much pressure from back home. He called it 'Newpanews' [Newport News, Virginia]. He'd say, 'Man, I wonder what they're thinking back in Newpanews.' "

Bethea's high school coach, Harlan Hott, said, "He was the type you thought would turn out to be a lawyer or doctor."

Bethea left Dallas after the '83 season amid rumors he was a cocaine abuser. He bounced around the USFL. In 1985 he pleaded guilty and paid a $1,000 fine for setting three fires in Rainier National Park, in the state of Washington. In 1986 his wife (and high school sweetheart) divorced him, citing his drug problems. Thurman says, "They'd had problems before because they couldn't have children. It was really sad." Bethea soon was arrested for assaulting his wife. Police found $61,375 in his pockets, which he had stolen from a safe in his mother's attic. He received a suspended four-year sentence.

In early 1987 he moved back into his old neighborhood in Newport News. He applied for a job at a 7-Eleven where he was a regular customer. Either he was rejected or no job was open. Three weeks passed. On the night of April 22, 1987, Bethea cashed a $166 unemployment check and bought cheap beer and a pack of cigarettes. Then, allegedly, he robbed the 7-Eleven and another convenience store with a stolen .38 automatic pistol.

Some time after midnight Larry Bethea walked into the backyard of a boarding house where a childhood friend was staying. He put the stolen gun to his temple and pulled the trigger.

Larry Bethea. Don Smerek. Rafael Septien. Thomas Henderson. D. D. Lewis. Duane Thomas. John Niland. Bob Hayes. Lance Rentzel. Ed Jones. So many lost souls. So many chances for a father figure to guide, to touch, to save. Yes, many people who heard Landry give his Christian testimony wrote to tell him what impact he had on their lives. But what of the people who heard him speak nearly every day for six months a year? What of his players? Why did the most important man in FCA have so little positive impact on his own players? On those in his front office? If God were in Landry's heart, wouldn't it be impossible to keep from mixing bi'ness with God's love? With charity? With what Staubach calls good works?

No, Landry couldn't be held responsible for the behavior of all 434 who played for him over twenty-nine years. He was coaching pro football, not teaching Sunday school. The game's object is to knock people down. How can an NFL coach be held accountable for the after-hours hellraising of his gladiators?

But this NFL coach was Billy Graham's John the Baptist.

I always admired Landry for not forcing his religion on his teams or organization. He didn't preach or make Bible studies or chapel services mandatory. Yet even if a Christian never said a word, wouldn't his actions alone inspire or influence those under and around him? I can't remember many players voicing "love" for Landry. They lived in awe or fear of him. But I sensed no love between players and coach. Was it unfair of me to wonder how my favorite Bible verse fit in Landry's Cowboy context? In 1 Corinthians 13 it says, "If I speak in the tongues of men and of angels, but have not love, I am a noisy gong or a clanging cymbal. And if I have prophetic powers, and understand all mysteries and all knowledge, and if I have all faith, so as to remove mountains, but have not love, I am nothing. . . . Love is patient and kind. Love is not jealous or boastful; it is not arrogant or rude. Love does not insist on its own way. . . . So faith, hope, love abide, these three; but the greatest of these is love."

Was it unfair for me to start wondering how Landry the evangelist could challenge FCA audiences to carry God's banner against alcohol, drugs, and sexual permissiveness when so many who played for and worked with him were contributing mightily to what he called "this devastating problem"?

So many wins. So many lost souls, so near to and far from God's Coach.

On a Sunday at Candlestick, Cowboy Mystique was buried for good in the same soggy end zone in which it was born in the 1972 playoffs.

This time, until the end, the "new" Staubach had a nice game.

Danny White was sixteen of twenty-four for 173 yards and two touchdowns. But in the end San Francisco drove eighty-nine yards in thirteen plays against the mighty Flex. On third down from the Cowboy 6-yard line, Joe Montana faded and was chased from the pocket by Ed Jones and D. D. Lewis. Montana: running right, searching, double-pumping, falling backward, letting go for . . . whom? To this day many Cowboys say Montana admitted to them he was trying to throw the pass away.

Dwight Clark went up into the fog and got it. The Catch. San Francisco 28–27.

But fifty-one seconds remained. Danny White threw a perfect post pass to Drew Pearson, who was all but gone. But 49er cornerback Eric Wright dived, grabbed the back neck of Pearson's jersey, and somehow held on. Pearson went down at the 49er 44. A near-Hail Mary.

Still, plenty of time for one more completion and a field goal.

White, fading, looking. White, sacked. White, fumbling.

Tex Schramm said, "If Drew had broken free of that tackle, Danny's whole career would have been different. He would have become known as a Super Bowl quarterback. I'd like to think we'd have won that Super Bowl [San Francisco 26, Cincinnati 21]. That could have been a springboard for us into the '80s. But . . ."

Young Tom Landry, in his days at the University of Texas.

The man in the hat, in his last game as coach of the Cowboys. *AP/Wide World Photos*

Roger Staubach: Only his team mates knew just how great h was, and how tough.

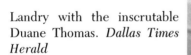

Landry with the inscrutable Duane Thomas. *Dallas Times Herald*

The twinkling eyes and devilish look—Don Meredith, a natural for television. *Dallas Times Herald*

Clint Murchison with his wife Anne, the former Mrs. Gil Brandt. *Dallas Times Herald*

H. R. "Bum" Bright, seated before his legendary tapestry. *Phil Huber*

Butch Johnson, the master of the spectacular, goes horizontal for a touchdown against Denver in Super Bowl XII. *AP/Wide World Photos*

Two who resisted the Cowboys' mystique: Pat Toomay and Pete Gent.

"Every girl's dream"—the Cowboys' cheerleaders. *AP/Wide World Photos*

The biggest talent, the biggest mouth, the biggest headlines: Hollywood Henderson was a dynamo on the field, the center of attention off it. *Dallas Times Herald*

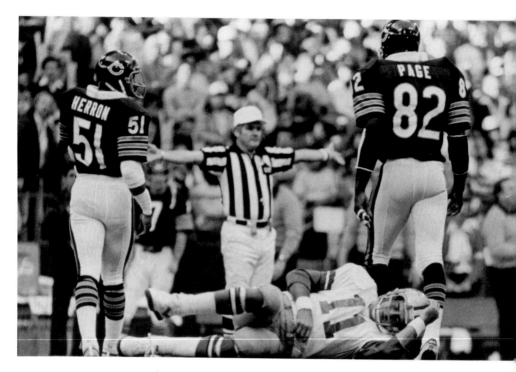

Danny White, down for the count after fumbling against Chicago in 1981.
AP/Wide World Photos

The brain trust in the war room before the 1983 draft: Gil Brandt, Tom Landry,
Tex Schramm. *Dallas Times Herald*

Thurman's Thieves, in the photo that caused all the trouble. Top Row: Michael Downs, Billy Bates. Middle Row: Rick Easmon, Victor Scott, Dextor Clinkscale. Bottom Row: Ron Fellows, Dennis Thurman, Everson Walls. *Dallas Morning News*

Jimmy Johnson and Jerry Jones at Mia's, as all hell was about to break loose. *Dallas Morning News*

God's Coach, waving to the masses on Tom Landry Day, 1989. *Dallas Times Herald*

11

ONE DAY in the fall of 1983, Bum Bright got a call from Tex Schramm. Bright barely knew Schramm, who asked, "How would you like to buy the Cowboys?"

Bright said, "You mean the Dallas Cowboys? I got no more interest than a man in the moon. I've been to two games in my life."

And Schramm said, "Clint wants *you* to buy the team."

More likely it was Schramm who wanted Bright to replace Murchison as absentee owner. Talk about a Bright idea. Schramm had all but found a Murchison clone, at least in appearance, camera shyness, and net worth. Bright and Murchison could have passed for brothers on flattop haircut alone—a style you didn't see a whole lot of in 1983, even in Texas. Bright's was gray-white, as were the wingtips of eyebrows much longer than his hair. Bright's eyebrows, resting above lightly tinted black-framed glasses, gave his face a hint of scholarly wisdom, as did the tapestry on his office wall. Hand-woven in England, it nearly brought to life the sword-in-the-stone legends that fascinated Bright as a child. Bright's heroes were Arthur and Lancelot, not Cowboys. To Bright, Tom Landry was just a football coach.

Harvey Roberts Bright was just an Okie from Muskogee, Okla-homa. But he was no "Bum." The nickname came from his dad. As a red-faced infant, wrapped in blankets, Harvey reminded his dad of a little railroad bum. "Bum" stuck. Bright, one of the fifty richest men in the world in '83, still takes an impish satisfaction in his paradoxical nickname. Last laughs make Bright smile his little tulip-shaped smile. Bright likes to humble people who think they're big shots. For Bright, the happiness money can buy is power. Money can make giants—like Landry—seem even shorter than Bright's five feet ten inches.

When Bright was four his family moved to Dallas, where his dad ran a pharmacy. At Highland Park High School, Bright really was too small to play football, but at halfback he survived on guile and guts, as he would in the larger game of empire building. Bright roughnecked for a while in the Oklahoma oil fields before deciding he'd rather have people roughnecking for him. With his parents' financial aid, he enrolled at Texas A&M. After graduation he began trading oil leases and, well, you can guess the rest. Another Texas Millionaire Fairy Tale.

Oil. Real estate. Trucking. Banking. "A dealoholic," a friend says. "He will never be able to stop making money. He's obsessed. Not so much with spending it. With *making* it."

Ah, there's where Schramm slightly miscalculated. Key differ-ence between Bright and Murchison: Bright mostly made; Murchi-son mostly spent. Murchison inherited his fortune. Murchison was driven by pleasures of the flesh. Murchison was more of a play-oholic. Murchison owned his own tropical island, Spanish Key. Murchison's life had become a can't-take-it-with-you spree.

Bright still has a fear of going broke. During business hours he often looks as if he has just bitten into his last lemon. He arrives for work at 7 A.M., six days a week. His life is built on the military routine and discipline he learned at A&M and in the Army Corps of Engineers. Collectors' swords and pistols are crossed on his walls. There's a little Scrooge about him, as employees scurry to avoid his wrath, which can echo in a nasal-bass twang much bigger than his body. But he softens quickly when talking about each grandchild in the long row of office pictures. In business he'll do anything to beat you short of cheating you.

Bright's one vice is cigarettes, which he carefully lights, smokes, and extinguishes one after another. Bright says, "I run all my com-panies. I'm not off to Acapulco or Europe."

He had known Murchison since they were boys and occasionally had lunch with him at the old Statler Hilton downtown. "One time he had some movie star waiting for him up in a room and wanted me to come up and meet her," Bright says. "That's not my game."

Bright's only game is Texas A&M football. The tile in his office bathroom is done in A&M maroon and white. He says, "A&M is my team." While serving a four-year term as chairman of A&M's board of regents, Bright made national headlines in 1981 by striking a deal, through Gil Brandt, to hire coach Jackie Sherrill away from Pitt for a then-outrageous $1.6 million package. Of course, Bright demanded nothing less than $1.6 million worth of results, which Sherrill eventually gave A&M, along with an NCAA probation for recruiting violations.

But the Cowboys? In 1983 at age sixty-three, he didn't have time to waste on any pro football team. Schramm made a couple of runs at Bright. No interest.

Then Bright got a call from Charles Pistor, chairman of the board of RepublicBank Dallas. Bright sat on RepublicBank's board and held 3.7 percent of its stock. Brandt recalls Pistor saying, "When I go to Singapore or Tokyo or Mexico City or Paris or London and introduce myself, people give me a blank look. Then I say 'Dallas,' and they say, 'Oh, Dallas Cowboys.' If we could be the bank of record for the Cowboys, it would be of great benefit to the bank. You're our largest shareholder and it ought to interest you. Why don't you buy the Cowboys?"

Pistor gave Bright the most favorable loan possible. But Schramm gave Bright the old "great fun, bad investment" speech. Bright says, "Tex told me we might make a million a year and we easily could lose a million a year. Clint wanted $85 million for the team and the stadium, which was an awful lot. But Tex said, 'We'll be the premier team of the '80s. With all the new owners coming into the league, we're way ahead of everybody. You'll be able to sell the team for $250, 300 million.' Well, we [Bright & Co.] were making more than $8 million a month in oil income alone, and I thought we could swallow the depreciation pretty easily. We kicked it around and I finally thought 'Aw, it'll be fun.'"

Fun? Bright wasn't even interested in going to road games, which interfered with A&M games. No, this purchase was much more business than pleasure. The Dallas Cowboys were about to be bought by the one man in America who really had no feelings about them, one way or the other. The NFL's biggest business was about to be owned by a man who was strictly business. What goes around had come around.

While Murchison remained in awe of Landry, Bright remembered him as a fellow he had turned down for the A&M coaching job.

Enduring memory of Butch Johnson: Visitors' locker room, Philadelphia's Veterans Stadium. The Cowboys had beaten the Eagles 17–14. Johnson sat in front of his locker, smoking a cigarette. Behind him, on top of his locker, his tape player rocked the room with Queen's "Another One Bites the Dust." Johnson wore only the shorts he had worn underneath his silvery game pants. Magic Markered on Johnson's shorts was his motto: "It don't mean a thing without the ring." Without the Super Bowl ring.

"What hurts me the most," Johnson says now, "is that I was one of their best team players. Despite what people thought, I was one guy who wanted to do whatever it took to win."

Indeed, Michael McColly "Butch" Johnson made as many big catches per down played as probably any NFL receiver ever. For sure he made more spectacular catches per capita. "Butch," said Danny White, "makes the tough catches in the tough situations." As teammates often said, "Drew [Pearson] makes *the* play. But Butch makes plays." Drew made the game-winning catch. Johnson made game-saving catches. Johnson wasn't a starter, but he was a passing-down star. He was from Los Angeles and had an appreciation of art, jazz, and things Hollywood. But he had rigid priorities. When it was time to work, Johnson worked. When it was time to play, Johnson played like a champion. When it was time to unwind, well, crank up the volume.

Once, before a late '82 Monday night game in Minnesota, I ran into Johnson in the hotel lobby. Winning this game was important only for possible home-field advantage if the Cowboys made it to a third straight NFC championship game. They had lost their last two Super Bowl shots in Philadelphia and in San Francisco. Johnson kept saying it was critical that this NFC title game be played at Texas Stadium. That Monday, Johnson told me, "These guys just don't understand anymore, man. Girls were all over the [fourth] floor last night. You watch: We'll lose tonight and we'll live to regret it." They lost 31–27. They wound up playing the NFC title game in Washington.

"By 1982," Johnson says, "we really were no longer a football team. We had become rock stars with people lining up at hotels to see us. It was insane. Every player on the team had developed his own image, down to his attire. The biggest competition was dressing for the team plane. If you didn't have a mink or an Armani or something really sharp, other players would really talk bad about you. Hey, Tom had his image, too. We'd be warming up before games and look over at him in cold weather, and he'd have on his full-length cashmere coat and fur-lined hat. No sweatshirts for him. In the early years I'd look over and think, 'Damn, we got to win with this man dressed like this.'

"But by 1982 we had become reflections of reflections."

That was it. Leave it to Johnson to come up with the clutch line: reflections of reflections.

"We were Tex Schramm's media darlings. We were on national TV almost every week. But Tex marketed the package, not individuals. This was never Roger Staubach and the Cowboys. It was America's Team. But *we* weren't America's Team; Tom and Tex and Gil were. People on the outside had no idea what was really happening on the inside.

"Our games were no longer against other teams. They were against our own game films. We'd be walking off the field after winning a game and you'd hear 'Fuck, I missed a step on that play, and I won't be able to sleep tonight.' Tom was too smart to let a player have it during a game, with the cameras on him. Oh, he knew when to get you to the side and say, 'What the hell are you doing?' But the main way he tried to keep everybody in line was through the fear factor. I understand that an NFL coach has to deal with forty-nine very large egos, and his has to be the largest. But to control all his talent, Tom made everyone live in fear of losing their job. That fear slowly became hatred."

But Johnson became Landry's cross to bear because Johnson didn't have a job to lose. Landry had nothing to hold over Johnson's swelled head. Pearson and Tony Hill were the starting wide receivers. You could argue (as I did in print) that Johnson sometimes benefited on passing downs from the double coverage drawn by Pearson or Hill or even tight end Doug Cosbie. But Johnson was passionately convinced his performance merited more playing time, and he had the stats and the endorsements of assistants and teammates to back it up. Like Hollywood Henderson, Johnson had no fear of Landry. Unlike Henderson, Johnson had no credibility flaw. No cocaine addiction. No missed practices for "colds." For five seasons Johnson did everything asked of him. In the sixth, 1981, he began to ask something in return—play him or free him.

"Let me have a chance to be a star somewhere else," Johnson told Landry again and again.

Johnson says, "[Assistant] Dan Reeves kept telling Tom to start me and Tom just wouldn't do it. Dan said he just couldn't figure what Tom saw in Tony Hill. I'd had a conversation with [assistant] Mike Ditka in '78 that really made me start thinking. He said, 'I'm not supposed to be saying this, but we grade players on value to the organization, and the only player ranked above you is Randy White.' I returned punts and kickoffs, and on the big third-down plays I was often the one who had to cut in and block on the guards and tackles [Johnson, at 185 pounds, was known as a fierce blocker]. I was doing so many valuable things that Tom wouldn't trade me. What was I supposed to do? Quit trying? I felt like a lot of guys looked up to me. After [assistant] John Mackovic left, he told me, 'Butch, you were the conscience of that team.' Howard Cosell told me one time, 'Butch, you'll never get the credit you deserve from that organization.' It was really starting to get to me.

"I was rooming with Too Tall on the road, and one night he was talking about all the ink Billy 'White Shoes' Johnson was getting. He said, 'He's a great punt returner, but he's not half the receiver you are. All he has on you is that end zone dance he does.' That put the thought in my mind. In a preseason game at Texas Stadium I was having a good game against [Pittsburgh's] Mel Blount, a great player. I was thinking, 'Man, if I can take *this* guy . . .' I caught a touchdown pass and looked up in the front row and there was this lady raising her hands straight up and shaking like she was having an orgasm. I thought, 'Well, that looks good.' And I did it back to her. They showed it on a sportscast in California, and a newscaster said, 'That looks like an earthquake.' My relatives called and told me, and I started calling it the California Quake. I was really embarrassed about it at first. But people just pushed me into doing it. Even my teammates loved it. It just kept evolving. A kid sent me a letter and said, 'Why don't you add something "Texas" to it?' So I started pulling imaginary six-shooters out and shooting [usually at the refs]. It was wild. But I had to do something different. Stats alone weren't going to get me noticed by the outside world. Being an entertainer would."

Johnson mounted Schramm's international stage and said, "Hello, world!" Each time Johnson scored—he led the team with five TD catches in 1981—he rocked Landry with a California Quake. After decades of watching Landry's robots coolly flip the ball to the ref after scoring, Texas Stadium fans got a tequila-style kick out of the Quake. Johnson, a light-skinned black, wasn't quite so offensive to red-neck fans. Johnson, a TV reporter during the off-seasons, spoke with a no-accent California accent. Johnson made sense, even when calling Landry a "hypocrite." After all, Johnson produced.

Johnson says, "I think Tom knew I was everything black people enjoyed. I wasn't a joke. I was articulate and outspoken, and that community needed that. Tom just couldn't handle it."

Johnson became the most acclaimed dancer since Astaire. This wasn't just "White Shoes" Johnson's spontaneous "funky chicken" dance. Butch Johnson worked with a ballet teacher to choreograph an entire routine. Naturally, the networks all came to Dallas to do pieces. The *New York Times* and *Los Angeles Times* called to do features. David Letterman gave Johnson "Spike of the Year." Not bad for a second-stringer.

Teammates found high-fiving irony in the Quake because, as one said, "Butch can't even dance." On Greenville Avenue dance floors Johnson had very few moves. But here he was, dancing on Tom Landry's head.

"I just had to go on my own image campaign," Johnson says. "One time Duane Thomas called me. This was earlier, like '79. Gil had gotten him this job as maître d' at a restaurant called Papillon, where Gil often entertained guests. It was the night before a Monday night game, and Duane said Gil was bringing Howard Cosell for dinner and that maybe I should drop by. I jumped on the opportunity. At that time Cosell could make or break you nationally. So I just walked up to the table and introduced myself, and Howard said, 'Butch, have you had dinner?' I said no. He said, 'Have a seat.' Oh, Gil was pissed. I really gave Howard the juice [the inside info about the Cowboys]. And so, every time we played on 'Monday Night Football,' Howard had me for dinner. And during the game he'd really talk me up. Once I had the Quake, he'd just go crazy about me."

Landry was being driven crazy. Landry occasionally sought counseling from Dr. Don Beck, who also worked with Houston Oiler coach Bum Phillips. I sought Beck's advice on the Johnson dilemma. Beck said, "Tom focuses on a system performed by people, and Bum on people performing in a system. . . . Bum is more interested in what's natural. To him, playing is an art. Bum is a master of sensing moods, as opposed to engineering and manipulating people. . . . Butch is an egocentric achievist, but from the very beginning Bum would have sensed something was wrong and found a way to make everyone feel important."

Instead, Johnson openly challenged Landry's integrity. Johnson says, "I thought he was a hypocrite because of all the statements he made. In February he'd tell me and the press that all jobs would be open in camp. Then we'd get to camp and he'd say, 'Well, what I meant was . . .' I had more one-on-one conversations with the man than any player ever, and he could really screw you around. He'd say one thing to you, then something else twenty minutes later to someone else. Whatever fit the tone or the time. He would change his whole tune. He would just lie. After a while I wanted a third party in the room when we talked. He was a great chameleon.

"Sometimes I'd walk into his office, and instead of having me face him across the desk, we'd sit on the couch. I'd say, 'Hey, I was a psych major, too.' That game wouldn't work with me. I'd see a side others didn't. I'd see a man who wasn't as stoic as he pretended to be. I just kept saying, 'Let me out.' He didn't know what to do."

So, after a third straight NFC title game loss (Johnson: five catches, one for a TD), Landry announced: No more spiking. I asked Landry if the Quake offended him, and he gave me a classic yes/no Landry answer: "It doesn't bother me. I just don't like it." Landry also said, "Butch's is one of the more spectacular ones [spikes], so it looks like I'm picking on him. But I'm not. It's just a general feeling I have. Losing concentration has never been a problem for Butch. . . . It's what distractions do for the rest of your team. Some guys can not do much all week and just play the devil out of it on Sunday. But the young ones pattern themselves after what they see and say, 'I can do the same thing.' " Landry could dance, too.

Johnson told me, "I think Tom and I are a lot alike. We're both ambitious fools." Johnson also said, "They're burying me again. They're saying, 'Be a clone.' . . . But the real problem, if they wanted to acknowledge it, is that we're living on mystique instead of all-out playing football."

Landry sighed and concluded, "I'm sure Butch will come up with something else."

Butch sighed and concluded, "I'm working on something."

Little did we know it was the Cancun Quake. After three games the next season, Johnson took off for Cancun. As in Mexico. As in posh resort. Only Dallas Cowboys went to Cancun to "think." Johnson says, "One assistant coach actually told me to hold out. I just told Tom I wasn't playing anymore that season. Of course, he told the team and the media that I said I'd be back in a day or two, and some in the organization made it out to be a money issue, which it wasn't remotely. I was paid better than many of the starters. Tom called me four or five times [in Cancun] and he finally guaranteed to trade me at the end of the season if I'd go ahead and play.

"So I came back [in two days] and played hard. But I just had to get out of Dallas. I had learned a lot about shrewd business from that organization, which was the shrewdest, but I really didn't want to raise my kids in Dallas. Very, very few black players make it in business in Dallas. I didn't want to be another tragedy. Tex Schramm helped Drew Pearson [by getting Pearson an official NFL license for his now booming business of making and selling hats with team logos]. Tom always loved Drew. But do you think they would have helped me? . . . Dallas was such a paradox. Number one, it was the divorce capital of the world. It had a religious side and a party side, and the same people who appreciated religion seemed to be the people partying. The nicest clubs in the nation were in Dallas. I guess that was the only place people could go to spend all the money they were making. . . .

"So the season ended, and Drew had his accident, and I read where Tom was saying he was going to 'reevaluate' whether to trade me. I called him and said, 'Man, we had a *deal*. Our deal is *still on*.' After all I'd been through, no way was I going to let him back out."

A Bum Phillips, perhaps, would have made amends and made Johnson his starter and star. But Landry traded Johnson to Houston, for Mike Renfro, in early April 1984. Yes, Butch Johnson was gone just two weeks after Pearson's career came to a high-speed halt against a parked tractor-trailer rig one late night along LBJ Freeway.

Drew Pearson was always hustling. Undrafted free agents never quite trust their stardom. So Pearson hustled even harder during the off-season. He always had two or three businesses going, including Drew Pearson's Super Shine car wash. He did radio. He did TV. He made appearances all over the country. "It was frustrating," he

said. "I'd been to three Super Bowls and made $225,000 my last
season. I'd go around the league and find out these son of a bitches
were making twice as much as me, and they weren't even winning."

Pearson even managed, promoted, and starred for the Hoopsters, an unofficial Cowboys off-season basketball team. His younger
brother Carey Mark, or "Moose," served as equipment man. The
Hoopsters would fly to play the Redskins or Bears, but they also
would bus to play high school faculties in Texas, Oklahoma, New
Mexico—anywhere Pearson could swing a deal. Pearson paid other
players between $250 and $500, depending on the gate. He also
provided plenty of fried chicken and beer and a chance to be with
the boys—and girls. One player said, "If you wanted a girl, you
could always pick one up after the games. If you did drugs, you did
drugs. If you drank, you drank before and after the games. If we
were flying back, most guys stayed up all night and crashed on the
flight home."

On March 21, 1984, the Hoopsters bused to Coalgate, Oklahoma. Pearson had made a personal appearance the day before, in
Abilene, and he seemed "cranky tried," according to teammates. On
the bus ride home Pearson had a beer or two and, as usual, cleaned
up playing cards. Pearson's biggest victim was fellow receiver Doug
Donley. Donley and Pearson sometimes spent before-practice lunch
hours together sipping a cocktail at the Million Dollar Saloon.

Donley challenged Pearson to cut cards, double or nothing.
Donley cut to a nine. Pearson hooted. Pearson cut to a five. It wasn't
like Pearson to lose with a five.

"It was a weird night," Pearson says. "I was dressed in all black,
including my hat and sneakers. I had just picked up an all-black
Dodge Daytona with a five-speed [a tradeoff for Cowboy tickets]. I
usually drove New Yorkers, not five-speeds."

After the bus unloaded at the Cowboy practice field, around 1
A.M., Pearson told everyone he'd call them "within forty-five minutes" to say whether the Hoopsters would take the 10 A.M. or noon
flight to Washington the next day. Drew and Moose needed to wash
the uniforms. Drew needed to take Moose home. Drew admits he
was "overextended."

He says, "I remember getting on the freeway, and then it's all
a blank. There was no 'aaaaaa!' I just don't remember anything. I
woke up with my brother's head on my shoulder. I shook him.
'Moose, wake up.' He was limp. I walked out. He was dead. I have

no idea how I wasn't dead. I had a lacerated liver and fractured clavicle. But when you hit a parked rig going that fast. . . .

"I'm not a religious person. I mean, I pray every day, but I don't go to church every Sunday. But did the Lord pull my spirit out of that car or what? The experience didn't make me become a devout Baptist, but it made me think of things supernatural. Coach Landry never forced any religion on us. I just knew he was supposed to be a Christian. When I was playing, I'd watch him jump on a player and think, 'Goddamn, how can he do a player that way?' Now I see it's a cold business. But when I woke up in the hospital, I saw two faces. I saw Staubach's, which I expected to see, but I saw Coach Landry's, too. It was right in the middle of a minicamp, and he just didn't have time. But there I was on that cold-ass table, hurting like hell, and I'd open my eyes and look one way and I'd see Coach Landry. I'd look the other way and I'd see Coach Landry. That's when I knew he was a genuine Christian."

Not long before the accident Pearson had blasted Landry in a *Dallas Morning News* interview, characterizing his coach as callous and uncaring. Landry had called Pearson to his office and told him how hurt he was by the story. Landry probably would have told most players how the remarks would hurt *them*. Landry did seem to care about Pearson.

Landry talked Pearson, at age thirty-three, out of trying to make a comeback. He gave Pearson a job as a scout and assistant coach. Schramm helped save Drew Pearson Enterprises. "The NFL had turned us down flat," Pearson says of his official hat logo license. "But once Tex got involved, the NFL called us."

Hats, a "bi'ness" Landry could appreciate.

But within two weeks in 1984, Landry had lost two of the best big-play receivers ever to play.

When Mike Ditka was Landry's receivers coach, a story circulated in the locker room about what a "crazy mother" Ditka was. After one practice, as the receivers ran halfhearted sprints, Ditka challenged them to a fistfight. Right there. All at once. Drew Pearson, Butch Johnson, Tony Hill, Billy Joe DuPree, Doug Cosbie—"Come on, you pussies!" yelled Ditka, as Landry looked on.

No takers.

Now, of course, it seems that every other Chicago Bears practice ends with head coach Ditka challenging half the squad to a rumble. But in the Cowboy structure, Ditka seemed to have enough loose screws to build an entire robot. He was Landry's token maniac.

But Ditka also was as shrewd as Schramm. Ditka knew he could get away with an occasional explosion as long as he paid the proper homage to Mount Landry. Ditka kissed Landry's, well, hat. All his top assistants did: Ditka, Dan Reeves, John Mackovic, Gene Stallings. Today they tell interviewers that coaching under Landry was among their "greatest" experiences, but it wasn't then. One thing they learned in Dallas: It isn't always wise to be honest, especially about legends.

Under Landry they always filled newspaper stories with awe about him. They publicly accepted their ridiculously limited input and responsibility. They arrived early for coaches' meetings and mostly deferred to Landry's one-way thinking. "Assistants," says Drew Pearson, "could act like little kids, peeking around the corner to see if Landry was coming. They were even more afraid of him than the players were. Once when I was coaching, my daughter didn't have a ride home from school, and I absolutely had to go get her and miss some of practice. The other assistants said, 'You can't miss practice.' They thought I was fucking crazy. But I just said, well, I'll have to suffer the consequences. Coach Landry didn't really say anything."

Yet Pearson, who lasted just one year as an assistant, had no life-or-death ambition to become a head coach. The others knew if they could live with their head coach, they'd have a better chance of becoming one. Serving under God's Coach made for a blinding resume. If an assistant was good enough for Tom Landry, he was good enough for an owner in search of a Landry.

Yet Reeves often complained privately, bitterly, about Landry's inflexibility. Meanwhile, Reeves came in second for four or five head coaching jobs. But finally Landry helped Reeves get the Denver job. Three Super Bowls later, Reeves will tell you the suffering under Landry was well worth it. Reeves was replaced by Mackovic, who gave up his head coaching job at Wake Forest to be Landry's quarterback coach. After his first training camp, Mackovic was in semishock. "I just don't do anything," he told me confidentially. Yet Kansas City owner and Dallas resident Lamar Hunt kept reading about Landry's bright young assistant. After just two years under

Landry, "young Landry" was hired by Hunt to coach the Chiefs.

That infuriated Stallings. His defensive backs told me, "Gene went crazy in our meeting today. He was saying, 'How could John Mackovic get a job when I've been here for ten years?'"

Stallings' lip-biting paid off in 1986. Cardinal owner Bill Bidwell, long in awe of the Cowboy franchise, decided to try beating Landry with one of his own. Stallings' general reputation among players: warmhearted assistant who might not have the big-picture, snap-judgment command to be a successful head coach. But all Bidwell saw was a chip off the block. Stallings' long association with Landry didn't hurt after the 1989 season, either, when the Cardinals fired him and Alabama soon hired him. A source in Phoenix says, "A lot of people in the organization found that Gene's reputation was better than he was."

Associating with God's Coach certainly didn't hurt "crazy" Ditka. When the Bears called Ditka in 1982, several Chicago writers called me to ask if the guy was sane. I told them I wasn't sure he had enough handle on his temper to last as a head coach, but I stressed that Ditka knew how to play the game, on the field and behind the microphone.

One morning at camp I wandered into the TV room of the coaches' dorm and found Ditka, intently watching a soap opera.

"You always watch this?" I asked.

"Don't tell anybody," Ditka said, grinning. He eyed me a second and said, "You don't swallow the party line around here, do you? I like that."

And Ditka winked at me.

As Bears coach, Ditka actually became a phone pal of Landry's. They talked once or so a week. Landry volunteered to serve as a character witness when Ditka was arrested for DWI in 1985. You got the feeling Landry wished he could be a little more like Ditka, not to intoxication, but a little more spontaneous and outwardly emotional. But did Ditka and Reeves keep in touch with Landry the way you do a tough professor or a commanding officer? It's difficult to imagine Ditka or Reeves calling Landry to shoot the breeze or, for that matter, Landry chatting at length with anyone but Alicia. But in a profession without much security or mercy, continuing a relationship with Landry can't hurt your image.

Landry delighted in talking to the media about the success of his "sons," Ditka and Reeves, especially as the Cowboys were less and less successful. But he never was able to replace what Ditka and Reeves did for his Cowboy teams. They could keep a Butch Johnson from flying off the handle and the Lid from flying off Landry's locker room.

Before I left for camp one early '80s summer, I talked to a friend about my religious struggles. Sunday-only Christians were turning me away from church services. Was I wrong to think I could worship God on my own? And in God's eyes, where did financial security stop and greed start? And why did God make it so unfair for us sexually? Why, if you commit to one woman, doesn't your first-kiss heat automatically grow the longer you're with her? And why . . . You know, basic meaning-of-life questions. My friend suggested I kick them around with Landry. Well, I said, he wouldn't have time. But maybe at camp . . .

Thousand Oaks is a Paradise Found, a hilly bedroom community about an hour's drive north and west of L. A. International Airport. In July and August, you can tan by day and wear sweaters at night. Purple mountain majesty and Pacific beaches are both fifteen minutes away. Everywhere you turn is another perfect California family: handsome, athletic dad; striking, athletic mom; 3.2 cute, athletic kids. On the northern edge of Thousand Oaks, at the base of some scenic mountains, lies California Lutheran University, best known as the summer home of the Dallas Cowboys. It's a pretty little campus, a greenhouse of flowers and trees, with six two-story stucco dorms grouped in a semicircle across the street from the football "stadium," which might seat a thousand or so in the bleachers.

Media members were grouped in one dorm, known as the Third World Dorm. But I opted for the Howard Johnson's, about five miles down a busy fast-food, shopping-center street called Moorpark and just off the Ventura Freeway. The student maids didn't always clean the Third World bathrooms, and with up to four ink-stained wretches per suite, well, I'd sacrifice feeling "just like a Cowboy" for the HoJo's. Besides, the media dorm was known for its sunup curfew. As a bleary-eyed Schramm said one late camp morning, "Why isn't there a curfew for management?"

So I didn't really mind driving back and forth for practices and lunchtime interviews in the dining hall, which the poor Cowboys shared with hundreds of autograph seekers attending the John

Wooden basketball camps. Landry always sat at the last long table in the back, the coaches' table. He always arrived at the same time—something like 12:05:30—and ate in about seven minutes and fifteen seconds. The fifteen seconds were for getting grapes from the salad bar to take back to his Spartan dorm room, where he watched more film than a Dallas censorship board. Sometimes assistants were eating at the table when Landry sat down. But very little was said.

And so it surprised me my first day at camp that summer when Landry approached me near the salad bar and said he wanted to introduce me to some guests of his from Dallas. They were mostly fellow members of a company board upon which Landry sat, out for a look at the team. We chatted briefly; no big deal. But I hadn't seen Landry approach a writer about anything. My courage grew: Maybe I would try to take four minutes and forty-five seconds of Landry's time to ask some personal religious questions.

The next morning, back at the Howard Johnson's, I was on the phone when someone knocked at my door. I was on a security floor—the room key opened the entry door—and I assumed the maid was knocking. I put down the phone and carelessly flung open my door.

It was not the maid. It was Mike Trope, accompanied by a very large assistant. As the country's most successful '70s agent, Trope had represented Tony Dorsett when Dorsett first signed with the Cowboys out of Pitt. When Dorsett grew unhappy with that contract and talked of replacing Trope and holding out, I wrote a column about it. Schramm and Brandt showed the column to Trope, he said later. Brandt referred to Trope as "the one agent I like to deal with. He's a pro. You always know you can get a deal done with Mike." (Ultimately, Trope did in fact renegotiate Dorsett's contract.)

Meanwhile, Trope sued me over that column for $40 million and later testified in a deposition that Brandt and Schramm had encouraged him to do so. And now, as I opened the door, he and his assistant had come to serve me the papers. Caught off guard, I accepted the papers and closed the door. Only then did my mind [or imagination] begin to work. How had Trope gained access to my floor? How had he known what room I was in? Most hotel clerks won't tell someone what room a guest is in. Most clerks insist visitors use the house phone to have the hotel operator contact the guest. Trope hadn't called me. Could Brandt have told him what room I was in? Wait a second: Was this why I had been put in the same room for the second straight year? I remembered the room number only because it was 222. I also remembered Brandt boasting once that he "knew the people" at the Howard Johnson's. Was this "Brandt's" room? Good Lord, what if my phone was tapped?

All but quivering with Cowboy paranoia, I walked down to the lobby to call my attorney on the pay phone. As we talked Trope and his assistant came out of the restaurant, conferred briefly, then walked over to where I was using the phone. Trope casually examined a brochure for the Hollywood Wax Museum and said, "I wonder how Skip would look in wax."

On the immediate advice of my attorney I tried to ignore Trope and keep talking into the phone. I was so rattled, I was saying things like, "Well, you know, Mary had a little lamb . . ." Trope and his assistant soon left. But I was so shaken I actually borrowed a knife off my room service tray to carry with me at all times. Now I truly was inside the Dallas Cowboys.

I never did ask Landry if he'd counsel me about religion.

In his former life he was known as Special Agent Mandrake. Among Cowboy players who feared him he was a Mandrake the Magician. His real name (I think) was Larry Wansley, and he was fresh from the FBI where he had worked on many infamous cases, including Patty Hearst's. In April 1983, Tex Schramm hired Wansley to be the Cowboys' security director. "Drugs," said Schramm, "will be one of his main responsibilities."

Another Cowboy first: hiring an ex-FBI agent to combat a drug (and image) problem. An FBI investigation of cocaine use by several prominent Cowboys had inspired a new name: South America's Team. NFL drug counselor Carl Eller said every team had "at least one problem user." But America's Team? "Say it ain't so," said CBS's Dan Rather in a special report.

Schramm went so far as to admit, "If I went back and read *North Dallas Forty* today, I would settle for its being that way versus the problems we have today." That way: booze, painkillers, a little reefer.

Landry backed the hiring of Wansley, saying, "Right now I am more concerned with individual players than the team. I know that is new thinking for me, but I'm old enough where I think that way now. I just don't want to see [what happened to Thomas Henderson] happen with any more of my players. We need to be more aware and help people who need help."

That sounded good. But it appears Wansley was hired more for appearance than results.

Wansley was a distinguished looking black man who seemed out of place in camp shorts and T-shirts. His manner was mild and polite, his voice calm and soothing, his hair and mustache trimmed like Highland Park hedge. In his usual suit, silk tie, and wire-rims, you couldn't picture Wansley yelling, "Freeze!" But if you were a Cowboy and your behavior was anything less than Landry's, you started dreaming of Wansley's pleasant smile.

"I had a bad dream about him," safety Dennis Thurman told me with an uneasy chuckle. "It's just that you don't like the idea of somebody spying on you through your bedroom window. You don't want to live in a police state. You want to keep a private life."

But Wansley first had to concern himself with the team's public life, specifically its relationship with Joe Campisi, known as the "Godfather of Greenville Avenue." Campisi's Egyptian Lounge, on Mockingbird near Greenville, was long known for its best-in-Dallas pizza and dim, smoky atmosphere. Part of the charm of waiting in line for a table was wondering who might have used the ashtray. Campisi was known to be close to the Marcello family of New Orleans; he attended the 1989 wedding of Michael Marcello. In fact, Clint Murchison was an acquaintance of Carlos Marcello, the most feared mob boss in the South. A 1978 FBI wiretap established a direct link between Murchison and Marcello.

At the very least, NFL security considered Campisi's a gamblers' hangout and advised Wansley that Cowboy ties to Campisi had to be severed. Gil Brandt and Campisi were so close that a framed letter from Brandt hung on Campisi's office wall. Brandt often entertained out-of-town guests at Campisi's VIP tables. Cowboy players frequented the restaurant, mostly because the food was good and free and they never had to wait for it. Landry was known to love Campisi's pizza.

At the direction of NFL security, Wansley made Campisi's off-limits for all players and staff. That, however, didn't stop Campisi from visiting Brandt in his office. Says scout John Wooten, "I just couldn't believe Tex let Gil get away with that." Campisi continued catering the Draft Day lunch for the staff and media. Joe himself greeted us from behind the serving line.

Some players kept eating at Campisi's.

A source says, "So many in the organization had such a long-time relationship with Campisi that Wansley was handcuffed." Of course, it's very possible Cowboy officials and players did nothing at Campisi's but eat pizza and sign autographs, but the restaurant's reputation raised serious questions. Was Campisi privy to inside info on injuries or game plans? At Campisi's, would Cowboy players be more susceptible to bribes or even game-fixing temptations? Two local bookmakers told me "word out of Vegas" had it that an occasional Cowboy game was fixed. Naturally, I laughed. They had no proof beyond, "Well, what about Campisi's?"

For sure, it didn't look good. For sure, Wansley was unable to put an end to it. Did Landry's image, Schramm's league influence, or Murchison's vast power keep NFL security from pressing the issue?

Larry Wansley soon traveled with defensive end Harvey Martin to the Hazelden Foundation clinic in Minneapolis. From the *Dallas Morning News:* "Landry emphatically stressed that Martin was sent to the five-day assessment program 'to evaluate it for us. I wanted to get one of our leaders to do it and Harvey agreed. We didn't send Harvey there to dry out. I don't feel he's involved [with drugs] right now. A year or two ago, I don't know.'"

Says black scout Wooten, who was closer to black players than most Cowboy coaches were: "Tom liked to know what Gil could find out about players [in the '70s] so they could be 'kept in line.' But when the drug thing hit, Tom just didn't know how to deal with it. He let Thomas Henderson go to hell. Then he let Harvey go to Hazelden and lied about it. He said it was just a visit to see what the place looked like. After that, Harvey knew they'd lie for him. He was lost.

"Tom was approached and told we were going to lose this team to drugs. But he just didn't seem that interested in doing anything about it. He just couldn't believe the effect it could have. Everything was going to be all right. The team was still close enough to a Super Bowl that just a little more and it would be okay."

Was it that Landry couldn't comprehend the impact cocaine could have or that he didn't want to comprehend it?

"Oh," says Wooten, "it was like with Tex and Gil. Tom knew a lot of the things they were doing, but there was some of that 'right hand doesn't know what the left is doing.' And there was a part of Coach Landry that was just naiveté."

Not long after the Hazelden trip, according to several players, Wansley confronted Martin in the locker room and asked for a urine sample. Voices rose. I'm not sure of the outcome because Martin and Wansley refused comment the day I asked them—at Martin's hastily called retirement press conference. For "the beautiful Harvey Martin," Dallas native, Super Bowl MVP, actor who starred as Lucifer in a Dallas production of "Damn Yankees," it was an inglorious sendoff.

My favorite camp pastime was listening to Dr. Bob Ward, the Cowboy fitness guru. As a marathon runner and weight-lifting addict, I was easily enthralled by Ward's mystical wisdom. He quoted Far Eastern philosophers I hadn't heard of and sold me vitamins I couldn't find in my health-food store. Only Tex Schramm would have hired Dr. Bob, who lived in another dimension of sinew and endorphins.

"Tex," says Ward, "created me."

Naturally, Ward was a California native, from Huntington Beach. In 1982 he was almost fifty and looked to be nearing forty. He had the ruggedly handsome face of an ex-star and the at-peace aura of a martial arts expert, which he was. Ward's weight fluctuated, depending on how much distance he was running, but he averaged a linebackerlike 220. He could lift more weight than most of his players, for whom he set up printout regimens. Ward had a master's degree in physical education from the University of Washington, a doctorate from the University of Indiana, and was track coach for eleven years at Fullerton College before being discovered by Schramm.

Ward gave off Cowboy Mystique like charged electrons. He introduced the team to a $3,000 isolation tank in which Cowboys could reach the "alpha state," Ward said, "and increase learning ten to one." Ward said that, floating in 250 gallons of body-temperature salt water, Danny White could better absorb video of the Redskin secondary.

And if the tank didn't actually work, maybe the Redskins would think it did.

Ward and All-Pro defensive tackle Randy White often could be seen after a camp lunch going at each other with Kung Fu sticks, to improve White's hand-eye quickness and "escapability" from clutching blockers. Ward smiles and says, "Oh, our Cowboy myth was very important to us. Randy and I had been working a lot with martial arts, and everywhere we played, reporters would want to do a story on it. Randy thought the stories really had an effect on the guy trying to block him."

The steroids probably did, too.

White was the most successful of several Cowboy steroid users in the late '70s and early '80s. White came to the Cowboys in 1975 as a middle linebacker at maybe 235 pounds. When the Flex overwhelmed him, even at strong-side linebacker, White was moved to defensive tackle. Landry had to find someplace for the second pick in the entire draft. And White, driven maniacally to succeed in football, had to find some way. Injecting steroids, coupled with lifting massive amounts of weight, helped White bulk up to around 270 pounds and turn into a raging Incredible Hulk.

He told me, "Man, I'd look across the line at those Steelers with their sleeves rolled up on those huge arms and, well, I had to do something. I figured they were using steroids, too."

Larry Cole, who played next to White, said, "Randy was a 'little man' who became a big man." A "Manster," as Charlie Waters called him—half man, half monster. White was so strong, so quick, so crazed during games that he often blew through a blocker as if the poor fellow had the molecule density of a ghost. White was Dr. Bob's most devoted disciple.

So when steroid scandals first hit the headlines at the Pan-Am games in August 1982, I did a column on Cowboy steroid experimentation, quoting Ward on the twelve-week steroid cycle he tried. He experienced a "tremendous drop in fat," a 34 percent increase in overall strength, and added ten pounds, to 225. The only side effects—so far, I wrote—were moodiness and aggression. On the sidelines at Washington, Ward had "gone after" a Redskin defensive back, "which isn't my nature."

Ward said about 25 percent of the Cowboys had used or were using steroids. Ward said, "Man was not created equal, so why shouldn't he use every form of technology to get better?"

Ex-defensive end Pat Toomay, who left Dallas just before Ward arrived, said, "Tex just brought in Ward because he envisioned the day all players would be bionic."

I wrote, "Landry, who tightropes between his religious image and Super Bowl realities, takes a see-no-evil stance on steroids." Landry told me, "We haven't dispensed any, so we don't know." Well, assistant coach Ward certainly knew where to find them, and Ward was reprimanded for talking to me about steroids.

Landry told me he was "opposed to steroids because there are enough controversies about detriments health-wise." But he added, "The bad thing about sports is that people are afraid to get behind. If they hold, you gotta hold, too. That's not right, but that's the American way."

I assumed that meant that if you're going to coach in the NFL, and other teams are using or abusing steroids, then you have to, too. The day after my column appeared, a Cowboy star asked me, "If we're supposed to take steroids to get bigger and stronger and shots to play with pain, why wouldn't we be tempted to use a little cocaine at night to forget all the pain and pressure?"

December 11, 1983. Cowboys and Redskins, both 12–2, going at it for the division title at Texas Stadium.

Earlier I had interviewed Danny White about what it was like to play quarterback for Landry. He said, "I very sincerely believe that one of the hardest things about being a Dallas Cowboy quarterback is making a decision whether to do what Coach Landry *tells* you to do or what he *means*." White told of how play messenger Doug Cosbie sometimes brought in "36 switch" and told White, "I think he means 37."

White said, "It can create confusion."

On the play that turned the Redskin game—and Cowboy season—White suddenly decided to do what he thought Landry meant. This time Landry thought otherwise. Chaos, and Washington, reigned. On fourth and one, White audibled to a play sending fullback Ron Springs off tackle. Against what amounted to an eleven-man line, the play took too long to unfold. Springs was thrown for a loss, as was Landry.

A CBS camera captured a rare flash of emotion, which was replayed repeatedly through the coming weeks. "No, Danny!" Landry yelled as White audibled. "No, no!" That became an epitaph for White's career. Washington 31–10.

That off-season, after the Cowboys were eliminated by the Rams in a wild-card playoff game at Texas Stadium, Gary Myers of the

Dallas Morning News conducted an anonymous poll of Cowboys. Which quarterback did they prefer, White or Gary Hogeboom? "Boomer," as he was called, had a quick, classic release followed by passes with vapor trails. He was taller and heavier than White and appeared to be sturdier when sacked. Hogeboom even drank beer with the boys—not a hobby of White's. The boys mostly voted for Boomer.

Again and again Landry blamed the poll for creating a quarterback controversy. "When a newspaper does a poll like that," Landry said, "what are you gonna do?" Landry vacillated through camp. Landry waited until his final preseason media conference to name a starter. Clearly flustered, Landry announced he was going with Pozderac. Phil Pozderac was an offensive tackle. Landry meant Hogeboom, or "Hoggenbloom," as Landry often called him.

Schramm was promoting 1984 as the Silver Season, a sterling twenty-fifth for the Cowboys. Yes, the Cowboys would honor themselves for all they had accomplished. The "Hogeboom era" dawned like a Pacific sunrise in Anaheim on "Monday Night Football" as the Boomer completed thirty-three of forty-seven for 343 yards. The Cowboys upset the Rams 20–13. A P.R. aide, who had seen Hogeboom wandering through the hotel lobby that afternoon, told him, "You're not going to be able to do that anymore. You'll be mobbed."

By the end of a 9–7 season Hogeboom could have slept in hotel lobbies. The Cowboys had missed the playoffs for the first time since '74. Schramm said, "We're having a hard time living up to ourselves." The Silver Season had been tarnished all the way down to the midseason banquet honoring ex-owner Clint Murchison, who did not appear well.

I visited the Murchison estate once, on a Saturday morning in late 1981. Murchison had surprised me by agreeing to an interview. He wasn't doing many.

What was surprising about the twenty-five-acre estate is that it stuck out like a green thumb on a busy six-lane street, Forest Lane, near the congested intersection of Preston Road. Yes, Murchison's 6200 Forest Lane address was a Hail Mary pass from four corners of shopping centers. Murchison had created his own semitropical island right in the middle of residential North Dallas.

But it had taken him two days a week for twelve years to complete. Murchison designed every inch of the 43,500-square foot, one-story, horseshoe-shaped house, which covered an acre itself. He had supervised the placing of every piece of limestone, which had been imported from Acuna, Mexico. Murchison carefully chose the most exotic trees, shrubs, and flowers that would survive in Dallas, and had them planted at precise angles.

I pulled off Forest Lane into a manicured jungle and headed cautiously up the long driveway beneath overhanging foliage. I didn't want to hit one of the peacocks. A servant answered my ring. Another accompanied Murchison, in short-sleeve blue shirt, black slacks, and black slippers, into the living room. As we exchanged pleasantries my attention was drawn to the open Bible on an ornate stand. Was it for show, like all the Oriental artifacts? I figured so. In our brief chat we stuck to the religion of football.

Later I learned that the former Mrs. Brandt had undergone a religious conversion soon after becoming Mrs. Murchison. Anne told the *Dallas Times Herald*, "God had to give me everything to prove to me that it was worth nothing without Him. He [Murchison] was my god, and I had to begin to deal with that when none of that [Murchison's money] made me happy, not even what I considered to be [Murchison's] wonderful love." Four months after the marriage, therapy helped Anne "work through all the guilt" and "forgive myself." She said, "All my life I had sought the perfect love, and I have found it in Jesus Christ."

Anne went so far as to tell *People* magazine that she "lets Jesus handle even the little things. Like I pray for parking spaces."

By 1980, Anne even had begun to tame her husband. Clint dried out and quit drinking and drugging. Bedford Wynne said, "Oh, Anne was not well liked by Clint's friends. She refused to allow any liquor in the house anymore. Even in the end, when we knew Clint was dying, she wouldn't let his friends bring any alcohol over for one last drink."

Clint began attending Shady Grove Church in Irving, not far from Texas Stadium. The mostly blue-collar members were "charismatic" Christians who spoke in tongues. Murchison had gone from one extreme to the other.

He also was on his way from riches to rags, financially and physically. In business Murchison had followed his father's advice—borrow!—to a fault, or default. On status alone the owner of America's Team had been able to borrow from banks all over the country—America's Scheme. But now, as the Murchison empire collapsed just ahead of the Texas economy, banks everywhere wanted their money back.

The Cowboys had to be sold.

"The first time I actually tried to talk to him on the phone," Bum Bright says of the negotiations, "he just couldn't even speak. It was embarrassing. I just couldn't interpret what he was saying. I finally said, 'Clint, I want to see you.' "

Murchison wasn't looking so well, either. His motto—"Don't worry, it won't happen"—finally had failed him. By 1983 he was diagnosed as having a rare degenerative nerve disease, olivoponto-cerebellar atrophy. His mind still functioned as brilliantly as ever, but his speech and mobility were going.

Was this somehow a result of twenty-five Silver Seasons of some of the wildest living since Caligula? Was Murchison being punished for his sins of the flesh? Had he been left only what he was intended to use most—his mind? And the obvious question: Was Murchison finally turning to God in desperation? Or had he asked God into his heart before his world crumbled? Was Murchison finally happiest, spiritually, when everything worldly was lost? "I'd like to think that was the case," said Wynne, "but only Clint could tell you that for sure."

Bright (along with some minority investors, including Schramm at 3 percent) agreed to buy the Cowboys and their stadium for about $84.5 million. Originally Bright took only 17 percent, though Schramm told him that NFL rules prohibited a general partner of less than 51 percent. Bright was led to believe the rule had never been bent, but Schramm arranged for him to be approved if he would sign a letter giving Schramm full power to be the Cowboys' "league representative"—to, in effect, operate as owner on all league matters. Bright says, "We were learning Pete Rozelle worked for Tex and wouldn't do anything without Tex's approval. . . . At the time I had full confidence in Tex." Bright even told his introductory press conference, at the league meetings in Hawaii, "If you think Clint Murchison was invisible, you ain't seen nuthin' yet."

Bright later learned that "invisible" Clint had an invisible partner. Brother John owned 50 percent of the team, which meant the Murchison brothers had violated the 51 percent rule.

Bright also shakes his head over memories of the March 19, 1984, closing of the Cowboy sale. He says, "It had to be at 7 A.M.

because a Saudi bank needed a [Murchison] note paid by 2 P.M. There were eleven different lawyers [mostly representing members of the Murchison family, who wanted their rightful shares]. There was a lot of hostility and maneuvering. When everybody got paid, there was $365,000 left. But Henry Gilchrist [Murchison's lawyer] said, 'Condition precedent to closing: legal fees!' I said, 'Aw, Henry, send him a bill.' But Henry said, 'I've been sending the son of a bitch a bill for two years.' . . .

"So in the end poor old Clint got not a penny."

Clint Murchison lasted three more years. At his funeral he was eulogized by Tom Landry. "Tom's words," said Bedford Wynne, "were very moving." Tom and Clint had made so much possible for each other.

12

MY 1985 prediction column brought an avalanche of hate mail. I called a spade a spade and dug an 8–8 grave for the Cowboys. They simply weren't as good as NFC East rivals Washington and New York. Throw in games at Cincinnati, Houston, and San Francisco, and another with Chicago, and 8–8 seemed gracious. If I could have known the Cowboys would lose at Detroit and St. Louis, predicting 8–8 would have qualified me for Tex Schramm's P.R. payroll.

The Cowboys were opening with the Redskins, the defending division champs, on a Monday night at Texas Stadium. For my punch line I wrote, "Washington 24–10."

I sagely reasoned that Redskin quarterback Joe Theismann would be the first of many quarterbacks to exploit the Cowboy secondary. Imagine: The Cowboy computer had completely rejected five of the eight Cowboy defensive backs. So had every other NFL computer. Of the five undrafted free agents, three were starters: safeties Dextor Clinkscale and Mike Downs, and cornerback Everson Walls. The other starting cornerback was a seventh-round choice, Ron Fellows, a wide receiver in college. On passing downs, in came free agents Bill Bates or Ricky Easmon, and eleventh-rounder Dennis Thurman. The only credentials belonged to second-rounder Victor Scott, who sometimes performed as if he shouldn't have been drafted.

The Cowboy computer had coughed at these guys because they were slower than Monday night games. Yet I also noted that the Cowboy secondary was "one of the NFL's most cohesive units" and that "as the secondary goes, so go the Cowboys."

But the defensive backs didn't get that far in the column. They hit the word "slow" and hit the ceiling. Then they hit poor Theismann like bats out of hell. They intercepted six Redskin passes and recovered a fumble. The game ended with the Texas Stadium crowd mock-singing "Happy Birthday" to Theismann. Dallas 44, Washington 14 ended so late that I didn't have time to go down to the interview room. Instead, I remained in the press box, force-feeding myself crow as I wrote the next morning's column.

In the middle of the interview room, before six or eight mini-cams, the defensive backs gathered and chanted my name. Walls all but pressed his nose against one minicam and said, "How slow are we now, Skip?"

An amused Danny White watched this scene and came up with a nickname. White, ironically, was not a favorite of the defensive backs. But he told reporters, "They're like thieves—Thurman's thieves."

And a *dynamic*, as Charlie Waters would say, was born. Here, from nowhere, was a force even Tom Landry couldn't control. Here was a love never before shared by Dallas Cowboys, an honor among Thieves. Thurman's Thieves. All the king's horses and all of his men, and these guys put Landry together again.

After the 1985 season new Cowboy offensive coordinator Paul Hackett reviewed the two upsets of Washington and the two of New York and said, "For that team to win the NFC East was one of the all-time great upsets in the history of sports. People just couldn't see it because it happened over several games instead of in just one."

It happened mostly because the Cowboys intercepted thirty-three passes, at all the right times. The Bears led the NFL with thirty-four, but then, the '85 Bears won the Super Bowl with one of the all-time dominant defenses. At Texas Stadium the Bears beat the Cowboys 44–0. At Cincinnati the Cowboys fell behind 50–10, before losing 50–24. At San Francisco the Cowboys lost 31–16. For that matter Detroit led Dallas 26–0, before winning 26–21.

The '85 Cowboys weren't very good, but they stole the NFC

East. Rather, the Thieves did. The Thieves made possible a franchise-record sixty-two sacks—seven and a half by blitzing defensive backs. Many sacks by Cowboy linemen were "coverage" sacks—nobody open, quarterback finally goes down.

The Thieves were a remarkable bunch of rejects. Particularly Everson Walls, who in '85 became the first player ever to lead the NFL in interceptions three times. In 1981 he was one of 117 rookies, including 25 defensive backs, Brandt brought to camp. At the first exhibition game in Dallas, Walls was identified on press box rosters as "Emerson" Walls. The Cowboy P.R. department hadn't even realized that Walls was from Dallas. Not only that, but Walls grew up in the lone black neighborhood in North Dallas, Hamilton Park, just up the street from the Cowboy practice field. Talk about right under your upturned nose.

Walls went undrafted because he was a slow cornerback, usually a deathly combination. He also had clashed with legendary Grambling coach Eddie Robinson. But Walls could control receivers with his superior upper body strength. He had Butch Johnson's big-play hands and "football" speed—an untimable burst as the ball neared. Walls had a burglar's instincts. Walls simply knew how to play cornerback.

The day after the draft Walls chose Dallas over four or five interested teams simply because he loved the Cowboys. He says, "All my teammates at Grambling hated the Cowboys. They wouldn't let me hear the end of it when the Cowboys lost to Pittsburgh in the Super Bowl. They hated the way the Cowboy organization treated black players. Dallas never had signed anyone from Grambling."

The odds against Walls even making the '81 team were somewhere over the rainbow. But "Emerson" made the starting lineup. And the Pro Bowl.

Says Clinkscale, from another black college, South Carolina State, "The defensive backs were like illegitimate children who had found a home. But we caused a lot of resentment. What hurt us most is that when we finally were accepted into the family, we were still treated like illegitimate kids. It was like, 'We'll feed you, but keep your emotion to a minimum.' "

September 29, 1985. Astrodome, Houston. Dennis Thurman had an idea. He called his Thieves together on the sideline and explained a new "double blitz": two defensive backs charging from the same side. Thurman was sure it would throw Oiler quarterback Warren Moon and his young blockers for a loop and a loss. Thurman's suggestion led to twelve sacks and four interceptions of Moon. The Cowboys scored late to win 17–10.

"Dennis didn't have great size or speed," says ex-linebacker coach Jerry Tubbs, "but as a leader and winner you didn't find 'em any better." In 1985 Tubbs had a feeling Thurman would be the NFL's first black head coach. Thurman was coaching defensive backs for Gene Stallings in Phoenix in 1989 when Art Shell became the first for the L.A. Raiders.

Thurman's personality bounced off the locker room walls. He was from Santa Monica, on L.A.'s beach, and could talk "black" or "white" with equally overpowering wit. Thurman liked to talk big, to put pressure on himself, then have to live up to it. That's how he made it to Southern Cal, made all-American, and made Landry's '78 Super Bowl roster. One of Thurman's closest friends was Magic Johnson. Like Magic, Thurman had made-for-ESPN ESP. Thurman could sense an opponent's next move. Thurman had the same feel for football that Magic did for basketball.

Before the 1985 season Landry talked to Thurman about being a player-coach. Nothing was formalized. But once Thurman became the highly publicized leader of the Thieves—the most serious threat yet to Landry's control—Thurman's coaching days in Dallas were over.

"Before that season," Thurman says, "Coach Landry came up with a new slogan, 'Get the Job Done.' We knew the talent had slipped, but we could still feel a little mystique in those magic uniforms. So we knew we had to utilize it, drain it. We had T-shirts made with 'Get the Job Done.' And that year, when we had to, we got it done.

"Not only were the drafts falling off, but we kept seeing the coaches keep one guy when it was clear to everybody on the team that another guy was better. Like Mike Walter versus Jeff Rohrer [both second-round linebackers]. Walter was just a better athlete, but he got cut and went on to San Francisco to become a starter on three Super Bowl teams. You'd think, 'What is going on?' "

By 1985 it appeared Landry preferred to win with inferior cogs. How much satisfaction or credit could he gain with superior talent?

Clinkscale, Thurman's favorite partner in crime, says, "There was so much decay. Even on the coaching staff. Coach Landry was more comfortable with the old-school coaches, the Southern gentlemen. Even Gene [Stallings, the defensive backs coach] was a racist from way back. When Gene was coaching at Texas A&M, he supposedly said, 'There's not a colored boy in America could play for me on scholarship.' Man, did Gene change. He matured and we matured right along with him."

Man, did Stallings mature at age fifty, his last season in Dallas, as he coached the Thieves. Here was a dyed-in-the-cotton Texan who played under Bear Bryant at A&M. Here was a man with a Johnny Cash drawl who had been taught that black boys could run but not think. Here was Stallings coaching blacks who could think much faster than they could run—black "thieves." Lord a'mighty, Stallings was having to open his mind with a crowbar. He even was having to challenge a hermetically sealed mind—Landry's.

Clinkscale says, "In our defensive back meetings, Gene would say, 'Now Tom doesn't agree with this, but this is the way we're going to do it.' At first we'd do it, and he wouldn't back us up. But more and more he did. He kept telling us that winning hinged on how the secondary played. We all but abandoned the Flex. We were playing more of a '46,' like the Bears, attacking, blitzing almost every down. The only way for the Flex to survive was to incorporate what we were doing.

"Ernie [Stautner] was defensive coordinator, but more and more, Gene was untitled coordinator. Ernie [who called defenses from the sideline] would get panicky during games and listen to Gene, and Gene listened to us. At Houston, Dennis suggested the new blitz to Gene, and Gene told Ernie what we were going to do. But when it led to twelve sacks, Ernie was threatened. More and more he resented Dennis, not for his wit but for his wisdom. But Gene backed us to Coach Landry."

Significant development: By 1985 players no longer feared Landry's film sessions the way the Cowboys of the '60s and '70s had. Referring to *The Wizard of Oz*, Clinkscale says, "The curtain had been pulled back. The wizard had been exposed. Film sessions just weren't that tough. Oh, I remember him getting on Walls and Dorsett a couple of times, but nobody thought it was any big deal." Players tended more to roll their eyes at the great and powerful Landry than cower before him. Far fewer starters feared losing their jobs to great young understudies. There weren't any. And thanks to the NFL players' union, even salaries on the NFL's weakest union team, in Dallas, had risen far above middle-class levels. As Pat Toomay said, "For $250,000 [about Thurman's salary] you can take any shit anyone wants to dish out."

By 1985, perhaps, Landry was underpaid for what he was beginning to take.

After the Oilers came the Giants, in New Jersey, prime time Sunday night. Clinkscale stunned his teammates and coaches and perhaps the Giants by saying Giants quarterback Phil Simms was a "facade" and that the Giants would not win the division. This inspired the memorable response from Simms: "Who the hell is Dextor Clinkscale?"

Frederick Dextor Clinkscale usually kept his considerable thoughts to himself. At the time he had a brother working for IBM, another in medical school, and another in law school. Dextor was living their fantasy: third-year starter for the Dallas Cowboys. But Dextor wanted to be a lawyer. The only football Dextor truly enjoyed playing was the video-game variety. Dextor was drawn to the NFL game's cerebral nuances. If only he didn't have to run into people. He had taken a free-agent flyer with the Cowboys, his favorite team, only because his mother insisted. Tom Landry's starting strong safety, responsible for busting up power sweeps, readily admitted, "I don't like contact."

Here was a Cowboy who lived alone in a condo near the practice field, was pursued by models and Cheerleaders, yet preferred to spend evenings at malls, people-watching and mingling. Here was one Cowboy who didn't smoke anything or drink a drop of alcohol. Here was a Dallasite who was a regular at church and Bible study, yet was quick to say, "I constantly wrestle with the devil." Here was yet another stranger-than-fiction Cowboy.

"Maybe the smartest player we ever had," Jerry Tubbs said. "Not fast, but great quickness. Very effective."

And Clinkscale, with backup vocals from Thurman, spread the word through the New York papers: "The Thieves are coming. Lock up your jewels." Thurman says, "Guys on the team were very upset with us, but we said those things to help propel the team to another emotional level. Man for man, the Giants were better than we were. We couldn't go to New York and win at the nonemotional level we were used to."

Security was beefed for Clinkscale at the Marriott Marquis in

Manhattan. The pressure weighed on him until "my back was so knotted I played in intense pain." He was told Simms had offered $1,000 to any teammate who knocked Clinkscale out of the game.

Simms nearly took care of the entire band of Thieves by himself. He threw for 432 yards, including touchdown passes of 51, 23, and 70. But with about three minutes remaining and a 29–27 lead, Simms fumbled a snap, which the Cowboys recovered at the Giants' 19. The Cowboys couldn't move, but Rafael Septien made a thirty-one-yard field goal. Dallas 30–29. Simms quickly passed the Giants to the 50. But his next pass, with 1:16 remaining, was intercepted by Walls. The Cowboys stole away with another victory.

"Simms threw a party," says Clinkscale, "but he gave out too many gifts."

Thurman chimes, "What we told the press came to fruition. We said Simms was good but not great. We said he'll put up good numbers, but before it's over he'll do something to self-destruct. That's exactly what Coach Landry told us in the meeting, but we said it publicly and we were made out to be the bad guys."

Perhaps the Thieves should have chosen white hats that afternoon in St. Louis. The Cowboys hit town for a Monday nighter at 6–2. Browsing through the Union Station mall, Walls checked out a little freestanding circular shop called Hats in the Belfry. He paid $50 for what he calls "an Indiana Jones fedora. It was sweet. I didn't buy it just for fun." By the pre-game meal every Thief had patronized Hats in the Belfry.

Clinkscale smiles and says, "We bought hats similar to Landry's but with a little more flash. It was like, 'If he can wear one, we can, too.' The same hat he wore could make you look like a gangster or make you look astute. Was he a genius? Or was he a cold, uncaring man who could have you bumped off at any time?"

Were the Thieves good or evil? Shrewd or foolish? Were these "hoods" Robin Hoods? Was Landry the Coach of Nottingham? Whatever, the Thieves made Landry's holy symbol, the hat, their symbol. Talk about a hat trick.

Lightning was about to strike.

With kickoff at 8 P.M., the Thieves had agreed to do a live TV interview at 6:25 for Dallas station WFAA. Interviews weren't often done before games, but this one, staged just outside the Busch

Stadium locker room, would be quick. For this one the Thieves decided to wear their new Landry hats. Several defensive linemen and coaches immediately decided the Thieves had bats in the belfry.

Tubbs, a small-town Texan who starred at Oklahoma, says, "As a general rule the typical old-fashioned white player and coach has a success-oriented, serious outlook with no show. No frills. It's more of an English-type attitude. The blacks don't buy into that, on the whole, so some of the guys really resented the hats and the interview."

Tubbs referred mostly to defensive linemen Randy White and John Dutton. But this clash wasn't strictly black and white. Defensive lineman Jim Jeffcoat, who is black, also resented the Thieves. Bill Bates, who is white, was considered a Thief and had a hat to prove it. But what happened that night on the sideline definitely had racial undertones.

In the third quarter St. Louis scored on an eight-yard sweep to take a 14–10 lead. On the sideline Thurman approached linebacker Rohrer and end Jeffcoat the way an assistant coach would. Thurman says, "They had blown an assignment, and I was just trying to clear it up. On 'jet' the defensive end had 'contain' [responsibility to turn in a sweep]. On 'fly' the linebacker had 'contain,' and the end was free to go to the football. One thought 'jet' and one thought 'fly,' and neither contained the touchdown play. I was trying to do something positive. I said, 'You guys just need to communicate.' But Randy White jumped in and said, 'What the fuck are you talking about?' He was in a rage. Totally out of control. He wanted to fight."

Too bad an ABC camera didn't follow this action.

Clinkscale: "Randy said, 'Sit your ass down, Dennis.' Dennis said, 'Randy, I'm not talking to you.' Randy kept on, and Dennis got excited and swore back at him. I had to grab Dennis because he wouldn't back down. He was saying, 'That sorry motherfucker. He ain't shit to me.' "

The rest of the way, the Cowboys weren't much to the Cardinals, either. St. Louis 21–10.

More Clinkscale: "Later, I was in the shower with Randy and his Ed McMahon, Dutton, and maybe Randy's drugs had worn off because he was sane again. He said, 'Dextor, I don't see what everybody's mad about. You and I cuss each other out all the time.' Which was true. Once, Randy missed a tackle and got up and said, 'Tackle the motherfucker, Dextor.' And I said, 'You tackle the motherfucker.' We got in the huddle and he said something else, and I said, 'Ain't nothing between you and me but the huddle.' He said, 'Shut the fuck up.' I said, 'Fuck you.' This went on all the time."

But this time the ill will wasn't washed away by a post-game shower. This was a clash of wills between the leader of the Thieves and Landry's anointed leader, White. This was black and White. The Thieves considered White a red-neck fisherman who had reeled in Landry. They resented that White wasn't criticized by Landry, to the media or in film sessions, even after not-so-great games. White almost always was portrayed by the media as a fierce competitor with a heart of gold. The Thieves saw him as a great player too hung up on guns-and-snuff macho to be the team leader. At one Pro Bowl, outside motel bungalows in Hawaii, Walls was "sickened" by a drunken Sumo-like fight he witnessed between White and the Bears' Dan Hampton, as White's wife and crying daughter pleaded for them to stop.

"Randy," says Thurman, "held on to that St. Louis incident for the rest of the year. Coach Landry certainly wasn't going to side with me."

Walls says, "Tom refused to admit Randy was a racist. Tom just said to us, 'Well, stop wearing the hats.' I said, 'Hell, no, I paid $50 for this hat.' It was all so crazy and childish."

The next week Landry called a captains meeting, attended by White and Thief Mike Downs. Downs reported back to the Thieves that White apologized and said, "I didn't see Dennis Thurman in front of me. I just saw a black guy wearing a gangster hat." This further infuriated the black Thieves.

A poster-style picture that soon ran in the *Dallas Morning News* further infuriated anti-Thieves. Dressed to kill, the Thieves posed as cold-eyed gangsters around Thurman, the only one who didn't wear his hat. Thurman's eyes said, "I'm the brains of this operation."

Schramm privately cussed the Thieves to reporters, who relayed the remarks to the Thieves, who relayed their indignation to Schramm. "We heard he called us some really bad names," Clink-scale says. "Then he came down [to the locker room] all nice and friendly and apologized. He said, 'Oh, I didn't say *that*.' He hated us, and I just couldn't understand it. He was an innovator, and so were we. But we had become a threat to him and Landry."

Yet somehow the Cowboys teamed again the following Sunday to all but rob the Smithsonian. How they won in Washington 13–7 may still be under FBI investigation. They had the shortest possible recovery/preparation time—a Saturday departure following a Tuesday morning return from the loss in St. Louis. But they pulled it off, intercepting Theismann three times, sacking him six times, and confusing him more times than he wanted to admit. "They did a great job disguising their coverages," Theismann said.

And disguising dissension. The next Sunday, at Texas Stadium, the same Cowboys lost to the Bears 44–0. Has an NFL team ever won and lost so spectacularly?

As I finished a recent interview with Dr. Bob Ward, the Cowboy fitness coach, he said, "You really need to talk to Walter Covert. It's very possible he had a lot to do with what happened in 1985."

"As in covert operation?" I said.

Ward smiled cryptically and said, "I don't know, so many weird things happened in those games. . . . You ought to talk to Walter about psychotronics."

Covert psychotronics at Cowboy games? Okay, I'd bite. Ward set it up. Covert agreed to drop by my home. I was surprised when he arrived in a cab. I asked what happened to his car. He appeared rattled. He said his brakes had just gone out. He indicated it might have been "another" attempt on his life. He said he was afraid to talk in detail to me.

"I just want to protect you," he said. He wouldn't say much more about psychotronics.

But Covert, I found, could quote at length from Einstein, Freud, Ben Franklin, Galileo, Shakespeare, Nietzsche, and the Bible. "Brilliant, brilliant mind," Ward says of Covert. I checked with a highly regarded Dallas doctor who knows Covert. "Brilliant but scattered," the doctor said.

Just how scattered I'll leave to you.

Ward met Covert in 1975, Ward's first season with the Cowboys. Lamar Hunt's North American Soccer League team, the Tornado, had offices in the same tower the Cowboys did. Covert says he came to Dallas to play for the Tornado. Now, at age thirty-eight, Covert still has the look of a European soccer player—slender, wiry, brownish hair parted down the middle. Covert grew up in Meridian, Mississippi, but went to college "in England" and played soccer "all over Europe."

His field is "bioelectronics." He said he is experimenting with technology that could cure cancer, regenerate bones, and allow athletes to achieve a high that would forever detoxify them from drug use. The technology, he indicated, could put some in the medical industry out of business and, if misused, could make a fortune for the wrong people. Sound like a "Batman" episode?

With the Cowboys, anything was possible. For sure, a Cowboys coach authorized Covert's experimentation on the Cowboys.

Ward says, "I just know there's a technology out there that very few people understand. The experimentation with it is supposed to be rampant behind the Iron Curtain. I like to put things in a context I can understand. There probably was a time people would have scoffed at the idea of the radio. Today you take it for granted. But do you know how it works? Very simply, radio waves are forms of vibrations modulated and changed back into a form that can be heard with the ears. What's so difficult about that?"

I gathered that Covert has a piece of equipment that somehow modulates brain waves. Covert said, "It has enormous potential for good as well as evil, like a hammer." Could it be used to hamper a team's performance as well as enhance it? "In the next few years," he said, "measures will have to be taken to guard against this technology, or some teams will get their lights knocked out."

In 1985, says Ward, Covert experimented "recreationally" on the Cowboys before key games. Clinkscale and Thurman say they never met any Walter Covert and weren't aware of any "brain machine." But Ward says, "It was unnecessary for them to know about it."

When I appeared skeptical, Covert said, "Einstein said, 'Great spirits always have encountered violent opposition from mediocre minds.' "

Ward asked me, "Do you believe in prayer?"

Yes, I said.

And Ward said, "Some people think the idea of prayer is far-fetched."

For sure, what the Cowboys did on December 15, 1985, was implausible. After that game I'd have believed Landry had discovered Flubber. Phil Simms and the Giants came to Texas Stadium to play for the division title. The Giants wound up with twenty-five first downs to the Cowboys' thirteen. Cowboy quarterbacks Danny White and Gary Hogeboom were hurt, leaving clipboard-carrier Steve Pelluer to play the fourth quarter.

And the same Cowboys who had just lost in Cincinnati 50–28 beat the Giants 28–21.

In the first quarter, the surest-handed Giant receiver, punt returner Phil McConkey, broke free on a post pattern and dropped a perfect pass. Late in the second quarter, as the Giants drove toward a 21–7 lead, at the Dallas 22, a Simms pass was batted and intercepted by Jeffcoat, who returned it sixty-five yards for a touchdown. The Cowboys quickly held. Giant punter Sean Landeta fumbled the snap. The Cowboys took over at the Giant 12 and scored again. In two minutes the Giants had gone from a potential 21–7 halftime lead to trailing 21–14. In the game, the Giants reached the Cowboy 22, 17, 25, 24, and 16 without scoring a point.

Midway through the fourth quarter, Pelluer faced a third-and-fifteen from his 48. Against a max-blitz, Pelluer hit rookie Karl Powe for twenty-eight yards. Pelluer? Powe? Covert? The Cowboys scored to lead 28–14. The Giants cut it to 28–21. Finally, Simms drove the Giants to the Cowboy 16. With time running out, Victor Scott intercepted to preserve the NFC East title.

Why didn't Ward continue using Covert? Ward says he hesitated to even mention psychotronics to Landry. Once, as Ward went over some ideas in Landry's office, Landry nodded off. "I just kept talking until he woke up," says Ward, who probably was hired for P.R. as much as IQ.

So Covert has taken his pschotronics elsewhere. As I took him home he said he wasn't sure how much longer he would live in Dallas. "There's a real struggle in this city between the light and dark forces," he said. "There has been so much greed here. Greed is the biggest problem on this planet."

I liked Covert. I wanted to believe him the way I want to believe in time machines. Only the Cowboys could have attracted a Walter Covert. But I pitied him, too.

Before he got out of the car, he wrote on a piece of paper the name "Marcello."

For the Cowboys' first pick in 1984, Brandt recommended Billy Cannon, Jr., who scored high in two key areas. He was the son of former Heisman Trophy winner Billy Cannon, which meant bonus publicity, and he had played at Texas A&M, Bum Bright's school. Bright says Brandt probably pushed for Cannon to score points with the new owner. Several Cowboy scouts say Cannon was a second-rounder at best. A neck injury ended Cannon's career before anyone could find out.

In 1984–85 one of those scouts was Drew Pearson, who doubled as an assistant coach. Pearson says, "In the early '80s we couldn't believe the shit they were bringing in from the draft. These guys didn't have it when they got there. . . . There was so much arrogance and complacency. You should have seen how Landry shot down the assistant coaches' ideas. It was like, 'Damn, what did I spend the last eight hours working on?' Man, I didn't want to do that for fifteen or twenty years."

Brandt sent out Pearson with a "black box" of devices to measure and time potential draftees. "I said, 'Just let me go out and see if the guy is a football player.' Let me see how fluid he runs, how natural an athlete he is. Let me get inside his head, see how many brothers and sisters he has, see what motivates the guy. Let me check the *human* aspect. But no."

Pearson was sent to Delaware to work out John Taylor. Taylor stood him up the first time, and Pearson had to make a second trip. "I came away raving about the guy. I had thrown all kinds of passes low and behind him, and he hadn't missed a thing. I went back and said, 'We cannot pass this kid up.' But Gil said something about drugs. I said there was no evidence of drugs, and Gil said, 'Why did he miss that first workout?' Gil totally dominated."

Taylor caught the winning pass in Super Bowl XXIII for the San Francisco 49ers.

John Wooten says, "By then it was almost like Gil preferred to lose with his guys than win with other people's recommendations. That's scary."

Wooten and Pearson suspected Brandt fabricated deficiencies to knock a potential draftee to Landry. "Then," says Pearson, "we had some injuries at receiver and needed to pick someone up, and Gil came in with his big, thick book [of current NFL players]. I wanted us to go with Raymond Butler, who was available and could still run. But Gil looked up Butler and said, 'IQ not high enough,' and slammed his book shut. We went with Gordon Banks [from Stanford]. Come on . . . They [Landry and Brandt] even talked bad about Jerry Rice. Jerry Rice! The best receiver in football today. They said his IQ wasn't high enough. I'm not saying a guy can be a dummy, but they always found company guys who never complained.

"They just couldn't stand any individuality. I said. 'Hey, if Thieving motivates these son of a bitches, let 'em wear hats and Thieve. If Quaking gets 'em in the end zone, let 'em Quake.' But they had to take all that away. If Tex had invented the Quake or the Thieves, they would have been all right."

Pearson quit after one season.

Doughnuts. Thurman and Clinkscale remember boxes and boxes of doughnuts on locker-room tables. This was before the divisional playoff game against the Rams in Anaheim. "Lots of guys," says Clinkscale, "were kicked back eating doughnuts. We had the look of a loser."

Especially Tony Hill, the one-time Pro Bowl receiver. Without Drew Pearson and Butch Johnson to push him, Hill often failed to push away from the table. His weight was as high as 235, earning him the nickname Fridge.

The Thieves did a low number on Ram quarterback Dieter Brock, who hit just six of twenty-two passes for fifty yards. But Eric Dickerson ran through the Flex at silent-movie speed for 248 yards on thirty-four carries. Danny White was a fright. Rams 20, Cowboys 0.

Yes, these Cowboys looked like the ones I'd written off for 8–8.

In the locker room I waited out the crowd of reporters around Landry and asked, one on one, if he planned to return the next season. "I'm not sure," he said, as always. "I need to get away and evaluate."

In hindsight it's easy to see this would have been the best time for Landry, at sixty-one, to go out a winner. Well, a division winner. Bob Ward says, "Every indication we got as assistants was that Tom was phasing out. He gave everybody more responsibility that off-season, and I was sure he was retiring."

If only he had, and saved himself and so many so much heartache.

That pointless day in Anaheim, Number 33 was no factor— seventeen carries, fifty-eight yards. Anthony Drew Dorsett was many things, but seldom no factor. Carrying the ball or dropping it in his not-so-private life, Dorsett annually led America's Team in headlines. He had two of the quickest feet in NFL history and

constantly put them in his mouth. He was called Hawkeye because
of his big eyes and extraordinary on-field vision. But out of uniform,
Dorsett often leaped before he looked.

After 20–0, Dorsett criticized his offensive line to reporters. He
was right: The many holes in the Cowboy line weren't the kind you
run through. But if my mail was any indication, the reaction of most
fans was, "Why can't the little [fill in expletive or slur] just keep his
mouth shut and run?"

Dorsett, it seemed, was respected much more by teammates
than by fans or perhaps management. At heart Dorsett was a Thief;
Thurman, Clinkscale, and Walls were among his closest friends.
They called him "T," short for TD, and they were in awe of his
acceleration and star quality. Clinkscale says, "Tony was the best I
ever played with. Somehow God let football find Dorsett because he
couldn't have played anything else. Well, maybe he could have run
track, but he probably would have been too lazy. He had no basketball skills to speak of. He was no dancer. He had zero hands. His
dimensions weren't big [five-feet-ten, 185]. But he had incredible
explosion and the ability to sustain it for distances. He was just a
blur, with very quick vision. And he was much, much tougher than
rumored to be. He had the heart of a lion. He was put together well
in his upper body so he could take a lot of punishment, and he did
take a lot.

"But he was spoiled by his college success [Dorsett won a Heisman Trophy at Pitt]. He didn't give a damn what color a girl was. If
he wanted her, he went after her. Italian, Hispanic, white, or
black—Tony didn't care. . . . He was very gullible. Innocently stupid. Too trusting. He could be arrogant, but he was really just a
super nice guy."

When I think of Cowboy cool, I flash on Dorsett climbing
slowly out of his midnight-black Porsche in full-length mink. As
Raider Matt Millen once said, "He's the slowest-walking, fastest-
running guy I've ever seen." Dorsett had a slo-mo strut that could
hypnotize every woman in Cafe Dallas. The baby-faced Dorsett was
as cute as an undone button.

But beneath the mink was another very lost soul. The Dorsett
I sometimes saw was as scared and lonely as he often made open-
field tacklers feel. Dallas swallowed him as if he were a free drink.
"Everywhere I go," he said, "somebody has another deal for me,
and most of 'em are bad. Most people are trying to stick a knife in

your back. It's to the point I can't have any friends, and that's a lonely feeling."

For Tex Schramm, Dorsett was a puppet on a purse string. Come contract time, Dorsett was Silly Putty in Schramm's hands. Schramm seemed fascinated with Dorsett's speed and style, and was said to have a soft spot for him. But Schramm also seemed to derive satisfaction from throwing his biggest star for losses in highly publicized negotiations. The most controversial came in 1985.

For a year Dorsett had stewed about how Randy White had held out until Schramm made him the team's highest-paid player. "We kept telling Tony to hold out," Walls said at the time. "He was one of the most underpaid superstars. I know fans haven't liked his attitude because he parties a lot. But he has been true to the organization. He has been our captain. He has run hard behind a make-shift line. Look at the record: Thirty-nine of the forty-one times Tony has rushed for more than one hundred yards, we've won. I mean, he'll definitely be a Hall of Famer."

Yet Dorsett's $450,000 salary was about half of what Walter Payton and Billy Sims were making. So, as camp approached, Dorsett decided to hire White's agent, Howard Slusher, and hold out. Slusher specialized in lengthy holdouts. Schramm so despised Slusher that he could barely say Slusher's name in press conferences.

But Schramm knew something the public didn't. The Internal Revenue Service had disallowed multiple tax writeoffs taken by Dorsett in 1979, 1980, and 1983. When Dorsett didn't have the reserves to cover the back tax and penalties totaling $414,000, the IRS attached his Cowboy wages and took two houses Dorsett owned. So when Dorsett failed to report to camp on time, Schramm mentioned something about Dorsett's "problems" on his KRLD radio show. KRLD sports director Brad Sham followed that lead, and "other indications," he says, and broke the full story the following day. Dorsett's teammates accused Schramm of leaking the story to make *his* financial problem (Dorsett's holdout) appear to be Dorsett's IRS problem. To fans, it probably appeared he had squandered millions on cars and minks, couldn't pay his taxes, and was holding up Schramm for even more money. Dorsett had three years left on a seven-year contract.

"Tony didn't leak the story," Walls said. "His teammates sure didn't leak it."

When I cross-examined Schramm, he denied leaking the story

and said he was "irate" Dorsett's problems had been smeared across the headlines. The somber Schramm acted like a forgiving father whose son hadn't listened. He said Dorsett was "a very confused and distraught individual, and we just want to help him." Schramm tipped reporters that he even had lent Dorsett $500,000 over the previous six months. Again, to the public, the stories read as if Schramm repeatedly had rescued his prodigal son of a . . .

But the money was a loan, not a gift—a loan that undercut Dorsett's bargaining power. After a meeting with Schramm, Dorsett fired Slusher and signed a renegotiated contract for $550,000 in 1985—still far below his market value. The new package improved Dorsett's long-term financial security, but with deferred dollars that would lose value. What a masterstroke by Schramm. He looked like a hero while reeling Dorsett back to camp for a steal of a deal. Dorsett even apologized to reporters for saying Schramm had "double-crossed" him. "I also want to apologize to America," said a penitent Dorsett, who never won a game against Texas E.

Dextor Clinkscale held out of the next training camp. He was entering the option year of his contract, and management had cold-shouldered him. But he insisted his protest wasn't really about money. "I'm going to play for what I'm worth," he told me, "or I'm going to play for free. If the NFLPA says I have to accept a salary, I'll give it to charity. I'll play damn good and say, 'I don't want your dirty money.' "

Now, he says, "I felt like I was innocently living in the Mafia. I couldn't believe all the things I was seeing behind closed doors of the team I grew up loving."

But in the end all Clinkscale wanted was for Tom Landry to say he loved him. "Just a little respect," Clinkscale says. He met with Schramm. He met with Landry. That, of course, was just what he got: very little respect.

He asked to be released, and was. Six teams were interested in him. He chose Indianapolis, for nearly double the financial package he had in Dallas. He lasted one season. "They really made me feel needed, but I was in love with being a Dallas Cowboy. My heart wasn't in it. It was the wrong girl."

*   *   *

Early that camp, as Clinkscale held out, Dennis Thurman spoke up and out for him. In a more subtle show of support, Thurman wrote a small 47, Clinkscale's number, on the towel he tucked into his practice pants. Soon, though, the coaches weren't being so subtle about Thurman's involvement in drills. "I'm just not getting much practice time," he told me.

At lunch one day a TV sportscaster who was tight with team management told me Thurman wouldn't be with the team by opening day. I said something like, "I just don't believe that. Thurman's too valuable. He's only thirty years old. As hard as he works out in the off-season, he could play five or six more years."

Even that year's media guide called Thurman, the NFC's leading active interceptor with thirty-six, "as valuable a nonstarter as can be imagined."

"Trust me," the TV guy said with a wink.

After I told Thurman about the tip, he went to Landry to ask about his status. "He said he isn't sure yet," Thurman told me uneasily, "but that it looks like I'm in his plans."

Unconvinced, Thurman had his agent ask Landry for a trade. Landry said no. Yet Thurman barely played until the fourth exhibition game, on a Saturday night, when he forced a fumble that was returned for a touchdown. On Monday, after practice, equipment man Jerry Fowler approached Thurman in the locker room and told him Landry wanted to see him.

"I could tell by Jerry's eyes what was up," Thurman says.

The meeting was brief. Thurman took a seat across the desk from Landry.

"If he felt any emotion," Thurman says, "he didn't show it. Oh, he tried to pacify me by saying things like, for my size and speed, I was one of the better players he'd seen in a long time. But he just said he was going with younger players, and that was that. Not once did he look at me. Not once. I know it's pro football, it's a business and all, but it was cold. I felt that distance he was noted for. A lot of guys felt it when they were released. Ron Springs, Mike Hegman, Ron Fellows, Dextor—they all felt the chill. He got up and shook my hand, but I felt no warmth, not that I really expected any.

"All I know is that he sure didn't cry the way he did [in front of the team] when he released John Dutton. To this day I can't understand that. Tom didn't even get emotional when Roger retired. You never knew."

Clinkscale says, "In my opinion Coach Landry got emotional over Dutton for two reasons. Number one, Dutton was the biggest trade the Cowboys ever made [coming from Baltimore in 1979 for the Cowboys' first- and second-round picks]. They really went out on the limb for him. They built him up to be sensational because he'd had some great years in Baltimore. But he just never was that good in the Flex. Landry had to make a really tough choice whether to keep him because he wasn't that productive anymore. That's part of why he got choked up. But Dutton was also one of those guys who professed to 'love and respect' Landry. You know: Randy White, Don Smerek, Dutton—all backed by Ernie Stautner. We couldn't believe how much Dutton could get away with in front of Landry. He could complain—just come out with a string of profanity—and the coaches would say, 'Oh, that's just Dutton, always cuttin' up.' We used to laugh about what would have happened to Ron Springs or Butch Johnson or even Dennis if they'd done the same things."

The night he was cut, Thurman said, "At least they [the coaches] could have done this earlier. With everybody cutting down, it's hard to get picked up now. I just think this is something they knew all along."

"Premeditated murder," says Clinkscale. "A lot of guys were even hot about the way Coach Landry let Dennis practice, then told him he was gone. Why not tell him in the morning?"

Many '80s Cowboys would remember the way Thurman's release was handled when Landry was released by Jerry Jones and complained it was mishandled. No, Thurman was no Hall of Famer. Landry certainly didn't owe Thurman a gold watch or picnic. Thurman made a nice living off the Cowboys playing a game he loved. But in the end he expected a little more consideration from a coach so loved by the masses. For living with eight seasons of Cowboy uncertainty and insecurity, for never missing a game with injury and making so many big plays, Thurman thought he "deserved just a little better."

Thurman was picked up immediately by new St. Louis coach Gene Stallings.

Thurman says, "Anyone who had the ability to think and reason and give a perspective Tom didn't want projected, Tom didn't want around. It was as simple as that."

Just after he heard Thurman was gone, Dorsett heaved a bitter sigh and said, "On this team you either go with the flow or you go.

Most teams don't mind if a guy's a little outspoken. But you don't do that stuff around here."

"A terrible blow for this team," Walls said.

The Thieves' ringleaders, Thurman and Clinkscale, had been sent up the river, and Landry had been a winner for the last time.

Recently, as Landry reflected on his twenty-nine seasons, he said, "The team I enjoyed the most was the '85 team that won the East. It was so outmanned. There was no reason why New York or Washington shouldn't have won the division that year. We won it because of guys like Mike Renfro. And Steve Pelluer coming in and throwing to Karl Powe. I enjoyed coaching them and seeing them perform."

No mention of the interceptions or sacks. The inference was, "That was my greatest coaching job." Maybe it was. But the Thieves say that quote says it all about 1985.

13

ONE EVENING in February 1986, I was working on a column at home. I wanted to catch the 10:25 P.M. sportscast, so, as a reminder, I flipped on the TV and turned down the sound. A moment later I glanced up and received the biggest shock since I first saw *Psycho*.

Side by side sat Tom Landry and Paul Hackett, smiling. Behind them, like the star of Bethlehem, was the silver Cowboy star on a blue background. This was the platform used for major Cowboy press conferences. Clearly, this was a major announcement.

Hackett had done it! I had warned him, and he had done it anyway. For God's Coach, I figured, all hell was about to break loose. Heaven help Hackett, too.

I met Hackett in 1976 when he was quarterback coach and offensive coordinator for John Robinson at Southern Cal and I worked for the *Los Angeles Times*. For a day-in-the-life story on college recruiting, I hit the talent trail with Hackett, and we hit it off. He was unlike any coach I'd dealt with, and perhaps I wasn't what he expected, either. We shared loves of playing basketball, listening to rock 'n' roll, and debating life's meaning. Hackett was the son of a political science professor who taught at the University of California-Berkeley. Hackett said he was the black sheep of his family for pursuing a career in football instead of the arts or sciences.

Hackett was the only coach I've known who could passionately discuss whether John Lennon was more talented than Paul McCartney. Hackett had the most extensive rock 'n' roll collection this side of Wolfman Jack. At heart Hackett remained in 1969, when Janis Joplin and Jimi Hendrix explored the same new realms Hackett did in the passing game. Hackett made a special trip to the store the first day the Beatles' "Abbey Road" album was available in CD.

Hackett was a football artiste in awe of musical genius. Hackett was strung tighter than an electric guitar and was prone to piercing highs and lows. He could bubble or boil over. He could get James Bond cocky—he had every Bond film on tape. He also could doubt himself and his profession to the point that he once asked if I could help him get a job as a disc jockey.

Hackett often looked as if he had crammed all night for a quantum-football exam. His hairline was retreating and his face had the ruddy glow of high blood pressure. During the season he'd live on Snickers and adrenaline, if necessary. He watched rival game film as if it were Agatha Christie: There! The free safety cheats one step left! We got him!

Hackett was driven to create unstoppable passing schemes and to make a quarterback believe in them. Hackett was a one-on-one teacher, communicator, motivator, brother figure. He had his quarterbacks and their wives or girlfriends over for dinner and rock 'n' roll dessert. He looked much more natural in T-shirts, jeans, and sneakers than coats and ties. Imagine Landry in jeans. Even nearing forty, with a wife and two sons, Hackett could think and speak hip. He loved to laugh, to get "gunned up" about going to a Fleetwood Mac concert, to gush about the "sheer greatness" of a Larry Bird–Magic Johnson game he'd watched.

In case you haven't noticed, Paul Hackett had very little in common with Tom Landry. I soon would wonder what Landry thought when Hackett was quoted in Dallas papers as saying he wanted to catch a Madonna concert after a Cowboy exhibition game in San Francisco. "I just think she's a major talent, and I want to see her perform," Hackett said. This guy was going to work in concert with Tom Landry?

Hackett was intensely faithful to wife Elizabeth and devoted to his sons: "I'd be nothing without them." But Hackett didn't even pretend to be religious. He had his reasons; I respected them. At least he wasn't a hypocrite. Hackett often blurted his heart to a reporter, a player, or his head coach.

Roll over, Beethoven. You, too, Coach Landry.

Hackett's claim to football fame was making a quarterback an extension of his soul. Not mind. Soul. A Hackett pupil became Hackett. Hackett wanted to know their moms, girl problems, politics, religion. Did he get too close to criticize? No. In the name of perfection, Hackett was relentlessly demanding in the classroom and during practice. Some vets thought he could go nearly as crazy as assistant Ditka once did. While Landry devastated players with monotone critique in front of their peers, Hackett could take apart a player one on one, as if the poor guy were standing in front of a speaker at a Rolling Stones concert.

But Hackett's tone was always, "You are *better* than this." At the University of California–Davis, Hackett was a pretty good quarterback with pretty meager talent. So his attitude was, "Do you realize how fortunate you are? If I had your talent, I might still be playing." Hackett worked the practice field like Mick Jagger working a stage. He pleaded, blasted, cheered. Everything was VERY GOOD or VERY BAD, and after practice Hackett was sometimes very hoarse. Landry, of course, used a bullhorn at practice to correct players from a distance, giving his voice a God-above omnipresence.

Hackett was the unLandry.

Again and again Hackett had helped make good quarterbacks great, great quarterbacks better. Hackett developed Steve Bartkowski and Joe Roth at Cal, Vince Evans and Paul McDonald at Southern Cal. Brian Sipe had an MVP season under Hackett in 1982 at Cleveland. San Francisco quarterback Joe Montana raved about "Hack."

From 1983 to 1985 Hackett was the creative collaborator of San Francisco coach Bill Walsh, who said, "Paul is the best young mind I've ever worked with." Hackett became Walsh's son of Flubber. Like Walsh, Hackett was an inventor prone to extreme highs and lows. After three seasons Hackett and Walsh were, as Hackett said, "about to put each other in the funny farm." Too many will-work, won't-work clashes had nearly pushed Hackett's mental and physical health over the edge. His lingering memory of Walsh was of coaches' meetings the morning after losses: Walsh, elbows on table, face in hands. "The Pose," Hackett called it, with a shudder.

Hackett called me soon after the '85 season ended and asked how I thought he'd fit on the Cowboy staff. "You wouldn't," I said. "Reeves and Mackovic constantly complained about how little input they had. You might feel like you'd gone from the funny farm to solitary confinement. Landry runs everything."

"Oh, come on," he said. "It can't be that bad."

"Maybe not," I said, "but it sure seems that way. Have you been contacted?"

"No," he said. "Nothing concrete. Just a feeler."

Soon Oiler general manager Ladd Herzeg interviewed Hackett for Houston's head coach vacancy. Hackett and Elizabeth flew to Houston for a highly publicized wining and dining. But Hackett came in second to Jerry Glanville and was told by Houston writers he had been "used" by Herzeg to show fans that the GM had made a "thorough search." Hackett was crushed. That was the last I heard from him until I saw him on my TV screen.

When I talked to Hackett a day later, he was back on top of the world. Cocky. Gunned up. He laughed and said, "I didn't call you because I knew you'd tell me not to come. But it's a lot better deal than you think."

Hackett got a kick out of a picture that ran that morning, showing him and Landry at the press conference. While Hackett is earnestly explaining his offensive philosophy, Landry is craning his neck sideways, turtlelike, with a squint that appears to say, "Who is this whippersnapper?" Hackett read nothing ominous into the picture; Landry had welcomed him publicly and privately. But Hackett thought the picture looked so funny that he taped it to his refrigerator door.

The picture would be worth a thousand Xs and Os. One day Hackett would call his experience under Landry a "tragedy."

Bum Bright didn't like what he was hearing about one of his many companies, Dallas Cowboys Football Inc. He still couldn't get comfortable with the idea of pouring money down the Cowboy drain. It just wasn't his penurious nature. Texas A&M was in the process of going to three straight Cotton Bowls, so saying he was "Dallas Cowboy owner Bum Bright" just didn't mean enough to him. His game plan for Cowboys Inc. was to make money by building a new ring of "Crown Suites" atop Texas Stadium—118 ranging from $300,000 to $1.5 million. They were completed by 1985. The projection was for all 118 to be sold by 1989, but by 1986 nearly one hundred remained empty. For Bright this was the Crowning blow.

The Tax Reform Act of 1986 had taken away depreciation advantages. "That," says Bright, "mostly was why the banks and savings and loans started to fail." Cowboy fans were a little more hesitant to invest $1.5 million (plus personal decorating and entertainment expenses) for a home away from home they might use only ten times a year. In the past they could count on two or three playoff games at Texas Stadium, but suddenly the team was showing the same dangerous signs the economy was.

Just after the '85 playoff loss to the Rams, Tex Schramm had said, "We won't be playing with the same deck next year." When a team has won its division and its GM vows to reshuffle, if not break out a new deck, something is wrong.

Bright had his theories. To beef up his limited football knowledge, Bright sought the thoughts of Texas A&M offensive coordinator R. C. Slocum—Slokes, as Bright calls him. Slocum, now head coach at A&M, impressed two points upon Bright. "He said all the big-name NFL coaches, from Gibbs to Walsh, had been to A&M to talk to the coaches and look at prospects, but not once had they ever seen Tom Landry. This was disturbing."

Furthermore, Landry was running basically the same offense he ran in the '60s. So Slocum recommended the Cowboys bring in some hot new blood. Slocum suggested Paul Hackett, with whom he had worked as an assistant at Southern Cal. "Best young mind in the game," Slocum told Bright.

Bright put his CEO in charge of football, Schramm, in charge of the hiring process. Schramm soft-sold Hackett to Landry, asking only that Landry interview him. When Hackett and Landry happened to be in New Orleans for an NFL scouting combine, they met in Landry's hotel room, but there was no meeting of the minds. "I probably shouldn't have paid so much homage to him," Hackett said much later. "I should have been more open with him about what I'm all about."

Hackett was so upset by the apparent waste of time that he called Slocum to vent his frustration, then left for the airport. Slocum called Bright. "I understood," says Bright, "that Paul had

taken his wife to meet Landry and that Landry had made her wait
outside and hadn't really given her the time of day. Well, I called
Tex." And Schramm called the New Orleans airport and had
Hackett paged. What are the odds against all this? Hackett, reaching Slocum, who reached Bright, who got hold of Schramm, who
successfully paged Hackett before his flight left? Yes, Hackett
heard the page and returned the call. Schramm asked him to reroute his return flight to San Francisco through Dallas. And by
that evening Hackett and his wife were sitting on the floor of
Schramm's office in the new Cowboys Center complex, which
Hackett called "a mind-blower." Schramm's luxury suite of an office wasn't yet furnished, but they sat Japanese-style on the carpet
and ate Chinese food.

The Hacketts were dazzled. Later I asked Hackett what
Schramm had promised. "Well, he just said that Tom wouldn't coach
much longer and that I'd put myself in a great position by being
here." Nothing in writing? "No way he could do that. But he gave
me great money, and I'll be able to learn from one of the masters for
a while, then we'll see what happens." There was a wink in his voice.

I said, "I just hope you realize what a silver-tongued devil
Schramm can be."

Yet, for a while, I was amazed at how gracefully Landry accepted Hackett, after all but rejecting him in the interview. It certainly appeared Hackett was forced on Landry and that Landry was
living with it. Most talk-show callers and media analysts viewed the
hiring as the first breach of Landry-Schramm autonomy. Had
Schramm finally made more than a suggestion? No, this was more of
a Bright idea.

Hackett was given a title that wouldn't sound quite so threat-
ening to Mount Landry, who had never had an offensive coordinator. Hackett, we were told, would be "pass coordinator." The
implication was that Landry would still control the running game—
and the offense.

But soon after Hackett arrived in Dallas, Landry and Alicia took
Paul and Elizabeth to dinner. The Landrys did not take new assistants and their wives to dinner. Then Landry handed Hackett his
playbook. "No, no," said Hackett. "I don't want to take your playbook. I'll just get another one."

"No, go ahead," Landry said, "you'll just rewrite most of it,
anyway."

Hackett detected no sarcasm. "He seemed very sincere and very open to my thoughts."

Hackett was interviewed so much during training camp that other assistants started calling him Hollywood Hackett. For reporters, Hackett had dual appeal. With Schramm's blessing, the P.R. department didn't do anything to discourage Hackett's label as "the next Landry." And Hackett didn't do anything to discourage interviewers. A Cowboy first: an assistant coach who spoke for the record as openly and entertainingly as predecessors did confidentially over beers. Hackett would rip or hero-worship players as if he were a fan sitting in front of the TV. No coachspeak. He hid behind no clichés or generalities or ifs. If a player was fat and lazy, as Tony Hill had become, Hackett told reporters, hey, he's fat and lazy. Hackett dealt in reality.

Hackett rebelled against anything phony or hyped. He despised the Cowboy "image." Yet, for Hackett, the sad irony was that he had been yet another victim of that image. "I got blinded," he said later. "I really had no idea what I was getting into. Tex can be so convincing. You read all this stuff about 'greatest organization in football,' and it's impossible to know what's really going on until you get inside it. For sure, I had no idea how far the talent had slipped. I mean, it was the Dallas Cowboys."

For a while Landry and Hackett, Mr. Inside and Mr. Outside, ice and fire, appeared to be teaming like Lennon and McCartney. Hackett traveled to L.A. to work out and "get inside the head of" UCLA receiver Mike Sherrard. Hackett's raves appeared to influence Landry's selection of Sherrard in the draft's first round. "This," Hackett told me, "is a very special human being. You have to understand, he didn't come from the same genes you and I did." Sherrard's mother had been an Olympic hurdler. His father, like Hackett's, was a political science professor, at Chico State in Northern California. "Mike has great ability," said Hackett, "and great work ethic and drive. An absolute stud. We will win with this guy."

And before camp was over, thanks to Schramm, Hackett inherited "by far the most talented player I've ever coached." Schramm had been at it again in the '85 draft, suggesting a fifth-round pick be gambled on Herschel Walker, who played for Donald Trump's New Jersey Generals in the United States Football League. Schramm was hoping the USFL would lose its lawsuit against the NFL and fold. The night the court ruled in favor of the NFL, the Cowboys were in London to play the first NFL exhibition in Europe. From his suite atop the London Hilton, Schramm capped a liquid celebration by calling Pete Rozelle.

"I love you, Pete," a sappy Schramm said over and over.

Two weeks later Herschel Walker was a Dallas Cowboy. Hackett was rocking and rolling with his new toys, Walker and Sherrard. If possible, Hackett was in irreverent awe of Landry–thoroughly impressed but unafraid of him. One day after a camp lunch, I happened to be walking with Hackett on one side of the street when Landry passed without a word on the other. "That man," Hackett said, "is 180 degrees from me. No matter what happens, win or lose, he does everything the very same way at the very same time every day. What *strength* he has. I've never seen anyone with that much discipline. I wish I had some of it."

"Maybe," I said, "you'll learn some."

Landry, concentrating on defense, was letting Hackett call all the plays through the preseason. "We've put in so much new stuff," Hackett said, "that I'm not sure he could call 'em if he wanted to."

Hackett was underwhelmed with quarterback Danny White's talent. But White was perhaps one of the few QBs in history who could have coped mentally with Hackett/Landry. Hackett believed in the Walshian philosophy made famous by Montana: The QB looks to receiver Number 1, then 2, then 3. "Basically," said Hackett, "you don't really care what the defense is doing. If the first option is covered, you go to the second." Basically, in Landry's scheme, the quarterback and receivers read and reacted to the defense. Combining the two systems was like combining solar systems. Planets collided in White's mind, but he didn't crack. "It was amazing how much we threw at Danny," Hackett said. "He was the buffer."

But wouldn't White need Bufferin? I kept asking Hackett how White could think and duck at the same time. I'd seen too much. White had a reputation for being "brittle," easily injured. How long would he last behind the Cowboy line, which had become more of a bread line? "It's hard to believe how bad it really is," Hackett said. "But we'll trick 'em."

Did the Cowboys ever pull a fast one on the Giants. On yet another "Monday Night Football" opener, the "Hack attack" generated 378 yards and thirty-one points against what would be the

NFL's best defense that season. The game winner was scored by Herschel Walker, from ten yards, on a draw play called by Hackett. Cowboys 31–28.

Anyone for a Crown Suite?

For the first time Landry was maintaining direct contact with the press box, where Hackett sat. No headset for Landry, though. How could he fit his hat over a headset? Landry used a telephone. Dial-a-play. "Coach and I are doing great," Hackett said. (He often referred to Landry as just "Coach," Hackett's term of endearment.)

Hackett said, "I suggest plays and Coach usually goes with 'em. Coach and I, we're okay." In effect, Hackett was calling the plays but Landry retained veto power. For Landry this was radical. Hackett had moved Mount Landry.

Hackett strutted his stuff for another "Monday Night" audience against the Cardinals in St. Louis. Cowboys 31–7. With two minutes left, as the Cowboy coaches vacated the press box, Hackett walked by my seat, leaned over, and whispered, "Bor-ring." The Cowboys would lead the NFL in scoring the first half of the season.

And at 6–2 (5–0 in the NFC East) the Cowboys met the Giants again, at Giants Stadium. The Giants were also 6–2. This game would make one team and break the other. Specifically, it would break Danny White, whose wrist was fractured in the first quarter by a blitzing Carl Banks. White was lost for the season.

And for the Cowboys, trailing 17–14, the season was lost in the dying seconds. White had been replaced by Steve Pelluer, who rang up 339 yards passing on twenty-eight of thirty-eight. But long completions to Tony Dorsett and Timmy Newsome that would have set up an easy tying field goal, if not a winning touchdown, were nullified by penalty. Both were on Number 75, tackle Phil Pozderac, who already had been called twice for holding. The Giants survived, and Poz became the punch line of more heartless jokes in Dallas than blacks, Mexicans, or New Yorkers.

Hackett was haunted by Pozderac but didn't hold it personally against him. Hackett blamed Brandt. "That guy," Hackett said of Brandt, "has screwed this franchise." After all, Pozderac hadn't picked himself in the fifth round of the '82 draft. He was a six-foot-nine-and-a-half Draft Day curiosity out of Notre Dame (Brandt always gave us heights to the quarter inch), but Pozderac was a much better story than player. "We cannot win in this league with the tackles we have," Hackett said, plunging into blackness after the game. "It is staggering how poorly this team has drafted for the last eight years. You compare this team to the 49ers, man for man, two-deep, and it's a joke."

The final irony was that Hackett was now stuck with a quarterback he had rejected as a 49er assistant. Before the 1984 draft, Bill Walsh sent Hackett to the University of Washington to check out Pelluer's mental and physical makeup. Hackett wasn't impressed. "There just wasn't any pizzazz about him," Hackett said. The Cowboys took Pelluer in the fifth round, and now he was all Hackett had.

Before that preseason's game in London I'd bumped into Pelluer in the hotel elevator. He was wearing a flowered shirt and a camera around his neck, as if this were his first time in Hawaii. He said, "Mr. Bayless, I'm Steve Pelluer." No Cowboy ever had called me mister. Pelluer further surprised me by saying he was on his way to a disco, the Hippodrome, that a lot of the Cowboys were howling about. It was around 5 P.M. I imagined Pelluer standing outside the Hippodrome snapping pictures.

But the next morning at practice I heard that Steven Carl Pelluer, of all the nice young men, had been one of five Cowboys who missed curfew. "Maybe," Hackett said, "he's ready to become a quarterback." Hackett certainly didn't condone missing curfew, but in Pelluer's case it at least indicated Pelluer had snipped one apron string. At age twenty-five—and six-feet-four, 210 pounds—he still had the look of a towheaded kid away from home for the first time at a summer camp. He remained admirably close to his parents and grandmother, but the Hippodrome Cowboys weren't sure if Pelluer was leading them into NFL battle or just across the street, as he did old ladies.

But in the final eight games, Sweet Number 16 proved he was as tough as any Lee Roy or D.D. who ever played. Unfortunately, that was about all he proved. Pelluer was racked and sacked and packed in ice, game after game. Pelluer won only once—he was sacked eleven times in that one, at San Diego—but he won Hackett's respect. Hackett said, "I'm not sure any quarterback ever has taken a worse beating for a longer period and kept getting up."

But the more Hackett tried to "trick 'em" to compensate for turnstile blockers, the more he overloaded Pelluer's dizzy brain. Landry didn't help, either, telling the media Pelluer was a better scrambler than Roger Staubach. Often, Pelluer could remember only one option—run! He carried forty-one times that season for 255 yards, a 6.2 average. "I was so sore some Monday mornings," Pelluer says, "I couldn't get out of bed. I hope I never go through anything that bad again, physically or mentally."

After the Cowboys fell behind 34–0 at Washington and lost 41–14, then lost to Seattle 31–14 on Thanksgiving, the inevitable happened. Landry all but disconnected his phone to the press box. Landry told the staff they were asking too much of Pelluer and Landry began to eliminate Hackett plays from the game plan. More and more the offense looked like old times. From 6–2 the Cowboys finished 7–9.

The thirty-three interceptions of Thurman's Thieves the season before fell to seventeen. The Cowboys simply didn't have enough players who made plays.

The final three weeks of the season were as tough emotionally on Hackett as on Pelluer. More and more, Hackett was tormented by trying to coach football in what *Newsweek* had called the "Emerald City of the Cowboys"—Cowboys Center. "TexWorld," I called it in my column. Schramm had attempted to create his very own kingdom, a master-planned community called Valley Ranch in the undeveloped prairie out near Dallas–Fort Worth Airport. You exited the airport extension of LBJ Freeway at MacArthur and dropped down one of the steepest hills in North Texas into what appeared to have been a flood plain. Before the 1986 season, the population of Valley Ranch was projected for twenty-five thousand in the many different neighborhoods of upper-middle-class apartments, condos, and townhomes—The Villas, Quail Hollow, River Bend, Canyon Crest, Tree Tops, Reflections, Barrington Court . . .

But as this is being written, a signpost at the Valley Ranch entrance says, "Population: 8,007." From above it still looks like a large apartment complex in the middle of nowhere. It appears that two-thirds of the two thousand five hundred acres remains undeveloped. You have to drive a half mile from the freeway before hitting the first buildings. The many hot shops and restaurants never materialized. The busiest business in "town" still seems to be the 7-Eleven, the place to see and be seen. Imagine: a 7-Eleven is the new Cafe Dallas. You often see Cowboys and Cheerleaders in the 7-Eleven. An employee told me it's the busiest 7-Eleven in Dallas–Fort Worth.

Death Valley Ranch, I began to call it.

Soon after buying the team, Bum Bright was stunned by the reports he was getting from the construction site of Cowboys Center, the team's new two hundred-acre complex on the far side of Valley Ranch. "That," Bright says, "was our first indication of the very bad business practices. I don't believe Tex really cared how much it cost. Right away the contractor had to be replaced." What was finally completed was an eighty-thousand-square-foot structure of Arizona sandstone. These above-ground catacombs were just one endless story high—an "unbelievably bad design," says a source close to Schramm. But Cowboys Center inspired story upon media story. Remember what Dorothy said? "He really must be a wonderful wizard to live in a city like that."

Cowboys Center housed executive offices, the Dallas Cowboys Travel Agency, the Cheerleaders Dance Academy, *Cowboys Weekly*, the ticket office, a souvenir shop, a TV studio, a media library and, oh yes, a locker room. The Jacuzzi was so big it was called Lake Landry.

But much of Schramm's vision never got off the ground. Cowboys ShowPlace, a video hall of fame, couldn't be funded. Neither could an ice arena, hotel, sports medicine clinic, or restaurant pavilion. Still, Cowboys Center had the feel of an amusement park. It seemed that more tourists wanted to see where America's Team lived than fans wanted to see their sorry Cowboys play.

Hackett was outraged.

"This is no place to prepare a team to play the game of professional football," he said. "I mean, our coaches' meetings get interrupted by tour groups. It's a joke! Just take a look at that locker room. How can a team feel like a *team* in there?"

Dressing cubicles were grouped in four alcoves—four upper-class Valley Ranch neighborhoods. The configuration encouraged cliques or, worse, every man for himself. It was as if each player had his own locker room condo, and perhaps butler and maid. The ambiance was more that of a country club golf locker room than of scarred helmets and stinking practice jerseys. The one Spartan feature of Cowboys Center was the weight "room," which was outside. It was covered but open to the Texas elements, which discouraged or hampered lifting weights in heat or cold or blowing rain. "Makes absolutely no sense," Hackett said. More planning, it appeared, had gone into the Dance Academy.

But Hackett's deepest frustration was the mood that seeped like poisonous gas from Landry and the coaching staff. The "living dead" was how I described the Cowboys Center atmosphere in columns before Hackett arrived. By December, Hackett was saying, "The place is like a morgue. Nobody laughs. Nobody seems to look forward to getting up and going to work. Nobody whistles while they work. Landry says something in a meeting and *that is it*. Nobody says a word. I'm sorry, but I just can't live that way. If I have something to say, I'm going to keep saying it. I don't care if anybody listens or not, at least I can live with myself."

Hackett couldn't believe Landry and staff called it a day by 6 P.M. Some assistants did arrive earlier than Hackett, who was in by 8 A.M. But he came to believe that was as much to impress Landry as to accomplish much. Hackett wanted the staff to stay late together two or three nights a week. "Let me tell you," Hackett said, "every other staff is working later than we are, and just about every team is practicing longer and harder than we are. How can we compete in this dog-eat-dog league?" Hackett suggested having dinner catered on just one night, Wednesday, so the staff could put in a few extra hours. But the idea, he said, was greeted with little more than cleared throats, from Landry on down. "All I hear is, 'It's just not done that way here,' " Hackett said. "Nothing has changed around here in twenty-seven years. That was fine when the Cowboys were winning. But we're not winning."

Sometimes after lunch I'd walk past assistants' offices and see them nodding off at their desks. Occasionally, said Hackett, *Landry* dozed during coaches' meetings.

"Look, he's a great coach, a legend," Hackett said, "but we have got to *do* something."

Hackett was losing patience as fast as he was losing input.

Assistant Jerry Tubbs, a man of gentle perspective who was with Landry from start to finish, says, "We were playing a little tougher teams the second half of '86 and we had the injuries, and Tom told us he was just going to have to cut down on some of Paul's stuff for Pelluer's sake. That had to be so frustrating for Paul. That's when all the trouble started. Paul was so bright. He thought he saw things with such clarity, and when others didn't see it, he just boiled over with emotion. It just spilled right out of his mouth. It was just very, very unfortunate." Tubbs pauses, struggling with his role in the Landry-Hackett clash. "I started to say something to Paul that first year—I should have said something. I finally did later, but by then it was too late."

A first-year assistant just didn't let his emotion spill out during coaches' meetings. It just wasn't done. Landry wasn't one to lash back, but he knew how to humble an upstart player or assistant. He simply took away what mattered most. In Hackett's case, it was creativity. Hackett had gone from Walsh's frying pan into the ice.

He began to tell me Landry and Schramm weren't happy that he associated with the likes of me. "They think I'm being disloyal," he said. Yet from the start Hackett had been up front with Landry about his ten-year relationship with me. The first time Hackett mentioned we knew each other, Landry said, "You gotta watch him. He's from L.A." This amazed and amused Hackett, who knew me as a guy from Oklahoma City who had worked for two years in L.A.

But one evening at camp Schramm saw Hackett and me on our way to the gym to play basketball. We certainly weren't trying to hide our intentions, though perhaps we should have. The next day an incredulous Hackett said, "He told me I couldn't play with you anymore."

That night media correspondents would get drunk with Cowboy coaches and staffers, but Hackett and I couldn't play some one-on-one basketball?

The sorry irony was that I was so uncomfortable professionally with our relationship that I quoted Hackett only when necessary. This frustrated me because I often read so many enlightening Hackett quotes in rival publications. He certainly didn't ask me to campaign for a new head coach or undermine Landry. On the contrary, he asked from the start that I try to ignore him. Sometimes our casual conversation provided me with unique insight into the team's internal decay, but details or anecdotes he mentioned only reinforced themes I'd already written about. Mostly I bit my lip and tried not to say, "I told you so."

"Man, they [Landry, Schramm, and staff] think you are really evil," Hackett said, grinning and shaking his head. "Some of 'em call you 'the devil.' "

"*The devil*," I said.

Hackett, who seldom read my column, said, "They say you can really be tough."

I said, "I just try to write the truth as I see it. I wrote glowing tributes when they won, and now I'm seeing the wheels come off. Wouldn't you write the truth if you had my job?"

"I suppose," he said, amused at the thought of having my job. Under Walsh, Hackett had been taught that the press was the enemy. "It's just that they fear you because they can't control you the way they do everybody else. What I can't believe is that everything this organization does is predicated on how the press will react. It's always, 'What will the press say?' Hell with the press. Who cares what the press says? Is that going to make us win or lose games?"

"Well," I said, "the press helped create the Cowboy Mystique that got you here."

The same power soon would keep Hackett in Dallas.

University of Southern California officials called Hackett soon after their season ended and offered him the head coaching job. Hackett had been popular among alumni in his five years at USC and was a unanimous choice to replace Ted Tollner. Paul and Elizabeth flew to L.A. and even looked at houses and schools. The Trojans were, as always, deeper than the Pacific in talent. Many of Hackett's old Trojan chums wondered why he was even flying back to Dallas. Who could turn down Heisman U?

But first Hackett needed to talk to the man who hired him, Schramm. And Schramm, silver tongue flicking away, told Hackett he had "made a commitment" to pro football and needed to be patient. Again, Schramm hinted that Landry wouldn't coach much longer and that Hackett very well could replace him. Again, no promise. But Hackett had to ask himself: Would he rather be head coach of the USC Trojans or of the Dallas Cowboys? Did Hackett want to return to the year-round grind of college recruiting and fund-raising? Or did he want to be able to spend more off-season time with his family? Did he want to raise his sons in L.A., which he and Elizabeth hadn't much liked? Or did he want to remain in their "dream house," which was in a wooded, family-oriented addition another twenty minutes from Dallas beyond Valley Ranch. Hackett worked for the Cowboys without really living in Dallas. The Hacketts could have lived in their kitchen alone. Swimming pool, basketball court—who needed L.A.'s traffic and smog?

Hackett slowly talked himself into thinking, "What the hell, Danny White will be back. Maybe I can hang in one more season and see what happens."

Hackett turned down USC.

Soon after the news hit the papers, Bum Bright received a call from Schramm. For the last ten seasons under Murchison, Landry had worked without much more than a year-to-year handshake. But now Schramm told Bright that Landry wanted a three-year contract. What's more, Landry wanted $1 million a year. "Tom's argument," says Bright, "was that four other coaches got $1 million. I believe he said Walsh, Gibbs, Shula, and Noll. Tex told me that Clint had always kept him and Tom on par, so he wanted a raise, too. I said, 'Tex, the buckets are empty.' I told him to give Tom a three-year contract that could be terminated after each year [like the standard NFL player's contract]. I told him to give Tom $800,000 the first year, $900,000 the second, and a million the third. But I specifically told him not to give Tom a guaranteed three years."

Schramm says he doesn't remember those instructions and that Bright "was always very specific."

Whatever, Schramm gave Landry a guaranteed three-year contract, setting the stage for a Shakespearean tragedy. It appeared Hackett's decision to stay had so concerned—threatened?—Landry that for the first time he demanded contractual security.

Then again, why had Schramm gone to bat with Bright for Landry? Loyalty? Fear? Image? Why would a man who had just indicated to Hackett that Landry wouldn't coach beyond another season give Landry three more years?

Bright says, "Tex wanted to benefit from the association with Tom's wholesome image. And Tex feared Tom's power with the press. Tex didn't want to look bad."

A team source says, "It's like wanting to stay married for appearance' sake, but you hate your wife."

Yet perhaps Schramm was thinking the way Hackett was. Thinking, selfishly, "Danny will be back. Hackett's still here. Maybe we can carry that 6–2 record on into the second half of next season. Maybe we're still magic."

Hadn't the Giants routed the Broncos in the Super Bowl? Hadn't the Cowboys come within a Pozderac of beating the Giants twice? Maybe . . .

The next morning Hackett glanced at the sports page of the *Dallas Times Herald* just to see if the Mavericks had won. He noticed a little box at the top of the page: "Landry Signs Three-Year Deal." He read the short story twice, just to make sure he was awake.

"I nearly fell out of my chair," he said. When he asked Schramm "what the hell was going on," Schramm turned up his palms and said, "It was out of my hands." For the first time Hackett wasn't sure whom to believe. He said, "This place is unbelievable. No one ever tells anyone anything. Tom never says anything to Tex. Tex never says anything to Tom. We [assistants and players] are never made aware of anything. We just have to read about it in the paper. You never really know who's responsible for anything."

"Deniability," they call it in Washington. With the Cowboys the buck had never stopped.

Under new coach Larry Smith, USC was on its way to three consecutive Rose Bowls. Hackett was on his way to, as he later described it, hell.

Early the next camp, the Cowboys scrimmaged the San Diego Chargers in Thousand Oaks. Hackett was "gunned up" about getting a full camp with Mike Sherrard, who had held out for a while as a rookie. Sherrard had lived up to Hackett's draft expectations, establishing himself as a premier deep threat. He had caught forty-one passes for a team-leading 744 yards (18.2 per catch) and five touchdowns. But in the scrimmage, as Sherrard took off on a route, one cleat hit the opposite shin, freakishly shattering it. The bone protruded through the skin. Sherrard hadn't even been hit, and he was lost for the season.

He wouldn't play again for the Cowboys.

As Sherrard was carried to an ambulance, Paul Hackett cried. Two weeks later I went to visit Sherrard in Los Robles Hospital, not far from camp. He said, "You won't believe this, but Coach Hackett has been up to see me every night. Hasn't missed a one. He even has his family out here and he still comes. I feel like the rest of the organization just forgot about me as soon as I was hurt. But Coach Hackett, he cares."

Schramm had done his damnedest to limit Gil Brandt's responsibility. Brandt no longer negotiated contracts. Brandt no longer was in sole charge of scouting the NFL for trades or waiver-wire acquisitions. But Brandt remained on the loose in college football, which set up a classic Brandt escapade during camp. First-round pick Danny Noonan, a defensive tackle from Nebraska, was a contract holdout. Brandt had known Noonan and his parents since Noonan was a sophomore, so he slipped into Lincoln and looked for Noonan in the Nebraska University weight room. "I know every plaque on the wall in there," Brandt said.

Noonan wasn't around, so Brandt took Noonan's mother, Donna, to lunch. During holdout negotiations agents consider this sort of unauthorized contact dirty pool. Noonan's agent, Tom Condon, called new Cowboy negotiator Joe Bailey, cussed him out, hung up, and broke off talks.

Schramm said he hadn't been aware of Brandt's mission but backed him nonetheless. Schramm said, "I'll do anything to get Noonan to camp. My first consideration is to get Noonan in, not the ego of the agent."

Schramm's response so infuriated Condon's partner, Tony Agnone, that he told Dallas reporters, "They're sitting there saying they were totally justified in doing that. How can they justify trying to negotiate behind our backs? How can they be that arrogant? I would at least lie about why I was in Lincoln."

At camp, Brandt had told me he was playing a lot of golf because "I just don't have that much to do." But now he was back in the headlines, back in full strut. When I asked about Agnone's remarks, Brandt dismissed them with, "I went for the good of the fans and the team." Maybe so, but Brandt's tactics helped keep Noonan out of camp. By September, Landry was saying, "Noonan missed so much of camp that it's just going to be hard for him to be productive this year."

Worse, the Cowboys are still waiting for Noonan to be productive after three seasons.

Oddly enough, Landry soon agreed to undertake a kind of mission on Brandt's behalf.

Dorothy "Dot" Comer came from oil-and-gas wealth in Highland Park, where she had been taught to believe in God and God's Coach. She even attended Highland Park Methodist, Landry's church. She says she occasionally had dreams that she one day would marry someone affiliated with the Cowboys even though "I didn't know anyone who even *knew* anyone affiliated with the Cowboys."

She met Gil Brandt in the Denver airport after noticing the name tag shaped like a Cowboy helmet on his briefcase handle.

They dated, she says, for four and a half years. They often ate at the finest restaurants with the most famous college coaches and their wives. Dot had Cowboy stars in her eyes.

"I guess I have to question myself for marrying him," she says now. "But here was one of the most highly recognized and thought-of people in his field. I thought, gee, he must be some neat guy."

After all, he was Tom Landry's right-hand man. At Highland Park Methodist, Dot married Brandt on June 28, 1979, a few months after the Cowboys' last Super Bowl appearance. Dot and Gil had one child, Brig, born in August 1980.

Dot filed for divorce in July 1987, alleging adultery and "cruel treatment."

Soon after the '87 season began, Dot was surprised by a call from Landry, who asked if he could drop by on a Saturday before a home game. She knew Landry only from team or NFL functions and then only to say hello. The Brandts lived two minutes from the Landrys but didn't socialize with them.

Dot was even more surprised by what Landry had to say about Brandt. She assumes he came at Brandt's request. She says, "I guess Tom felt I was a fairly stable Christian and he obviously is, too, so he came to speak on Gil's behalf. He came thinking my only beef with Gil was adultery . . . and at one point, he said, 'Dot, of all the people I work with, Gil would be the last one I'd ever suspect of something like that.' I thought to myself, 'Tom, do you have blinkers on or what?' What I found so hard to believe was Tom's naiveté. I can't imagine that he didn't know (anything about Brandt's behavior)."

By '87, it was difficult to believe Landry wouldn't question Brandt's character. So many players drafted for character, like Noonan, soon questioned Brandt's. So many stories were exchanged so often by Landry's loyal assistants. Wouldn't he have heard one or two?

Publicly, Landry continued to say he was "too busy to keep up with that Gil." Landry and Brandt appeared to have no relationship beyond talking occasionally about draft picks or player acquisitions. On the way to home games, Landry did pick up Brandt (and Dot's son by her first marriage, Todd, who carried Landry's sideline phone cord). But Brandt traveled alone to colleges several days a week and usually met the team for road games. It wasn't as if Landry and Brandt worked together closely or daily. Yet here was Landry, intervening to vouch for Brandt's fidelity after Dot had filed for divorce. Consider the impact such words from Mount Landry were supposed to have on her. Could Landry have renewed her trust in Brandt? Was Landry actually so locked into his world that he was oblivious to Brandt? Was Landry's religious influence being manipulated by Brandt? Or did Landry see or hear more evil than he let on? Was he simply acting out of loyalty to a man who had done so much to help make him a success?

"I just don't know," Dot says. "Maybe Tom was just too preoccupied with game plans and strategy to know anything [about Brandt]. Or maybe he felt an obligation to Gil, enough devotion to make one visit for him."

But Dot wasn't swayed by Landry's testimony. She says she already had seen too much. "I told him about the time I found the dirty laundry. I told him about the underwear [she found] and about other things. If I'd been one of these wives who was hurt or torn up and wanted to do anything to save the marriage, I might have been affected by what Tom said. But I didn't have an ounce of love left for the man. I told Tom I appreciated his coming by because I knew he was so busy, but I just said the adultery was a drop in the bucket as to what was wrong with the marriage. I just let it go at that."

After a two-year, five-month legal battle, the divorce was final in December 1989. "When I filed," Dot says, "Mr. Brandt was flabbergasted. He thought I was so enamored with his position with the Cowboys that he couldn't believe I'd do it. He was saying, 'You'd give up *that*?' I said, 'I didn't marry that. I married *you*. I have to live with *you*.' "

Buddy Ryan wasn't enamored of the Cowboys, either.

The 1987 NFL players' strike began for Cowboy fans with Ryan's "replacement" team visiting Texas Stadium. Philadelphia coach Ryan had made it four-letter clear he wanted as little as possible to do with his "scabs," whom he'd all but chosen out of the classifieds. Ryan's heart was with his real players, whom he wanted to remain on strike "till they take care of business." The Cowboys, on the other hand, had persuaded a few stars to cross the picket line. Here came Randy White, Ed Jones, Tony Dorsett, Danny White, and Mike Renfro, contracts between legs. The Cowboys were known as the weakest team in the union.

"We're a league-wide joke," said player rep Doug Cosbie. "Our guys are just too afraid of management to participate in a strike."

Schramm had taken a Barnum-like fancy to a leprechaun of a quarterback named Kevin Sweeney who had set an NCAA record for passing yards at Fresno State. Hackett wasn't much of a Sweeney fan, which was why the Cowboys hadn't taken him until the seventh round. Hackett considered Sweeney too short (a shade under six feet), too slow, and too unathletic to do anything but lean back like a missile launcher and throw deep. "Oh, he can really throw the home run ball," Hackett said. "But is that all there is to playing quarterback? Come on, is this the guy who's going to get us back to the playoffs?"

Schramm loved Sweeney in part because fans loved him. Sweeney was a cuddly underdog who shook his fist and slapped butts and hurled bombs. After watching White and Pelluer throw so many deadhead interceptions, it wasn't hard to fall for Sweeney by default. Strike sign at Texas Stadium: WHITE'S A WEENIE, WE WANT SWEENEY.

Schramm said, "I just like the look in Kevin's eye." To Schramm's chagrin, Landry cut Sweeney just before the '87 season began. But as the strike loomed, Schramm sweet-talked Sweeney (against his lawyer's advice) into returning to Dallas to lead P. T. Schramm's Flying Scab Circus. If the Cowboys couldn't win games and fans against real NFL teams, by golly they'd return to glory before the real players returned to work.

In Dallas, a nonunion town, it had come to this.

In the first strike game, before an intimate 12,370 at the Meadowlands against the Jets, Sweeney completed just six of fourteen passes, but three went for TDs. Dallas was back, 38–24. So were Cowboy fans, who turned out 40,000 strong for Ryan's Eagles, considered the worst of the strike teams. On the Cowboys' first play Landry called a reverse that split end Kelvin Edwards took sixty-two yards for a TD. Ryan took off his headset and fired it at the turf. The Cowboys led 21–3 after a quarter on the way to a 41–22 waltz across Texas Stadium.

Afterward I asked Hackett about the reverse. Against the Eagle scabs it seemed almost like running up the score on the first play. Wasn't it something of a junior high stunt that was beneath Landry's dignity? Hackett just shrugged and gave me a "don't ask *me*" look. He said another play had been scripted, "but at the last second

Coach decided to go with the reverse. I didn't even know what was coming."

Landry, it appeared, was trying to show the Cowboy faithful that he could still come up with those "exotics." For God's Coach it had come to this?

Calling Landry a hypocrite and a phony, Buddy Ryan vowed revenge. He would get it two weeks later in Philadelphia, with his real team. With time running out on a 30–20 lead, Ryan called a pass. The Cowboys were called for interference in the end zone, giving the Eagles first down on the 1. Keith Byars plunged for the eye-for-an-eye TD. With that, Ryan carved in brimstone a national reputation as the anti-Landry—a run-it-up scoundrel. Ryan had chosen to get even with the wrong saint. But few fans seemed to understand the genesis of Ryan's hatred. Landry was above question.

Except, that is, when it came to his employer.

Bright had gotten caught up in Sweeneymania only because his customers had. The final strike game, at Texas Stadium on "Monday Night Football" against a Redskin team of all scabs, drew the largest crowd of the Cowboy season. Yes, 60,612 flocked to see "Kevin from Heaven," as I called Sweeney. But Landry, apparently hoping to stockpile one more victory, started Danny White. Many fans were furious enough to demand their money back. In Bright's suite his friends were on him like stink on the Cowboys.

Even with White and Dorsett and other stars, the Cowboys lost 13–7 in what had to be one of Joe Gibbs's finest coaching jobs.

Bright says he waited two days to cool down a little before meeting with Schramm. Bright remembers Schramm going immediately into one of his "acts"—rages. "Tex's nose even turns blue," says a Cowboy source. He paces. He wrings his hands. He curses. This time, says Bright, Schramm was cursing Landry. "He was saying, 'That son of a bitch. That son of a *bitch*.' He was mad about Sweeney and even about how Tom wouldn't ever question Gil."

Bright remembers this exchange: "Tex, it's a goddamn business. Call Landry and let's fire him."

"No, we can't do that just yet."

"Okay, call him and I'll fire the son of a bitch."

"No, let me handle it my way."

The more the two talked, the more Bright realized it was going to cost him $1.9 million to fire Landry—for two more guaranteed seasons. Bright was losing enough as it was, and not just on Cowboys

Inc.; Bright was on the way to losing something like $200 million in banking and real estate.

Bright: "That's when Tex said something like, 'Oh, yeah, I forgot to tell you . . .' That's when I found out he had signed Tom to three years. Tex, of course, was very apologetic. He had all kinds of excuses about how the contract had gone on to Tom's lawyers and he [Schramm] had gotten busy and . . ."

And so it was, seven weeks later, that Bright made his first national headlines—Buddy Ryan-like headlines. Following a 21–10 Cowboy loss to lowly Atlanta at Texas Stadium, Bright was called at home by a *Dallas Morning News* reporter. Bright was asked how he felt about a loss Schramm later called "the absolute low point of my years with the Cowboys." Counting strike games, the Cowboys were 5–8. Bright told the reporter, "I get horrified sometimes at our play calling. I've heard we're not using certain players because they haven't been brought along yet. Maybe the problem is we can't utilize the talent of certain guys because we don't have anybody to direct how to use them. It doesn't seem we have anybody in charge that knows what they're doing."

The following week three columnists from other cities called me to ask about this "lunatic" owner who had the gall to criticize Tom Landry. For years the national media had been conditioned by Cowboy lore. Clint Murchison: greatest owner ever. God's Coach: never bothered by owner. Cowboys: most stable front office in NFL history.

Hence, Bum Bright: does not compute. "Who is this geek named Bum?" an L.A. sports columnist asked me. How could I begin to explain? How could I fight perhaps the strongest public perception in sports?

Two weeks later Bright made his third and last visit to Cowboys Center, for the annual Christmas party. When he spotted Landry, he moved through the crowd toward him, with Schramm in close pursuit. Landry hadn't helped matters with Bright by treating the owner as if he actually *were* invisible. Bright found Landry aloof and unapproachable. But Bright walked right up and said, a touch sarcastically, "Well, Tom, I guess you want me to give you a vote of confidence."

Bright remembers Schramm leading him away by the elbow before Landry could reply.

14

A COUPLE of months after the 1987 season Paul Hackett called and asked if I'd meet him for dinner. This surprised me only because we didn't have much of a go-to-dinner relationship. Hackett, I found, had an announcement to make.

We met at the same restaurant, China Terrace, where I'd bought him a welcome-to-Dallas dinner two years earlier. I thought about how dramatically his life had changed since then. This time you might say our conversation, like the food, was sweet and sour. We talked hoops and music through the main course, then he hit me with the news as the fortune cookies came. Perhaps his fortune should have said, "Man who leaves 49ers and turns down USC deserves fate in Dallas."

Hackett told me he was officially "on probation."

"What?"

"I'm not supposed to talk to you at all anymore. I'm supposed to be very careful about what I say to the media. I've even been assigned a P.R. coach to help me learn what to say and not to say in interviews."

"A P.R. coach?"

Hackett shrugged and tried to smile. His spirit seemed broken. He had heard from several sources around the league, as had I, that hints dropped by Landry to other coaches had damaged Hackett's reputation. Hints that he was disloyal, impossible to work with, and blindly ambitious. When Landry spoke, others listened.

"I may never get out of here," Hackett said.

Landry had told Hackett that for one season he was to be seen and not heard. During coaches' meetings he was to listen instead of blurt. His input into the game plan would be minimal at best. During games he could communicate with Landry only through assistant Al Lavan, who stood near Landry and had a direct line to Hackett in the press box. Landry had announced he would be his own offensive and defensive coordinator, a dual burden shouldered by no NFL coach that I knew of. Hackett was to turn down his practice field volume, work quietly with the quarterbacks, then go home when the rest of the staff did.

If he didn't, he was told, he would be "let go." If he earned no demerits for a season, he might earn back some of his game plan responsibility. Landry, who had never fired an assistant, appeared to be giving Hackett a P.R. lesson. Instead of firing him he was making Hackett's working conditions so intolerable that he would probably quit. Firing Hackett wouldn't look good, especially to Bum Bright.

Naturally, Hackett's first impulse was "I am outta here." But Hackett's national reputation had plunged with the Cowboys' records. Thanks, perhaps, to word spread by Landry, Hackett no longer was the first or second name mentioned for the latest college or pro vacancy. It had been quite a while since the one-time Boy Wonder had been contacted by an ego-stroking athletic director or GM. He had nowhere to go.

Hackett said, "I have to decide whether to quit or to just try to relax for a season and regroup emotionally. Maybe going home at six every night would be good for me for a while." Son David would be a senior at Southlake Carroll High School. David was a backup receiver for a Dragon team that would be favored to win the state championship (and would). David wasn't wild about moving.

"So maybe it's best that I just blend into the woodwork like everyone else," Hackett said, "and look forward to going to the Dragon games. Then maybe something will open up. But you're going to have to help. You can't even mention me in the paper. I'm going to try not to talk to anybody [in the media]."

Hackett had been "called on the carpet" for several statements he made to reporters other than me. After a Hackett critique of Tony Hill appeared in the *Dallas Morning News*, Landry told Hackett, "What you said has forced me to get rid of him." What Hackett said was simply the truth; Hackett was quietly cheered by Cowboys and other assistants who had no respect for Hill. Hill tried to make it with the 49ers but soon was out of football for good.

Hackett acted as if he'd soon be out of a job, too, if he didn't start listening to Benny Goodman music. Hackett, like Bright's A&M, was on probation. He even dropped one last little bomb on me: Landry had talked to him about religion. I hadn't heard of Landry ever "witnessing"—sharing his faith in Christ—one on one with a player or coach. To me this indicated the depth of Landry's respect for and frustration with Hackett.

That night Hackett resolved to turn himself into a Cowboy clone. Through the season we continued to talk, briefly and periodically, but not once did I quote him in my column.

Jerry Tubbs says, "That last year, Paul did everything in his power to get along. And I told Tom that. Paul was just tremendous."

"Tremendous" also did not appear in my column as I wrote about the 1988 Cowboys.

During the time-out, with 3:20 remaining at Three Rivers Stadium, I glanced down at the Cowboy sideline summit and wondered how Steve Pelluer kept from yelling, "Everybody shut up!" Another first for Tom Landry: He had kept four quarterbacks. As if Pelluer wasn't suffering enough self-doubt, he now had Danny White, Kevin Sweeney, and Scott Secules making suggestions and competing for his job. No NFL team carried four quarterbacks on the active roster. The fourth canceled a developing rookie, valuable backup, or special-teams performer.

But Landry seemed overwhelmed by what to do with five camp quarterbacks—including Paul McDonald, a Hackett favorite who probably had the best preseason of the five. McDonald was cut. To explain his quarterback moves, Landry often ducked behind his infamous "feel." He would say, "I just have a feel for which quarterback to go with." It was never clear if this "feel" was heaven-sent, instinctive, or Landry's wily way of saying, "No comment." When Landry narrowed his eyes and told a media conference, "It will just depend on my feel," reporters (and readers and viewers) tended to nod along hypnotically. Yes, Landry had a Plan.

But by 1988 I wasn't sure Landry had a Clue. His "Achilles feel," I began to call it. I often looked at my notes after Landry interviews and realized his responses were little more than nonsensical non sequitur nonanswers. Hackett had grinned and told me, "Coach tells us (in coaches' meetings) how he really likes to give you guys the runaround."

All we knew for sure going into the opener in Pittsburgh was that Pelluer would start. Whether he would finish was up to the "feel."

Pelluer was the perfect on-field extension of Landry. Too perfect. Pelluer *was* Landry. Pelluer says, "We were really a kindred spirit. I see a lot of him in me." Pelluer was religious to this depth: He was baptized in a neighbor's swimming pool as part of a Valley Ranch Baptist Church service. Pelluer came from a long line of stars at Washington and Washington State, most of them defensive stalwarts. "Steve," said Hackett, "was taught that the team absolutely comes first." Pelluer was more of a follower than a leader. Pelluer tried to do exactly as Coach Landry said. During games this sometimes turned huddles into muddles.

If Landry mixed up the play, Pelluer tried to run it as called. Worse still, under fire Pelluer's brain tended to short out as Landry's sometimes did. Scout John Wooten says, "Steve was like a product of a broken home. Hackett would tell him one thing, Landry another, and everybody on the sideline would be yelling something else to him. Steve would call a play and break the huddle, and they'd still be yelling something different from the sideline. Staubach got the same treatment, but he'd just ignore it and run what he thought was right. Then he'd get back to the sideline and say, 'Were you guys trying to yell something at me?' "

So there stood Pelluer, amid the Tower of Babel on the Three Rivers sideline. Landry, assistant Lavan, and the other three quarterbacks all appeared to be talking at once. The Cowboys trailed 24–21. Third and two from the Steeler 4-yard line. On the previous play Pelluer had bolted from the pocket for eight yards before meeting several linebackers head-on. A similar scramble had left him so groggy in an exhibition game against the Bears that Pelluer couldn't remember any plays. Was he woozy now? "No," Pelluer said later, "I was fine."

But was Landry? His training camp theme had been, "This is now Herschel's team." As in Herschel Walker, around whom the Cowboy image and offense would revolve. So, with the game on the line, did Landry want the ball in Herschel's hands? No, on the sideline he told Pelluer to run "37," a pass to fullback Timmy Newsome. But once in the huddle Pelluer called "36," the wrong play for the right formation. Why didn't Newsome, an intelligent veteran, correct Pelluer? Newsome said, "There are over one hundred plays, and a lot of times I leave the huddle and think maybe there's been a mistake. They're always changing things. They could have talked about anything on the sideline."

Pelluer rolled right while his blocker (Walker) and receiver (Newsome) went left. Perhaps a quarterback who didn't fear he was one play from the bench would have thrown the ball away and taken the tying field goal. But Pelluer forced an off-balance wobbler back into the middle of the end zone, apparently intended for tight end Doug Cosbie. Three Steelers could have caught the pass. Steeler David Little did intercept.

Yet reporters might not have known Pelluer called the wrong play if, before we were allowed in the locker room, Landry had told the team to protect its quarterback during media interrogation. Instead, as we gathered first around Landry, he immediately volunteered that "we just called the wrong play." Eyes widening, I exchanged glances with a veteran Cowboy reporter. We had learned long before that "we" usually meant "he," the quarterback. Not once in eleven years did I hear Landry accept even partial blame.

The veteran reporter pressed for details. Landry made it clear Pelluer had failed to repeat the play correctly in the huddle. Landry had called the right play; "we" had called it wrong in the huddle. So several of us vultures peeled off from Landry and descended on Pelluer. Wearing nothing but a towel, Pelluer spent the next twenty minutes explaining to wave after media wave how he mixed up the play Landry called on the sideline.

Despite completing fourteen of eighteen for nearly two hundred yards in the second half alone, Pelluer became "Wrong Way" Pelluer. And the Cowboys were off and stumbling. Often Pelluer would feel he was being held under in that neighbor's pool. So, for that matter, would his coach. The more the Cowboys lost, the further Landry reached back into the past for what had worked before. "Back to the Future," I called Landry's script. He would coach the Flex. He would devise and install the game plans. He would show the world his systems would prevail again. After all, he was Tom Landry. Everyone told him so. Everyone counted on him. He couldn't quit. Tom Landry never quits. He couldn't change. God's Coach never changes. His greatest strength was perseverance.

And it had become his greatest weakness. In a column soon after the Pittsburgh loss I wrote, "Will anyone ever save this poor man from himself?"

Landry and Pelluer collaborated again two weeks later against the Giants at Texas Stadium. This time, after planning all week to give the ball to Walker in "plus" territory, inside the 20, Landry called a pass on second-and-goal from the Giant 9. With an unblocked pass-rusher in his face, Pelluer threw blindly into the end zone and was intercepted by Harry Carson.

Giants 12–10. Ed Smith had seen enough.

He had come on the scene fairly anonymously with Bum Bright's ownership group in 1984. Ed A. Smith, Jr. didn't even live in Dallas. He commuted from the fashionable River Oaks section of Houston, where he had made his fortune owning and running barges. Here was yet another Billy Bob Alger, originally from Nevada, Texas. Smith says he took 15 percent of the Cowboys because "not only were they America's Team, but they were loved all over the world, in China, in India, everywhere. I based my decision on history . . . on Landry and Schramm's attitude at the time. The Cowboys were the outstanding franchise in the NFL."

Nobody knew much about Smith other than he rode team charter flights to every away game. Unlike Murchison and Bright, Smith looked more like a stereotypical Texas zillionaire. At seventy he had wavy hair the color of silver dollars and wore boots with his suits, a Vegas-style cowboy. His wife, approximately Smith's age, was conspicuous only because of her silver beehive and miles of mink.

For four years Smith remained as silent as Bright. But by nature Smith was a man of Wild West action. He didn't first go after Landry through the newspapers to satisfy his frustration and ego; he called Landry after the loss to the Giants.

"I'd had it up to here," says Smith, who now owns 27 percent of the team. "I figured it was costing me around $100,000 a game to own my portion, and I just couldn't stand to watch it anymore. I mean, Valley Ranch was costing something like a million a year just to maintain, just mowing the grass and clipping the hedges. It was extravagant, grandiose beyond reason. And on top of that, Tom and Gil were living off their laurels. Tom had a huge ego. His attitude was 'I'm a legend' because he read it every day in the paper. He kept saying, 'Just give me three more years,' but he had the thing so far down he couldn't ever come back. Bum should've said, bang, 'Landry, you're gone.' But Bum just didn't have the courage. You've got to be hard-nosed when you're in the public eye. You've got to be able to take the scathing [sic] of the press.

"Schramm was no help, either. He had become a legend, too. He was living like a king out there [at Valley Ranch] and wouldn't listen to anybody. He had a stranglehold on the organization and he had Rozelle by the ying-yang. At least I finally voiced my criticisms to Landry. At least I wasn't a hypocrite."

From Houston, Smith called Landry at his office. "I just wanted to know why he called two passes after he had first and goal at the 9. He said, 'You're second-guessing me.' It was an amicable discussion, but there was no meeting of the minds."

So a few weeks later Smith let Landry have it in an interview with Dallas's KDFW-TV. He didn't mention he had called Landry. But Smith was stunningly critical, especially for a guy virtually unknown to most fans. Media people I talked to were equally critical of Smith. "Blowhard" was the term I kept hearing.

Later that season it was reported that Smith accosted Landry as he walked off the field after a chaotic loss in Cleveland. Smith says he knows nothing about that. But he did call Landry again, to get the coach's side of another Cowboy collapse, in Philadelphia. "I will say he was good about taking my calls," Smith says.

But others on Landry's staff wondered if Hackett was good about taking Smith's calls, too. Buddy-buddy calls. On plane rides home Hackett occasionally went over stat sheets with Smith. But it wasn't as if they rendezvoused in the back of the plane. Hackett and Smith talked in the first-class section, in plain sight of the head coach. "Look," Hackett said, "one of Tom's biggest problems is that he can't even talk to those guys [owners]. I mean, Tom can be such a nerd. He just doesn't even know how to communicate with somebody. You just feel sorry for him. You have got to be able to make those guys feel a part of what's going on. They're paying the bills."

Smith admits he was a Hackett sympathizer. "Poor old Hackett worked his tail off for Landry, and Landry resented it because he didn't hire him. Hackett should be a head coach in the NFL right now, and because of certain things Landry said to [Miami coach Don] Shula and others, Hackett may never be a head coach in the NFL. That doesn't show a lot of character [on Landry's part]. It shows a little weakness, especially when you're professing how great thou art. What Landry did to him was a disgrace."

Precisely the word I used for the game in Philadelphia.

I fought through the locker-room door amid the usual soccer riot of notepads, microphones, and minicams. This was the visitors' locker room at Philly's Veterans Stadium, where I had scribbled down so many mightier-than-thou words from so many Cowboy stars. There, just to the right, was where Butch Johnson held court. Across the piles of jerseys, and down six or eight stools, was where Charlie Waters and Cliff Harris always sat, side by side in blue-sleeved undershirts and shorts, slashes of black grease still under their eyes, putting another Cowboy victory in such quotable perspective. Back in the glory days, which suddenly seemed a century ago, the Cowboys usually danced with the Eagles for a while, then stomped them. "We always let them and their fans get their hopes up for a while," Butch Johnson said, "then burst their bubble. It's even better that way."

But as I made my broken-field run through this locker room, feeling the discarded tape stick to the bottoms of my shoes, I saw only shell-shocked faces and tight lips. None of these zombies would have much to say. The one man I wanted to hear was Landry, whose interview would be conducted in an unused room to the left. I raced for position. When fifty-odd people pin Landry against a cinderblock wall, you'd better be no worse than three-deep. Even after inexcusable losses, Landry did not raise his voice. Half the time I couldn't hear his answers.

Unfortunately, I heard these.

Thanks mostly to Steve Pelluer, the Cowboys had led Philly 20–0 in the second quarter. The third and fourth scores had been short field goals, meaning the lead could have been 28–0. Pelluer finished the game thirty-two of forty-six for 342 yards. Big-league numbers.

But the game had turned like a cold-front wind on one Pelluer play with 2:25 left. Leading 23–17, the Cowboys faced third-and-three at the Eagle 23. Cowboy kicker Roger Ruzek had made three of three field goal attempts. Three points here, it appeared, would just about finish Philly. Once again the choice seemed fairly obvious for the coach of Herschel's Team. You hand the ball to 230 pounds of Herschel Walker. Even if he's stopped cold, Ruzek is left with a reasonably makable forty-yarder.

As usual Landry struggled with the decision. The call came in late, as the thirty-second clock ticked under fifteen. The Cowboys already had rolled up fifteen penalties for 126 yards, many of them delay-of-game, false-start, or illegal-motion infractions caused by huddle confusion. The Cowboys were on their way to leading the NFL in penalties for 1988, with 141 (nearly nine per game). They probably led in wasted time-outs, too. If the call came in late or if, say, a play was called for two tight ends and only one was in the huddle, Pelluer sometimes called time to avoid a five-yard delay penalty. Most of the fans who wrote me blamed "that brainless Pelluer." To most fans it was inconceivable that Mount Landry was panic-prone.

But these Cowboys appeared to be coached by Slim Pickens in *Blazing Saddles*. I often was embarrassed for Landry. How could anyone who knew even a little about football watch this slapstick offense and think Landry was adding to his legend?

This time Landry called "fake toss 30 QB keep left." Pelluer didn't question the logic because Landry had called Pelluer's number. To Pelluer the coach was displaying faith in his quarterback. Again, Landry had put the game in Pelluer's hands. And in the clutch this Cowboy QB could be the shakiest gun in the West. Even worse, this play called for the right-handed Pelluer to roll to his left and make a snap decision on whether to run the ball or throw awkwardly across his body to fullback Newsome in the flat.

Newsome was covered. Eagle defensive end Clyde Simmons, all six-feet-six of him, wasn't blocked. As Simmons did a one-man wave in Pelluer's face, the quarterback cut loose a prayer of a pass.

Pelluer was flagged for intentional grounding—minus twelve yards and loss of down. The Cowboys had to punt. And Randall Cunningham led the Eagles on what seemed longer than a cattle drive, eighty-five yards in sixteen plays, the last a two-yard touchdown pass with four seconds remaining.

Eagles 24, Cowboys 23. Incredible: The Dallas Cowboys were snatching defeat from the jaws of victory.

A Dallas TV reporter sympathetically asked Landry to explain the third-and-three play. Landry's eyes were locked on the opposite wall. You could almost see him frantically yanking the mental levers that worked the great and powerful Landry. He said he, uh, called a, uh . . . "safe pass" because the ball was on the 30 and he wanted to get within field goal range.

Thirty? I flipped back through my notebook play by play. I'd written third-and-three at the 23. Another newspaper reporter politely corrected Landry.

"Huh?" Landry said, staring over our heads. "No, the ball was on the 30." His tone hinted of condescension, as if it were ridiculous to even question a man who had been calling plays under pressure for twenty-nine years.

But no, the ball had been on the 23. If, say, Jerry Glanville, then coach of the Oilers, had made a similar blunder, he would have been turned into a headline laughingstock in Houston. But in Dallas it was difficult for me to criticize Landry's lapses without fans criticizing me for taking a cheap shot at the lovable old nutty professor. All three Dallas–Fort Worth papers would make mention of Landry's "on the 30" mistake the next morning, but it wouldn't become An Issue on talk shows. You could have shown some Cowboy fans a tape of the play, and they still wouldn't have believed the ball was on the 23. If Tom Landry said it was on the 30, it was there, sure as God is in heaven.

As I left the locker room I walked past Hackett, who in rumpled suit with tie askew looked as if he'd just been to his own funeral. "What a tragedy," he said. "Tom just lost it. Completely lost it. It was total chaos on the sideline. Steve Pelluer played his heart out, and now he'll be the goat again. I just don't know how much more of this I can bear to watch."

Hackett wasn't being critical of Landry. He was hurting and rooting for him. Hackett no longer had any delusions of one day succeeding Landry. He simply wanted the Cowboys to win a few so some coach or GM or college president would think enough of Hackett to give him a job—a way out. But that day in Philadelphia, Cowboy Mystique was officially laid to rest. No one was going to say, "What about Hackett? After all, he's been with the Dallas Cowboys."

The Cowboys were 2–6.

*   *   *

Don Beck called the week after the "on the 30" debacle. Beck had met independently with Landry and Schramm. Beck said, "I'm just afraid Tom is coming apart emotionally."

I first met Dr. Don Beck in the late '70s when he worked with Oiler coach Bum Phillips. As a sports psychologist Beck could offer a coach motivational strategies. He could provide psychological profiles of "problem players." He could suggest ways to create—or re-create—image or mystique or dynamic. If nothing else, he was a good listener for a coach or GM feeling the NFL pressure to win or else.

Beck ran the National Values Center in Denton, just north of Dallas. Beck and his partners had worked with Schramm on and off for twenty years. Beck was meeting more and more with Landry.

Beck called occasionally to pick my brain on the Cowboy collapse. He read my column and said he appreciated my insight into people. Of course, I sometimes thought, "If Landry and Schramm knew Don Beck was talking to me, they'd flip." But I honestly tried to help by sharing with Beck off-the-record gripes from players, assistants, and front-office people. One week in 1987, for instance, we talked about Landry's increasing inability to inspire an under-talented team. During our discussion Beck hit on the idea of doing a "reverse George Allen." When Allen had coached the Redskins, he was known for serving ice cream after practice. So Beck suggested to Landry that he break the runaway tension with an ice-cream social. Landry actually tried it, after a Friday practice.

Two days later the Cowboys won at New England in overtime. But that was the last I heard of ice cream. Landry just wasn't an ice-cream socialite.

But now, in late October 1988, Beck no longer asked about motivation techniques. He said he and Schramm were discussing "a graceful exit." Beck told me, "We must find a way to allow Tom to ease gently into the sunset without compromising his pride or his legend." Schramm and Beck had arrived at this strategy: Hire the best young coach in the country and have him serve as Landry's assistant head coach for a season while Landry does a victory tour through NFC East cities. If Landry would announce that 1989 was his last time around, perhaps even the Redskin organization would honor him with some sort of pre-game ceremony. After all, most rival fans respected Landry as deeply as they hated the Cowboys.

Meanwhile, it could appear to Cowboy fans that Landry was teaching "the next Landry" everything he knew. Schramm's first choice was University of Miami coach Jimmy Johnson. When speculation hit the papers that Philadelphia owner Norman Braman was interested in Johnson, Schramm went as far as calling Johnson. Johnson says, "He just wanted to know if Norman Braman had contacted me. I said, no, he hadn't. Tex asked if I'd be interested in the Cowboy job. I said, well, sure I would. That's about where we left it."

And that was about where Schramm left it with Beck. Soon after the '88 season ended, Beck said, "I'm afraid Tex is afraid to even broach the subject with Tom. Besides, it's probably a pipe dream to think a Jimmy Johnson would accept working with Tom or that Tom would accept working with a Jimmy Johnson. I just don't know what's going to happen. Tom seems almost lost. Something just has to change."

I promised Beck I would write none of this in my column. Anyway, had I tried, some fans would have accused me of writing fiction.

Schramm did go as far as inviting Johnson to sit in the Cowboy box at the Super Bowl, which was conveniently in Miami. What a scene that must have been: Landry, Johnson, Schramm, and Brandt in the same room for four hours. Oh, to have been a fly on the walls of those minds. Within months Brandt would despise Johnson and Landry would criticize him. But on that Super Sunday perhaps Schramm wanted to see if he sensed any "graceful exit" rapport between Landry and Johnson. Johnson doesn't remember any.

By then Johnson must have been wondering if Landry, Schramm, or Brandt had any idea what his old friend Jerry Jones was up to. "Maybe the biggest mistake I could have made," Johnson says, "would have been moving up as head coach [after a season under Landry] and me being the only change in the entire organization."

After road games he often caught me as I left the locker room. I seldom saw him after home games because only Cowboys requested by reporters were brought across the hall to Schramm's interview room. Nobody ever seemed to request Mike Hegman.

All he had done was start at strong-side linebacker for ten years. Often he walked up beside me after games and, like a ventriloquist talking to a dummy, asked me the same question almost without moving his lips. Hegman didn't want the coaches to see him initiating conversation with a sportswriter, let alone this one.

Hegman asked me, "Coaches say anything about me, man?"

The coaches almost never did.

Hegman's eyes would dart. "How'd you think I did?"

The fact was, I seldom could remember if Hegman had even played. So I'd tell him, "Well, you didn't do anything really wrong."

He'd sigh and say, "That's what it's all about."

Michael William Hegman, age thirty-five, was the inevitable end of Landry's Flex. He had perfected the art of seldom making a mistake or a play. He could do precisely what Landry taught, little more. He was simply the most amazing player I never watched. Given a choice, Number 58 would have worn a jersey without a number. He played longer with less publicity than any America's Teamer—170 games over twelve seasons. He seldom was hurt or heard. Hegman tried not to say or do anything that would draw attention to the $350,000 he was making. Dextor Clinkscale, who played in tandem with Hegman on the strong side, said, "He had good size and speed, but I don't think he ever ran quite as fast as he could or hit as hard because he didn't really want to be noticed. He wasn't obsessed with being number one. He was motivated more by comfort."

In Hegman, Landry had created his scariest monster—one that was harmless. For ten years Landry had failed to find anyone agile enough of body and mind to replace Hegman in the Flex. Finally, though, midway through the '88 season, Landry surprised me [and Hegman] by cutting him. Things were that bleak. No warning. No obvious replacement. No sendoff press conference or ticker tape.

Not much was made of Hegman's passing in the next day's newspapers. I wrote a bittersweet eulogy, lauding Hegman's ten-year survival. The day the column appeared, Hegman left a message for me to call him. I expected he was upset over what I'd written. But he said, "I just want to thank you for that column. You were just about the only one who wrote anything. No matter what you thought of me, I played a long time for Tom, and I played hurt. He called me in and said I'd been released and that pretty much was it. It was cold, man, real cold. I just thought I deserved a little more."

*   *   *

By the fall of 1988, Bum Bright needed and wanted to sell the
Cowboys. Schramm was desperately and unsuccessfully trying to
put together an ownership group. A partnership headed by Roger
Staubach made an offer just for Bright's 40 percent of the team. But
Bright was surprised that a man "with Roger's reputation" would ask
Bright to sell out on his limited partners—leaving them, in effect,
with new management. No, Bright insisted on a full buyout. Oil
baron Marvin Davis, who had looked at several for-sale football and
baseball franchises, added the Cowboys to his list. He, too, just
wanted to buy Bright's interest. No dice.

   Many of the "some 100" potential buyers voiced a similar fear—
the "Landry problem." Why pay $180 million, Bright's steep price
tag, for the inevitable responsibility of having to fire sixty-four-year-
old Tom Landry? "It scared some people off," says a source close to
the sale. "And if they wanted to bring in another coach immediately,
well, Tom was still owed a million dollars for '89 on top of the
publicity beating they'd have to take."

   But none of this scared off Arkansas oil man Jerry Jones, who
had called out of the metallic blue from Cabo San Lucas. Jack Veatch
of Salomon Brothers, which was handling the sale for Bright, wasn't
quite sure what to make of Jones. "He seemed reasonably qualified," Veatch says. "He said if I needed references to call [Arkansas
athletic director] Frank Broyles or [Oklahoma coach] Barry Switzer
or Jimmy Johnson." Veatch arranged for Jones to take a tour of the
Valley Ranch facilities—and to meet Schramm.

   "I was just like a fan," Jones says. "I was in awe of Tex."

   Then again, Jones soon admitted to Veatch that "Tex really has
the job I'd want to do. I'd want to be president and general manager." Veatch remembers Schramm saying, "Oh, God, I need this
guy like a hole in the head."

   From the start Jones told Veatch and Bright, "If I buy this
team, I want to bring along my good friend Jimmy Johnson as coach."
Jones and Johnson were teammates and roommates at the University of Arkansas. "If that's a problem," Jones told them, "just tell me
now so I won't waste any more of your time."

   No, Bright told him, that would be no problem. "Bum and
Jerry really related to each other personally," Veatch says. "Bum is
nothing but a promoter [wheeler-dealer]. And Jerry's one of the best
promoters I've run into. But at that point [October 1988] Jerry just
faded out of the picture for two months. We didn't hear from him."

But Bright did hear from Mavericks owner Don Carter, who had a deeper love for the Cowboys than the NBA team he owned. Carter, a Dallas native who actually wore a cowboy hat and boots to work, owned a Texas Stadium box and a van painted in Cowboy colors. Carter worshiped Landry. So did Carter's mother, Mary Crowley, who had started their multimillion-dollar business, Home Interiors, from scratch. Landry knew Carter's mother well from Christian functions. "She's one of the great Christians I've ever known," Landry said. "You don't have to ask if she's a Christian. You just know it."

Carter probably would have eased down Landry much slower than any other new owner. "We would have pulled on Tom's wisdom through the transition," says Carter. Yet Carter also would have included Hackett in his plans. "Boy, Hackett was the one who got the worst of it. There had to be a way for Hackett and Tom to . . ." Carter interlocked his fingers.

As Carter and Bright horse-traded, the fates of Landry and Hackett dangled. Carter offered more than anyone did for the team, but Bright wanted to sell Texas Stadium, too. Carter didn't particularly want to get involved in stadium operation. The egos of these Texas millionaires did not interlock like fingers. Carter's "final offer" led to Bright's final answer: No dice.

For sportswriters, the Monday night radio shows of Landry and Schramm were required listening. They were back to back on KRLD, and in effect they were the only "conversation" these two had all week. Schramm listened to Landry's remarks as he waited in the wings. Then Landry listened to Schramm's as he drove home. You never knew when Landry would fire off a little radio-waves memo to his GM, or when Schramm would take one sip too many and fire back. It made for gripping theater if you knew what to listen for.

For sure, you occasionally could hear the tinkling of ice in Schramm's glass.

One night in early November, Landry slipped in, "If I was doing what's best for me, I would have quit a couple of years ago, probably . . . but I want to do what's best to rebuild this team for the future."

Translation: Tex, I've decided to keep coaching until I get this team back to the playoffs.

As much as Schramm feared losing his arm-in-arm association with Landry's image, didn't he fear being linked with a loser? Didn't he have a "Landry problem," too? Hadn't his P.R. machine helped create an unfirable monster? Surely Schramm, known for his football vision, could see Landry truly might have to coach forever to get this team back to the playoffs.

But Schramm would challenge Landry only from a distance, from behind the microphone, between the lines. Schramm would not say, "It's time for Tom to consider stepping down." But he would say things like, "If the teacher doesn't teach, the student doesn't learn." He would say, "Something drastic needs to be done. You have to realize how many lives are affected by what's happening."

He would campaign openly for his favorite QB, Kevin Sweeney.

Finally, when the Cowboys fell behind 26–0 at the half on the road against the Giants, Landry succumbed to Schramm's weekly radio suggestions and replaced Pelluer with Kevin from Heaven. And lo, all heaven broke loose. Scrambling and flinging like Fran Tarkenton, Sweeney completed nineteen of thirty-seven for 189 yards and three touchdowns. Not a bad half's work. But then, the Giants didn't appear to take Sweeney too seriously. The Giants still won 29–21, breaking only a light sweat.

By the way, the second-half plays were called by a forgotten press box observer named Paul Hackett. He said, "Coach just got overwhelmed in the second half, and I had to take over."

Overwhelmed?

"He just . . . lost it," Hackett said, as if he were about to do the same thing.

Yet the following night on KRLD, Schramm told Cowboyland, "We have seen the dawning of a new era." Landry on his show had been evasive about whether Sweeney would start the following Sunday night against Minnesota. But the next day, Tuesday, with all three TV stations going live at Landry's 11:30 A.M. media conference, Landry gave in to P. T. Schramm's hucksterism and named Sweeney starter. Lines immediately formed at the ticket office. What price dignity?

Hackett just hoped Sweeney wouldn't get hurt. He said, "What we ought to do is put Kevin on a white horse and let him gallop down the tunnel and into the stadium to a standing ovation. Are you believing this stuff?"

The Vikings weren't. Sweeney was ten of twenty-eight for ninety-three yards with four interceptions. The final Viking score came when Sweeney was sacked in the end zone for a safety. Vikings 43–3.

I kept hearing there was one other reason Landry couldn't quit: He needed the money. His son, Tom Jr., was yet another get-poor-quick victim of the black-gold market. Tom Jr. had plunged heavily in oil deals and hit too many dry holes. Tom Jr. sometimes had taken his dad down with him.

As a lawyer, one of Tom Jr.'s specialties was bankruptcy.

An oil-business associate of Tom Jr.'s says, "He left his law practice during the oil boom and became a big Las Vegas guy—the exact opposite of Big Tom. He was as into flash as Big Tom was against it. He was the typical Texas oil man—big belt buckle and boots. He was on the fast track, shucking and jiving and using his father's name a lot. He'd want a bigger cut of the pie because he was Tom Landry Jr., then he'd pull Coach Landry into the deal. In the end, Coach Landry had to bail him out of the drilling business."

Big Tom victimized by greed? It happened to the best of 'em in Dallas. "But the last couple of years," the associate says, "as Tom Jr.'s cash flow faded, he really seemed to tone down his life-style and got closer to his dad."

You wonder if the Landrys would have named their firstborn Tom Jr. if they'd known Tom Sr. would become God's Coach. Talk about a cross to bear.

The week before the Washington game at RFK Stadium, I bumped into ex-Steeler quarterback and CBS commentator Terry Bradshaw. He lived just outside Dallas and worked out at the same club I did. In the hall outside the locker room Bradshaw literally pinned me against the wall, gripping my shoulders to squeeze home his point.

"Look, the sad truth is that the game has passed Tom Landry by," Bradshaw said. "It is a young man's game. Tom just isn't willing to put in the hours these other guys do. Why should he, at his age? He had a great run, but he should have gotten out of it several years ago. You know it and I know it. You have got to tell the people in your business to quit treating Tom like such a god and making it even harder for him to quit."

Bradshaw was reacting in part to what had happened the Sunday before in Cleveland. The Cowboys were penalized a club record seventeen times for 142 yards. Late in the game, trailing 24–21, the Cowboys faced third-and-four at the Cleveland 22. Pelluer was back at quarterback. Landry called a play in a way it hadn't been practiced. Herschel Walker, who was split out right, didn't quite understand. Receiver Kelvin Martin, also wide right, wasn't sure, either. Before calling signals, Pelluer actually had to trot to the flank to reroute Walker and Martin.

Pelluer's pass for Martin fell incomplete. Browns 24–21. In the final paragraph of my column I referred to Landry as "Mount Senility." I know: It was too strong. I overreacted. I was hearing too much from players, from Hackett, from Beck, and now from Bradshaw.

The following Sunday, as I settled into my press box seat at RFK, I felt a hard tap on the shoulder. It was Vito Stellino, a veteran pro football reporter who had covered Bradshaw's days in Pittsburgh and now worked for the *Baltimore Sun*. Stellino was ready to pin me against the press box wall. He said, "How in the world could you refer to Tom Landry as senile? My God, this is maybe the greatest coach who ever lived. He sure doesn't look or sound senile to me."

How could I even begin to debate that? Stellino was talking about the image; I was writing about the reality. But who would believe Thomas Wade Landry was losing it on the sideline? Who'd believe he sometimes dozed off in coaches' meetings? For that matter, who wanted to read it if it was true? Millions drew upon Landry's faith and strength. But how many more games could Landry lose for how many more seasons without losing some of his aura and credibility? This sharply dressed emperor had fewer and fewer clothes. At what tragic point would the masses see Landry as I did?

Already a call-in poll conducted by the *Dallas Times Herald* had indicated Landry was no longer above doubt. The yes-or-no question was "Should Tom Landry retire?" For what it was worth, 7,367 said yes; 4,172 said no. You could argue that "real" Cowboy fans—those who owned boxes or held season tickets—wouldn't stoop to calling a newspaper poll. You could say Christians wouldn't think of participating in such heretical nonsense. Who knows? Maybe Schramm and staff frantically called the "yes" number several thousand times. For sure, the *Times Herald* received several hundred cancellation threats. Publicly, Landry made light of the poll, saying only that Alicia no longer allowed the *Times Herald* in the house.

But had Landry lost all perspective on himself? Had the guy from Mission forgotten how he came to be one of the world's most sought-after Christian speakers? *By winning.* Isn't that really all most fans care about? Most fans I've known invest emotionally in a team only in the hope that it will win and make them feel better about themselves. Would Landry have been sought by the Graham Crusade if the Cowboys had remained a .500 team into the '70s? No, he probably would have been fired.

Most people wouldn't have worshiped a devout loser.

I often prayed for guidance before I wrote about Landry. I often asked, "Use me for Your good." And "Give me vision I don't have." What many readers couldn't understand was that I did not "hate" Tom Landry. By 1988 I didn't think he was much of a football coach, mostly because so many who played or coached told me he wasn't. But when I wrote, I tried to separate the coach from the man. I thought Landry, away from football, was a pleasant enough guy who lived cleanly and dedicated much of his time to good causes. But if I'm paid to write the truth, as best I can substantiate it, should I let my feelings for Landry affect my view of his coaching?

This is the dilemma of the sports columnist: If Tom Landry returns your calls and calls you by first name, is your objectivity deflated? Should being able to tell your friends and relatives you know Landry "personally" assure him of godlike status in your writing? If he treats you nicely, should you treat him that way in print, no matter his coaching performance? Would he return your calls and be quite so nice if you couldn't help shape public opinion of him? For that matter, would Schramm buy dinner for a sportswriter and get drunk with him just because the writer was a hell of a guy? I knew a lot of media people who thought they'd been welcomed into the Cowboy "family" simply because Schramm and staff enjoyed their company. Maybe so. Maybe I was too fanatical about not being sucked in, but what was I being paid to do? I wasn't a "beat" writer whose job was to report the day-to-day Cowboy news. I was a columnist paid to express an opinion. Was my job to get close to Landry? Perhaps get him to open up to me a little more, in exchange for using all his quotes in a "wisdom from Mount Landry" context? Was I supposed to write only about Landry's image? To give readers

what they'd come to expect for twenty-nine seasons? Was I wasting
my time and theirs trying to write about the real Landry for a Dallas
newspaper?

What was I doing? Aren't sports basically the opiate of the
masses? A nights-and-weekends soap opera in which we can lose
ourselves? Pills of vicarious thrills? Don't, as Thoreau said, the mass
of men (and women) lead lives of quiet desperation? Don't most
people just want me to give them a quick morning fix, a chuckle or
sigh or harrumph over some disposable-as-newsprint opinion about
last night's game? I was a sportswriter, for heaven's sake. Was I
supposed to make a reader think about anything deeper than why
the Cowboys weren't scoring inside the 20? Did the mechanic in
Mesquite or the waitress in Euless really care about what truly was
going on at Valley Ranch? Weren't there enough problems in the
world without my questioning how a great Christian such as Tom
Landry could live with himself, his business, his organization?

If people paid $25 to watch the Cowboys, what did I owe them
for the twenty-five-cent price of my newspaper? The truth? Were
advertisers, who basically paid my salary, hesitant to buy ads in the
Times Herald because I didn't hesitate to criticize Landry? God,
what a dilemma.

I couldn't forget what Charles Champlin once told me. Champlin was the nationally renowned film critic of the *Los Angeles Times*.
When I asked why he didn't write occasional feature stories about
actors and actresses, he said, "I don't want to even meet those
people. I don't want to have any personal feelings for them one way
or the other. I have to critique their work." I recall he used a
Landry-like example, Charlton Heston: "What if I think he's a great
guy and he makes a bad movie?"

I thought an okay guy, Landry, was making a bad movie.

For me this forced a final question: Could I be a Christian and
judge Landry? Judge not, lest I be judged? Wasn't I throwing
printed stones at Landry from a glass house? I took my job a lot more
seriously than I took myself. Really, who was I to judge? I hadn't
played or coached pro football. All I did was study the game and talk
to lots of people who knew far more about it than I did. But when
I criticized Landry, lots of readers must have thought I was the boy
crying wolf. Lots of Christians probably thought, "How low can you
stoop to sell papers?"

All I knew was that the more I prayed, the stronger I believed in what I was saying. Again and again I wrote that it was time for Landry to become a full-time evangelist or enjoy the Hall of Fame retirement he deserved. I wrote, "I don't want to have to watch the men in white designer coats dragging Tom Landry off the Texas Stadium sideline."

Yet, though the Cowboys were 2–12, they had come close in five losses. Was I being hypercritical? Overemotional? That day in Washington, Pelluer hit twenty-one of thirty-six for 333 yards and three touchdowns, the last giving the Cowboys a 24–17 victory. Pelluer says, "I was beginning to figure out how to handle everything."

On the suggestion of thirteen-year center Tom Rafferty, a game ball was awarded Landry in the locker room. The Dallas–Fort Worth media made it sound like a Ronald Reagan movie. Landry said, "It was like we won the Super Bowl."

I was thankful I didn't bump into Vito Stellino after the game.

The following week, in the season finale at Texas Stadium, Buddy Ryan's Eagles had their way with the Cowboys, 23–7. The loss assured the Cowboys of the NFL's worst record, 3–13, and first pick in the draft. Conveniently, UCLA quarterback Troy Aikman was on his way to Dallas for the Cotton Bowl, allowing Landry to avoid negative themes on his Monday night radio show. Landry assured fans he would "get a good look at Aikman."

He also slipped in a statement that sent shudders through Bum Bright and all who were quietly involved in the sale of the team. Landry said he planned to coach "into the '90s." With Aikman, Landry would have another excuse for another "three-year plan" back to the playoffs.

And at 3–13 he had enough of an excuse to fire Hackett. But that wasn't the only head that rolled. Landry simultaneously fired a fan favorite, a co-living legend, Ernie Stautner, the Hall of Fame defensive lineman. For twenty-three seasons Stautner had been a loyal yes-man under Landry. But at 3–13 Landry needed scapegoats. He needed to show fans he was doing something. So he announced that his top offensive assistant (Hackett) and his trusty defensive coordinator (Stautner) were being replaced by Jerry Rhome and George Hill.

Stautner bitterly blasted Landry, saying the head coach repeatedly ignored his draft and strategy suggestions through the '80s. "I'd suggest defensive linemen to Tom and Gil, but they wouldn't listen," Stautner said.

Yes, it had come to this.

After his year of being P.R.-coached, Hackett made a graceful exit. No parting shots. No comment. He seemed relieved—until he began job hunting. Landry agreed to put in a good word for him with colleges, not NFL teams. Hackett interviewed to be head coach at Stanford, a position he had turned down five years before. This time, despite Landry's recommendation, Hackett was turned down. He struck out at Washington State and SMU, too. He sought several NFL jobs, but other managements were leery of his, uh, complications with Landry. Finally, growing desperate, Hackett took a job as offensive coordinator at the University of Pittsburgh.

I couldn't believe how far he had fallen.

I talked to him a few months later. He chuckled once, in disbelief, and said, "Well, I'm forty-two years old, and I don't have a nickel in the bank. We took a huge hit selling the house [losing something like $50,000]. We were just financially devastated, and now I'm making half the salary I was in Dallas. We're living in a nice little house in a nice neighborhood, but it just has one bathroom."

From the "next Landry" to one bathroom.

"But you know," he said, "I still have the greatest wife in the world, and I go to work every morning with a smile on my face. Isn't that what it's all about? None of that morose, holier-than-thou bullshit. No one dissects every word I say. Right now I'm not even talking to the media. I'm just coming down off a tragic situation. But you know, looking back, it was a lot more tragic for Tom. He went through some very heavy stuff. It had to be devastating."

15

YOU WOULDN'T exactly describe The Man Who Fired Tom
Landry as a coldhearted businessman. Associates and rivals say Jerry
Jones is a likable guy who gets so high on deal-making that he'll stay
awake for days figuring ways to close one. "He often has called me
at 5 A.M. with an idea," an associate says. "I'll say, 'Jerry, it's five in
the morning.' He'll say, 'It is?' He's just a guy from Little Rock who
doesn't have the sense to see that something is impossible. When
most 'good businessmen' would say, 'Well, there's no way,' Jerry is
saying, 'How 'bout this?' I'm not saying he won't do 'whatever it
takes' to do a deal. Who doesn't? But you wouldn't call him ruthless.
He's more relentless."

Jerry Jones, the American Dreamer, was relentlessly trying to
buy America's Team. From a distance you'd have made his odds
longer than the Cowboys' Super Bowl odds. Yet if you knew Bum
Bright, you knew Jones had an even-money chance. Says Salomon
Brothers broker Jack Veatch, "Start with the fact that both are deal-
oholics. They just love to negotiate. And both are self-made men
who like to talk about their days as undersized football players who
played on guts."

Jerry Buss, owner of the Los Angeles Lakers, was probably a little too "I'm from Hollywood and you're not" for Bright. Buss indicated to Veatch he was ready to make an offer that would make Bright forget about Jerry Jones. But Buss had been too slow to fly to Dallas, strap himself in across the desk from Bright, and *deal*. For Bright, dealing was testing your manhood with millions at stake. For negotiating sessions, Bright loved to make a militaristic entrance through a side door of his office, flanked by aides, and all but play Stratego with a rival general. For Bright, victory was trapping a bidder in an unscrupulous plot or a bogus bluff and making him "flush"—redden with castrated humiliation—in a roomful of aides and lawyers.

Bright made Jones "flush." Bright had to "woodshed" Jones, take him aside and tongue-lash him for a backdoor maneuver. But Bright decided right away that Jones's heart was in the right place. Jones simply was tap dancing as fast as he could, trying to find a way to put together a $140 million package that would keep him in the running with dozens of "big boy" bidders. Besides Buss there was a Japanese group said to be "price insensitive." A source close to the sale says, "The Japanese were ready to make an offer with no real sense of how much the Dallas Cowboys were worth. To them it was like, 'Oh, Dallas Cowboys! How much? Two hundred million? Three hundred?' Landry might have coached for another century if the Japanese had bought the team. But World War II had a profound effect on Bum. He just wasn't comfortable with the thought of selling the Dallas Cowboys to the Japanese, whether or not the league would have approved it."

One Saturday morning Bright's negotiating team met Jones's team around a conference table. Lots of suits and briefcases and failing deodorant. Jones had informed Bright he was prepared to make a formal offer, but as the meeting began he nervously announced the offer was slightly less than the figure discussed the day before. Bright interrupted: "Jerry, you're a nice young man, but you don't have enough money to buy the Dallas Cowboys. Either that or you're not offering enough."

Bright fondly remembers that Jones was red-faced. The meeting lasted "one minute." Bright marched out of the conference room to the beat of closing and clicking briefcases.

But Jones wouldn't give up. Jones was unembarrassable. And though poker-faced during sessions, Bright got a kick out of this one-time poor boy from Little Rock trying so hard to buy the Dallas Cowboys. Perhaps Bright thought it would be fitting for a guy from Little Rock to own the mirage known as America's Team. Bright's philosophy: "Don't get mad. Get even." Was selling to Jones his way of getting even with Landry-Schramm-Brandt? Bright could have let any bidder pull the sword from the stone, to use Bright's favorite legend. He could have sold to several bidders who would have considered it a sacred privilege to carry on the Cowboy tradition. But Jones, who wanted Schramm's job, came packaged with a coach who wanted Landry's and Brandt's. Did this make him more attractive?

Bright says, "I just thought Jerry would make a great owner."

But didn't Bright sense Jones might sandblast the Landry-Schramm-Brandt monument and all but highlight it with Razorback red? Change it for the better, perhaps, but definitely change the holy heck out of it? Didn't Bright like Jones's relentless naiveté? For all the millions Jones had made in oil and gas—by hook or (some say) crook—Jones could be something of a Jethro Bodine. In some ways he could be foolish and gullible. What set him apart from most self-made millionaires is that he had a big heart, with which he often thought and spoke. "Too often, probably," he says. Did Bright see in Jones a P.R. rube who would take the P.R. fall on the "Landry problem"?

"Absolutely not," Bright says. "I told all buyers that I would fire Tom Landry. If I'd had any idea what was going to happen to Jerry, I'd have taken the fall. Jerry got a very bad rap."

In fact, before the sale was finalized, Veatch kidded Bright that gawkers soon would be driving slowly past Bright's home the way they did the window from which Oswald fired.

But to this day you'll have a hard time finding a Cowboy fan who holds Bum Bright responsible for the firing of Tom Landry. A "coldhearted" Jones did the deed "without mercy." Or so it appeared. In truth, Jones was played for the fool by Tex Schramm. "It was Tex's job to fire Tom," says Bright.

Landry would play Jones's P.R. stupidity for all it was worth, too. Jones knew how to make a deal, but he knew nothing about making public opinion. "Jethro" Jones was about to dive headlong into a nightmare-come-true.

"Looking back, I wish I could change a few things," says Jones, understating for once. But looking back, Jerry Jones was the best thing that could have happened to Tom Landry. To this day I believe God used Jones to free God's Coach from himself. Crazy? So was what happened.

The week of February 20, 1989, Bum Bright went so far as to tell aides he and Jones were "hitched." They had the foundation of a deal. "But until that Saturday morning [February 25]," Jones says, "I guarantee you there were two hundred deal-breakers still on the table."

On Wednesday night, the twenty-second, Jack Veatch interrupted final negotiations with a warning. "I said, 'Wait a second, guys, we're dealing with Tom Landry here. He's a great figure. I'm just not sure we can keep this thing a secret much longer.' Jerry really underestimated the backlash."

Perhaps what Jones and Bright underestimated was how much Veatch was telling many members of the media. In particular he was keeping Channel 5, KXAS-TV, apprised—in part, perhaps, because the station had done a nice profile story on Veatch, who had been a classmate of Staubach's at the Naval Academy. Veatch says he met with Channel 5 reporters that Wednesday. "I got them to hold the story *because* of Tom Landry. They sat on it for four days. They understood the problem, but it was like, 'Hey, this is going to break in the papers any moment.' "

Bright says, "We were doing great until Channel 5 blew it. We had kept Schramm and Valley Ranch completely in the dark, and we would have done everything with class and dignity."

Maybe so. But Bright was a skilled veteran of dealing with the media through the hirings and firings of Texas A&M coaches and the acquiring of banks and businesses. He had to know the story could or would break. Jones had been interviewed "maybe once or twice in my life." The question is, by this point, what did Bright really care about treating Landry with class and dignity? Had Landry treated Bright that way?

On Thursday night at ten the story broke like a dam—or a damn!—on Channel 5: "Arkansas oil man Jerry Jones has bought the Dallas Cowboys . . ." Furthermore, a Channel 5 reporter standing in front of the University of Miami said Jones was bringing in Jimmy Johnson to replace Landry. The entire story was attributed to "sources." Bright's right-hand man Jim Francis denied on camera that the team had been sold to Jones. It hadn't been. Schramm told Channel 5 he knew nothing about it. He didn't.

The following evening Channel 5 softened its scoop from "has bought" to "appears will buy." Jones insists, "Channel 5 made an educated guess, was all. I promise you, they could have shot themselves in the foot. In my view, if four days earlier Bum Bright had thought it was necessary, he would have called Coach Landry. But we just did not have a deal. And I had no idea of the impact the media was about to have. I'd just never dealt with that quantity or quality of reporting."

But the next morning, Friday, as Jimmy Johnson and his wife slipped aboard Jones's jet in Miami, the media massed at Valley Ranch for Landry's reaction to Channel 5's bombshell. Why would Johnson, the highly visible coach of the highly successful Hurricanes, risk being recognized in Dallas? Mostly, says Veatch, because of minority owner Ed Smith. Jones didn't know Smith but desperately needed him to close the deal. Smith agreed to take 27 percent and put up some $18 million—on one condition: Smith insisted on face-to-face assurance from Johnson that he indeed would leave Miami to coach the Cowboys. Smith didn't want Jones getting cold feet at the base of Mount Landry. He wanted a guarantee that Landry would be fired.

Friday afternoon Smith met with Johnson and was satisfied. Meanwhile, the minicams were following Landry through another bi'ness-as-usual day at the Ranch. Landry kept saying, no, he hadn't heard a thing about what was going on. Landry kept doing the same things at the same seconds he had for thirty years. That night, televised scenes of Coach Landry, jaw set, forging ahead while terrible rumors swirled, touched and outraged Landry lovers.

I half-wondered why Landry didn't just call Bright and ask if there were any truth to Channel 5's story. But I didn't know that the last time Landry had called Bright was in 1959, to interview for the A&M job. They simply didn't communicate.

So Landry fiddled diligently; Rome burned. I doubt he could even smell smoke. Him fired? No way.

That evening Jones and Johnson and their wives checked quietly into an Embassy Suites hotel across I-35 from Bright's office tower, whose lobby had turned into a national media convention. The Jones-Johnson reservation was made for a Jerry Petty, Bright's son-in-law. So far Johnson had avoided media detection. "We still did not have a deal," Jones emphasizes. So why didn't they just order room service? Call out for pizza or Chinese?

Instead, Jones asked a motel employee to recommend a "quiet little out-of-the-way Mexican place." The guy suggested Mia's.

Mia's was one of Dallas's most popular Mexican restaurants. Mia's also was Tom Landry's favorite.

Even so, Jones and Johnson might have survived if, perhaps, the Lord hadn't worked in one more mysterious way. A *Dallas Morning News* reporter, Ivan Maisel, had been assigned to watch for Jones and possibly Johnson at the Mansion on Turtle Creek, where Jones had been staying. Maisel and a photographer had camped from 4:30 P.M. to about 7:30 when Maisel gave up and took his fiancée to dinner. She had been out of town and wanted a Mexican food fix. She wanted to go to Mia's.

What are the odds?

Johnson says, "The way the guy at the hotel described the place, we thought there'd be two or three customers." But as usual, thirty or forty customers were waiting for a table. And one of them was a stunned Maisel, whose dinner break had become a huge break. Maisel approached as Johnson and Jones ordered beers at the bar. "I'm thinking, 'Oh, me,'" says Johnson. "He said, 'Jimmy, can I get some quotes?' I said, 'You've got to understand the position I'm in. I've got no comment.'"

So Maisel went to Plan B: Call the newspaper, perhaps for a photographer. Make that Plan C: Mia's, he found, had no pay phone. Maisel didn't want to alarm Johnson and Jones by walking past their table and out the front door, so he slipped through the kitchen and out the back and called from a Chinese place down the street.

A photographer arrived as Jones and Johnson were in mid-fajita feast.

Johnson says, "Rather than trying to hide behind napkins and look like a couple of villains, we just asked that we move the beer bottles off the table."

Say cheese (enchiladas)! Johnson and Jones smiled for the camera. The color picture ran on the front page of Saturday's *Morning News*. No, these two "villains" weren't hiding behind napkins. They were grinning across the table at each other *at Coach Landry's favorite restaurant!* The most damaging aspect of the picture was that Johnson and Jones appeared to be having such a good time at Landry's expense. To Cowboy fans it looked as if the Johnsons and Joneses were on their way to dance on poor Tom's fresh grave.

Bright aide Francis says, "That picture will go down in Dallas lore with Ruby shooting Oswald."

That same evening Bright instructed Schramm to be at his office the next morning and to let Landry know he probably ought to "stay in pocket this weekend, just in case." The Channel 5 story had rushed the negotiation. The Mia's picture sent it careening through the longest day of Jones's life.

Jones and Bright met around 6 A.M. Before Schramm arrived they shook hands on a deal. Slight complication, though: They didn't have time to negotiate "twenty or thirty points," says Jones, "involving about 10 percent of the total value." The final price was about $150 million. So maybe $15 million remained on the bargaining table. "I couldn't believe it," says Jack Veatch. "They had nothing in writing. No letter of intent. Just a handshake. And they were about to fire Tom Landry."

But what else were they going to do? The world had known they had a deal before they had one, they say. The P.R. damage was done. What now? Wait until Monday to tell Landry?

Bright asked Schramm to call Landry at home and arrange an immediate meeting. A servant told Schramm that the Landrys were out. Schramm and Veatch began calling around looking for Landry. Several hours later they discovered he had left for his getaway home in Austin. To Bright it seemed Landry was playing very hard to get. Heating, Bright called Bob Alpert, who developed the Hills of Lakeway where Landry had a home on the eighteenth fairway. Bright had done some business with Alpert, and with his help, he finally tracked down Landry at another course, Hidden Hills, and instructed an employee to go out and find Landry and "tie him up if you have to."

Schramm finally got Landry on the phone. Schramm told him, "It doesn't look good."

Schramm got directions to Hidden Hills. Schramm told Landry "we're" coming down. We? "Tex suggested I go," Jones says. "Technically, according to the team charter, only the president and general manager could fire the coach. But I've always felt strongly in any of my businesses that if there's a hard job to do, I should do it myself. I just wanted to show Coach Landry I was man enough and honorable enough to face him."

But what if P.R. discretion had been the better part of valor?

What if Jones had said, "Bum, you said you'd deal with Landry, so I'll just lay low for a couple of days until the smoke clears"? What if Jones had gone back to Little Rock instead of on to Austin? What if he had waited until the following week to tell the media: "I informed Mr. Bright six months ago I wanted to start fresh with my dear friend Jimmy Johnson"? But Jones, new owner of America's Team, already was intoxicated with the power. Unlike the camera-shy Murchison and Bright, Jones gets camera-high. He lights up in the limelight. Perhaps a part of him wanted to go down in history as the man who flew to Austin to break the news to Thomas Wade Landry.

That, obviously, was what Landry thought. When Jones and Schramm arrived, Landry immediately accused Jones of "grandstanding." Jones says he was stunned by the charge. "I really thought I was going out of my way to do the right thing." Jones says Schramm backed him in front of Landry.

But what was really happening no longer mattered. As always with the Cowboys, what counted was appearance. For the moment Schramm had to be thanking his lucky stars for "Jethro" Jones. A sale source says, "Tex said later that night that Jerry took all the pressure off him."

In one night Jones created a national image he may never live down. His script was being written scene by scene by P. T. Schramm. Schramm suggested they fly straight back to Dallas for a media conference at Valley Ranch. Jones says, "Tex just thought we had kept the media in the dark for so long that we should give everybody the story."

Jones, soaring, viewed it as a celebration. After all, he had just done the impossible and bought the Dallas Cowboys. In fact, while Jones was in Austin, an El Paso group had contacted Bright and "guaranteed" it would top Jones's price by $20 million. Bright says, "I had made a deal with Jerry and was going to honor that, but I gave Jerry the chance to sell to the El Paso people if he wanted." If Jones wanted, apparently, he could have sold the Cowboys for a $20 million profit the same day he bought them. A source says, "Jerry took about thirty seconds to think about it and said, 'Tell El Paso to kiss my ass.' "

He had done it! He owned the Taj Mahal, the Statue of Liberty, the Grand Canyon, the Dallas by-God Cowboys!

And he was about to address the mourning masses.

Yes, masterfully, Schramm played the media conference as a wake. At this point, remember, Schramm and Jones had spent most of sixteen straight hours together talking philosophy and had agreed to try working together. Says Cowboy P.R. director Greg Aiello, "Everyone thought Jerry and Tex were going to work out as a Mr. Inside (Schramm) and Mr. Outside (Jones)."

KRLD radio went live with the 8:30 P.M. state of disunion. It took place on the same stage from which Landry always addressed his team and the media. It was theater of the absurd. It became known as the Saturday Night Massacre.

Jones made a grand entrance followed by an entourage of family and business partners, maybe twenty people trying to squeeze onto the right side of the stage. They were joined on stage by Ed Smith and family. Bright quietly took a chair on the left side. Schramm presided.

Asked how the meeting with Landry had gone, Schramm broke down in midsentence. He struggled to say, "It was very, very sad. . . . It's tough to break a relationship you've had for twenty-nine years." Schramm's scene was made for TV and radio and front-page, full-color pictures. Lights, cameras: Poor Tex had lost his "best friend." Schramm's face was longer than the '88 season had been. This was the Schramm who indicated to Bright he "hated" Landry? If Schramm was actually moved to tears, it was over losing his budgetless control.

How could Jones possibly have followed Schramm's act? A skilled politician wouldn't have tried. A P.R. specialist would have sighed deeply and said, "Tonight belongs to Coach Landry and Tex Schramm and their three decades of greatness. I am humbled by the opportunity to own the Dallas Cowboys. But I've had nothing to do with creating this franchise and it just isn't appropriate for me to answer any of your questions yet."

For most stunned fans it was a time to look back instead of ahead. For Jones it should have been a time to ask Bright to lay Landry to rest. Instead, Jones was grinning ear to ear. Jones looked as if he hadn't slept for two weeks, which he pretty much hadn't. Jones took the microphone as if he were Conway Twitty about to sing his greatest hits for an adoring audience.

Jones said, "This is like Christmas to me. The Cowboys are America. They are more than a football team. . . . My entire office and my entire business will be at this complex. I intend to have an understanding of the complete situation, an understanding of the player situation, of the jocks and socks. . . ."

That was it, for most fans and media people. Not only had this

Arkansas hillbilly grinned and fired Landry, but Jones was spitting on the sacred Cowboy tradition of silent ownership. This wild man was even going to hang around the locker room trying on jocks and socks. Jones immediately became known as "Jocks and Socks" Jones.

But he was just getting warmed up. Though, prudently, Jimmy Johnson had returned to Miami, Jones said, "What Jimmy will bring us is worth more than if we had five first-round draft choices and five Heisman Trophy winners. History will show that one of the finest things that ever happened to the Dallas Cowboys is Jimmy Johnson."

Jones's family and friends cheered and clapped as if this were an Arkansas Razorback pep rally. You could almost hear the lynch mobs forming across Dallas. Jones wasn't through: "There is no substitute for winning. And we must win! We will win! Winning is the name of the game! We're going to win this year!"

I wanted to stick some socks in Jones's mouth. He was speaking as if everyone thought of Landry the way Bright and Smith and other insiders did. Throughout negotiations Jones had heard about the "Landry problem," and now he wanted to tell Cowboyland the problem had been solved! Shoot, Jones had heard from Johnson that Tex himself had talked to ol' Jimmy about replacing Landry. And here he, Jerry Jones from Arkansas, had delivered the very coach chosen by Schramm to be the next Landry! Pig, sooooie!

Jones, perhaps, was lucky he lived to see Sunday morning. The only Landry problem that Cowboy fans knew of was Jocks and Socks Jones.

Landry didn't miss a chance to run up the score, either. Landry struck while the irony was hot. Landry flew back from Austin on Sunday and went straight to clean out his office. He made no secret of it, so the minicams massed. Landry gladly, though sadly, allowed the media into his office to follow his every sigh and shake of the head. Landry dressed perfectly for the part: open-collared flannel shirt, work-in-the-garden pants, bifocals, no hat. As the film rolled, Landry sorted through his files, discarding some papers, keeping others. Occasionally he almost smiled over some Memory Lane memento. He moved slowly, deliberately, as if what Jones had done to him had suddenly aged him twenty years.

It appeared to fans that Jones had waited until Landry was in Austin, playing golf with his family, to show up and tell him to vacate his office by the next afternoon. Who was this Hooterville menace? Everything had happened so fast that stories of the firing had grown into fish stories. Shark stories. I was told by a team source that Jones and Schramm had taken a golf cart to go after Landry and had caught his family foursome on the first green. I could just picture Jones walking straight across the green to Landry, stepping in everyone's line and saying, "Tom, I'm Jerry Jones. I've always wanted to meet you. By the way, big guy, you're fired."

But upon further review, as they say in the NFL, I found that Landry (and family and loyalists) were waiting for Jones and Schramm near the Hidden Hills putting green. In the living room of a sales office overlooking the course, Jones told Landry of his dream of working with Johnson, his best friend, but that he'd love for Landry to stay on in some capacity. Either way, Jones assured him, he would be paid $1 million for 1989.

"I honestly don't know what else I could have done under the circumstances," Jones says. "After the Channel 5 story hit, we were in a can't-win situation."

All Jones could have done was let Schramm go alone to Austin. Instead it appeared Jones had ordered Schramm to go along and witness the firing of his best friend. And through the entire Saturday night news conference Bright was asked only one question, near the end: "Mr. Bright, what did *you* think about Tom Landry?" Bright spoke the briefest, truest words of the night: "To be honest, I didn't say fifteen words to Tom Landry in the five years I owned the team."

For Sunday's paper I wrote that Bright, in effect, had fired Landry. But that wasn't what people wanted to read. Jones already was "The Man Who Fired Tom Landry." In Texas, Jones was the easiest target since Oswald. Oh, how Tom Landry needed Jerry Jones. If Bright had fired him quietly, it just wouldn't have been the same.

But there, on Sunday night TV specials in Dallas, was poor, evicted Tom, cleaning out 270 victories' worth of memories. Charlton Heston couldn't have played the suffering any more convincingly. By Sunday night Tom Landry had become the most sympathetic figure since B.C. became A.D. It actually was as if Landry had risen from the 3–13 dead. All was forgotten and forgiven. The losing, the drafting, the firing of Ernie Stautner—all gone.

God's Coach was free to become his image.

By Monday I was getting calls from sports columnists and talk shows all over the country. Landry had been widely quoted on how "mishandled" his firing was. No, he did not turn the other cheek. He did not say, "They were put in a bad spot by the Channel 5 story. I had that happen to me several times before I could tell a player he was cut." Landry said "mishandled." So everyone said, "Mishandled!" Landry said, "They flew to Austin to see me for nothing. It was obvious I wasn't going to be the coach." So everyone said, "Jones flew to Austin just to rub it in!"

But Landry said, "I'm not bitter at all." So everyone said, "Landry is the only one handling this with any class."

The entire country seemed to be outraged. It seemed as if every national leader, from President Bush to Billy Graham, was called for comment. What were they going to say except what a shame it was? Many Texas politicians and Dallas powerbrokers spoke angrily of Jones's insensitivity. Day after day the newspapers smoldered with "poor Tom" quotes. He was Tom of Arc, a martyr for the ages.

I wrote that I was relieved and happy for Landry. But for most readers, probably, my emotions were incomprehensible blasphemy. My final frustration came after I spoke to or heard from several Cowboys and ex-Cowboys who expressed this off-the-record sentiment: "He finally got treated the same way he treated us." The same players were quoted in the papers as saying, "It was a shame it had to end that way for such a great coach."

On the morning of April 22, 1989, a Saturday, I exited I-35 into downtown Dallas and hit traffic. Big-game traffic. Downtown was usually dead on Saturday morning. I edged my way to the *Times Herald* parking garage and walked the last few blocks. Already, the throng was five-deep along Commerce.

Where was I? In front of their faces, hundreds of kids and grownups alike were holding up giveaway Landry masks on a stick. It looked as if everyone in Dallas had turned into a Landry look-alike. Was this my punishment, my personal "Twilight Zone"? Hawkers were selling Landry T-shirts and buttons and, of course, hats. Yes, this was the "Hats off to Tom Landry" parade. The hottest selling item appeared to be a button that said "I (Xed-out heart) Jerry Jones."

For nearly a month Tom Landry had been honored the way perhaps no living human ever had been. As Pete Rozelle said when

Landry was fired, "It's like Lombardi died." But Landry had gone to heaven on earth. In Dallas many groups honor themselves by honoring outstanding people. Landry could have received a proclamation, award, or gift daily, for breakfast, lunch, and dinner. Perhaps he still could.

America's Team had risen and fallen. Its coach had fallen and risen.

Within a week of Landry's removal, Dallas politicians and merchants conceived of a Landry Day. An organizer told me, "The thing just got out of hand. Everybody wanted a piece of it." Again and again Dallasites heard on TV and radio that "up to one hundred thousand people may be in downtown Dallas." Lots of people might have come to see how many people would come. It had been a long time since Dallas had experienced an Event.

It had to be the largest crowd in downtown Dallas since the Kennedy motorcade. But it was difficult to tell whether the biggest attraction was Landry or the floats and classic convertibles full of Cowboys and ex-Cowboys—nearly one hundred of them. The ex-stars used the occasion as an excuse for a weekend reunion. And, as one ex-superstar told me, "Why should we let Tom get all the credit for what we accomplished? You think this many people would have showed up just to see him?"

So here came the parade, if not charade: the Dixie Style Cloggers . . . the Apache Belles . . . the Grambling Marching Band . . . Shriners in go-carts . . . Miss Fort Worth . . . and Cowboys, Cowboys, Cowboys. America's Team lived. Cameras clicked. Good times rolled. Look! There's Coach Landry!

In the final convertible rode Tom and Alicia, waving. Now, outwardly, Landry appeared as overwhelmed as he sometimes was inwardly during games. Tom Landry was waving at thousands wearing his face. His expression was somewhere between embarrassment and disbelief. Mine was more of the latter. All this for a Landry whose teams had missed the playoffs four of his last five seasons, hadn't won a playoff game since the '82 season, and had finished 3–13 in '88? Perhaps Landry should have been wearing a button that said, "I (heart) Jerry Jones."

Tom and Alicia had become the closest thing in America to a royal couple. More people probably had less reason to dislike Landry than any other living legend. Maybe you didn't care for Ronald Reagan's politics. Maybe you couldn't swallow Billy Graham's religion. But Landry wasn't *too* political, *too* religious, *too* outspoken. Landry could play a great "sheepishly humble honoree." What church, school, or civic group in America wouldn't want to say it honored Tom Landry?

Wasn't Landry the perfect role model for all ages, male or female? Wasn't he what every American should aspire to be? And he belonged to Dallas. Maybe Dallas no longer had a great football team. Maybe SMU's football program had gone down in national flames. Okay, even Texas governor Bill Clements had been party to an SMU player payroll. And yes, the basketball Mavericks had collapsed around Roy Tarpley's drug and alcohol problems. And maybe the only stock sold in baseball's Rangers was laughingstock.

But Dallas still had Coach Landry, and it wasn't ready to let him retire. Landry wasn't ready to, either. He finally could be Himself, full-time.

The parade wound up at City Hall Plaza, along with a crowd estimated at fifty thousand. Cowboys were seated in one roped-off section, dignitaries and media in another. Emcee Roger Staubach began by reading a telegram from President Bush. "Tom," it began, "the love and respect the people around the country have for you is evident today. . . ." Staubach read another from Billy Graham. "As you know," it began, "there is no one I have more respect for than you, as a Christian, a professional, and a leader. . . ."

A call from Bob Hope was hooked into the loudspeakers. Hope was making an appearance in, of all places, Port Arthur, Texas— home of Jimmy Johnson. Hope said to Landry, "You've done so much for the whole country. Not just Texas, but everywhere. You've brought such wonderful entertainment to us over the years. . . ." Then Hope swung into his routine. "You've had winning teams for so long that a lot of people thought Tom Landry was the capital of Texas. . . . Seeing Tom Landry without a hat is like seeing Tammy Bakker without makeup."

In a way no one outside his football teams had seen Landry without his makeup.

A 180-voice choir sang "The Battle Hymn of the Republic." Governor Clements made Landry an honorary admiral in the Texas Navy. Braniff and Southwest Airlines gave Tom and Alicia free passes for the rest of their lives—gifts of gold for constant travelers. Landry finally got to the podium and said, "You just have to ride in a parade down that street and see the faces of you people—you're overwhelmed. You don't know what to say. You don't know that it's happening."

Was it? Landry was helicoptered to Texas Stadium to coach one last game. His Cowboys, with an intense Staubach throwing to Drew Pearson, beat the Redskins in a flag-football game 22–0. A receiving line allowed the Cowboys a final opportunity to shake Landry's hand and wish him well. Dextor Clinkscale said, "Some guys wanted to go through it just to see if Coach Landry could remember their names. He just winked a lot."

All in all, I suppose, Landry Day was a warm-as-the-temperature tribute. My regret was that it hadn't happened on April 22, 1979. The lone perspective was lent by Walt Garrison, who spoke the way he ran, straight ahead: "It should have been done when he was more successful. I'm sorry it's today, but I'm glad it's happening."

A notable absentee at Landry Day was Tex Schramm. Four days earlier Schramm had announced he was leaving the Cowboys to start a new branch of the NFL that would stretch across Europe. Today Dallas, tomorrow the World League of American Football. Schramm said he left town ahead of Landry Day because he didn't want to "detract from the total focus on Tom."

Perhaps. But did Schramm think he was so beloved that he could split the adoration on Landry Day? Did he envision disrupting ceremonies as thousands lined up for his autograph or began chanting, "Tex! Tex! Tex!" Or was it that Schramm just couldn't bear to watch?

A Cowboy source says, "Tom had become a hero, and Tex just couldn't believe what was happening to *him*."

What was happening was that lawyers for Bright and Jones were finally examining Cowboy financial records, and Bright and Jones were realizing to what extent Schramm was "living like a king at Valley Ranch." They discovered that, though Bright had told Schramm to freeze salaries two years earlier, some had been increased or supplemented by large amounts of overtime. Schramm, it appears, took care of his loyal employees to the end. Then again, he wasn't paying them with his money.

Schramm denies all this.

Why didn't Bright periodically review Schramm's spending? A

source says, "Don Wilson [the Cowboy treasurer] would only let the Bright people see what Schramm wanted them to see."

Bright says, "You know, I've always trusted all my CEOs. When this office was built [Bright moved to a new office in 1989], I was asked if I wanted bugs installed in the offices of my top people. I was told it was common practice nowadays. Well, I couldn't live with myself if I had to go in and pop out a tape each night to check up on my people. We caught one CEO cheating on us and [Bright slams the desk] fired his ass. But Tex . . . well, it's like having your top salesman fudging on his expenses. You let it go because he's producing."

But the longer Jerry Jones officed at Cowboys Center, the more he realized many of Schramm's staff were no longer producing. Jones fired about half of them and kept the ones who "want to work as hard as I do." This enraged Schramm to the point that, according to Jones and sources close to Schramm, the two nearly came to blows. Schramm, it appears, quit as he was being fired.

According to several sources, Schramm demanded a severance package that included the funding of a $1.2 million annuity; a Texas Stadium box adjacent to the press box; and cars and legal/accounting expenses for ten years. A source says, "Jerry's approval by the league owners was held up until Tex was taken care of. It was almost like extortion. Jerry's lawyers were ready to sue the NFL." Jones says he went along with the annuity and the box. Jones wasn't obligated to give Schramm anything, but Schramm deserved that much, Jones agrees.

Landry couldn't have done it without Schramm.

On Draft Day, 1989, new Cowboys coach Jimmy Johnson set up two "war" rooms. One was for Johnson; the other, basically, for Gil Brandt. Johnson allowed photographers to take a few pictures of him and Brandt "getting their heads together." But once the draft began, Johnson alone made trades and final decisions behind a closed door.

Johnson had firsthand knowledge of the worth of Brandt's opinions. On Draft Day of 1988, the Cowboys were jubilant when wide receiver Michael Irvin, who played for Johnson at the University of Miami, "fell" to Dallas on the eleventh pick of the first round. The Cowboys rated Irvin the best player in the entire draft. "This," Schramm said, "will speed our return to the living."

Johnson wasn't so sure: "It was funny that Gil and I were supposed to be so close, but he never asked me one thing about Irvin.
We were hearing from other teams that Irvin might not go until the
second round. He made a lot of big plays for us, but we had several
receivers faster than Michael." Irvin's speed was the main reason he
was seen as just a second-rounder.

Oblivious to Johnson's doubts, Brandt had been strutting since
the "Saturday Night Massacre." It appeared he was the lone member of the Unholy Trinity who not only would survive but thrive. A
team source says, "Everybody thought Gil had Jimmy fooled. They
were supposed to be such big buddies. But really, Jimmy just used
Gil to help prepare for that first draft, which came so quickly [two
months after Johnson was hired]."

Soon after the draft Jones met with Brandt in the scouting
library and told him the Cowboys no longer would need his services.
Brandt soon confronted Johnson and said something like, "I thought
we were friends." How many times had Brandt heard that from
players?

Johnson just shrugged. Business was business. Johnson says,
"Really, I don't let myself get close to anybody."

Brandt, the man who knew "everyone," had been done in by a
coach he was "close" to. Gil Brandt, who "made and broke" Tom
Landry, suddenly didn't appear to have a close friend or a direction.
He continued to operate out of Cowboys Center for a couple of
months. The Cowboys went to camp. Rumors surfaced that Brandt
might become a player's agent. Johnson and Jones feared that
Brandt, alone in the Cowboy offices, might be using classified draft
information to help launch his new career.

They called back to Valley Ranch and left orders with security
guards: Gil Brandt was no longer to be allowed on the premises.

In the end Bum Bright didn't make such a bum deal by buying the
Cowboys. He made around $40 million from the sale, he figures.
Perhaps that made him feel a little better about being "sucked in" by
Landry-Schramm-Brandt.

In the very end the lawyers uncovered about $600,000 worth of
expenses that hadn't been negotiated. Should Bright or Jones have
to cover them? Bright offered to flip a coin.

"Flip for $600,000!" Jones said. "I'd walk from El Paso to Texarkana for $600,000." Jones sighed: one last test of his manhood. Okay, he said. Flip.

"But none of us had any change," Bright says, loving this part of the story. An aide left the room to borrow a quarter. Here were the two men who determined the fate of Tom Landry, flipping for six hundred grand. That about summed up the "most stable organization in sports."

Jones flipped the quarter, but he flipped it so hard it hit the ceiling and came to rest in an empty ashtray. As it ricocheted, Bright called tails. Jones hurried to the ashtray: tails it was.

"Oh, well," Jones said. "You deserved to win."

Bright later sent Jones a replica of a two-tailed quarter, mounted in a glass ball. The inscription: "Jerry, you will never know for sure."

For around $150 million, give or take $600,000, Bright had sold Jerry Jones a gleaming monster. Many times in the next year, it would turn on him. Sometimes, perhaps, Jones would wish he hadn't had that hangover in Cabo San Lucas.

16

EARLY IN Jimmy Johnson's first camp at Thousand Oaks he was visited in his second-floor dorm room by offensive linemen Crawford Ker and Kevin Gogan. They barely made it through the doorway before looking at each other with wide eyes and saying, "Wait, this was Landry's room." You imagine Ker and Gogan forming crosses with their forefingers and backing into the hall.

Johnson grinned as he told the story. "They wanted to know if I had trouble sleeping, if I'd seen any ghosts," Johnson said. "I told them I didn't have any idea whose room it had been."

I suspected Johnson knew exactly whose barracks-style throne room he occupied. And if Landry's ghost appeared at night, Johnson probably rolled his eyes and said, "Thanks for leaving the cupboard so bare, big guy. You really had everybody fooled, didn't you?"

Now Johnson shrugs and says, "I really had no idea how far the talent had slipped. I mean, they were the Dallas Cowboys, and it looked like they were competitive in most of their losses."

Maybe 3–13 was a final achievement for Landry. Johnson says he inherited no more than two or three capable starters. Two or three out of twenty-two positions? And Landry's last Cowboys won three games? The three wins, like some of the losses, were close calls—by three over Phoenix, six over Atlanta, and seven over Washington. Landry was perilously close to 0–16.

That was one reason Johnson hit Cowboy camp with body language that said, "I refuse to pay homage to Tom Landry." Another reason was that the new regime remained bitter over the way Jones was criticized—by Landry, then the world—for flying to Austin to face Landry and assure him he'd be paid a million bucks. A source near Jones and Johnson says, "Jerry and Jimmy thought Landry would forgive and forget sooner or later. After all, he was supposed to be such a big Christian. But they didn't even get a good-luck note from him."

To that most fans would say, "The nerve of those hillbillies! Any coach but Landry would have sent 'em exploding cigars."

But the JJs, as they were called, refused to pay tribute to an organization that echoed with untold hypocrisy. Many in the new regime wondered if any fans realized what had been going on in the name of Tom Landry. They couldn't believe it when Landry paid tribute to Clint Murchison in interviews, saying, "He was the key to the whole thing." Landry even had suggested Texas Stadium be renamed Murchison Stadium.

Holy Cowboy.

Jones felt that the previous regime made him seem almost Landry-like. Salomon Brothers' security people say Jones's closet was cleaner than most multimillionaires' they scrutinize. Jones says, "Sure, I've done some things I'm not too proud of, but good gosh, almost all my free time has been spent around my family." Yet Jones didn't attempt to hide his weekend tradition of "honky-tonkin' "—moving from club to club with family and friends. Jones readily admitted to reporters that he "likes to look at and be around pretty women." Jones often came across in newspaper and magazine articles the way, well, Murchison and Schramm came across privately.

Perception: reality.

Jones: devil incarnate.

Johnson began to bristle at questions about having to live up to Landry. Clearly Johnson thought Landry's image had little to do with the coach he'd been for years. Johnson refused to wear a Landry hat over his Corvette-style hair or to claim he had suddenly "found God" while sleeping in Landry's old bed. Johnson's Miami teams, which entered the Orange Bowl through fake smoke, had come across in public the way Landry's old Cowboys had in private—play hard, party hard. I'd heard from other college coaches that Johnson was a crack blackjack player who could probably make more money in casinos than coaching. As an escape in Miami, Johnson used to hop a powerboat for a quick trip to Nassau for a few hands of black-jack. He also was an occasional guest of Donald Trump or Don King at championship fights, where Johnson loved to tan in the limelight, then hit the gaming tables.

Imagine the reaction of Bible Belt fans who might have read the first column I wrote on the "new Landry" from camp. My first interview with Johnson took place one evening in the coaches' dorm. I was surprised at how open he was. Johnson seemed almost thank-ful for the chance to talk about his life-style.

He said, "If I'm going to work sixteen or eighteen hours a day and go long periods without a day off, then I'm going to do whatever I want with my free time, within reason. As long as I'm not hurting anyone or doing anything illegal, I'm not going to worry about what anybody thinks. Playing blackjack is a great hobby. But I'm very careful. I don't go into sports books [where bets can be placed on games]. I don't play dice or roulette. I purposely don't go to the dogs or the horses because I don't want to be perceived as a gambler. But it is very relaxing to sit and play blackjack. I love the excitement of it. It is a release."

Landry had to be thinking, "Thank you, God, for Jimmy Johnson."

Johnson concluded our interview with, "I have a great amount of respect for Tom. I meant no harm to him. I started to call him, but what do you say? I told Tex to tell Tom to call me if he felt like it."

But the more the JJs appeared to be godless J.R.s, the more fans remembered the Landry of the '70s. Landry was greater than ever. A "best-wishes" note to Jones, call to Johnson, or encouraging remark from Landry might have signaled to Landry fans that it was okay to root for the new regime. But why turn down the fire under Tom of Arc?

"Jethro" Jones couldn't keep from putting his "bare" foot in his mouth. He treated the Cheerleaders publicly as Schramm had treated them behind office doors—as pinups. Jones questioned an old rule prohibiting Cheerleaders from appearing at functions where alcohol was served or Cowboys were present. Half the squad threatened to quit; the director did. Mothers across Texas were outraged. How dare this thrillbilly sexploit the Dallas Cowboy Cheerleaders!

Many fans were equally upset over the way Jones spent fourth quarters of exhibition games on the sideline. "I just love the game of football," Jones said, appearing genuinely surprised at the criticism. "I like to be down where I can hear the hitting and what the players yell back and forth. I'd think any fan would love to be down there." But Murchison or Bright never set foot on the field. After victories, Jones ran off the field arm and arm with Johnson. And—another eventual break for Landry—Cowboys II won exhibitions at San Diego and in L.A. over the Raiders. It took John Elway four and a half quarters at Mile High Stadium to beat them in overtime. The team came home to a near-sellout and beat the Oilers—who played their starters all the way—in the final exhibition on a last-second field goal. Little Rock 'n' Roll! In Dallas, keeping up with the Joneses took on a whole new meaning.

The attitude around town seemed to be, "Well, if these new guys can win, we can live with 'em."

Johnson had retired Danny and Randy White at least a season before Landry would have. He dumped Landry starters Mike Downs and Jeff Rohrer. He put Steve Pelluer on the trading block. He said he would start rookie quarterback Troy Aikman and play rookie quarterback Steve Walsh.

Johnson wasn't just tearing a page out of Landry's bible. He was tearing them all out.

Tom and Alicia Landry left for Europe as the season opener neared in New Orleans. Tom was recognized often as they toured Switzerland, Austria, Germany, France, and Italy. Meanwhile, on cue, the new Cowboys got lost in the NFL. In New Orleans their emotion was punctured 28–0. Johnson says, "If we'd won that game, the emotion might have carried us, but we just couldn't recover from that." The following week the Cowboys blew a 21–7 halftime lead and lost in Atlanta 27–21. As they returned for the home opener, Jones announced that his special guest would be Elizabeth Taylor. She even participated in the coin toss. "Mizz Taylor is even more beautiful up close," Jones said. Bible Belters might have forgiven and forgotten if the Cowboys hadn't played like cats on a hot tin roof.

Washington 30–7.

A week later at Texas Stadium the Giants won 30–13. The

preseason anticipation that rose like eyebrows suddenly turned to condemnation. BRING BACK LANDRY banners appeared at Texas Stadium.

Right on cue, the Landrys arrived back in Dallas. Suddenly Landry was available for interviews. His phone number or address hadn't changed. Media people could call him anytime for his thoughts on the new Cowboys. Dial-a-dig? Again and again he said, "Gosh, I don't want to second-guess . . ." Then he second-guessed nearly everything Jones and Johnson did. "Well," Landry would say, "I wouldn't have done it that way." He said he wouldn't have released Danny or Randy White. He wouldn't have traded Pelluer. He wouldn't have started Aikman or drafted Walsh. When Johnson traded Herschel Walker to the Vikings for three potential starters and eight draft choices, Landry told several interviewers, "Well, I can't imagine me doing that."

Landry indirectly blamed Paul Hackett, who had very little input, for Landry's final 3–13 record. He told longtime Cowboy beat writer Frank Luksa, now a columnist for the *Times Herald:* ". . . I kinda lost control of the basic thing I could do so well, and that was to win games in the [last two minutes]. . . . I always had the right answer in the two-minute period. . . . It wasn't anyone's fault. I was just trying to make a transition and then I realized it wasn't going to work. We lost so many times with the wrong movement, the wrong execution, or the wrong something. That's lack of having complete control of the system. . . . It was mainly just the load on [Pelluer]. We used sort of a 49ers system, which is okay if you're in it long enough like a [Joe] Montana."

Landry's final season had been Pelluer's third in the "new system," which by then had become pretty much the old system. But, said Landry, with a new quarterback coach and total control, his Cowboys would have gone 8–8 in '89. Of course, with Johnson's Cowboys 0–5, this was gospel music to Dallas's ears.

Yet Landry told a Baptist convention he "doesn't dwell on the past" and that there was "no animosity in my heart" toward Jones and Johnson. Maybe not, but his many interviews twanged faintly of bitterness. Landry sounded like a living legend who just could not accept that he had been fired for any reason but owner incompetence. Yes, Jones had martyred Landry. But Jones had taken away the one thing Landry loved to do: coach. God's Coach was now completely image. Maybe his heart ached for those sideline TV closeups—for calling plays, telling the media how it all happened, accepting congratulations at Mia's.

Schramm politely refused comment on Jones or Johnson.

But Landry, who seldom criticized other coaches, became Jimmy Johnson's Buddy Ryan. Landry didn't out-and-out blast Johnson. But when Tom Landry said he wouldn't have done that, most people thought, "Johnson should have stuck with college football." After four losses Johnson boiled over and ran off several more Landry leftovers. Johnson had attempted an old-new transition but says, "We just needed to start over."

Said holdover assistant Bob Ward, "Johnson completely destroyed our myth." Burned Rome to the ground. The Cowboy soap opera became "As the Door Revolves." The most minor Johnson cut or pickup was gleefully criticized by the many Landry loyalists in the media, who still drank to the good ol' days with Schramm and staff, who had offices five minutes from Valley Ranch.

Landry wasn't going to ride into the sunset, either. He wasn't retiring to Austin or Palm Springs. He wasn't offered any other NFL job, coaching or front office. He stared permanently over the JJs' sagging shoulders. Oh, were they easy targets. Landry might as well have been back in his B-17, tailgunning winless pigeons. As the Cowboys fell to 0–8 Landry became more visible than ever. Banquets, grand openings, testimonials—there seemed to be dozens of Landry clones accepting plaques and offering humble thoughts on the new guys.

It was no wonder Jones soon suffered an irregular heartbeat. The guy who seldom slept couldn't sleep at all. Too many critics and cocktail parties. Jones says, "They call the condition a 'party' heart." His doctor told him to key down and cut out the alcohol—or else. In months Jones looked as if he had aged years. His face was lining faster than a John Madden telestrater. Speaking and interview requests poured in from all over the country. Suddenly Jerry Jones, a guy from Little Rock, was Very Important. What he said Mattered. He had bought the Dallas Cowboys and been transformed magically into a philosopher-king. What do you think about abortion, Mr. Jones? The environment? Gorbachev? Jones kept trying to answer. Jones was being devoured.

Toto, I've a feeling we're not in Arkansas anymore.

"There were many times," says Jones, "I wondered just what I had gotten myself into."

The new Cowboys won an NFL-worst one game—13–3 in Washington, where Landry won his last one.

Landry's first appearance at a Cowboy game came, of course, in New York. Maximum national publicity. Plus the Giants were Landry's old team, which allowed him to sit with the Giants' hierarchy. A source close to Jones says, "We had to pay him $90,000 that month to root for the Giants." Landry used the occasion to announce plans for his authorized biography, at a Giants Stadium media conference. The tone of most next-day New York and Dallas newspaper stories: "Tom Landry watched in horror as the team he coached for twenty-nine seasons . . ." New waves of publicity swept the Dallas papers as it was announced that Landry was a candidate for the Texas Sports Hall of Fame and the Pro Football Hall of Fame. Landry was all over TV and radio doing commercials. Thomas "Hollywood" Landry even was represented by the Kim Dawson Agency, which made its reputation representing models.

Naturally, sportswriters began wondering in print how the same Landry who was a first-year cinch for the Pro Football Hall of Fame hadn't been enshrined in the Cowboy Ring of Honor. A source close to Jones says, "After all Jerry had gone through, you couldn't expect him to be real excited about putting Landry in the Ring of Honor. It might have been a good P.R. move, but Jerry has some pride, too. He wants to wait until the Cowboys are winning again so he can enshrine Landry on equal footing."

Landry's touché? He said he might not accept enshrinement if it's offered. "I don't know if I would or not," he told WFAA-TV. "I'm divorced completely from the Cowboys, and I don't see any reason to change that." The only group Landry wasn't going to let honor him was the one that martyred him.

Finally, on January 14, 1990, a Dallas columnist besides me criticized Landry for something other than play calling. Randy Galloway of the *Morning News*, a Dallas-area native, took his first chink out of Landry's image with a column about Jones's "Tom problem." Galloway wrote, "This is [Landry's] revenge, and strangely enough, revenge seems important to him. . . . Tom is playing to the crowd, and the crowd is loving it, of course. . . . Actually, it is Jones who is turning the other cheek in regard to the Landry situation. Once the losses began to stack up, Tom refused [in interviews] to let the JJs off easy. . . . Maybe they don't deserve it. But then again, a man of such strong religious convictions is usually quicker to forgive than the rest of us heathens. Could it be that Tom was really more like us than we ever thought?"

It was mildly surprising when Tex Schramm began showing up for Cowboy home games. Wouldn't he feel uncomfortable, a guest at a party he always had thrown? A fan who once had been Caesar? But there was Schramm in the box Jones gave him, number 280, a glass partition away from the press box.

Psychologist Don Beck told me, "Tex has really taken this hard. He just isn't doing well with it."

During one game Schramm told a *Sports Illustrated* interviewer, "You live this for twenty-nine years. You were part of creating it. . . . When you look out there, it's kind of like a dream, a nightmare. Sometimes I can't believe it isn't the same anymore. Everybody says, 'Gee, great, now you can retire.' Well, when you retire, you're supposed to do something you want. This is what I want. My life is being in the arena. I miss this."

The designer uniforms, the Cheerleaders, the Texettes, the press box, the open bar, the televised power, Tex's Stadium—it was all still there, just out of Schramm's reach. Somewhere, perhaps, Bum Bright was smiling his little tulip-shaped smile. Schramm, perhaps, had been suspended in his version of Dante's *Inferno*.

Schramm's last moment in the Texas Stadium sun—the glare of TV lights—came the day Jerry Jones enshrined Lee Roy Jordan in the Ring of Honor. (Jones was booed heavily as he introduced Jordan.) Schramm, you'll remember, had refused to allow Jordan in the Ring, apparently over a contract holdout. But before and after the halftime enshrinement Schramm was able to answer one last round of media questions about the sixteen-year feud.

Who listened over Schramm's shoulder to make sure he didn't fly into a rage? Bedford Wynne, the original Cowboy owner. When last we saw Wynne, he was on his way to dry out from near-lethal alcoholism.

I was stunned to learn Wynne counseled alcoholics, drug addicts, and codependents at his Family Recovery Inc. Imagine: Bedford Wynne, who lived as fast as any man in Dallas, now advising against it. Wynne, best friend and accomplice of Clint Murchison, now an antialcohol evangelist. At sixty-six Wynne remained one of Schramm's closest friends, but no longer his drinking buddy.

As Schramm did interviews, Wynne told me, "I'm a little worried that Tex has had a little too much to drink. But I think he's doing fine."

I asked if Wynne were counseling Schramm. "Oh, I'm working on him," he said very seriously. "You know, I was the one who introduced him to bullshots. But alcoholism is the only self-diagnosed disease. No one can tell you you have a problem but you."

Wynne agreed to talk to me for this book. I dropped by his office in a North Dallas tower, and we talked at length about the flights of fantasy he used to take on America's Team charters. "Sometimes I'm not sure it all really happened," he said.

He was excited about moving from the sixth floor to the fourth—more space for larger group meetings. He gave me a tape of Thomas "Hollywood" Henderson addressing a high school assembly. "I never would have believed it," Wynne said, "but Thomas is for real. There's no more powerful speaker against drugs and alcohol." Unless, of course, it was Wynne.

That night, while speaking to a group, Bedford Wynne died of a heart attack.

In December 1989 I called Gil Brandt to see if I could interview him for this book. "Yeah," he said, "I knew last May you were writing a book." He did? I didn't. He said, "Your mother told a friend in the beauty shop. That's how I found out." My mother lives in Oklahoma City.

Brandt said he "probably" was doing his own book. I asked what else he was going to do. He said he didn't know. "Sports has really changed a lot. The [money] numbers these guys are getting now, it's just a different business and I'm not sure I want to be in it."

Or was it that nobody wanted him to be in it? No other team had offered Brandt a job. The Draftmaster may have fooled fans and media people, but apparently he didn't fool rivals.

As word spread that I was writing my book, many people called to tell me what "Gil Brandt is really like." I heard from people who worked for him and people "close" to him. Some wanted to talk, then backed off. Some still fear Brandt's influence in Dallas.

John Wooten, who worked under Brandt and replaced him as pro personnel director, says, "The only thing you couldn't quite understand about Gil was that he just tore the hearts out of people when he didn't have to. He had it all—power, money, recognition. Why did he have to be so insecure? Without being an owner or general manager he was the most powerful man in the NFL. He ran college football. He all but ran the city of Dallas. It seemed like everyone from the mayor to the chief of police owed him a favor. Was he insecure because he didn't really know the game?"

Or was it that the man from nowhere couldn't help treating people the way he once was treated?

I saw Brandt from a distance at the Super Bowl. He was hanging around the press box entrance. Perhaps 90 percent of the writers at the Superdome had interviewed Brandt in the past. Maybe a writer would ask what he was doing, what he thought of the 49ers and Broncos. Maybe some owner would see a Brandt quote in Monday's papers and remember that he built America's Team.

Paul Hackett was calling from a car phone. He was "gunned up," barreling down a Texas highway to recruit a junior college star for the University of Pittsburgh. When Pitt's Mike Gottfried was fired, Hackett finally became a head coach.

"After all I went through," Hackett said, "this thing just fell in my lap. I got the best quarterback in the country [Alex Van Pelt], and he'll just be a sophomore. We get a great house right in the middle of campus, and we're putting a jukebox in the basement."

The Hacketts had been to see Paul McCartney in concert the night before in Pittsburgh. What a life.

A year after being on probation under Landry, Hackett had coached Pitt to a 31–28 John Hancock Bowl win over Bum Bright's Texas A&M . . . which was coached by R. C. Slocum, who had recommended Hackett to Bright. Mysterious ways?

After the game Hackett told reporters, "The things I hear myself saying, the things I do—they are so much like Tom Landry it amazes me."

A few weeks after I interviewed him for this book, Dextor Clinkscale called back with a postscript emotion. Clinkscale has moved back to his hometown of Greenville, South Carolina, which had been a recent stop on Landry's whirlwind itinerary. Being an ex-Cowboy, Clinkscale was asked to share the head table with Landry before he spoke at an FCA luncheon. Clinkscale did so warily.

He said he was surprised by the coach he never knew.

"He was different," Clinkscale said, struggling for the right words. "He was so . . . so *nice*. I don't know how else to describe him. He was . . . friendly. I actually felt some warmth from him. He was just like a regular guy. He said his wife had been on him about eating dessert, but he ate it anyway."

Clinkscale ended up having his picture taken with Coach Landry, who smiled for the camera. This was the man Clinkscale, as a free-agent rookie, went to Dallas to meet. And now Landry had come to Greenville, free at last to be a regular guy.

For perspective these days I like to go to Cafe Dallas. I can still smell those early-'80s nights when people stood in one-hundred-yard lines, perfumes colliding around them, as they waited to get into Dallas's wildest nightclub.

Cafe Dallas has been several different clubs and restaurants since it closed. As this is written, it stands empty. For Lease: lust in the dust.

Sometimes I like to take a Sunday drive past the Murchison estate on Forest Lane. For two years it has been overgrown with weeds. For Sale: America's Dream.

In the last few years Dallas has changed dramatically—changed for the better. Cowboyville has been knocked off its high horse. Boom turned to bust, if not dust. Imagine: an NFL record fourteen straight losses at Texas Stadium.

I've often wondered if this was God's wrath for the Unholy Trinity, for the unlikely partnership between Landry and Murchison, for the unbearable way this city flaunted its '70s wealth and Super Bowl Cowboys. In 1989, Dallas was the only multiple-sport town without a single playoff team. The city's lone championship in the '80s was won by our indoor soccer team, the Sidekicks, which may have been punishment in itself.

Yes, Dallas and its Cowboys have taught me a few valuable little Sunday School lessons. Many deeply unhappy "friends" taught me all about sex without love and singles bar romance. Cowboy Cheerleaders who wouldn't turn my head on the street taught me the powers of costume and makeup. Many North Dallasites taught me money can only rent happiness. Dallas taught me what can happen when you invest your city's self-worth in the fortunes of a football team. Many in the Cowboy organization taught me life is hard enough without alcohol or drugs. So many Cowboys taught me that great athletes are just like we are, only worse. Coach Landry taught me you can't believe everything you see on TV. Catholics taught me how to worship seriously instead of socially. Many Christians, who believe being "saved" saves them from ever having to obey a commandment, gave me a tour of hell on earth. I owe so much to faithful churchgoers who believe the more they put in the offering plate, the more they can drink, cheat, lie, make, and spend. They flourish miserably.

For me Dallas has been a great place to grow up, from age twenty-six to thirty-eight. The '80s made Dallas a much better place to live. We Dallasites coined a new word: humility. Really, Dallas is a lot like Landry. Once you get it away from Texas Stadium, there's a lot to like about it. It's clean, upbeat, proud, friendly. The quality of life is high.

But as a columnist I stay in Dallas because things just keep happening, things I couldn't make up. Columns just keep writing themselves. There's still enough material to outfit a Highland Park socialite for a year, still bolts of hypocrisy and pretension. Dallas continually makes me examine my faith, check my Porsche oil.

How could I leave Death Valley Ranch now? A gas deal Jerry Jones made with Arkansas gubernatorial candidate Sheffield Nelson is being reinvestigated. The $175 million deal, it is alleged, might have cost rate-payers extra millions. It definitely made Jones enough to buy the Cowboys. Jones insists everything was aboveboard. But Jack Veatch of Salomon Brothers says, "Naturally, I live in fear something could happen. It would really be a black eye for everyone, even the city." Though it appears unlikely, what if Jones had to sell the team? What if the highest bidder was a Landry lover? What if Landry made a triumphant return?

In Dallas, you never know.

In December 1989 I called Tom Landry to let him know I was writing this book. He said he would answer my questions if he decided against doing his own book—that he'd let me know one way or the other.

He didn't call back.

But when we talked he sounded busier and happier than ever.

"Gosh," he said, "I'm overwhelmed. Every church, every prayer breakfast is a possibility [for a speaking request]. But we're trying to accommodate 'em all."

Landry was opening an office with Tom Jr. They were back in the oil business. They were investing and consulting. Tom Jr. was going to "manage me," said Big Tom. Landry had become a one-man conglomerate—the Michael Jackson or Jordan of evangelical martyrdom. He is chairman of the Dallas International Sports Commission and a key member of President Bush's Drug Strategy Council. He says he plans to do more commercials, perhaps some acting, speaking all over the world.

I'd been told Landry could just about name his price to address the business groups on his waiting list. What, twenty thousand dollars a pop? Thirty thousand? No motivational speaker was hotter.

But he was probably keeping the first weekend in August open.

Yes, in January voting, Landry was a first-ballot selection for the Pro Football Hall of Fame. But no, he did not choose Tex Schramm to present him, as some Cowboy followers probably anticipated. Landry chose Roger Staubach—"the kind of image you want for pro football," as Landry once said. Naturally, Staubach said he was honored.

So Landry no longer had football, but he had more fame and fortune than ever. Funny, he often warned his teams, "Fame and fortune are fleeting." I even read where Alicia said, "After the season ended last year, he looked so worn, tired, and thin—but not anymore. He's relaxed, rested, and happy."

Of those who helped create America's Team, Landry was by far the most successful survivor. Or so it appeared. Was he truly happy with himself? Or did he vaguely feel as if he had made a Faustian bargain for his preeminence? Who knows what's really in a man's heart? So many players weren't sure Landry had one. So many times he altered his answers to fit the questions. How could you really trust anything Landry said in interviews? In the end, did he have any idea who he was?

I can draw some conclusions only from Landry's actions. Did he sometimes use his Christianity to justify what had to be done in his "bi'ness" of pro football? Yes. Did he sometimes use his image to satisfy his ego and greed? Well, yes. Did he look the other way as his owner and business partners used his image? Sometimes. Could he be uncaring and unforgiving? It appeared so.

Was God's Coach a great coach? In '60s and '70s results, yes. In reality, no. Staubach, Brandt, Schramm, and even Murchison deserve credit for Landry's first-ballot Hall of Fame election.

Did Landry cure cancer or invent television or land America's Team on Mars? No, his team won some football games, was all.

But in the final analysis, has Tom Landry helped make the world a better place? No question.

Perhaps that's a sad commentary on our society, but Landry influenced many, many lives for the better. For whatever reasons he gave generously of his time to spread God's word. No matter the truth, many people thought Landry was a great coach and a perfect Christian. The perception has made for positive reality, I suppose.

But the truth was that Landry was just an overwhelmed guy from Mission. He didn't set out to become God's Coach, it just happened. As Schramm's monster grew out of control, Landry hung on for dear life. That's the Landry I liked: the guy behind the curtain frantically yanking the levers that worked the great and powerful Mount Landry. He actually came fairly close to living up to an inhuman image he didn't discourage. He faced dilemmas and criticism few of us do. He was strong. He was weak. But one thing about Landry: He kept trying.

As Staubach said, Landry was "just a pretty darn good guy." That's all. If you judge him as your next-door neighbor instead of God's Coach, he comes off pretty darn well. For all his failings he didn't steal or cheat on his wife.

It's just that he couldn't heal the sick or raise the 3–13 dead. Unfortunately, many in his vast congregation believed he could. In the end, Landry probably did, too. But like the exposed Wizard of Oz, all he really could do was tell the cowardly lion, "You're confusing courage with wisdom," and that many "heroes" pull their "fortitude out of mothballs once a year and parade it. They have one thing you haven't got—a medal." Remember? The Wizard gives him a medal.

The lion hadn't needed a medal to help kill the wicked witch. The lion, of course, had courage all along. So do a lot of people who thought they needed to look to Landry for strength.

All along, Landry was just like the rest of us, scared, sometimes wondering what it all means. What did I learn from closely observing Landry? That God doesn't need a coach.

*   *   *

It was near midnight in University Park, not far from the SMU campus. Jerry Tubbs and I stood in his front yard, letting the fall breeze calm us after a long session about the rise and fall. Tubbs was my favorite person in the Cowboy franchise. You didn't have to wonder if God was in Tubbs's heart. You just felt it.

Whatever you believed or didn't, Tubbs could make you feel better about the world. When I doubted, Tubbs helped revive my faith in a basic goodness. It was more what he did than what he said. You could see him do unto others and love his neighbor, but you didn't hear him tell the media about it. He wasn't a big drinker, smoker, cusser, carouser—or bragger.

Tubbs was one ex-star who didn't take himself seriously. He didn't have to keep reminding you that he was Jerry Tubbs and you weren't. You had to study the media guide to learn that Tubbs, as a senior at Oklahoma, won the 1956 Walter Camp Award for the nation's outstanding player. He never said, "Back when I was the Cowboy middle linebacker . . ." Tubbs hoped people would respect him for what he did today.

He was perhaps the least publicized Landry assistant. He didn't ask to be on the sideline during games so the cameras could find him. He was content to coach his linebackers from the press box and be a lifelong assistant. He didn't pretend to be anything more than a slow-talkin' bald guy from Breckenridge, Texas, who knew a little about football. Sometimes it was difficult to interview Tubbs because he began interviewing you. His nature was so gentle that it was hard to believe he was known as the hardest hitter in Cowboy history. Only the scar running from his lip to his chin reminded you.

Winning was important to Tubbs, but not at the expense of his principles. "The most important thing," Tubbs always said, "is being a good person." After losses Tubbs never seemed to lose perspective. It was always, "Well, I'm just going to have to work harder and coach better next week." Or "Oh, well, I'll bet the sun still comes up tomorrow."

I never heard Tubbs blame a player, and I never heard a Cowboy bad-mouth Tubbs. I heard Cowboys knock every Landry assistant but Tubbs. Thomas Henderson loved Tubbs. All the players and ex-players quoted in this book said they respected Tubbs. Often Tubbs called players who had been cut to say how much he appreciated what they'd done for the team and told them to "stay in touch." Quietly, Tubbs had a profound impact on many lives.

Tubbs always seemed out of place on America's Team. He might have been the only Cowboy coach or executive who wasn't trying to be something he wasn't. Tubbs was real. For all of Landry's twenty-nine seasons, Tubbs stuck by him as a player and assistant.

Tubbs was fired with Landry. By 7 A.M., he would be on the road to his farm, an hour's drive from Dallas, to tend his eighty-five head of cattle. Yes, Tubbs was now an honest-to-goodness cowboy.

He sighed and said, "I've had a lot of time to think. You know, sure, there were some things I wanted to change. There were times I wanted to say something. But when you work for a man, well, you do have the right to quit at any time."

That's one thing I couldn't understand about the many Cowboys who hated their coach and organization. Their criticism was often valid, so why didn't they just quit? Landry didn't force them to sacrifice their bodies for his cause. But they, like Landry, often benefited greatly from Cowboy fame and fortune. Yes, he left many Cowboys with physical and emotional scars. But in return, so many profited. They got what they paid for.

Tubbs, as usual, was looking for a metallic-silver lining. He said, "When you work with a guy every day, it's easy to see his faults. Hey, everybody's got 'em. But you see all the foibles, and maybe you just don't realize the guy's greatness. It's hard to be a big guy because everybody sees your warts. And Tom is really a big guy. Everywhere I go in this country, people just think Tom is God. Who else is there, really? Of the great players and coaches, who's more respected than Tom?"

"Tom is good for the country, prob'ly."

Tubbs thought for a moment. "As you get older you get a little better perspective on things. When I was a kid and I first started going to church, I didn't like to see other people in church say one thing and do something else on Saturday night. I wanted to see everybody do right. But you know, they were prob'ly better because they did go to church. At least they made the attempt."

I was quiet. The Dallas night was quiet. Tubbs, toeing the curb, seemed to be trying to tell me something. "Oh, I'm sure Tom was aware of some things that were going on. But it's kind of like running a stop sign out in the country. It's something that shouldn't be done, but you don't spend a lot of time worrying about it."

Pause.

"Go easy on Tom, will you?" Tubbs said.

Forgive him.

"None of us are anywhere near perfect," Tubbs said.